Ideas Against Ideocracy

Ideas Against Ideocracy

Non-Marxist Thought of the Late Soviet Period (1953–1991)

Mikhail Epstein

BLOOMSBURY ACADEMIC
NEW YORK • LONDON • OXFORD • NEW DELHI • SYDNEY

BLOOMSBURY ACADEMIC
Bloomsbury Publishing Inc
1385 Broadway, New York, NY 10018, USA
50 Bedford Square, London, WC1B 3DP, UK
29 Earlsfort Terrace, Dublin 2, Ireland

BLOOMSBURY, BLOOMSBURY ACADEMIC and the Diana logo
are trademarks of Bloomsbury Publishing Plc

First published in the United States of America 2022
This paperback edition published 2023

Illustrations by Sergei Rozhin

For legal purposes the Acknowledgments on pp. viii–ix constitute an
extension of this copyright page.

Cover design by Eleanor Rose
Cover illustrations © Sergei Rozhin, 2018; Background image © Getty Images

Library of Congress Cataloging-in-Publication Data
Names: Epstein, Mikhail, author.
Title: Ideas against ideocracy : non-Marxist thought of the late
Soviet period (1953–1991) / Mikhail Epstein.
Description: New York : Bloomsbury Academic, 2021. | Includes bibliographical references and index. |
Summary: "This groundbreaking work by one of the world's foremost theoreticians of culture and scholars of Russian philosophy gives for the first time a systematic examination of the development of Russian philosophy during the late Soviet period. Countering the traditional view of an intellectual wilderness under the Soviet regime, Mikhail Epstein provides a comprehensive account of Russian thought of the second half of the 20th century that is highly sophisticated without losing clarity. It provides new insights into previously mostly ignored areas such as late Soviet Russian nationalism and Eurasianism, religious thought, cosmism and esoterism, and postmodernism and conceptualism. Epstein shows how Russian philosophy has long been trapped in an intellectual prison of its own making as it sought to create its own utopia. However, he demonstrates that it is time to reappraise Russian thought, now freed from the bonds of Soviet totalitarianism and ideocracy but nevertheless dangerously engaged into new nationalist aspirations and metaphysical radicalism. We are left with not only a new and exciting interpretation of recent Russian intellectual history, but also the opportunity to rethink our philosophical heritage"– Provided by publisher.
Identifiers: LCCN 2021013845 (print) | LCCN 2021013846 (ebook) | ISBN 9781501350597 (hardback) | ISBN 9781501350610 (epub) | ISBN 9781501350603 (pdf) | ISBN 9781501350627
Subjects: LCSH: Philosophy, Russian–20th century. | Philosophy and religion–Soviet Union. | Soviet Union–Intellectual life.
Classification: LCC B4231 .E668 2021 (print) | LCC B4231 (ebook) | DDC 197–dc23
LC record available at https://lccn.loc.gov/2021013845
LC ebook record available at https://lccn.loc.gov/2021013846

ISBN: HB: 978-1-5013-5059-7
PB: 978-1-5013-8091-4
ePDF: 978-1-5013-5060-3
eBook: 978-1-5013-5061-0

Typeset by Integra Software Services Pvt. Ltd.

To find out more about our authors and books visit www.bloomsbury.com
and sign up for our newsletters.

Contents

Acknowledgments viii
Preface x

Introduction: Philosophy, the State, and Plato-Marxism 1

Part 1 The Philosophy of National Spirit. Conservatism, Eurasianism, and Traditionalism

1. The Search for National Identity. Traditions and New Challenges 9
2. The Neo-Slavophile Revival in Aesthetics and Criticism. Petr Palievsky and Vadim Kozhinov 13
3. Other Neo-Slavophiles and Nationalists of the 1960s–1970s 18
4. Nation as Personality. The Moral Conservatism of Aleksandr Solzhenitsyn 21
5. From Anti-Socialism to Anti-Semitism. Igor Shafarevich 32
6. The Philosophy of Ethnicity. Neo-Eurasianism. Lev Gumilev 37
7. Radical Traditionalism and Neofascism. Aleksandr Dugin 47

Part 2 Religious Thought. Orthodox Christianity

1. Major Expatriate Theologians 64
   a. The Revival of Theology. Georges Florovsky 64
   b. The Liturgical Philosophy of Alexander Schmemann 66
   c. The Existential Orthodoxy of Metropolitan Anthony of Sourozh 69
2. Science and Theology. Archbishop Luka (Valentin Voino-Iasenetsky) 72
3. The Christian Intuitivism of Boris Pasternak 75
4. Christian Socialism. Anatolii Krasnov-Levitin 78
5. Atheism as the Forerunner of Spiritual Rebirth 81
6. The Dialogue between Believers and Atheists. Sergei Zheludkov and Kronid Liubarsky 83
7. Christianity and the New Humanism. Secularization and the Intelligentsia 88
8. The Philosophy of Christian Synthesis. Aleksandr Men 93
9. The Generation of Neophytes and Theological Innovations 101
   a. Postmodernist Perspectives on Christianity. Tatiana Goricheva 103
   b. Christian Energetism. Sergei Khoruzhii 105

Part 3 Mysticism, Universalism, and Cosmism

1. General Features of Russian Mysticism 109
2. Religious Universalism and Metahistory. Daniil Andreev and *The Rose of the World* 110
   a. The Spiritual System of the World 112
   b. The Theocratic State of the Future and the Coming of the Antichrist 115
   c. The Feminine in Russian Thought. Sophiology and Materialism 118
   d. Andreev's Mysticism of Femininity 122
   e. The Internal Ironies of Theocratic Thought: Utopia as Eschatology 128
3. Cosmism and Active Evolutionism 131
   a. The Sources of Cosmism 131
   b. The Variety of Cosmist Perspectives 135
   c. Svetlana Semenova. The Theology and Technology of Active Evolution 142
4. The Religion of Absolute Self and the Abyss of Negativity. Iurii Mamleev 150

Part 4 Postmodernist Thought. Conceptualism

1. The Origins of Conceptualism 157
2. The Archaic Postmodernism of Andrei Siniavsky 161
3. The Satirical Metaphysics of Aleksandr Zinoviev 172
4. The Metaphysics of Emptiness. The Philosophical Installations of Ilya Kabakov 181
5. The Philosophy of Sots-Art and Morality of Eclecticism. Vitalii Komar and Aleksandr Melamid 193
6. Shimmering Aesthetics. Dmitrii Prigov 197
7. The Canonization of Emptiness. The Medical Hermeneutics Inspectorate 200
8. Postmodernism versus Soviet Utopianism and Western Demythologization. Boris Groys 203
9. Academic Postmodernism. Valerii Podoroga 211

Epilogue: The End of Soviet Philosophy and Strategies for the Future 215

1. The Critique of the Russian Ideocratic Tradition 215
2. New Metaphysical Radicals 219
3. Conceptualism versus Metaphysical Radicalism 224
4. The Symbiosis of Radical Metaphysics and Conceptualism 226

Conclusion 231
1. The Circular Paths of Ideocracy 231
2. The Comedy of Ideas and the Tragedy of Ideocracy 233
3. Philosophy and the Philosophical 235

Bibliography 237
Appendix: Original Russian and Other Foreign-Language Titles 246
Name Index 251
Subject Index 254

Acknowledgments

My work on this book took place over a period of almost thirty years, most intensively in 1992–5 and in 2016–20. It incorporated significant input from a number of institutions and individuals, and I am deeply grateful to all of them.

In 1992–4, this research, initially titled "Russian Philosophical and Humanistic Thought after 1950," was generously supported by funding provided by the National Council for Soviet and East European Research (Washington, DC). In the fall semester of 2020, a sabbatical leave from Emory University enabled me to concentrate on completion of the manuscript. I am deeply indebted to these organizations.

I greatly appreciate the collaboration with Bloomsbury Academic that I have enjoyed since 2012, when this press published my book *The Transformative Humanities: A Manifesto*. In 2019, Bloomsbury released the first volume of the current study, *The Phoenix of Philosophy: Russian Thought of the Late Soviet Period (1953–1991)*. Now I would like to express my gratitude to the press and to the collaborators, colleagues, and friends who were instrumental in my work on the present volume.

I am grateful to my former research assistant Thomas Stuart, who in the early 1990s helped me to type and edit the first version of this study, and to Dr. Anesa Miller, whose scrupulous comments helped me in editing the second version in the mid-1990s.

I would like to express my deepest appreciation to the editor of the final version, Dr. A. S. Brown, who has played the most significant role in the preparation of this book. I am extremely grateful to Dr. Brown for his most dedicated, responsible, and intellectually generous help. Dr. Brown has made a thorough editing of the entire final draft, offering his invaluable advice in stylistic, terminological, and technical aspects. His devotion to the project was amazing, and he was extremely open and responsive to my queries and opinions and initiated many productive discussions that led to the significant improvement of the manuscript. We exchanged hundreds of emails while consulting on all aspects of this work, including the organization of the textual material and modes of expression for certain concepts. There was no issue regarding which Dr. Brown did not provide his most thoughtful, illuminating, and timely input.

My special thanks to Sergei Rozhin, an illustrator based in St. Petersburg, who designed nine excellent graphic portraits of philosophers for the book.

I would like to extend my sincere thanks to Haaris Naqvi, Editorial Director at Bloomsbury, who was instrumental in making the publication of both companion volumes possible. I am deeply grateful to him for his interest in the proposed manuscripts and his patient guidance and generous advice throughout my work on them. My thanks also to Bloomsbury editor Rachel Walker and editorial assistant Rachel Moore, who kindly helped me at various stages of the editing and publishing process.

My colleagues and friends at Emory University, Drs. Juliette Apkarian, Elena Glazov-Corrigan, and Vera Proskurina, were generous in providing the necessary creative atmosphere in my department and helping me to obtain the release time necessary for my work on the project.

My wife, Marianna Taymanova, is a permanent source of support and encouragement, and her advice has been most valuable and formative throughout all my work.

Preface

The ideal society we have described can never grow into a reality or see the light of day, and there will be no end to the troubles of states, or indeed of humanity itself, till philosophers become kings in this world, or till those we now call kings and rulers really and truly become philosophers.

—Plato, *The Republic*, trans. H. D. P. Lee

That kings should become philosophers, or philosophers kings, is not likely to happen, nor would it be desirable, since the possession of power invariably debases the free judgment of reason. It is, however, indispensable that a king—or a kingly, i.e. self-ruling, people—should not suppress philosophers but leave them the right of public utterance.

—Immanuel Kant, *On Eternal Peace. Second Supplement*, trans. Karl Popper

I ask you, where are our wise men, where are our thinkers? Who has ever thought for us? Who thinks for us now?

—Petr Chaadaev, *Philosophical Letters* (Letter 1)

This book discusses the major trends of philosophical and religious thought in the Soviet Union in its later, post-Stalin period, from Stalin's death in 1953 to the collapse of the state in 1991. This is the epoch of changing relationships between state power and intellectual life under the specific mode of production of ideas in a totalitarian society. The very phenomenon of totalitarianism can be explained as a regime of ideocracy, or the "dictatorship of ideas" that endows intellectuals with the most powerful and at the same time the most vulnerable role in society, dividing them into orthodox "ideologists" and heterodox "intelligentsia." The struggle in Russia between the intelligentsia and ideocracy, or between intellectuals at the service of Reason and Spirit and, on the other hand, intellectuals at the service of power, constitutes one of the most dramatic episodes in the world history of ideas.

The roots of this drama go back to Plato's vision of philosopher-kings and a society ruled by all-powerful ideas. Surprisingly, the Russian Revolution, albeit conducted under Marxist slogans, had inaugurated a political regime more like a Platonic ideocratic state than an economically driven Marxist society. How could the most radical and militant wing of Russian materialism led by Lenin and Stalin have in fact promoted the most extreme of all idealistic utopias, a kind of Platonic state of ideas, to the rank of world superpower?

Countering the traditional view that under the communist regime, Russia was an intellectual wasteland, this book offers a coherent account of Russian thought in the latter half of the twentieth century. It provides new insights into such previously neglected or under-investigated areas as late-Soviet Russian nationalism and Eurasianism, religious philosophy, cosmism and esotericism, and postmodernism and conceptualism. Rarely in the history of thought has philosophy been so liberating a force as it was in Russia from the 1950s through the 1980s. The philosophical thought of the late Soviet period played no less a role in the collapse of the Soviet system and communist ideology than had Marxist philosophy in its formation. Studying the philosophy of this period can enable us to understand the intellectual forces behind perestroika and the origins of some of the powerful political movements that shape Putin's Russia even today.

I have already investigated late-Soviet thought in my previous book *The Phoenix of Philosophy: Russian Thought of the Late Soviet Period (1953–1991)*,[1] which covers four major movements: late-Soviet Marxism, structuralism and neo-rationalism, personalism and liberalism, and culturology, or the philosophy of culture. This new book logically proceeds from the previous one and completes it with an investigation of four other highly influential trends: nationalism and Eurasianism, Orthodox religious thought, mystical universalism and the philosophy of cosmic evolution, and postmodernist thought and conceptualism. These movements, to different extents, have strong ideological, political, and even geopolitical consequences as manifested still today in Russian politics, sometimes in the most provocative and aggressive ways.

Philosophical ideas and religious visions have traditionally had enormous impact on Russian political goals and strategies. Russian thought has sparked renewed interest among academic and nonacademic readers due to contemporary global confrontations. In his book *The Road to Unfreedom* (2018), Timothy Snyder traces the sources of contemporary Russian geopolitics to the philosophy of Ivan Ilyin (1883–1954). But Ilyin died the year after Stalin did, and the more recent and direct sources of present-day Russian moves are to be found in Russian thought of the post-Stalin period. One cannot understand contemporary Russia, in the historical context of its global ideological claims and transformative projects, without looking in depth at its more recent philosophical heritage.

Thus, with this new volume, *Ideas Against Ideocracy*, the entire field of Russian philosophy of the latter part of the twentieth century is for the first time systematically explored and presented, both to specialists in Russian intellectual history and to the

[1] New York, London: Bloomsbury Academic, 2019, 312 pp. These two books, *The Phoenix of Philosophy* and *Ideas Against Ideocracy*, in fact represent a single research project, conditionally divided into two volumes. The cross-references between them are important for understanding the entire scope of Russian thought of this period.

general public interested in Russian culture, religion, and social thought.[2] This period is also important in the cultural context of European and Western philosophy and the history of ideas. With Russia's renewed importance in global politics, readers will better understand the intellectual trends that have shaped the Yeltsin and Putin regimes and contemporary protest movements. The Russian intellectual scene of this period is unique in world philosophy: it is a history of thought struggling desperately to escape its own self-imprisonment—the shackles of an ideological system created by the efforts of thought itself.

* * *

The structure of the two companion volumes, *The Phoenix of Philosophy* (published in 2019) and *Ideas Against Ideocracy*, is identical. Each volume is divided into four parts. Each part begins with an overview of the major trend in question and a history of its formation. The subsequent chapters are devoted to individual authors who represent the most characteristic approaches and subspecies of the general trend, considered mainly chronologically.

The Contents of the First Volume

The Phoenix of Philosophy: Russian Thought of the Late Soviet Period (1953–1991)

Introduction

The Role of Philosophy in Russian and Soviet History
Philosophy and *Filosofia*: The Scope of the Concept
Three Philosophical Awakenings
Existing Scholarship and Its Limitations
Major Trends of Russian Thought in the Post-Stalin Era
The Structure of the Book

Part I. Vicissitudes of Soviet Marxism

1. From Lenin to Stalin
2. Stalin's Later Thinking: From Class to Nationality

[2] Russian philosophy of the latter half of the twentieth century has remained a blind spot on the intellectual map of the world. Russian philosophy of the preceding era has been explored more or less systematically in the well-known historical surveys of Nikolai Lossky, Vasilii Zenkovsky, Sergei Levitsky, and Frederick Copleston. However, regardless of the time of their completion, these narratives end abruptly in the mid-twentieth century, as if to imply that nothing significant occurred thereafter. The last names mentioned in these four most comprehensive surveys are those of Sergei Bulgakov (1871–1944), Vladimir Lossky (1903–58), Lev Shestov (1866–1938), and Boris Vysheslavtsev (1877–1954), respectively. For more detail, see *The Phoenix of Philosophy*, Introduction (1–13).

3. The Renaissance of Early Marx. From Class to Humankind
4. The Renewal of Dialectics. Evald Ilyenkov
5. The Philosophy of Human Activity. Genrikh Batishchev
6. The Renewal of Ethics. Iakov Milner-Irinin
7. Discussions around Aesthetics. Mikhail Lifshits and Aleksandr Burov
8. The Philosophy of Science. Technology and Nature
9. The Marxist Critique of Bourgeois Philosophy
10. The New Moralistic and Grassroots Turn in Marxism. Arsenii Gulyga and Iurii Davydov
11. Revisions of Orthodox Marxism in the Era of Glasnost. S. Platonov
12. The Self-Destruction of Soviet Marxism. Aleksandr Iakovlev
13. Back from Science to Utopia. Mystical Neo-Communism

Part II. Neo-Rationalism. Structuralism. General Methodology

1. From Formalism to Structuralism. The Fate of the Formal School
2. General Premises and Particular Features of Russian Structuralism
3. The Philosophy of the Semiosphere. Iurii Lotman
4. General Methodology and the System of Thought-Activity. Georgii Shchedrovitsky
5. Reflective Analysis. Vladimir Lefebvre
6. Probabilistic Philosophy of Nature and Language. Vasilii Nalimov
7. Phenomenology and the Theory of Consciousness. Merab Mamardashvili

Part III. The Philosophy of Personality and of Freedom

A. Personalism

1. Personalist and Existentialist Trends in Russian Thought
2. Nature and Personality. The Writer Mikhail Prishvin as Thinker
3. The Religious Existentialism of Iakov Druskin
4. Between Historicism and Personalism. Lidiia Ginzburg
5. Personalism, Pluralism, and Spiritual Universalism. Grigorii Pomerants
6. Russian-Jewish Personalism. Boris Khazanov
7. Personal Freedom and Planetary Consciousness. Mihajlo Mihajlov
8. The Paradoxalist Boris Paramonov. Sexual Liberation against Nationalism
9. Joseph Brodsky as Thinker. Privacy as the Ultimate Value

B. Liberalism and Westernism

1. Liberalism, Conservatism, and Religiosity
2. Freedom and Solidarity in Emigre Thought
3. Skepticism and Pluralism. Aleksandr Esenin-Volpin
4. Liberal Dissident Scholars. Arkadii Belinkov and Andrei Amalrik
5. Liberalism and Science in Political Thought. Andrei Sakharov
6. Liberal Historians. Natan Eidelman and Aleksandr Ianov
7. The Paradoxes of Late-Soviet Westernism

Part IV. Culturology, or, the Philosophy of Culture

1. The Concept of Culture in Culturology
2. Dialogism and the Methodology of the Humanities. Mikhail Bakhtin
3. Dialectical Idealism and the Phenomenology of Culture. Aleksei Losev
4. Culture, Myth, and Imagination. Olga Freidenberg and Iakov Golosovker
5. Philosophy and Philology. East and West. Dmitrii Likhachev and Nikolai Konrad
6. Dialogical Logic in the Interaction of Philosophies and Cultures. Vladimir Bibler
7. The Philosophy of Culture and Christianity. Problems of Hermeneutics. Sergei Averintsev
8. Living-Thinking through the Diversity of Cultures, Georgii Gachev

Conclusion

Introduction: Philosophy, the State, and Plato-Marxism

The academic community in the West tends to be suspicious of the very phenomenon of Russian philosophy, at best categorizing it as "ideology" or "social thought." But what is philosophy? There is no simple and universal definition, and many thinkers consider it impossible to formulate one. The most credible attempt seems to be a nominalistic reference: philosophy is that which Plato and Aristotle, Kant and Hegel engaged in. Perhaps the best-known and most widely cited—if slightly eccentric—definition belongs to A. N. Whitehead: "The safest general characterization of the European philosophical tradition is that it consists of series of footnotes to Plato. I do not mean the systematic scheme of thought which scholars have doubtfully extracted from his writings. I allude to the wealth of general ideas scattered through them ... European philosophy is a series of footnotes to Plato."[1]

If so, Russian thought must be viewed as an important part of the Western philosophical heritage, since it provides perhaps the most elaborate set of footnotes to Plato's most mature and comprehensive dialogues: the *Republic* and the *Laws*. Questions of social ethics and political philosophy, of the individual's relationship to the state, of adequate knowledge and virtuous behavior, of wisdom and power, of religious and aesthetic values, of ideas and ideals as guidelines for human life—all of these are central to Russian philosophy and exemplify its continuing relevance to the Western tradition. Moreover, the very status of ideas in Russian philosophy mirrors Plato's vision of them as ontological entities, "laws," or ideal principles—as distinct from mere epistemological units or tools of cognition. The Platonic tendency to integrate philosophical and religious teachings, and to implement them politically, culminated in twentieth-century Russia. In discussing Russian philosophy, especially of the Soviet period, we must inevitably consider the practical reality of "integrative" Platonic conceptions within the final outcome of the Soviet ideocratic utopia, in which philosophy was called upon to rule the republic as the supreme religious and political authority.

Accordingly, Russian philosophy deserves an honored place in Western intellectual history. Nowhere have Plato's teachings on the relationship of ideas to the foundation of

1 Alfred North Whitehead, *Process and Reality* (Glencoe, IL: Free Press, 1979), 39.

the state been incarnated so vigorously and on such a grandiose scale as in communist Russia. To *philosophize reality*, to transform it into a transparent kingdom of ideas, was considered the goal of thinking. This is why thought itself, in the very moment of its triumph, became a prisoner in the Crystal Palace that Soviet ideocracy erected on a philosophical foundation. In the Soviet state, more than anywhere else in history, philosophy became a supreme legal and political institution, acquiring the power of a suprapersonal, universal reason, which in its unrestricted dominion was equivalent to madness—since, being a state philosophy, it ruthlessly victimized individual thinkers. Russia has suffered not from a lack, but from an excess of philosophy. In other countries, the supreme value and highest level of authority is assigned to religious beliefs, or to economic profit, but in communist Russia, it was philosophy that served as the ultimate criterion of truth and the foundation of all political and economic transformations. Loyalty to the teachings of dialectical and historical materialism was the prerequisite of civic loyalty and professional success.

If we attempt to single out a central tenet of Russian philosophy comparable to that of rationalism in French philosophy, or empiricism in English philosophy, this would be "holism" or "totalism." Such diverse Russian thinkers as Petr Chaadaev and Vissarion Belinsky, Ivan Kireevsky and Aleksandr Herzen, Vladimir Solovyov and Vasilii Rozanov all put forward the category of "integrity," "wholeness," "totality" (*tsel'nost'*, *tselostnost'*), or "all-unity" (*vseedinstvo*), which presupposes, first and foremost, the unity of knowledge and existence, of reason and faith, of intellectual and social life. Grigorii Skovoroda (1722–94), often called "the first original Russian-Ukrainian thinker," expressed the following credo in his prayer to God on sending a new Socrates to Russia: "I believe that knowledge should not be limited to the high-priests of science and scholarship, who stuff themselves to overflowing with it, but should enter into the life of the whole people."[2]

Ivan Kireevsky (1806–56), a founder of Russian Slavophilism, sought to inaugurate "an independent philosophy corresponding to the basic principles of ancient Russian culture and capable of subjecting the divided culture of the West to the integrated consciousness of believing reason."[3] Characteristically, Kireevsky derived this tendency of Russian philosophy from Plato, as opposed to "the mind of Western man [which] seems to have a special kinship with Aristotle,"[4] that is, with one-sided abstract rationalism. Invoking the legacy of Eastern Christian thought, Kireevsky asserts that

> in Greek thinkers we do not observe a special predilection for Aristotle, but, to the contrary, the majority of them overtly prefer Plato ... probably because Plato's very mode of thinking presents more integrity [*tsel'nost'*] in the exercises of the mind, more warmth and harmony in the speculative activity of reason. This is why virtually the same relationship that we observe between these two philosophers of

2 Gregory Skovoroda, "Socrates in Russia," in *Russian Philosophy*, ed. James M. Edie, James P. Scanlan, and Mary-Barbara Zeldin (Knoxville: The University of Tennessee Press, 1987), 1: 17–18.

3 Ivan Kireevsky, "On the Necessity and Possibility of New Principles in Philosophy," ibid., 213.

4 Ibid., 182.

> antiquity [Aristotle and Plato] existed between the philosophy of the Latin world as elaborated in scholasticism and the spiritual philosophy that we find in the writers of the Eastern Church, the philosophy that was especially clearly expressed by the Holy Fathers who lived after the defection of [Catholic] Rome.[5]

This inclination to relate Russian thought to Plato as opposed to Aristotle became a hallmark of the Russian intellectual tradition, which assumed that "in Plato's teaching, religion and philosophy are in the closest contact, but already in Aristotle's system, philosophy makes a decisive break with religion."[6]

These two thinkers stand at the source of Western civilization: Plato, with his dualistic split between the material and the ideal realms, and Aristotle, who sought to mediate between these extremes by arguing that ideas were present in objects themselves as their inherent forms. According to Sergei Averintsev, an outstanding Russian cultural scholar and specialist in antiquity:

> Russian culture encountered Plato more than once. In ancient Russia, this encounter took place through the mediation of the Platonic Fathers of the Church. In the nineteenth and twentieth centuries, the mediators were Schelling and the Russians Schellingians, including the great Tiutchev, then Vladimir Solovyov, Vladimir Ern, Father Pavel Florensky, and Viacheslav Ivanov. Ancient philosophy was studied by opponents of positivism and materialism, who were more or less romantically inclined, and who naturally took up Plato's poetic dialogues rather than Aristotle's boring treatises. And the encounter with Aristotle never took place … Educated society in Russia has, so far, not read Aristotle.[7]

From Averintsev's point of view, it is only to be regretted that Russian civilization chose the Platonic model, developing it with a relentless consistency that led directly to the realization of Plato's ideal government, where the order of things was strictly subservient to the order of ideas. From this perspective, Soviet philosophy embodied the final stage of the development of Plato's ideas. In this stage, the project of ideocracy was both practically realized and theoretically exhausted. In a certain sense, Russian philosophy of the past two centuries summarizes and explicates more than two millennia of the Platonic tradition and points a way for a return to foundations that are separate from the idealistic and ideological spheres.

From the 1920s through the 1940s, the kingdom of communist ideas succeeded in equating itself with social reality. However, beginning in the mid-1950s, stimulated by Khrushchev's denunciations of Stalin in 1956, this "ideal republic" increasingly

5 I. V. Kireevskii, *Kritika i estetika* (Moscow: Iskusstvo, 1979), 272.

6 A. I. Abramov, "Otsenka filosofii Platona v russkoi idealisticheskoi filosofii," in *Platon i ego epokha*, ed. F. Kh. Kessidi (Moscow: Nauka, 1979), 222.

7 Sergei Averintsev, *Ritorika i istoki evropeiskoi literaturnoi traditsii* (Moscow: Shkola "Iazyki russkoi kul'tury," 1996), 328. Averintsev directly counterposes the two philosophers thus: "If Plato is the first utopian thinker, then Aristotle is the first thinker to look the utopian spirit straight in the eye and overcome it" (ibid., 320).

revealed itself to be illusory and disconnected from reality. Religious and personalist philosophy, culturology, structuralism, scientism and the philosophy of thought-action, phenomenology, liberalism, and nationalism—all of these intellectual movements and methods were attempts to de-ideologize the social sphere. Thought tried to free itself from subjection to ideocracy by putting down roots in authentic, concrete forms of being, such as the empirical credibility of science, the existential uniqueness of personality, faith in a living God, the spiritual integrity of humankind, the rational design of the cosmos, the symbolic meanings of culture, or the organic soul of the nation; or by challenging the master discourse of Soviet ideology through parodic imitation. In its transition to its post-Soviet stage, Russian philosophy ultimately came to a sort of postmodernist skepticism and pluralism, a conceptualist style of thought that ironically reproduces and exaggerates the world of abstract ideas in order to demonstrate their artificial and chimerical nature. All that remained of the principle of ideocracy by the late 1980s was a museum of obsolete ideas, a carnival sideshow of ideological curiosities.

What role did Marxism play in the Platonic drama of Russian philosophy? Marxism, which deduces all ideas from the economic base of society, would seem to be diametrically opposed to Platonism. But Marxism, it should be recalled, represents a reversal of Hegelian idealism, the final moment in the self-development of the Absolute Idea. What is principally new in Hegel, as compared with Plato, is the progressive historical development of the Idea; but the end of this process is postulated as the universal state (presumably conceived on the model of the Prussian monarchy), which embraces the totality of the self-cognizant mind. Both Platonic and Hegelian idealism culminate in the concept of the ideal state. Although Marx removed this ideal from the causality of the historical process, it remains in his system as a teleological motive and grows into a vision of a future communist society.[8]

Plato, Hegel, and Marx represent three stages in the development of idealism in its progressive symbiosis with social engineering: (1) the supernatural world of ideas; (2) the manifestation of the Absolute Idea in history; and (3) the transformation of history by the force of ideas. For Plato, ideas are abstracted to a transcendental realm. For Hegel, the Idea is already ingrained as the alpha and omega of the historical process: it generates, and at the same time consummates, history in the course of its progressive self-awareness. Marx abolishes the idea as the alpha of history in order to emphasize the omega point: the prospect of the historical culmination of unified humanity in the transparent kingdom of ideas, the self-government of collective reason.

Moreover, Marxism potentially proves more staunchly idealistic than even Platonism. According to Plato, the world of ideas exists in and of itself without

[8] On the totalitarian implications of Platonism and its connection with Marxist philosophy, see Karl R. Popper, *The Open Society and Its Enemies* (London: Routledge and Kegan Paul, 1966). Comparisons of Marx and Plato are scattered throughout the book and can be traced using the subject index. In particular, Popper remarks: "The whole idea—which was not Marx's invention—that there is something behind the prices, an objective or real or true value of which prices are only a 'form of appearance,' shows clearly enough the influence of Platonic Idealism with its distinction between a hidden essential or true reality, and an accidental or delusive appearance" (2: 165).

necessarily demanding historical embodiment. For Marx, ideas are inseparable from the material process and seek realization and implementation. In Marx's own words, "theory also becomes a material force as soon as it has gripped the masses."[9] The message of "militant materialism," as realized in Russia by this term's coiner Lenin and his disciples, was that the power of "progressive" ideas should not be *abstracted from* but rather *attracted to* material life, even subordinating and transforming the economic base: hence, the institution of five-year plans that subordinated the entire development of the country to idealistic projections. Whereas ideas in Plato and Hegel still soared above the earth, constituting a separate sphere of Supreme Mind or Absolute Spirit, in Soviet Marxism they were grounded in the foundation of material life, from heavy industry to everyday reality, and from the rituals of party purges to ceremonial tidying-ups of neighborhoods. In this view, the ruling ideology would not forgive the slightest flaw or deviation from the purity of ideas: ideas had descended into the substance of Being, and they therefore demanded the complete submission of every person at every moment of their life. Soviet materialism proved to be an instrument of militant idealism, craving ever newer sacrifices for the altar of sacred ideas. This occurred in strict correspondence with another of Marx's statements: "As the revolution then began in the brain of the *monk*, so now it begins in the brain of the *philosopher*." But it only *begins* in this way, "for revolutions require a *passive* element, a material basis."[10]

For all these reasons, the dominant intellectual movement of the Soviet epoch was not just Marxism, but more specifically *Plato-Marxism*—an idealism that asserts itself as the regulative principle of material life. If Plato, from the idealist assumptions of his philosophy, deduced the system of the communist state, then Marx, proceeding from communist assumptions, deduced a system of ideocracy, a dictatorial state that was realized through the efforts of his most consistent and determined Soviet followers. Materialism became an ideology, and the very phrase "materialist ideology" came to sound perfectly natural to Soviet ears. No less natural, therefore, is the term "Plato-Marxism." Marxism is the flip side of Platonism, and the eventual collapse of the Soviet ideocratic state can be viewed as a sort of death sentence for both. The relatively brief Soviet period of just over seventy years sums up the two millennia of Western thought that followed Plato's quest for the world of ruling ideas. Among these footnotes to Plato that Whitehead believed to be "the general characterization of the European philosophical tradition," Soviet philosophy appears to the attentive eye as the final entry, signifying "The End."

One cannot but recall in this context a debate between two outstanding thinkers of the mid-twentieth century, Alexandre Kojève (1908–68), a French philosopher of Russian origin (his original surname was Kozhevnikov), and Leo Strauss (1899–1973), an American political scientist and historian of philosophy, of German-Jewish

[9] Karl Marx, "A Contribution to the Critique of Hegel's Philosophy of Right. Introduction." Translated by Annette Jolin and Joseph O'Malley. Available electronically: https://www.marxists.org/archive/marx/works/1843/critique-hpr/intro.htm

[10] Ibid.

origin.[11] In their debate on "tyranny and wisdom," they came to opposite conclusions. Kojève, who was strongly influenced by Hegel and Heidegger, assumed that "politics is derivative from *philosophy*"[12] and, conversely, that philosophy needs politics in order to realize its ideas (even at the price of their temporary distortion)—and thus to accomplish its ultimate goal: the construction of the universal and socially homogeneous state. At this point, according to Kojève, both history and philosophy achieve their end and negate themselves by merging into one. History dissolves in the Absolute Idea, which comes to complete self-realization in the universal state, whereas philosophy, being itself only a preparatory stage, a "love of wisdom," enables the full manifestation of wisdom, "Sophia," in political institutions. Leo Strauss bitingly responds that, indeed, "the coming of the universal and homogeneous state will be the end of philosophy on earth."[13] Yet the effect of such a process will be far less sublime than what Kojève envisioned; the result will be, rather, the political persecution and physical extermination of philosophers.

Although the Soviet historical experiment is rarely mentioned in this debate, it is implicit throughout. No wonder, since Kojève, a Russian émigré, emerged from the ideological movement known as Eurasianism, which, as early as the 1920s, expressed qualified support for the Soviet regime as an embodiment of the Hegelian impulse to the Absolute State. Eurasianists designated this "highest" type of state as "ideocratic," that is, ruled by and ruling through the power of ideas. This was one of the first, and most euphoric and euphemistic, formulations of what later came to be known as "totalitarianism."

As the ideocratic state demonstrated clearly in the USSR, the attempt to construct society according to the precepts of philosophy brings about their mutual destruction rather than fulfillment. A society subjected to the rule of ideas gradually disintegrates economically and morally, whereas philosophy subjected to the rule of politicians degenerates into catechism and propaganda and also disintegrates physically as its practitioners are persecuted and exterminated. This result is quite predictable, since the state conceived as the embodiment of Philosophy cannot tolerate any philosophy other than its own.

Philosophy itself, however, survives both its martyrs and its persecutors. Today, from the perspective of post-Hegelian and post-Marxist historicism, we are in the privileged position of being able to see what happens after the collapse of the ideocratic state, that perfect synthesis of "tyranny and wisdom." Although Strauss was essentially correct in his assessment of the perils of such a union, one cannot deny a kind of surplus value in such an experiment. Ironically, Kojève was not far in error in his prediction that "the coming of the wise man must necessarily be preceded by the revolutionary

[11] I owe a deep gratitude to Dr. Eve Adler (1945–2004) of Middlebury College, who drew my attention to this dialogue.

[12] Leo Strauss, *On Tyranny. Including the Strauss-Kojève Correspondence*, ed. Victor Gourevich and Michael S. Roth (New York: The Free Press, 1991), 173.

[13] Ibid., 211.

political action of the tyrant (who will realize the universal State)."[14] By this he meant that "Sophia," or "absolute reason," would be manifest after all *philosophical* aspirations toward wisdom have been realized by the revolutionary action of a tyrant. But what happens, in fact, is that wisdom accumulated by history denies the value of revolution itself, of all the philosophical illusions and temptations that led to the establishment of the universal state.

In the aftermath of the totalitarian regime, the mutual negation of "philosophy and society" in their attempted synthesis turns into the negation of synthesis itself, both on the part of politicians who cut back their ideological claims, and on the part of thinkers who withdraw their political aspirations. This sort of wisdom, born of historical experience, draws a clear line of demarcation between politics and philosophy while challenging the effectiveness of the "wisdom-tyranny" union, and becomes possible only in the aftermath of a futile though continuous and comprehensive ideocratic experiment. What gives a unique and universal significance to the "deferred" wisdom of Russian thought in the late and post-Soviet periods is its ability to pronounce a competent judgment on Platonic and Hegelian conceptions of the ideal state from within the "attained" reality of this very state.

[14] Ibid., 175.

Part I

The Philosophy of National Spirit. Conservatism, Eurasianism, and Traditionalism

1. The Search for National Identity. Traditions and New Challenges

The search for national identity, or *natsional'naia ideia*, is central to Russian thought of the nineteenth and twentieth centuries. If we attempt to single out one concept that has united the majority of intellectual trends, this concept would be "Russia" itself, not merely as a geographical or historical reality, but as a philosophical idea that remains to be properly defined or embodied. In a certain sense, the concept of *Russia* plays the same unifying role in Russian philosophy as do *Tao*, *Logos*, and *Geist* in the Chinese, Greek, and German traditions, respectively. Beginning with Petr Chaadaev (1794–1856), considered to be the first truly original Russian thinker, the most pertinent question has been: "Who are we?" What is the ultimate destination of the Russian people, its mission in the world?

This question famously divided Russian intellectuals into two opposite camps: Slavophiles, who believed in the particularity of the Russian spirit and mission as superseding an older, disintegrating European tradition; and Westernizers, who advocated the historical achievements of the West as a model for Russian development retarded by her semi-Asiatic past. This polarity of "introverted" and "extroverted" orientations can be traced from the 1830s–1840s onward. However, with the October Revolution of 1917, both Slavophilism and Westernism took new directions, sometimes even merging in unexpected syntheses. Being a militantly internationalist platform, communism initially provoked strong opposition among nationalist adherents of the old regime, including the White Guard movement, but the most original trends of postrevolutionary nationalistic thought attempted to reappropriate communism as an organic part of Russia's historical destiny, as the hope for its spiritual revival and ascent to future political dominance.

Among the postrevolutionary movements that anticipated the resurgence of late-Soviet Russian nationalism, the first was the *Scythians*, a branch of left-populists led by the philosopher, journalist, and historian Razumnik Ivanov-Razumnik (1878–1946). Immediately following the October upheaval, these thinkers identified it as a radical break with Western civilization. The name "Scythians" refers to the ancient tribes of nomadic warriors who from about the ninth century BCE until the fourth century CE had extended their influence all over Central Asia, from China to the northern Black

Sea. The northeastern-most corner of the Roman Empire that they inhabited would become the southernmost region of the Russian Empire. According to the cultural myth propagated by Ivanov-Razumnik, Russians, as the offspring of the Scythians, symbolize both barbarous opposition to the refined and decadent West and its eventual successor in the progression of world civilizations. The October Revolution eliminated (at least formally) two of the three principles upon which the Russian Empire was founded, autocracy and Orthodoxy, but the third, *narodnost'*, "folk spirit," not only survived but revealed its messianic potential as the destroyer of individualistic European societies. Hence Aleksandr Blok's defiant challenge to the West in his poem "The Scythians" (dated January 30, 1918) was inspired by the movement of that name: "Come, fight! Yea, we are Scythians, / Yea, Asians, a squint-eyed, greedy brood."[1]

The next postrevolutionary movement to anticipate late-Soviet Russian nationalism was *Smenovekhovstvo* ("Change of Landmarks"), founded in 1921 by Nikolai Ustrialov, a professor of jurisprudence with a Hegelian philosophical disposition.[2] Though a member of the liberal party of Constitutional Democrats and an enemy of the Bolsheviks, he came to believe, with Hegel, that everything that is real is rational and therefore that the Bolshevik Revolution could not but result in the historical advancement of the Russian people. From this point of view, history has its own morality, distinct from the notions of individual virtue and sin; thus it is the duty of the Russian intelligentsia to cooperate with the Bolsheviks, despite any personal disagreements with their violent methods. The goal of politics, according to Ustrialov, is the creation of a powerful state, and the Bolsheviks' professed internationalism, he felt, masked a welcome will to Russian global dominance under the slogan of proletarian solidarity. Change of Landmarks emerged in émigré circles, but in the 1920s it became popular also in Soviet Russia itself among members of the intelligentsia who, despite many reservations, tried to justify their collaboration with the Soviet regime on the basis of national rather than class solidarity. It has even been speculated that the official ideological shift in the late 1920s, from an internationalist revolutionary strategy to the internal politics of socialist construction "in one country," was due in part to the influence of the Change of Landmarks.

Another movement, Eurasianism, albeit less overtly political than Change of Landmarks, was intellectually more profound and proved more enduring in its influence. It was founded by philologist Nikolai Trubetskoi, geographer Petr Savitsky, theologian Georges Florovsky, historian Georgii Vernadsky, and philosopher Lev Karsavin.[3] Eurasianists put a greater emphasis on the Orthodox Christian identity

1 Trans. cited from Babette Deutsch and Avrahm Yarmolinsky, eds., *Modern Russian Poetry* (New York: Harcourt, Brace, and Company, 1961), 134.

2 The movement received its name from the collection *Smena vekh* (*Change of Landmarks*) published in Prague in 1921.

3 The Eurasianist manifesto *Exodus to the East. Presentiments and Accomplishments. The Affirmation of the Eurasians* was published in Sofia, Bulgaria in 1921; some of these materials of early Eurasianism were reprinted in post-Soviet Russia in I. A. Isaev, ed., *Puti Evrazii. Russkaia intelligentsiia i sud'by Rossii* (Moscow: Russkaia kniga, 1992). The latest collection of articles on the evolution and cultural and political impact of Russian Eurasianism is Mark Bassin, Sergey Glebov, and Marlene Laruelle, eds., *Between Europe and Asia: The Origins, Theories, and Legacies of Russian Eurasianism* (Pittsburgh: University of Pittsburgh Press, 2015).

of the Russian people and accused Change of Landmarks of a political compromise with Bolshevism. They based their views on the specificity of the Russian Empire as a geographical and historical formation different from both Europe and Asia. Russia is not a mono-ethnic but a supra-ethnic unit—a whole continent, encompassing a community of nations, of mostly Slavic and Turkic origin, in the same way that Europe encompasses the community of Roman and Germanic nations. It should not be perceived as a single country, comparable to England, France, or China, but as a continental conglomerate, on a par with Europe or Asia. Eurasianists criticized both monarchic and democratic types of government, advocating instead *ideocracy*, "a regime in which the ruling stratum is selected by the quality of loyalty to one overall ruling idea [*obshchaia ideia-pravitel'nitsa*]."[4] Categories of "class" or "nation" are too narrow to serve as a basis for ideocracy, since they divide the state rather than unite it; the idea of "humanity" is too broad, since it does not justify the existence of a distinct state. What is needed is the concept of a "separate world," Eurasia, that embraces a variety of classes and nations but remains self-enclosed in its distinction from other worlds, namely Europe and Asia.

Eurasianists assessed the Soviet Union as an imperfect ideocracy, divided by class polarities. They condemned its materialistic and atheistic doctrines but recognized the organizational power of communism and collectivist ideals. "Under ideocratic structure, the last remnants of individualism will disappear and the human being will realize not only himself but also his class and nation as fulfilling certain functions within an organic whole united in a State."[5] One of the peculiarities of the Eurasian state would be the subordination of the socioeconomic sphere and property relations to the dominance of ideas, unlike the West in both its capitalist and socialist variants, where the ideological and political spheres are derived from economic conditions. Many Eurasianist concepts would prove to be close to the ideology of Italian fascism and German national socialism, especially the glorification of a state, governed by a one-party system and based on the priority of national or transnational ideas, which interferes in all spheres of economic, cultural, and religious life and subjects the individual to the "symphonic" personality of the state itself.

The Eurasianists' original intellectual impetus was exhausted by the mid-1930s, but on the whole they demonstrated a better potential for adaptation to late- and post-Soviet ideological needs than did traditional Slavophilism. The main difference between the two movements can be formulated as the opposition between "back-to-the-soil" romanticism and an ethnically motivated will to political and technological domination. Eurasianism succeeded in freeing Slavophilic ideals from their dreamy nostalgia for a pious and patriarchal Rus, integrating them rather into a broad futurist project of a powerful totalitarian state. Early Slavophilism exalted the spirit of communality as exemplified by the Orthodox Church, while Eurasianism found

[4] N. S. Trubetskoi, "Ob idee-pravitel'nitse ideokraticheskogo gosudarstva," *Evraziiskaia khronika* (Berlin), no. 11 (1935). Available electronically: https://www.gumilev-center.ru/ob-idee-pravitelnice-ideokraticheskogo-gosudarstva/

[5] Ibid.

its most alluring ideal in the collective will of the state. Eurasianism, as an attempt to mediate the opposition between nationalism and communism, between religious traditionalism and technological pragmatism, between the Asian and European constituents of the Russian historical identity, proved to be a common denominator for many of the ideological tendencies arising with the erosion of official Soviet Marxism. The far left and far right, former communists and new nationalists, technocrats, and nativists, adherents of Orthodox and Islamic fundamentalism—all could potentially find a middle ground in the Eurasianist synthesis.

The period of the 1930s–1950s was marked by increasing nationalist tendencies, both in Soviet society and in émigré circles; in the latter, several minor pro-fascist parties formed. The prophecies of Change of Landmarks and Eurasianism about a nationalist reorientation of Soviet communism came true, especially with Stalin's ideological campaigns of the late 1940s and early 1950s, condemning the internationalist stance of earlier communism under the name "bourgeois cosmopolitanism." These nationalist tendencies, apart from their narrow political motivation, lacked theoretical novelty or philosophical depth, as their fundamentals had already been formulated in the wake of the revolution.[6]

Nationalism reached its nadir during Khrushchev's "Thaw," when, with the revival of communist ideals in full swing and with the establishment of communist regimes in Asia, Eastern Europe, and Cuba, internationalism was at its most fervent stage since the time of Lenin. In the philosophical context of this period, structuralism was showcasing the insights of scientific analysis, and the triumphs of the Russian space program served to reinforce the motivations of technological progress with its global appeal.

A new impetus for Slavophilism can be observed in Russian thought beginning in the mid-1960s with the exhaustion of the Thaw and of the impulse for social and intellectual innovation. Aleksandr Solzhenitsyn's novella *Matrena's House* (1963) and Vasilii Belov's *Business as Usual* (1966) laid the foundation for the new literary movement of "village prose," which was echoed in aesthetics and cultural theory. The celebration of scientific reason, penetrating deeply into the humanities as well, provoked resistance on the part of some conservative scholars. Opposition gradually arose within the younger generation of traditionalists, who identified the wave of rationalism as a symptom of Western influence and who, in their polemics against it, for the first time in Soviet intellectual history openly employed Slavophilic arguments. Even at the height of the campaign against cosmopolitanism, with its glorification of everything genuinely Russian, Stalin's ideologists never made recourse to the Slavophile legacy, which was unanimously condemned as reactionary and archaic. Notably, from its nineteenth-century outset, Slavophilism had stood in intellectual opposition to governmental policy, reproaching Peter the Great and all the emperors who succeeded him for their Westernist orientation, and it was characteristic that the resurgence

[6] The most comprehensive review of the tendencies toward the convergence between communism and nationalism in postrevolutionary Russian ideology (1917–30) remains Mikhail Agurskii, *Ideologiia natsional-bol'shevizma* (Paris: YMCA Press, 1980).

of Slavophilism in the 1960s likewise took the form of opposition to Westernist tendencies in Soviet ideology. Thus the pattern of evolution of the "Russian idea," from Slavophilism to Eurasianism, is repeated in condensed form in the 1960s–1980s: the Slavophile revival of the 1960s–1970s, which culminated in the programmatic writings of Solzhenitsyn, gives way to Eurasianism as the prevailing form of nationalist ideology of the 1980s and especially of the post-Soviet epoch.

2. The Neo-Slavophile Revival in Aesthetics and Criticism. Petr Palievsky and Vadim Kozhinov

The nationalist revival found its first academic expression in the writings of a group of young researchers at the Moscow Institute of World Literature whose point of departure was the rejection of structuralism as applied to literary studies.[7] Petr Palievsky (b. 1932), the initial spokesperson of this "anti-positivist" trend, was the author of several articles devoted to the image (*obraz*) as the central unit of artistic creativity.[8] For him, the sign (*znak*), which structuralists held up as the primary element of the semiotic approach to language and literature, is deficient as an instrument of analysis, since it presupposes an arbitrary and conventional connection between the signifying and the signified. Palievsky points instead to the image, to its integral relationship to reality: the image, in his view, is not merely the representation of external being but is at the same time the full-fledged being of this representation. The image, then, is not a variety of sign (e.g., an "iconic sign"); rather, signs are degraded images, reduced to conventional and instrumental usage. Palievsky accuses structuralists of bleeding literature of its unique vitality by turning it into a system of signs, hence failing to distinguish literature from language and its pragmatic functions. And indeed, structuralists could be said to subscribe to the famous formalist assumption that literature is merely a particular use of language, its "poetic function" (Roman Jakobson).

For Palievsky, structuralism is a reductive methodology which, in relegating literature to a substratum of verbal signs, undermines its aesthetic specificity. In his view, structuralism "does away with individuality by establishing it as a simple combination of general principles .... From the very start, in undertaking to dismember 'artistry,' structuralism dismembered it into such elements as were not elements of art. Setting out in search of the *specific*, it came to obtain the most *nonspecific*."[9] Rather than taking literature as an extension of syntactic and lexical structures, Palievsky views its essence as transcending the referentiality of pure semiotics. By its use of the image, literature imparts to signs an extralinguistic significance, which overcomes the arbitrariness of the designation. For example, the word "blue," as a linguistic unit, signals a specific

7 On structuralism and semiotics in Russian thought, see Epstein, *The Phoenix of Philosophy*, 77–92.

8 Palievsky's key essays "The Internal Structure of the Image" and "The Artistic Work" were published in an influential three-volume set on literary theory by the Institute of World Literature: *Teoriia literatury. Osnovnye problemy v istoricheskom osveshchenii* (Moscow: Izd. AN SSSR, 1962–5).

9 P. V. Palievskii, *Literatura i teoriia* (2nd ed. Moscow: Sovremennik, 1978), 69, 70.

color which has nothing to do with the characters making up this word or the sounds of their utterance; however, as a literary image, "blue" harbors the potential evocations of gentleness, peacefulness, wisdom, innocence, etc., which are given by the blueness itself as its inherent spiritual quality. When we read literature, we perceive not letters or words, but images as presentations of persons, landscapes, and objects in their lifelike totality. Without naming it (and perhaps without even realizing it), Palievsky appeals to the phenomenological or eidetic approach to artistic imagery.

In Palievsky's theory of the image, these totalities are grasped not through rational analysis (as in structuralism) but by a kind of holistic intuition. Moreover, this intuition is theorized as a uniquely non-Western and particularly Russian spiritual predisposition in opposition to Western rationalism. In his commentaries on the Russian classics, Palievsky underlines this organic and holistic nature of the Russian national spirit, as manifested in Pushkin, Dostoevsky, and Sholokhov. Palievsky does not exclude other nations from this kind of spirituality: for instance, among American authors, he admires such Southern writers as Faulkner, who in his view challenged the rational impetus of technological civilization and its emphasis on individualism by appealing to a deeper intuition of kinship, community, and tradition. At this earlier stage, neo-Slavophilism is not so much a nationalistic doctrine as an irrationalist and conservative reaction against the ideologies of scientific progress, which had allegedly exterminated, especially in Russia, traditional folk culture.

Many of Palievsky's other works are devoted to defending realism as a Russian cultural tradition and condemning all kinds of avant-gardism, which he regards as artistic extensions of technological positivism. He makes no patriotic exceptions for the Russian avant-garde, blaming equally Picasso and Chagall, Joyce and Khlebnikov for an anti-natural bias, a compulsion to remodel reality as an aggregate collage of discrete mechanical parts devoid of organic unity. Curiously, in his total denunciation of avant-gardism and modernism, Palievsky coincides with the position of the staunchly orthodox Soviet Marxist Mikhail Lifshits (described in *The Phoenix of Philosophy*). Both Lifshits and Palievsky chuckle over the cult of genius that led avant-gardists to appoint themselves messiahs and see them rather as self-promoting hucksters. Palievsky was an influential figure in the 1960s–1970s, but later his lack of productivity and preoccupation with administrative functions pushed him to the margin of the Soviet intellectual scene.

A far more stable and active presence was that of Palievsky's colleague and collaborator, Vadim Kozhinov (1930–2001), who was one of the most prolific literary critics and ideologists of the 1970s–1990s and remained an unfaltering defender of Slavophile ideals. Early in his career, Kozhinov concentrated on the theory of the novel and was a follower of Mikhail Bakhtin, whose works he helped to bring to public attention. Some of Bakhtin's later publications were edited by Kozhinov and introduced with his commentaries. Increasingly, however, Kozhinov's focus began to shift toward Slavophilism, and he was among the first in the Soviet context to argue publicly the merits of its philosophical legacy, claiming that it had anticipated the critique of rationalism and the Enlightenment and the existentialist challenge to abstract truth leveled by Western thinkers of the twentieth century.

In Kozhinov's view, the Slavophile tradition represents a continuation of the Platonic philosophic trajectory, as opposed to the Aristotelian—the path taken by Western thought. He traced the Slavophile vision of Christianity to the neo-Platonic teachings of the Byzantine Church, which emphasized the unity of human capacities of mind and soul, unlike the analytical approach of Aristotle, who abstracted logical categories from an intuitive (and allegedly superior) faculty. From a Slavophile perspective, the Western metaphysical tradition, which insists upon the opposition of subject and object, individual and collective, etc., is responsible for the degradation of human personality by individualism and the destabilization of society through political leftism and partisanship.

Furthermore, for Kozhinov, rationalism in thinking leads to violence in action. Thus he evaluates the history of Western colonialism as one of assimilation by conquest, while Russia's expansion to the South and East has proceeded in a spirit of mutual respect and interdependence. The non-Christian nomads of the steppes were treated as dignified neighbors, and even the eventual repulsion of the Tatar-Mongol hordes from Russia in the fifteenth century was followed by a process of peaceful integration, as enemy leaders were welcomed into the Russian aristocracy, to the point of becoming its elite. "The Russian people displayed a strikingly peaceful and friendly attitude toward the peoples residing in territories absorbed by Russians. If we compare the attitude of the Russian people toward the Chudes, Mordva, and Karelians dwelling in the land of Novgorod with the attitude, for example, of Americans to Indian tribes, we can clearly see an immeasurable difference."[10]

Similar reasoning allows Kozhinov to explain the Western ecological crisis. Attributing a prevailing Judaic influence to Western Christianity, he argues that the Old Testament emphasis has led to an anthropocentric mentality by which the ostensibly inferior nonhuman world is considered solely in terms of its practical utility. Kozhinov claims that, as Eastern Orthodoxy takes little account of the Old Testament, Russians managed to avoid such "Semitic" influence and established a more harmonious relationship with the natural world. This claim runs counter to the glaring fact of a grave ecological crisis in Soviet and post-Soviet Russia, but attributing these problems to Jewish undercurrents in the Bolshevik revolution that produced the Soviet system is a characteristic neo-Slavophile move.

Another mark of Russian moral superiority is the Slavic capacity for repentance and self-condemnation. Kozhinov draws many parallels between Russian and Western atrocities, claiming that the Russian people are actively remorseful for past mistakes, while Westerners tend to erase them from their historical memory. For example, he cites August 24, 1572, the day of both the end of Ivan the Terrible's reign of terror and, in France, the St. Bartholomew's Day massacre of Huguenots, claiming that more people were slaughtered on this one day in France than in eight cruel years of Ivan's *oprichnina*. Moreover, everyone in Russia recalls with poignant shame the execution of five Decembrists in 1825, while most Europeans have forgotten that 10,000 Parisian

[10] Vadim Kozhinov, *Razmyshleniia o russkoi literature* (Moscow: Sovremennik, 1991), 96.

revolutionaries were killed or injured in June 1848. Kozhinov notes that this latter event was condemned even by Aleksandr Herzen, the foremost Russian apologist of the West, who wrote after witnessing this massacre that, compared with the bourgeoisie that wrought it, Cossacks are meek lambs. Why then, wonders Kozhinov, are the Russian people singled out in the West as the cruelest among European nations? It is due only to the depth of the Russian conscience, which demands a forthright moral self-condemnation, that Russian history is depicted as a continuum of crimes and oppression. Kozhinov offers the example of Russia's greatest epic song *The Tale of Igor's Campaign* (twelfth century), which, unlike its Western medieval counterparts, does not portray the triumphs of a gallant figure, but instead the tragic disgrace of a prince doomed by his own hubris. In symbolic support of his claim, Kozhinov points to the relative importance of Christmas and Easter in Western and Russian Christianity. Christmas is the West's most celebrated Christian holiday, whereas in Russia it is Easter. On the one hand, we have a celebration of Christ's joyous appearance on earth; on the other, the mystery of the resurrection through suffering and death. Kozhinov compares the latter to the fate of Russia, which has died painfully and resurrected itself from ruin several times in its history.

Kozhinov argues that Russia shares a greater affinity with Asia than with Europe. He cites numerous examples of thematizations of the Caucasus in Russian literature that express a spirit of genuine brotherhood with Asian peoples. He recalls the last pages of *Diary of a Writer*, where Dostoevsky recommends that Russians overcome the "servile fear that Europe will call them 'Asian barbarians' .... Our hopes, perhaps, lie more with Asia than with Europe."[11] Ironically, Lenin, though invariably hostile to the "reactionary" and "arch-vile" (*arkhiskvernyi*) Dostoevsky, expressed similar sentiments shortly before his death, proclaiming that Russia must unite with Asia in the struggle of Eastern nations against Western imperialism. Thus, on this point, Russian patriots and Soviet leaders were in complete agreement, and Kozhinov often enjoys the opportunity to emphasize their solidarity in anti-Westernism.

Nevertheless, Kozhinov's quintessential understanding of the Russian national character, borrowed from Dostoevsky's well-known encomium of Pushkin, is its openness to other nations and to humanity in the broadest sense. A Russian is often ashamed of being only Russian because he feels himself primarily to be human. With this point, Kozhinov attempts to transcend the traditional divide between Russian Slavophiles and Westernizers by pointing to a universal mission for the Russian nation to unify world civilization under the banner of brotherly love. Westernizers wanted Russia to join one of the existing cultural worlds (the Roman and/or the Germanic); Slavophiles called on Russia to create a new, sovereign civilization. Both positions, for Kozhinov, lose sight of Russia's true destiny: not to imitate other nations, nor extol its own narrow nationality, but to embrace the spirit of all other nations and initiate a permanent dialogue among them. At this point Kozhinov reasserts his faithfulness to Bakhtin's "dialogic poetics," arguing that "it is specifically Russian thought that was

[11] Ibid., 51.

able and was obliged to create the aesthetics of dialogue."[12] Kozhinov counterposes Bakhtinian "polyphony" to Hegelian "monologic" philosophy, allegedly a manifestation and justification of European egocentrism. "The active, firm and coherent, and exclusively national self-assertion characteristic of the life and culture of, for instance, England and France, or in other forms, of Japan or Turkey, is not characteristic of Russian being and consciousness."[13] Russia's specificity, then, is to be free from any specificity, to overcome its own national limits. To be Russian means to be panhuman. This is somewhat reminiscent of Orwell's "All animals are equal, but some animals are more equal than others." All nations are human, but Russia is more human than other nations, it is the quintessence of humanity. "All-encompassing humanness [*vsechelovechnost'*] ... lives in the very depth of the Russian national character."[14] What appears as a refutation of nationalism is in fact its most ambitious manifestation, since a single nation is proclaimed to be more universal than all others.

That is why Kozhinov vehemently denounces "cosmopolitanism" and "superficial, mediocre international culture," or rather "semiculture," claiming it to be "omnivorous" and neglectful of national spirit. Ever since Stalin's campaign against "cosmopolitans," this term in Russian has usually implied Jews, "Zionists," or the "Judeo-Masonic conspiracy" against Russia. In 1987 Kozhinov initiated a debate on the "Khazar yoke over Russia," arguing that this people, which had professed Judaism and had in the seventh to eleventh centuries established a mighty empire in a vast territory of the southeastern European plain (from the Caucasus to Kiev), had been the oppressor of Russians (in the same way one could speak of the Roman yoke over the ancient Germans who later seized Rome, just as Slavs eventually seized and destroyed the Khazarian state). One of the earliest texts of Russian literature, Metropolitan Ilarion's "The Sermon on Law and Grace" (1049), traditionally considered a manifesto of rising Russian statehood as directed against Byzantium, is now reinterpreted by Kozhinov as an attack on Judaism, specifically as embodied in the Khazarian Kaganate. Even the subsequent Tatar yoke, according to Kozhinov, inherited certain crucial aspects of the Khazars' domination of Russia. For example, during the battle of Kulikovo (1380), the decisive event in the history of Russia's liberation from the Tatars, the Horde's troops, according to Kozhinov, represented not so much Tatar-Mongols, but the forces of cosmopolitanism, organized by slave-owners and merchants from a Genoan colony on the Black Sea. This was a "battle of the Russian people first and foremost against global cosmopolitan aggression, since the aggressive politics of Mamai [the Tatar khan] was increasingly determined by the interests and policy of the international speculators of Genoa and Kaffa."[15]

[12] Kozhinov continues by again contrasting this Russian penitential tendency with Western hubris, quoting the Slavophile Ivan Kireevsky: "A man in the West is almost always satisfied with his moral state; almost every European is ready to strike his breast with pride and proclaim to himself and others that his conscience is quite clear before God and man. On the contrary, a Russian man always feels his deficiencies deeply, and the higher he ascends on the ladder of moral development, the less he is satisfied with himself" (ibid., 60–1).

[13] Ibid., 61.

[14] Ibid.

[15] Ibid., 57.

Thus, all-encompassing humanity and "cosmopolitanism" are, for Kozhinov, irreconcilable, because genuine humanity is achieved only through national self-consciousness. Lest panhumanness, as exemplified by Russians, degenerates into "rootless" cosmopolitanism, exemplified by Jews, it must be continuously reinforced by national spirit. In other words, if to be Russian means to be human, then to be *really* human means to be Russian. This ideal, which had a definite Christian impetus in Dostoevsky, appears rather abstract in Kozhinov, since he is not inclined to identify his position in religious terms. Like most of the neo-Slavophiles who emerged in the 1960s, Kozhinov had been raised in an atheistic or at least secular milieu, and Orthodox Christianity appears to him primarily as an indispensable attribute of Russian historical tradition. This is the inherent paradox of the Slavophilism of the 1960s–1980s: it follows the formal patterns of its nineteenth-century religious-minded predecessors, like Aleksei Khomiakov and Ivan Kireevsky, but is for the most part devoid of the original justification located in Orthodox Christianity, which conceived of the nation as a "God-bearer." Thus neo-Slavophiles were left to conceive of the Russian nation as merely a "nation-bearer" or even a "self-bearer," which appears to be a tautology and absurdity at the same time.

3. Other Neo-Slavophiles and Nationalists of the 1960s–1970s

Besides Palievsky and Kozhinov, who represented the more intellectualized branch of neo-Slavophilism, there was another group of critics concentrated around the journal and publishing house *Young Guard*. This group, led by two literary critics, Mikhail Lobanov (1925–2016) and Viktor Chalmaev (b. 1932), took an anti-intellectual stance, claiming that the contemporary Soviet intelligentsia had betrayed the common people by becoming a transmitter of Western influences. In an article entitled "Enlightened Philistinism" (1968), Lobanov condemned "Americanism of the spirit," an ethical corruption wrought by bourgeois materialist temptations, whose major proponents were found among the Soviet educated elite. He assumes that "the temptation of bourgeois prosperity is the people's greatest mortal enemy."[16] Lobanov's critique of the bourgeois mentality is not grounded in a traditional Marxist position, but derives rather from a nationalist commitment. In his view, genuine culture comes not from education but from national soil: "It is the uneducated folk who give birth to enduring cultural values."[17]

Whereas Lobanov focuses on the opposition of the bourgeois value system to that of the common Russian people, Chalmaev attempts to restore the nationalist tradition by asserting the continuity of pre- and postrevolutionary Russian spiritual identity. He finds a common denominator in the tradition of patriotic conquest spanning several centuries of Russian history, beginning with Aleksandr Nevsky's repulsion of German

[16] Mikhail Lobanov, *Stranitsy pamiatnogo: literaturno-kriticheskie stat'i* (Moscow: Sovremennik, 1988), 304.

[17] Ibid., 299.

invaders in the thirteenth century, continuing with the victories of Dmitrii Donskoi, Ivan the Terrible, and Peter the Great, and finding its ultimate expression in the Soviet period with Stalin's defeat of the Nazis. In this way, Chalmaev echoes the typical Soviet valorization of Russian military might, but he includes among his cult heroes certain Orthodox saints, such as Sergius of Radonezh. Tracing the roots of national identity to Byzantium, Chalmaev identifies it as the self-sacrificing spirit that moves the Russian conscience to deny self-interest for the sake of higher moral ideals: "There is something great which inspires our thought in the attempts of Peter the Great, Ivan the Terrible, and the reformers of the Church to accommodate to the benefit of our Motherland the Byzantine ideal of the renunciation of the mundane world."[18] Thus the Russian St. Sergius *and* Lenin and the Bolsheviks represent the same tradition of patriotism and self-sacrifice as an expression of moral integrity.

Lobanov and Chalmaev publicized their views with the tacit permission of the Soviet authorities, although they were often criticized harshly from a Marxist standpoint and were thus obliged to tone down their ideological escapades.

* * *

Nationalist ideas found a more explicit expression in samizdat publications, where they tended to be divided according to two distinct ideological tendencies. One of these may be characterized as a moderate, even liberal, nationalism; the other borders on national socialism.

The most outspoken proponent of the first tendency was the journalist Vladimir Osipov. In 1960, he organized one of the first samizdat journals, *Boomerang*, and was jailed for a period of seven years. During this term of "corrective" labor, he was busy correcting and refining his own ideas. As he himself explains: "In the past I was a materialist, a socialist, and utopian. The camp made of me a man who believes in God, in Russia, in the heritage of our forefathers."[19] In particular, he came to appreciate Stalin as the man responsible for putting a halt to the anti-Church and anti-patriotic activities of the Trotskyists. After his liberation, Osipov organized another journal (1971) called *Veche*.[20] This publication was tolerant of a spectrum of patriotic ideological nuances, but especially cultivated the heritage of the Russian Slavophile Nikolai Danilevsky (1822–85), a naturalist and economist who, several decades before Oswald Spengler, pioneered the use of biological and morphological metaphors in the comparison of national cultures, and denied the historical unity of humankind. Following Danilevsky, Osipov argues that national cultures differentiate themselves in much the same way as species within a given class of organisms: "There are no trees in general; there are firs, baobabs, haloxylon. By the same token, there is no extra-national humanity. Everyone belongs to a specific tribe."[21] Osipov insists that

18 V. A. Chalmaev, *Ogon' veshchei* (Moscow: Sovetskaia Rossiia, 1989), 266.

19 Vladimir Osipov, *Tri otnosheniia k rodine: Stat'i, ocherki, vystupleniia* (Frankfurt: Posev, 1978), 84.

20 This term refers to the ancient Russian tradition of self-governance by local assembly; the *veche* was a meeting of citizens to solve public affairs, as well as the place of this meeting.

21 Osipov, *Tri otnosheniia k rodine*, 32.

one cannot love other humans if one does not love first of all one's own nation. He gives a rather loose definition of "nation," asserting that "the striking specificity of the biological, of the blood, cannot be explained without mysticism. In a national living organism, some mystery is always present, something which is not susceptible to scientific experimentation."[22] Counterposing this mysterious phenomenon to the traditional Marxist understanding of "nation" as a commonality of economics and language, he emphasizes a unity of religious beliefs as the determining national characteristic. "A particular individual can do without religion. A particular nation cannot do without religion. Where the faith ends, the nation ends .... A people disintegrates before your eyes when its faith in God disintegrates."[23] Osipov attempts to follow the liberal tradition of Russian Slavophilism in recognizing that Westernism—with the exception of its Marxist version—was beneficial for Russia, although only in the spheres of technology, industry, and legal institutions. He regrets the ideological rift between nationalists and democrats (like Andrei Sakharov), believing that their interests ultimately coincide, since only nationalism can unite Russians in their struggle against the Marxist totalitarian state.

The antidemocratic nationalist tendency was expressed more aggressively by another samizdat author, Gennadii Shimanov (1937–2013), who spent most of his life working as a janitor or elevator operator in Moscow. According to Shimanov's doctrine, the state is the highest value, thus nationalist and communist ideals should work together to strengthen the power of the state. Shimanov believed that, inadvertently, the atheistic Soviet state was a tool of God designed for the creation of a new Christian world. "Only Soviet power, once it adopts Orthodox Christianity ... is capable of beginning a Great Transformation of the World."[24] Thus in his writings he attacks not only democrats, but also "liberal" nationalists, such as Solzhenitsyn and Osipov, for advocating a "dissident" nationalism hostile to the Soviet regime and communism. For Shimanov, communism is religious in its unconscious depths, since it keeps alive the people's aspiration for moral perfection and social unity.

In many ways, Shimanov's ideas echo those of the Eurasianist movement. "To protest against our regime is to go against God." "Soviet Power, beginning in 1917, accomplished an enormous turn and continues to change before our eyes, if they are capable of seeing." Shimanov shares the Eurasianist hope that the Soviet state will eventually renounce its atheistic stance and embrace the traditional religion of the Russian people. For Shimanov, freedom of thought and speech are harmful for Russia, and he routinely blames Jews and "cosmopolitans" for this dangerous liberalism. "It is time to give up the absurd prejudice that a greenhouse atmosphere of freedom of opinion and creativity is the best for the maturing of truth and great art." In Shimanov's view, when the Soviet Union rids itself of atheistic Marxism, the state must still remain

22 Ibid., 30.

23 Ibid.

24 G. M. Shimanov, "Kak ponimat' nashu istoriiu i k chemu v nei stremit'sia" (1974). Available electronically: http://chri-soc.narod.ru/sh_kak_ponimat_nashu_istoriu.htm. Further quotations in the text are from the same article-manifesto.

an ideocracy where only one ideology, that of Orthodoxy and patriotism, should absolutely dominate.[25]

4. Nation as Personality. The Moral Conservatism of Aleksandr Solzhenitsyn

Soviet-era Russian nationalism remained largely a marginal movement, known only on the domestic scene, until Aleksandr Solzhenitsyn (1918–2008) took up its mantle in the early 1970s. His ethical and social views permeate all of his well-known creative

Figure 1 Aleksandr Solzhenitsyn.

[25] The history of nationalist ideologies in the USSR, including in the period under consideration here, is explored in a number of books, including: Nikolai Mitrokhin, *Russkaia partiia: Dvizhenie russkikh natsionalistov v SSSR. 1953–1985 gody* (Moscow: Novoe literaturnoe obozrenie, 2003); Aleksandr Ianov, *Russkaia ideia. Ot Nikolaia I do Putina. Kniga vtoraia: 1917–1990* (Moscow: Khronograf, 2014); A. Iu. Kozhevnikov, *Russkii patriotizm i sovetskii sotsializm* (Moscow: Prometei, 2017). The first two books are written from a liberal and more objective standpoint, while the latter represents an apologia of Russian nationalism.

works and have been analyzed by hundreds of commentators. This chapter will thus restrict itself to discussion of his most general philosophical ideas as expounded in his articles and essays. Solzhenitsyn's receipt of the Nobel Prize for Literature in 1970—and the opportunity this afforded him to influence world opinion—marks the beginning of his intensive nonfictional writing. This work reveals a unique stability of basic themes and ideas throughout the subsequent years of his forced emigration to the West (1974) and return to postcommunist Russia (1994).

The Concept of Nation

The decisive component of Solzhenitsyn's thought is the concept of nation, identified as the unique personality of a people among peoples, just as individuals are differentiated among themselves. "Nations are the treasury of humankind, its generalized personalities; even the smallest of nations carries its own colors, harbors a special facet of God's design."[26] According to Solzhenitsyn, nation is the most organic and concrete form of social existence, a natural mediation between separate human beings and humanity as a whole, a "generalized personality" that overcomes the polarity of the individual and the generic. Therefore, any kind of humanism that ignores the nation and directly addresses an atomic individual or the entirety of humankind tends to be abstract and speculative.

> Contrary to the predictions of many sages of humanism and internationalism, the twentieth century has passed with a sharp increase of national feelings everywhere in the world, and this process is still gaining momentum; nations resist attempts at a global leveling [*vsemirnaia nivelirovka*] of their cultures .... But when we say "nationality," we do not have in mind *blood*, but always *spirit*, *consciousness*, the vector of preferences of a human being.[27]

Solzhenitsyn's fundamental philosophical concern is the moral criteria of the social sciences. Since nations are personalities, they should be subject to ethical evaluations, such as "noble," "mean," "courageous," "cowardly," and so forth. With regard to large communities, he observes, such assessments are typically dismissed as "irrelevant" and "unscientific" in the humanities of the twentieth century, wherein, by contrast, economic, social, political, and technological criteria are persistently imposed on the life of individuals. Certain individuals are deemed to be "progressive" or "reactionary," "oppressors" or "oppressed," depending on their belonging to a given class or social institution. Solzhenitsyn finds this tendency of the humanities to "dehumanize" individuals one-sided and hypocritical, and suggests as an alternative the relevance of moral criteria to evaluate entire societies. If the determinants of individual behavior are so readily—especially in Marxism—attributed to the given socioeconomic system,

[26] Aleksandr Solzhenitsyn, *Sobranie sochinenii v 20 tomakh* (Vermont-Paris: YMCA Press, 1981), vol. 9, 15.

[27] Aleksandr Solzhenitsyn, "'Russkii vopros' k kontsu XX veka," *Novyi mir*, no. 7 (1994). Available electronically: https://magazines.gorky.media/novyi_mi/1994/7/russkij-vopros-k-konczu-xx-veka.html

why, vice versa, should the actions of nations, societies, and states not be appraised on a scale commensurate with the criteria of individual behavior?

> [W]hy are the standards and demands so necessarily and readily applied to individuals, families, small groups and personal relations, rejected out of hand and utterly prohibited when we go on to deal with thousands and millions of people in association? … Human society cannot be exempted from the laws and demands which constitute the aim and meaning of individual human lives.[28]

Solzhenitsyn's position, however, seems controversial precisely from his own moral standpoint: by judging nations as individuals, one risks judging individuals as no more than members of their nations. If the Russian nation acts in a courageous or cowardly way, does this apply to all Russians? How does one distinguish between courageous and cowardly individuals if moral judgment refers to the nation as a whole? By treating nations as singular individuals, one paradoxically reduces individuals to the status of representatives of their nation—exactly the type of generalization against which Solzhenitsyn protests.

For Solzhenitsyn, however, nations, as distinct from political parties, states, trade unions, corporations, international organizations, and other pragmatic and mechanical collectives, are, like personalities, living entities, "very vital formations, susceptible to all moral feelings …. The profoundest similarity between the individual and the nation lies in the mystical nature of their 'givenness.'"[29]

The Problem of National Guilt and Repentance

Therefore, Solzhenitsyn advances a specific moral attitude: nations, like individuals, should first of all address themselves. It is *repentance* that sets the standard of moral consciousness. "Repentance is the only starting point for spiritual growth."[30] Solzhenitsyn's "suffering" and "repentant" patriotism revives the spirit of Russian literature of the nineteenth century and distinguishes him from the overwhelming majority of Russian nationalist thinkers of the 1960s–1980s, who vied with one another in extolling the virtues of the Russian character in its superiority to other nations. From this latter standpoint, Russianness is determined by blood and origin, and so tsarism and Bolshevism, Orthodoxy, and atheism are equally justified, inasmuch as they all serve to increase Russian power and influence in the world. Solzhenitsyn balks at such all-accepting and self-flattering patriotism. "Their general name for all this is 'the Russian idea.' (A more precise name for this trend would be 'National Bolshevism')."[31]

[28] Alexander Solzhenitsyn, "Repentance and Self-Limitation in the Life of Nations" (1973), in Alexander Solzhenitsyn, Mikhail Agursky, Evgeny Barabanov, Vadim Borisov, F. Korsakov, and Igor Shafarevich, eds., *From under the Rubble*, trans. Michael Scammell and A. M. Brock (Boston, Toronto: Little, Brown and Company, 1975), 106.

[29] Ibid., 109, 110.

[30] Ibid., 108.

[31] Ibid., 120.

Instead, Solzhenitsyn calls for national repentance, insisting that the Russian renaissance can only begin with an apology to other peoples for decades and even centuries of imperial self-assertion. Following the early Slavophiles, Solzhenitsyn condemns not only the Soviet but the "Petersburg" period of Russian imperial history, which was characterized by political arrogance and a superficial imitation of Western culture. Furthermore, along with an admission of guilt before other nations, Russians must repent of internal sins: the not-so-distant serfdom and concomitant enduring poverty of the majority of their own people, which is unprecedented among civilized nations. Above all is the call for introspection:

> For half a century now we have acted on the conviction that the *guilty* ones were the tsarist establishment, the bourgeois patriots, social democrats, White Guards, priests, émigrés, subversives, kulaks … wreckers, oppositionists, enemies of the people, nationalists, Zionists, imperialists, militarists, even modernists—anyone and everyone except you and I! Obviously it was *they*, not we, who had to reform.[32]

Solzhenitsyn warns that by externalizing rather than internalizing the source of guilt, a nation only proliferates its own misfortunes through endeavors to overcome them at the expense of other nations. There is nobody to blame but ourselves. Thus it is only by the act of a willing self-condemnation that Russia—and by extension all of humanity—can survive the mounting evils of the twentieth century, including the exploitation of nature and the oppression of weaker peoples. "We have so bedeviled the world, brought it so close to self-destruction, that repentance is now a matter of life and death."[33]

If a nation's duty in relation to the past is repentance, its future may be secured only by the imperative of *self-limitation*—the other of Solzhenitsyn's two key concepts employed in his ethical manifesto "Repentance and Self-Limitation in the Life of Nations" (1973). Repentance and self-limitation are interconnected modes of spiritual ascension through humility and are rooted in religious ethics; nevertheless, Solzhenitsyn emphasizes their importance for both believers and nonbelievers as a means for the physical and historical survival of humanity, which is otherwise liable to fall victim to its own greed, its destructive claims to full satisfaction of all needs and desires. For Solzhenitsyn, the ethical imperative of self-limitation should be applied to decision-making on every scale, from the individual to the corporation and the state. The ascetic discipline of self-restraint as practiced by separate individuals still remains to be adopted by nations and societies, since, from the beginning of history, they have practiced a policy of limiting other nations rather than themselves.

National Self-Arrangement versus Communism

This will for expansion across all boundaries, from the geographical to the psychological and the transcendental (the atheistic usurpation of God's place in the universe), is

32 Ibid., 117.
33 Ibid., 107.

ominously expressed in communism, which, for Solzhenitsyn, is the most dangerous disease afflicting humanity—one that may prove fatal. Like cancer, communism multiplies by invading the neighboring cells of other nations and by leveling individuals, reducing their differentiation and incorporating them into collectivist totalities: a purely quantitative progress that eventually kills the organism of humanity. The disaster of communism is that it exterminates qualitative distinctions comprising the organic being of individuals and nations. Everywhere that communism spreads, it bleaches culture of its national character, replacing it with an impersonal and mediocre internationalism. This is why Solzhenitsyn sees the last chance for salvation in a regeneration of national consciousness and its reorientation toward inner refinement instead of extension in the outer world.

Again, in his personalistic approach to nations, Solzhenitsyn valorizes introspection as a means of restoring the inner balance of spiritual life, recommending in particular that Russia cease the expenditure of its resources for the sake of global domination, turning them instead to the task of national "self-arrangement" (*samoobustroistvo*). In contrast to the Russian expansionist policy that long targeted the West and South almost exclusively, Solzhenitsyn proposes reorienting it toward the North and East, where vast expanses of land remain undeveloped—virgin land that symbolizes the self-contained integrity and original purity of the Russian spirit.[34] Though Solzhenitsyn is very close to Slavophile teachings and holds them in high regard, he distances himself from them when considering the historical experience of the last centuries: now that Russia has suffered so painfully from its self-destructive expansionism, it has neither the time nor the strength to take care of its Slavic brothers or preside over a federation of Eastern European nations. Solzhenitsyn attempts to dispel "the specter of pan-Slavism, which has so many times already ruined Russia, and is all the more so now beyond our strength."[35] At the same time, Solzhenitsyn is careful to distinguish his nationalism from isolationism, claiming that the deliberate self-isolation of Russia from the surrounding world would be a temporary period of recovery from the evils of expansionism, during which Russia would prepare itself for a renewed dialogue with the world on terms of equality and mutual respect.

Solzhenitsyn is sensitive to the critique of Russian nationalism offered by domestic and Western liberals who warn of the potential of a new totalitarianism emerging from a nationalist revision of communism. In Solzhenitsyn's view, the idea of nation is incommensurate with a communist system, as evidenced by the history of the suppression of national spirit under Soviet rule. With the same argument, Solzhenitsyn answers those critics who claim that Soviet communism was a Bolshevik perversion of the Marxist model, or that the success of the October Revolution could be attributed to

[34] In his famous letter to the Soviet leaders in 1973, Solzhenitsyn called upon them to reject the claims of world hegemony implicit in Marxist ideology and reclaim their Russian identity in order to prepare the nation for a possible war with communist China. This is typical for Solzhenitsyn's argumentation: to attempt to demonstrate the value of a truth via the practical necessity of its implementation.

[35] Solzhenitsyn, "'Russkii vopros' k kontsu XX veka."

traditions of Russian history that were essentially "communist" long before Bolshevism itself, since they downplayed the importance of private property and exaggerated the role of centralized government. Solzhenitsyn wonders ironically why communism's rise could not just as well be attributed to Egyptian or Chinese history, given the evident socialist tendencies in their economies and bureaucratic regimes. For Solzhenitsyn, Russia was not the initiator of communism but rather its first victim; he emphasized the revolution's facilitation by internationalist forces where the leading role was played by Jews, Balts, Georgians, and other national minorities. The ensuing regime was not a "distorted" Bolshevik interpretation of Marx, but the direct expression of original Marxist doctrine, which prescribes the application of "revolutionary violence" and a "dictatorship of the proletariat" as the only means to break the national resistance to internationalist utopia.

Solzhenitsyn fully recognizes that Russians are also guilty of adopting communism and oppressing other nations with its program of worldwide revolution, but he argues that, historically, Russia's crimes have been directed mostly against Russians themselves. Communism in Russia was tantamount to a protracted national suicide, whereby one part of society enslaved and destroyed another. Thus to restore national identity means bringing the nation to peace with itself by eliminating the class, party, and ideological conflicts tearing the country apart.

The Intelligentsia and the People

The decisive factor in this envisioned national reconciliation is the relationship between the intelligentsia and the people (*narod*). Here Solzhenitsyn enters a heated dispute with such liberals and "pluralists" as Grigorii Pomerants, Andrei Siniavsky, Mihajlo Mihajlov, and Boris Shragin, who question the very existence of "the people" in Russia in the sense meant by its venerators: as an organic unity molded by religious beliefs and moral traditions. These thinkers pin all their hopes, to the contrary, on the individual who challenges traditional values—a typical member of the intelligentsia, whose alienation from the people is viewed positively as a feature of historical dynamics. The implication is that the Russian people gave in to communist promises and became an easily manipulated herd, devoid of any spiritual substance. Solzhenitsyn's counterargument goes so far as to propose that, quite the opposite, it was the intelligentsia that betrayed the national tradition and functioned as the ruling class in totalitarian society. This is why it lost the spiritual identity of the prerevolutionary intelligentsia, which was emphatically self-sacrificial and repented its guilt of alienation from the simple people. Solzhenitsyn coins an expressive word for this new social stratum that gradually came to substitute, under the Soviet regime, for the genuine intelligentsia: *obrazovanshchina*, which has been approximated in English as "smatterers" and might also be rendered as "educated mob."[36]

[36] On the polemics of liberal and personalist thinkers, including Andrei Sakharov, Grigorii Pomerants, Boris Paramonov, and Mihajlo Mihajlov, with Solzhenitsyn, see Epstein, *The Phoenix of Philosophy*, 129–32, 138–9, 144–5, 164–6.

Solzhenitsyn's dissatisfaction with the West proved to be a direct continuation of his polemics with Russian Westernizers that began when he was still in the USSR. After Solzhenitsyn's forced emigration in 1974, his Western audience eagerly anticipated an unfettered condemnation of his native state and a corresponding glorification of liberalism, but they were quickly disappointed. Not only did Solzhenitsyn undertake a radical and merciless critique of liberalism, but he made clear that his critique of Soviet Marxism was founded on a nationalist rather than liberal platform. On Solzhenitsyn's own part, there was an even greater disappointment: he had expected to find in the West a strong spiritual commitment to the struggle against totalitarianism, but was alarmed to discover instead a political will slackening with the pursuit of private prosperity and hedonism. As he saw it, the danger of Western consumerism, liberalism, legalism, and individualism lay in their sapping the moral courage necessary to resist communist expansion fed by a spring of ideological commitments that people were willing to die for.

Solzhenitsyn's ethical approaches evince certain ambiguities, for instance his condemnation of Western intellectual and political leaders for their "cowardly" allowing of Vietnam to be lost to communism. Apparently, the concept of self-limitation does not apply to the United States' ultimate withdrawal from that country, which might well be read as an abandonment of outmoded expansionist policies. Thus Solzhenitsyn identifies some cases of self-limitation with virtue, others with cowardice. He also underestimates the potential of "hedonism": while it easily surrenders on the battlefield, it may win the war in the arena of consciousness, as was demonstrated by the ultimately peaceful collapse of communism.

Morality and Law

Solzhenitsyn's critique of Western ideology centers on the concept of "freedom." In the West, freedom is an extension of individualism that is limited only by the external restraints imposed by law. Thus individualism and legalism complement one another, since the law guarantees individual freedom so far as the individual agrees to recognize the authority of the law. Solzhenitsyn calls this a model of "mutual pressure," as limitation is imposed from without by a judicial system; to it, he counterposes his ethics of self-limitation, whereby individual behavior is restrained from within by moral law. Solzhenitsyn finds the Western concern for human rights laudable but argues that rights here are overstressed at the expense of responsibilities. Rights are a purely humanistic concept, whereas responsibility restores a religious dimension to humanity—as subordinated to the higher criterion of truth.

The relationship between legal and moral norms is one of the crucial questions considered by contemporary Russian thought. From a liberal perspective, lack of juridical awareness was the major negative factor of Russian history, such that Russia's much-needed turn to democracy should first of all be based on the establishment of legal institutions and procedures as the governing laws of social life: the creation of a legal state (*pravovoe gosudarstvo*). This is the only way to abandon the excesses of the administrative-command system, where the only law was the will of a central or regional party leader. From the standpoint of the enlightened conservatism championed by Solzhenitsyn, a system of jurisdiction indeed should be introduced in Russia, but still subjected to the governance of moral law. The most important decisions, on the state level, should be made not by the quantitative majority of voices, but by unanimous consent of the people or their legal representatives. In the concluding notes to his treatise *Rebuilding Russia. Reflections and Tentative Proposals* (the English title of what was originally called *Kak nam obustroit' Rossiiu* [*How We Should Arrange Russia*], 1990), Solzhenitsyn formulates this position quite clearly: "Moral principles must take priority over legal ones. And justice means conformity to moral law before any purely legal compliance."[37]

These two judgments, crowning the whole work of Solzhenitsyn and so insistently placed in a supposed complementarity, actually contradict one another. If morality is actually higher than legality, then justice should be determined first by the simpler legal law, and then by the moral one. Proceeding in the order proposed by Solzhenitsyn to solve all social issues first and foremost, we will never reach the legal law. And in principle, why bother with the "lower," once the "higher" has been achieved? Isn't this neglect of the law in favor of higher moral motivations a typical feature of authoritarian regimes and a long-standing, neglected misfortune of Russian statehood?

This position of moral fundamentalism was stated in a more thoroughly philosophical manner by the philosopher Iurii Borodai, who criticized Western judicialism for its insistence on purely formal (specifically, adversarial) relationships between people, as if they were potential enemies: "Suffice it to note that the fathers of European jurisprudence (Hobbes, Montesquieu) founded their legal conceptions on very remarkable axioms: 1) *homo homini lupus est* (men are like wolves to one another), and 2) the war of all people against all people."[38] Borodai connects the emergence of Western juridical norms with the destructive wars of the Reformation, which led to the devastation of two-thirds of Europe's population. In order to survive, society had to transform the armed war of all against all into a juridical war through courts and judges. This is why legal norms reflect the lowest stage of moral consciousness, which, in its highest development, would make legal procedures unnecessary, since every individual would be directed from within by his or her own morality: "From the standpoint of natural community, the most developed juridical consciousness is to conscience as the horse's hoof is to human fingers."[39] Both Solzhenitsyn and Borodai would be correct in terms of universal moral values, but in the reality of Russian history, the neglect of legal norms led not to the ascension of moral virtues, but to their complete degradation, to a despotic voluntarism that easily justified itself by the highest ethical considerations, such as "the welfare of the common people," "the self-sacrifice of the individual for the sake of society," and so on.

[37] Aleksandr Solzhenitsyn, *Rebuilding Russia. Reflections and Tentative Proposals*, trans. and annotated by Alexis Klimoff (New York: Farrar, Straus and Giroux, 1991), 105.

[38] Iurii Borodai, "Krest'ianskii trud i sel'skaia obshchnost'. Filosofsko-ekonomicheskie predposylki perestroiki agrarnogo proizvodstvsa," in *Chto s nami proiskhodit? Zapiski sovremennikov*, ed. V. Lazarev (Moscow: Sovremennik, 1989), 135.

[39] Ibid., 136.

The idea that morality can be a single and all-encompassing norm of behavior for an entire society proceeds from the romantic assumption that a nation is one organic whole, one soul and one body, which, therefore, is subject to the rules of individual morality. For this reason Solzhenitsyn is inclined to idealize agricultural communities, which preserve the spirit of collective identity and thus do not require juridical regulations. Solzhenitsyn seems to ignore that moral fundamentalism may ultimately be self-defeating: raising moral norms to the level of legal authority and state regulation would undermine morality itself as a factor of individual self-determination. Morality, functioning in the place of legal norms, is nothing but immorality institutionalized by a totalitarian state. This substitution of an individual moral sense for nationally legitimized moral norms permeates all of Solzhenitsyn's thought, both on the level of social science—where nation is subject to moral evaluation as a single person, and on the level of social practice—where moral norms function as, and instead of, legal institutions. But this triumph of collectivized and institutionalized morality proves, despite Solzhenitsyn's intent, the most severe restraint on the freedom of personal conscience, which is now completely regulated by the criterion of "the nation's conscience" or "the people's wisdom." In fact, few historical figures spoke of morality more than the Soviet leaders, who required from their citizens self-sacrifice and heroism in order to substantiate the power of the state. One morality for everyone means no morality for anyone, because an individual subjected to the moral prescriptions of the governing body, of a political and/or religious leader, cedes his or her power of decision to this authority, thereby becoming a mere instrument for state manipulations.

Morality and Religion

Solzhenitsyn claims to defend Christian values, but one often feels his deep attraction instead to what could be called an Old Testament mentality, common to the majority of Russian nationalist thinkers, who believe the nation (*narod*) rather than the individual is the "God-bearer" (*bogonosets*) destined to fulfill some higher religious and moral mission. Christian civilization is based on the division of moral and legal powers ("God" and "Caesar"), on the duality of individual and society, the former called to spiritual fulfillment and salvation, and the latter subject to its own "earthly" regulations, borrowed from Roman legislation. Any attempt to elide this duality, to subordinate society entirely to the governance of moral laws and spiritual goals can be seen, on the one hand, as a shift toward the theocratic aspirations of the Old Testament era, or, on the other, as a gesture of rising authoritarianism, which establishes a "substitution for God" in the person of a national, charismatic leader—the mundane messiah. To be sure, Solzhenitsyn is far from the conscious pursuit of theocratic goals: even the nation for him is not the highest value in and of itself, but owes its unique character to God, and only for this reason is endowed with self-consciousness.

Overall, Solzhenitsyn's position can be characterized as enlightened conservatism. By focusing on Christian values, he strives to avoid the extremes of militant nationalism and liberal democracy, both of which he vehemently decries. His conservatism is based on implicitly religious and explicitly moral criteria. Solzhenitsyn rarely exposes his religious views directly, and does not confuse his political conservatism with clericalism. He avoids bringing religion too close to church, and church too close to state. In fact, Solzhenitsyn's persistent hope for the spiritual revival of Russia hardly seems to rely on the Orthodox Church itself. "Will the Orthodox Church help us? During the years of communism, it has been smashed the most. Moreover, it was internally undermined by its three centuries of submission to state power, and has lost its drive for strong public action."[40]

Nevertheless, religious faith lies at the foundation of all his political and moral views. To a certain degree, he inherits didactic patterns of Russian medieval culture and attempts to translate the basic concepts of Orthodox spirituality, such as "conciliatoriness" or "communality" (*sobornost'*), "repentance" and "abstinence" (*vozderzhanie*, self-limitation), into the contemporary cultural and social language. Solzhenitsyn believes that the twentieth-century ethics of self-realization has its distant roots in the Renaissance affirmation of humanism and anthropocentrism. Solzhenitsyn recognizes that medieval religiosity placed too narrow a limitation on human physical nature, but he argues that the Renaissance represents a headlong rush to the other, far more perilous extreme. In its deification of individuality, the Renaissance began the trend of the celebration of human pride and "will to power," a mode that gave rise to the modern ethos of the exploitation of nature. Thus Solzhenitsyn not only blames the humanistic mentality for the sociopolitical crises of the twentieth century, both in Russia and the West, but prophesies that world history is now on the eve of a new radical transition tantamount to the transition from the Middle Ages to the Renaissance—but in the opposite direction.

> Is it true that man is above everything? Is there no Superior Spirit above him? .... If the world has not come to its end, it has approached a major turn in history, equal in importance to the turn from the Middle Ages to the Renaissance. It will exact from us a spiritual upsurge: We shall have to rise to a new height of vision, to a new level of life where our physical nature will not be cursed as in the Middle Ages, but, even more importantly, our spiritual being will not be trampled upon as in the Modern era. This ascension will be similar to climbing onto the next anthropologic stage.[41]

Monism against Pluralism

On the whole, Solzhenitsyn's system of views can be defined as ethical monism, which becomes clear from his polemics with the so-called pluralists (1982). In the late-Soviet context, the term "pluralism," which would become one of the key slogans of perestroika (first as "socialist pluralism"), owes its popularity to Solzhenitsyn, though

[40] Solzhenitsyn, "'Russkii vopros' k kontsu XX veka."

[41] Alexander Solzhenitsyn, "A World Split Apart." Harvard University commencement address, delivered June 8, 1978. Available electronically: https://www.americanrhetoric.com/speeches/alexandersolzhenitsynharvard.htm

he used it in a derogatory sense. "Pluralism" in Russian is consonant with "spitting" (*pluiut*) and Solzhenitsyn associates it with an indifferent, "devil-may-care" attitude toward the highest moral values. He recognizes that a plurality of views may have its own merit as a multiplicity of manifestations of one single truth but rejects the idea that there could be multiple truths themselves, and that such multiplicity may be a goal in itself. "It is strange that a simple plural number should be granted such status .... If there is no universal foundation, there can be no morality. 'Pluralism' as a principle degrades to indifference, to the loss of any depth, flowing into relativism, into absurdity, into a pluralism of delusions and lies."[42]

Solzhenitsyn calls pluralists those representatives of liberal and dissident movements who consider ideological diversity and tolerance to be the greatest achievement of contemporary civilization, especially as exemplified in Western institutionalized democracy. It is noteworthy that Solzhenitsyn argues his preference for "one truth" from the perspective of "rigorous sciences, based on mathematics." It would seem more coherent to connect morality with the humanities and social sciences, but Solzhenitsyn asserts that pluralism in these disciplines is symptomatic of their inferiority to the natural sciences: "The plurality of truths in the social sciences is a sign of our imperfection, not of our excessive richness, and why should we make a cult of pluralism from this imperfection?"[43] Solzhenitsyn's aspiration to a single truth draws, on the one hand, from religion, on the other, from mathematics, which was his professional field both before and after the war and his imprisonment in the Gulag. He appeals, that is, to both superhuman and nonhuman domains, thus dispensing with the sphere of the properly humanistic, in which pluralism has been doomed to reside due to its immanent imperfection. "The truth in the whole course of the world is one—God's truth, and all of us, sometimes unconsciously, are striving to approach and touch it."[44] For Solzhenitsyn, difference is meaningful and valuable only as a means to the progressive elimination of difference, as a mode of comparison between oneself and others that allows a person to recognize his or her mistakes, overcome them, and approach universal truth.

The greatest danger for the Western world, according to Solzhenitsyn, is the loss of distinction between "truth" and "falsehood," between undoubtable good and undoubtable evil. He characterizes this pluralistic principle as a call for "diversity for its own sake," as "centrifugal disarray" and "the entropy of thought."[45] To liberal thinkers, this centrifugal tendency represented the strongest challenge to all-encompassing Soviet centralism, but in his writings, Solzhenitsyn finds pluralism too weak to wage such historical-political combat. This is why he believes in the superiority of the centralist model, but proposes replacing the monism of political power with the monism of religious faith and moral commitment.

[42] Aleksandr Solzhenitsyn, "Nashi pliuralisty," *Vestnik russkogo khristianskogo dvizheniia*, no. 139 (1983). Available electronically: http://www.rodon.org/sai/np.htm

[43] Ibid.

[44] Ibid.

[45] Ibid.

From a pluralist standpoint, Solzhenitsyn continues the authoritarian thread in Russian history and for this reason displays a surprising affinity with Soviet ideology, condemning the bourgeois West for its moral degradation and relativism. From Solzhenitsyn's point of view, pluralism shares with Soviet totalitarianism an origin in atheistic and materialistic doctrines of the nineteenth century; both emerged as two complementary aspects of the same processes of secularization. The only alternative to both world systems would therefore be the restoration of religious absolutism, equally opposed to the anti-religious absolutism of the Soviet system and the irreligious relativism of Western democracy.

After his return to Russia in May 1994, Solzhenitsyn remained a staunch champion of the same fundamentalist principles he had consistently advanced since 1973. Ascribing the chaos of post-Soviet society to destructive and centrifugal tendencies unleashed by the pluralistic strategies of Gorbachev and Yeltsin, he left aside the fact that the communist empire had broken up under the pressure of these same centrifugal tendencies. Solzhenitsyn's enlightened conservatism held a strong appeal in the postcommunist climate of excessive instability, but at the same time it could not account for the democratic reforms that had led to the end of communism. This perhaps explains why Solzhenitsyn did not hasten to return to his motherland until his conservative stance could find some practical application. Only after totalitarianism was ruined by democratic reforms, did Solzhenitsyn's ethical and political monism come into its own right as a challenge to the extremes of pluralism.

However, despite all of Solzhenitsyn's attempts to distinguish the "genuine" Russia from the Soviet Union, it is their shared historical identity that lends his thought a certain ambivalence. He could not but rejoice at the fall of Soviet communism, and could not but mourn the demise of a strong, unified Russia, but how in reality could one have been preserved while the other perished? If in the 1990s, with the demise of the Soviet Union and the triumph of centrifugal forces, Solzhenitsyn's monism acquired political significance, it is only because the pluralists were right in their own time and succeeded in creating a new historical space that secured a relevance for Solzhenitsyn's preachings as well as the very possibility of his homecoming.

5. From Anti-Socialism to Anti-Semitism. Igor Shafarevich

In the late 1970s, the nationalist movement won another prominent supporter, the mathematician Igor Shafarevich (1923–2017). Within the spectrum of neo-Slavophile thought of that period, Shafarevich occupied the rightmost position. A significant theorist in the field of algebra and a privileged member-correspondent of the Academy of Sciences (from 1958 on), he originally appeared on the dissident scene as one of the most outspoken proponents of human rights and religious freedom. However, his position, even in the early 1970s, was closer to Solzhenitsyn's cautious conservatism than to Sakharov's liberal Westernism. In fact, he became famous as a contributor to *From under the Rubble* (1974), the collection of articles initiated by Solzhenitsyn;

here Shafarevich published fragments of what would become his book *Socialism as a Phenomenon of World History* (1977).

This work was the first investigation by a Soviet author to treat socialism not as a specific phenomenon of the nineteenth and twentieth centuries, but as a recurrent social structure, traceable to ancient Egypt and Mesopotamia. Contrary to the traditional view, which sees socialist states as proceeding from and implementing socialist teachings, Shafarevich argues that the reality of socialism as embodied in certain ancient Near Eastern societies anticipated the appearance of socialist theory by at least a thousand years. In this view, socialist ideology, while claiming to construct a distant future, in fact represents a regressive attempt to restore the primitive communality of the past. Such strivings for complete social leveling and elimination of all differences periodically interrupt the progressive historical tendency for psychological individualization and economic privatization that keeps humanity in a state of creative tension. Its ideological content may vary—from Platonic idealism to Christian millenarianism, or from Confucianism to Marxism—but the basic structure of socialism, according to Shafarevich, always remains invariable. The common denominator of the "Jesuit State" in Paraguay, Thomas More's "Utopia," and Russian Bolshevism is the suppression of individuality, private property, and family bonds in order to promote the absolute negation of social difference.

Socialism, therefore, thrives on destructive energy and suggests many parallels with what Shafarevich (following Freud) identifies as the "death instinct." As evidence, he cites the pessimistic views of socialists (Fourier, Saint-Simon, Engels) regarding the inevitable physical demise of Earth and humanity, and the "hero complex" peculiar to all revolutionaries—the desire to die for their cause. This inclination for self-destruction is inherent to the human psyche, and socialism is a powerful expression of this instinctive lure of Nothingness. "The death of mankind is not only the foreseeable result of socialism's triumph, it constitutes the goal of socialism .... Socialism is an aspect of mankind's striving for self-destruction, for Nothingness; specifically, it is its manifestation in the sphere of social organization."[46] This explains, according to Shafarevich, why philosophers who see Nothingness as deeply embedded in the foundation of Being, such as Heidegger and Sartre, demonstrate a strong proclivity for socialism, in its nationalist or Marxist form. "Understanding socialism as a manifestation of mankind's striving for self-destruction means understanding its hostility to individuality, its attempt to annihilate such forces as maintain and reinforce human personality: religion, culture, family, individual property."[47]

Shafarevich's book, though rather derivative and rife with long citations, made a strong impression on Russian intellectuals. For the first time, socialism was divorced from its specifically Soviet connotations, from the constraints of Marxist/anti-Marxist polemics, and treated as a metaphysical law responsible for periodic interruptions of the "normal" and "progressive" course of history. The author's impartial, scientific

[46] I. R. Shafarevich, *Sotsializm kak iavlenie mirovoi istorii* (Paris: YMCA Press, 1977), 365, 374.

[47] Ibid., 375.

approach to a hot-button social issue, in combination with his staunch loyalty to the ideal of freedom, won him wide public acclaim. Shafarevich's impartiality is demonstrated by his seemingly paradoxical defense of socialism as an option open to a free society. Just as suicide is the proving ground of unrestrained human self-determination, socialism is indispensable as evidence of the collective freedom of humanity. Socialism might lead to the world's enslavement, but at the same time it stands as a testament to the fact that "free will, given both to a person and to mankind, is ABSOLUTE, encompassing freedom even with respect to the ultimate question—the choice between life and death."[48]

Shafarevich's next book, *Russophobia* (1978–90), despite having been begun immediately after the publication of his first, could almost be the work of a different author. The entire conception of social dynamics is reversed: the source of destruction is now identified not with the socialist homogenization of society, but with an elitist challenge to the traditional values shared by the nation as a whole. Shafarevich borrows some of his principal ideas from the French historian Augustin Cochin (1876–1916), who explained the French Revolution of 1789 as a process of social self-destruction activated by a narrow group of intellectuals—members of philosophical clubs and masonic lodges. Cochin called this adversarial elite the "small people" (*le petit peuple*), as opposed to the "large people" (*le grand peuple*) that constitutes the organic basis of a given society. According to Shafarevich, this model, in which the "small people" destroys the foundations of traditional society, recurs throughout the ages, and may be identified with the English Puritans of the sixteenth–seventeenth centuries, the Freemasons and espousers of the French Enlightenment of the eighteenth century, the "Young Germany" and left Hegelian movements that gave rise to Marxism in Germany in the 1830s–1840s, and the liberals and nihilists in Russia of the 1860s–1880s. The common characteristic of the "small people," or the "anti-people," is its spiritual rootlessness and hostility to the organic way of life based on enduring religious and moral values.

The focal point of Shafarevich's conception is that he sees Jews as the twentieth-century incarnation of the "small people"; in his view, Jews are to blame for the destruction of the Russian Empire. "The most fatal feature of this entire century, which can be explained by an increasing Jewish influence, is the fact that liberal, Westernist, or internationalist phraseology often concealed antinational tendencies."[49] Shafarevich argues that the Soviet regime, with its internationalist claims, was in reality a Jewish occupation of Russia. He cites as evidence the disproportionately large representation of Jews in Russian revolutionary parties and in the earliest Soviet governments, their "leading role" in the repressive organs of the Cheka and in the destruction of the peasantry and the Russian Orthodox Church in the name of "collectivization" and "scientific atheism," respectively. Shafarevich's anti-Semitic (and hardly original)

[48] Ibid., 382.

[49] I. R. Shafarevich, *Russofobiia. Dve dorogi—k odnomu obryvu* (Moscow: Tovarishchestvo russkikh khudozhnikov, 1991), 75.

arguments were repeated in the late 1980s by numerous activists of nascent Russian fascism, who would subsequently take to skipping this ideological "middleman" and refer directly to Nazi propaganda.

According to Shafarevich, Jews' appetite for destruction is fueled by an irrational force he calls "Russophobia." This word was not a new one, but it was Shafarevich who theorized and popularized it. Russophobia is a hatred of everything Russian, including its history, customs, fashions, and its pagan and Christian beliefs. Shafarevich and his followers blame every failure and crisis in contemporary Russian history, from the October Revolution to the disintegration of the USSR and the proliferation of post-Soviet reforms of varying effectiveness, on the pernicious influence of Russophobes, including American presidents and influential Western businessmen. Within Russia, Shafarevich indicts not only such intellectuals as Andrei Amalrik and Grigorii Pomerants, but also creative writers of Jewish origin, such as Isaak Babel, Ilya Ilf, and Vasilii Grossman, for their allegedly innate "contempt and squeamishness" toward Russians and other Slavs. "[T]he ideology of the Small People: an arrogant/ironic, mocking attitude toward everything Russian, even Russian names; the notion that 'in this country, it has always been thus, and there can be nothing good'; the image of Russia as the 'Land of Fools.'"[50]

Shafarevich never specifies why Russianness should provoke such a negative reaction, but he does attempt to explain why Jews are the primary catalysts of Russophobic feelings. As a cosmopolitan people devoid of roots in any national culture, their "diasporic" consciousness makes them organically incapable of accepting a traditional, agricultural way of life, consistent with the truth of Nature.

> Why did it happen that it was specifically those of a Jewish background who proved to be the core of the "Small People" destined to play so fatal a role in this critical epoch of our history? … Here I would note only the most obvious reason: almost two millennia of isolation and a suspicious, hostile attitude toward the surrounding world.[51]

Shafarevich argues further, marshaling numerous citations from the Old Testament, that even before their diasporic period, Jews justified their hatred of other nations religiously, since, according to their messianic beliefs, all non-Jews are inferior to the "chosen people." One of the inconsistencies of Shafarevich's thinking is that he blames Jews for their extreme nationalism, while himself subscribing to the same ideology—provided the "chosen" nation will be his own. This self-defeating argumentation is characteristic of nationalism of whatever sort.

In any case, "nation" is almost a magic word in Shafarevich's lexicon: "[B]eing a member of one's nation makes one a participant in History."[52] The destruction of

[50] Ibid., 90.
[51] Ibid., 82.
[52] Ibid., 95.

national self-identity in Russia entails the loss of life's meaning: men become alcoholics and drug addicts, women abort their children, the people die out. "This is the end towards which the 'Small People' is driving, tirelessly working to destroy everything that supports the existence of the 'Large People.'"[53] Thus it is the task of Russian national self-preservation to create a weapon of spiritual defense against the "small people."

Shafarevich devoted his later writings, small in quantity and journalistic in style, to the critique of liberalism and Western democracy. Noting a strange sympathy for Stalin's regime on the part of such "progressive" Western intellectuals as Romain Rolland, George Bernard Shaw, and Jean-Paul Sartre, he explained this phenomenon with reference to the alleged internal affinities between Western liberalism and Soviet totalitarianism. Both, in this view, are hostile to traditional societies based on organic ties between human productivity and the natural environment. "Like Stalin's system of administrative command, Western technological civilization chose a technocentric ideology in opposition to a cosmocentric one. This is only another way to implement the familiar Utopia of the 'organization' of nature and society on the principle of the 'megamachine,' with maximal exclusion of the human and living element."[54]

This two-pronged attack on both the liberal West and communist Russia had been a standard tool of Nazi propaganda, but appeared rather new on the late-Soviet intellectual scene, where Soviet communism and Western capitalism were typically counterposed as two absolute polarities. From the nationalist-conservative point of view, communism and capitalism are two versions of the same technocratic paradigm, which was initiated, according to Shafarevich, by the "small peoples" of Europe—Huguenots, Puritans, and Jews—who, as the result of their migration to Germany, America, and Russia respectively, undermined the organic conditions of agrarian labor and laid the basis for (artificial) capitalist and communist economies. Now that Russia has finished with communism, Shafarevich argues, it would be unwise to take the path of capitalism, which leads to the same precipice. "The West is ill, but with another form of the same disease from which we would like to recover."[55]

For all his critical remarks, Shafarevich never presents his positive ideal, except insofar as he evinces an overwhelming nostalgia for the past, when the peasant lived in harmony with Mother Earth and followed the patterns of "calendar" culture as constituted by a mixture of Christian and pagan ritual. Shafarevich greatly admires "village prose," which resurrects the values of agricultural civilization as a model for a stable social structure that would preserve the unity of Man and Universe.

In his conservative views and his polemics with liberal thinkers—such "Russophobes" as Siniavsky, Pomerants, Ianov, Amalrik, and Shragin—Shafarevich often follows Solzhenitsyn, but the difference between the two authors is significant. Solzhenitsyn, like a biblical prophet, summons Russians to repent for their sins, whereas Shafarevich lays the blame on the demonic "small people," who, in his telling, would seem to be the sole source of metaphysical and social evil.

53 Ibid.
54 Ibid., 123.
55 Ibid., 140.

6. The Philosophy of Ethnicity. Neo-Eurasianism. Lev Gumilev

Most nationalistic thinkers in contemporary Russia emerged from the field of literature: they were fiction-writers, poets, journalists, critics. In this regard, Lev Gumilev (1912–92) stands out as one of the very few professional scholars. One would be hard-pressed to find him sinking outright to a level of nationalism we might term "vulgar," but his theories of ethnogenesis have provided a basis for ideological conclusions sometimes bordering on chauvinism and racism. Lev Gumilev was born into one of Russian culture's most illustrious families: his father Nikolai Gumilev was the founder of acmeism, a highly influential poetic movement of the Russian Silver Age; he was shot by the Soviet Cheka in 1921. His mother, Anna Akhmatova, an even more celebrated poet, devoted one of her most poignant long poems, *Requiem*, to the tragic fate of her only son, Lev, who spent fifteen years in Stalin's concentration camps for the mere crime of being the son of "infamous" parents. After his return from the

Figure 2 Lev Gumilev.

Gulag, Gumilev emerged in Leningrad as one of the most renowned historians and ethnologists of the 1970s–1980s. He authored numerous books, mostly dealing with the history, geography, and ethnography of Eurasia and with the interaction between Slavic and Turkic tribes in the vast region of the southern Russian and Mongolian steppes.

Serving as the ideological model for this research were the teachings of the "Eurasianists." If, for traditional historians oriented toward the West, the early history of Russia appeared to be an incessant struggle against the Tatar-Mongol horde and other Turkic tribes and nomads, Gumilev stressed the productive interaction between Slavs and Turks as two major cohabitants of the great Eurasian expanse. For him, "Russia" is the general name for a synthetic civilization of which Slavs are only one ethnic component. Gumilev's ethnological studies provoked a heated controversy: official Soviet scholarship accused him of overemphasizing the ethnological aspects of the historical process at the expense of social determinants, and of harboring a simplistic understanding of ethnos as a natural phenomenon formed by geographical environment and by impulses of "biospheric" energy.

Indeed, contrary to convention, which situates ethnology within the humanities, Gumilev attempts to base his ethnological research on the methodologies of the natural sciences. His most significant influence is the work of Vladimir Vernadsky (1863–1945), a great twentieth-century Russian scientist in several interconnected fields, including geology and biochemistry. The core of Vernadsky's thought is his theory of "living matter," the organic substance of life that determines the formation of both the inorganic and superorganic (rational) layers of the global ecosystem, including the biosphere and noosphere (the sphere of reason as a geological force). A variety of philosophical schools has made use of Vernadsky's legacy as a bridge between natural and humanistic phenomena. It matters, however, which direction one takes in crossing this bridge. One could, for instance, make an "ascending" interpretation of the noosphere as the vector of the spiritualization of matter, as in the evolutionary theology of divine cosmogenesis developed by the French Catholic thinker Pierre Teillard de Chardin (1881–1955). Conversely, a "descending" interpretation would attempt to derive all forces engaged in historical evolution from sources of material energy. Such an approach, reducing the human element of ethnology to natural laws, is elaborated by Gumilev, who argues for the priority of biological and chemical determinants in the historical process. Citing Vernadsky's theory of the biosphere as a reservoir of energy permeating and charging all living substances, including the human body, Gumilev explains ethnogenesis by the influence and infusion of cosmic energy. "Ethnos as a form of existence of the species *Homo sapiens* … preceded the creation of tools of production and social development …. The character of its development correlates with the fluctuation of biochemical energy in the living matter of the biosphere."[56]

[56] L. N. Gumilev, *Noosfera i khudozhestvennoe tvorchestvo* (Moscow: Nauka, 1991), 62.

Gumilev's most important work, *Ethnogenesis and the Earth's Biosphere*,[57] represents a philosophical and methodological summation of his more specialized historical investigations. This book, completed in the 1970s, could not be published until shortly before the author's death in 1990 because its method, though based on materialist assumptions, was, from the standpoint of official Marxism, suspect—an example of "*vulgar* materialism," reducing the social form of materiality to its more primitive chemical and biological forms. The historical scope of *Ethnogenesis and the Earth's Biosphere* may be compared to Arnold Toynbee's *A Study of History* (1934–61), though Gumilev rejects Toynbee's methodology, in particular, his principal conception of human civilization as a response to the challenge of a severe natural environment. Gumilev's book explores the fates of dozens of ethnoi, from the Spanish and Italian to the Egyptian, Arabic, and Mongolian, and covers several millennia of their ascension and decline. But it is not based only on empirical research; the author advances an original conception to account for ethnic processes all over the world, relying in particular on Hegel's and Marx's views of the role of passion in human history.[58] In his search for some decisive factor determining the seemingly variegated forms of ethnicity, Gumilev arrives at the concept of "passionate drive," or "passionarity."[59] This coinage is meant to signify the extent of passion, which for Gumilev is the key factor determining the historical activity of a given ethnos.[60]

"Passionarity" is the energetic drive that generates the formation and activity of an ethnos. "The work done by an ethnic collective is directly proportional to the

[57] An abridged version of this book (*Etnogenez i biosfera Zemli* [Leningrad: Gidrometeoizdat, 1990]) appeared in English translation as Leo Gumilev, *Ethnogenesis and the Biosphere* (Moscow: Progress Publishers, 1990). I will cite both the original and the translation, since they are not identical; in particular, the Russian edition has 528 pages, nine parts, and extensive indexes; the English has 384 pages, six chapters, and no indexes. For the reader interested in examining both editions, page numbers for citations from the Russian edition will be indicated in these notes in parentheses. Significantly, the last (ninth) part of the Russian edition, "Ethnogenesis and Culture," in which Gumilev's views on ethnic purity and his condemnation of "mixed," "chimeric" ethnoi are most directly expressed, is absent from the Progress edition, probably to avoid offending the foreign reader. For passages that are missing in the translation, I will cite directly from the original.

[58] "Inasmuch as the whole individuality, to the neglect of all other actual or possible interests and claims, is devoted to an object with every fibre of volition, concentrating all its desires and powers upon it—we may affirm absolutely that nothing great in the World has been accomplished without passion" (G. W. F. Hegel, *The Philosophy of History*, trans. J. Sibree [New York: Dover Publications, 1956], 23).

[59] In the original Russian, *passionarnost'*. The (anonymous) Soviet translator of Gumilev's book uses the term "drive"; however, Gumilev's term is a neologism in Russian, which some English-language commentators have since rendered (rightly, in my view) with an English neologism derived from the same root: "passionarity." Gumilev likewise coins the term *passionarii* to signify those people who embody ethnic *passionarnost'*; the English equivalent would be "passionarians," although the Progress edition, again, renders it as "people with drive."

[60] Definitions of "passionarity" and derivative terms like "passionary infusion" and "passionary overheating" are given (in Russian) in a glossary compiled by V. A. Michurin: "Slovar' poniatii i terminov teorii etnogeneza L. N. Gumileva." This is included as an appendix to L. N. Gumilev, *Etnosfera: Istoriia liudei i istoriia prirody* (Moscow: AST, 2004), which also features the author's account of how his theory of ethnogenesis came to be: "The Biography of a Scientific Theory, or an Auto-Obituary."

tension of drive [*passionarnost'*]."[61] Gumilev even proposes to calculate passionary tension as the amount of passionarity contained in an ethnic system divided by the number of individuals in that system. This is, however, solely an abstract notion, since Gumilev never goes so far in his scientific claims as to provide a mathematical means for quantifying the passionarity in a given ethnos. Nevertheless, he does make use of charts showing solar activity cycles in order to argue that the historical beginnings of new ethnoi chronologically correspond to periods of minimal solar activity, when cosmic radiation is more readily admitted to earth's atmosphere, giving rise to a greater frequency of mutation, hence to new passionarians and, correspondingly, to new ethnoi.

Not all members of a given ethnos are equally charged with passionarity; thus Gumilev singles out a specific category of persons who are its true founders and leaders, "passionarians." Whereas most people, both individually and collectively, are motivated by a desire for self-preservation, and therefore behave reactively in the face of social and natural cataclysms, passionarians are people who devote their entire lives to the pursuit of a particular goal and are ready to give their lives for its attainment.

> It must be an impulse strong enough to overcome the instinct of personal and even species self-preservation inherent in any organism, i.e., sacrifice that extends even to one's posterity, something, which is not observed in any animal species. But then there are no ethnoi among animals. Their communities lack the social form of the motion of matter and self-developing institutions.[62]

As examples of passionarians, Gumilev points to Alexander the Great, Hannibal, Joan of Arc, Jan Hus, Avvakum, and Napoleon, among others. The decisive feature of the passionarian is his or her capacity to charge other people with the energy of action ("passionary induction"). Thus, for example, a given division of soldiers may be composed of varied individuals, but the presence of a few passionarians among them would raise their level of passionarity and convert the unit into a passionate organism capable of decisive action.

The factor of passionarity allows Gumilev to divide ethnic populations into several categories. Inasmuch as passionarity is measured in relation to the instinct of self-preservation, three relative proportions become possible: those in whom passionarity exceeds the instinct for self-preservation are the passionarians, and Gumilev designates their "drive" as $P > 1$; those whose passionarity is equal to their survival instinct are called "harmonious" ($P = 1$); and those whose passionarity is less than their instinct for self-preservation are termed "sub-passionarians" ($P < 1$).[63] In a given population, the harmonious personalities, who are diligent but not super-active, constitute a decisive majority. Sub-passionarians are those satisfied by mere "bread and circuses"; according

[61] Gumilev, *Ethnogenesis and the Biosphere*, 217 (273).

[62] Ibid., 197 (253).

[63] Ibid., 269 (327).

to Gumilev, they are typically found among vagrant populations or are employed as soldiers of fortune who "do not change the world and do not preserve it, but exist at its expense."[64] The proportion of passionarians and sub-passionarians within a population fluctuates with the ascendancy or decline of a given ethnos. Thus, in Gumilev's view, "Ancient Rus was ruined by destabilization, which appeared as a consequence of a decrease in the passionary tension of the ethnic system or, more simply put, an increase in the number of sub-passionarians—egoists not capable of sacrifice for the sake of selfless patriotism."[65] Notably, Gumilev cites patriotism—and not for instance artistic or philosophical genius—as the most convincing form of passionarity.

Gumilev does not connect passionarity with any ethical norms. He recognizes its ability to produce both heroic deeds and terrible crimes, to create and to destroy; the only attitude excluded from passionarity is sluggishness and indifference. He is also careful to distinguish it from leadership as typically understood, arguing that it is the passionarity of the rank and file *within* "the pack" that often constitutes the true impetus for decisive action. For example, while Napoleon as a passionarian had no rival among the leaders of the monarchic European coalition arrayed against him, it was the greater proportion of passionarians in the ranks of the opposing forces that led to the downfall of a less passionate French force composed of fresh recruits. Thus, strong passionarity does not necessarily correlate with individual prominence.

According to Gumilev, passionarity is a factor of an ethnos's negentropy, which resists the inevitable tendency toward entropy—the dead equilibrium to which all closed physical systems are liable. However, ethnoi too are susceptible to the law of the gradual exhaustion of passionarity. First of all, the tendency for passionarians to perish prematurely in times of war explains why these persons rarely reproduce and pass on their passionary genes. Moreover, during peacetime, passionarians are apt to miss their callings and are forced into marginal status, alienated from societies in which moderate and cautious people enjoy greater success. Thus the fate of every ethnos is a gradual loss of passionarity and a multistage degradation into passivity and extinction.

More specifically, Gumilev identifies the following phases of ethnic evolution: the ascension, acme, fracture, inertia, obscuration, regeneration, relic, and memorial phases, after which an ethnos dissolves into nothingness. In the stages of ascension and acme, the ideal of victory prevails; next comes the ideal of success, followed by those of knowledge and creativity; then the search for well-being without risk; and finally, a quiet conformity adapted to the local biocenosis. The average term of existence for each ethnos is 1,000–1,500 years, after which entropy overcomes passionarity, ensuring this collective organism's demise. Gumilev charts the moral guidelines prevalent in each period of ethnic history. The phase of ethnic formation and ascension, for example, is inspired by such imperatives as: "It is necessary to correct the world because it is bad"; or "Be what you should be." The next stage, that of attaining the acme, demands: "Be yourself!" The transition to inertia is expressed as "We are tired of the great"; "Be

[64] Ibid., 229 (285).
[65] L. N. Gumilev, *Drevniaia Rus' i velikaia step'* (Moscow: Mysl', 1989), 682.

like me"; and later, in the obscuration phase: "Be like us." The memorial phase may be summarized as "Remember how fine it was."[66] In the last phase of ethnogenesis, people lose their memory of the past and even their sense of time. They enter a state of homeostasis, energy equilibrium with their natural environment, where their existence becomes almost identical to that of animals.

According to Gumilev, an ethnos cannot preserve itself in the status quo; it is either developing or deteriorating. Thus he describes the Chukchi people of northern Siberia as having lost the sense of time, not even noticing the change of seasons. Severe climate might be blamed for this exhaustion of spirit, but even the denizens of paradise are not immune to such entropy, as witnessed by the Onge people, who are "too lazy to live. They sometimes prefer to starve than hunt for food."[67] Gumilev never considers the possibility that each ethnos may have its own criteria for growth and degradation, and that the same modes of time orientation may be "progressive," "regressive," or "neutral" for different ethnoi. On the one hand, Gumilev criticizes ethnic elitism, which he sees, for example, in Karl Jaspers's concept of the "axis" time, according to which five great nations—the Greeks, Jews, Iranians, Chinese, and Indians—produced the greatest prophets, who from the eighth to second centuries BCE gave spiritual birth to contemporary civilization. On the other hand, Gumilev finds an original justification for those ethnoi that have traditionally been considered to be "backward," such as Native Americans and Black Australians, Eskimos, and Bushmen: these, he says, are "simply relics that have outlived their flourishing and decline."[68] Contrary to the traditional white chauvinist view of these ethnoi as still too young, hence in need of the "blessings" of Western colonization to enter into historical development, Gumilev believes them to be "decrepit" ethnoi whose best time is in the past: they have come to the last phase of entropy, to homeostasis; "that is why their material culture is so poor, and their spiritual culture so fragmentary."[69] This is a paradoxical "multiculturalism" that does not recognize the different values of differing cultures, but rather seeks to explain perceived deficiencies with reference to a universal process.

Gumilev pays considerable attention to the interaction among different ethnoi, and especially to the type of interaction that results in the formation of self-destructive ethnic complexes, which he calls anti-systems or "chimeras" (combinations of elements not organically united).[70] When two ethnic systems interact, a kind of cacophonous disruption occurs instead of a seamless harmony. "Let both systems be positive, ecologically and culturally, but when combined they generate an anti-system, an epiphenomenon that arises beyond the will of the participants."[71] Further:

[66] See the chart in Gumilev, *Ethnogenesis and the Biosphere*, 379 (491).

[67] Ibid., 373 (450).

[68] Ibid., 283 (360).

[69] Ibid.

[70] For Gumilev, the chimera (a mythical animal with the head of a lion, body of a goat, and tail of a serpent) symbolizes "a form of contact of incompatible ethnoi of different superethnic systems, upon which their originality disappears"; or, "the coexistence of two or more alien superethnic ethnic groups in one ecological niche" (*Etnogenez i biosfera Zemli*, 500).

[71] Ibid., 473.

> When heterogeneous ethnic systems and related "systems of consciousness," which are now called "cultures," overlap, then chimeras arise that are fundamentally different from ethnoi, although they are similar in appearance. The difference between an ethnos and a chimera is hardly perceptible. But while an ethnos passes through all ages, assuming it does not meet with a violent death, a chimera either exists or disintegrates. This means that the relationship between an ethnos and a chimera is the same as between an organism and a cancerous tumor.[72]

With ethnic combination or transplantation, people begin to lose their sense of organic connection with their geographical environment and turn to abstract thinking, which ultimately leads such thinkers to hate their natural milieu, and life in general. "Then, at the site of collision, there emerges either a symbiosis, with ethnoi existing in a single region independently of each other; or a chimera, when the interaction changes the structures and stereotypes of behavior. Then development is halted amid chimeric formations, and a complex of negative attitudes toward nature, culture, and even life as such arises."[73] As an example, Gumilev cites Gnosticism, which arose on the border between two prosperous ancient ethnoi, the Jews and the Greeks. The Gnostic worldview considers life on earth to be a hardship which the human soul must shed. In the same way, the collision between Hellenic and Persian civilizations in the third century generated Manicheism, a powerful anti-system that likewise identified life with evil. Adherents of this religion destroyed temples, icons, even human bodies, since the visible world was created by an evil god and must be subjected to annihilation.

Gumilev traces the history of such chimeric concepts through Christian heresies and socialist utopias, hinting that communist revolution in Russia may also have been initiated by the interaction of two ethnoi, Jews and Russians, resulting in a chimeric Soviet ethnicity based on the ideological subjugation of the natural environment—which is self-ruinous for the ethnos. Notably, Gumilev's analysis of Christian heresies and early socialist movements[74] has affinities with that offered by Shafarevich, and both authors see the Protestant and socialist movements as associated with a Manichean hatred for the world and grounded in a gravitation toward death. Gumilev's metaphysics includes the concept of the "infernal" vacuum as the opposite of life-generating nature. He dedicates *Ethnogenesis and the Earth's Biosphere* to the great cause of defending the natural environment against anti-systems that have millions of adherents all over the earth, and that hold up, as their ideal, the void.

In these terms, however, Gumilev himself may be viewed as a Manichean, since he insists upon dividing the world into two opposing forces of energy and vacuum. In his eyes, the force of anti-system would be irresistible if not for the new impetuses of passionarity, which infuse deteriorating ethnic systems with energy.

[72] Gumilev, *Etnosfera: Istoriia liudei i istoriia prirody*, 212–13.
[73] Gumilev, *Noosfera i khudozhestvennoe tvorchestvo*, 63.
[74] Gumilev, *Etnogenez i biosfera Zemli*, 472–83.

> Given how long humans have existed on earth, all ethnoi must long ago have entered into contact; then it seems that anti-systems would have supplanted ethnoi and replaced them, would have annihilated all life in its natural habitat .... But for some reason nothing of the kind has happened .... It is the impetus, mutation, giving birth to passionarity and imparting the original rhythm of the biological field to the newly arising ethnoi that destroys chimeras and their concurrent anti-systems.[75]

Thus, Gumilev proposes, the passionary impetus at the turn of the current era created Christianity, which dissolved Gnostic teachings, but Gumilev thus seems to lose sight of the fact that Christianity itself arose on the same ethnic border (between Jews and Romans) that originally produced Gnosticism. By the same token, Gumilev insists that a new impetus of the sixth–seventh centuries put an end to the Iranian anti-systems and gave rise to Islam. Both Christianity and Islam are positive systems for Gumilev, though he interprets Protestantism and Ismailism as expressions of life-denial. In general, his attitude toward religion is rather ambivalent; he celebrates the adoption of Orthodox Christianity in Russia, but simultaneously believes that theism may lead to the deterioration of ethnoi: "Anti-systems are often theistic, while the ideals of ethnic cultures are atheistic."[76]

Here again Gumilev's thought converges with Shafarevich's allegiance to an eco-morality that condemns theism, and primarily Judaism, for the negligence of nature and the divinely justified assertion of human dominance. Gumilev's extensive discussion of Khazar history[77] leads him to the conclusion that this ethnos, comprised of many sub-ethnic groups that converted to Judaism, was not only chimeric in itself, but also threatened to "chimerize" the Russian and other surrounding peoples. Although Jews themselves were averse to allowing anti-systems into their own communities, Gumilev argues that they deliberately introduced Gnostic and Manichean doctrines to other ethnoi in order to destabilize them: "They preferred to see Manicheans among their neighbors but not to admit them into their own domain. And since they, like metastases, penetrated into all civilized countries, they generally succeeded in achieving their goals, but not always."[78] Gumilev is also quite close to Shafarevich's concept of the "small people" that sows nihilism in order to undermine the ethnic stability of larger peoples. The only difference is that Shafarevich explicitly blames Jews for the destruction of contemporary Russia, while Gumilev limits himself to a discussion of the dangers the Judaic Khazar state posed for ancient Rus. One can also find interesting parallels between the right-wing critics Petr Palievsky's and Vadim Kozhinov's condemnation of avant-garde art in favor of traditional realism and Gumilev's proposal that "ancient

[75] Ibid., 484.

[76] Ibid.

[77] The Khazars, a people who inhabited a vast area in the lower Volga region in the seventh–ninth centuries, were defeated by the Russian Prince Sviatoslav in the tenth century and quickly dissipated.

[78] Gumilev, *Drevniaia Rus' i velikaia step'*, 151.

Jewish art was the prototype of abstractionism."[79] Jewish monotheism forbade the visual reproduction of God's creation, giving rise to nonrealistic tendencies, which prefigured the worldwide avant-garde movement of the twentieth century. Thus avant-gardism may also be explained (in accordance with the terms of Nazi propaganda) as a product of Jewish insidiousness, which infects European nations with a nihilistic hatred for reality, thereby setting in motion a progressive dissolution of national spirit.

In his naturalist bias, Gumilev goes so far as to propose that all philosophical and religious teachings may be mere epiphenomena of the vacuum that, like a black screen, repulses and distorts all biospheric impulses and hampers natural processes. Even personal consciousness, in his terms, is nothing but a black hole through which the vacuum emanates into the world.[80] In the final analysis, only nature and its vital energetic impulses are considered real and positive in the system of Gumilev's thought, whose conclusive thesis is that "we are not alone in the world! The near-Cosmos takes part in protecting nature, which it is up to us not to spoil. Nature is not only our home; she is us."[81]

Gumilev's preference for a natural rather than historical approach to ethnicity is not purely methodological, but also reflects his metaphysical assumption that history is a waste of natural forces, a kind of cosmic illness. Central to Gumilev's philosophy is the problem of historical time, which he discusses as a function of entropy, the tendency of energy to dissipate into nothingness. According to this view, history has no creative potential in itself; the impetus for artistic, scientific, or political creativity, as well as for violence and destruction, comes solely from impulses arising in the biosphere.

> [P]rocesses occurring in the course of time are entropic and inertial, but since now and then they are interrupted by creative flashes, producing new ethnoi and cultures, the end of the world does not come. Therefore, the history of culture is the struggle of the Creative force (energy) with Chronos (entropy); this is the manifestation of the second law of thermodynamics in the historical process.[82]

To what extent, though, is Gumilev's "Creative force" actually creative? To be sure, he disdains entropy and praises energy, but his theory suggests no criteria for distinguishing destructive manifestations of energy from constructive ones—even as, after all, passionarity in action may at times be more harmful than passionarity in decline. In his book on ancient Russian history, Gumilev himself observes that "the explosion of passionarity at first burns down the place where it emerges. In this conflagration, it is not just the weak, those capable only of admiring the masterpieces inherited from their ancestors, that perish, but also the masterpieces themselves."[83]

79 Ibid., 148.

80 "[B]lack holes have been punched from the Abyss into the World, and each of them is called 'a personal consciousness'" (Gumilev, *Etnogenez i biosfera Zemli*, 485).

81 Ibid., 485.

82 Gumilev, *Drevniaia Rus' i velikaia step'*, 590.

83 Ibid., 590.

This imparts a tragic dimension to Gumilev's theory, although the author himself does not always seem to be conscious of it. The same energy that creates culture arises to destroy it. Gumilev's passionarity recalls Heraclitus's fire, the mythical image-conception of the universe's self-creation and self-destruction through "everliving fire, kindling in measures and being quenched in measures."[84] It is unclear why Gumilev should disparage entropy and indifference if the energy in his system is as indifferent to values as entropy. Why condemn Gnostic and Manichean theories for deprecating the material world, if the passionarity Gumilev glorifies as the principle of life can all the more vehemently lay waste to that same world?

Another philosophical question underlying all of Gumilev's theorizing is the problem of free will. He distinguishes a hierarchy of levels of material organization ranging from the atom to the galaxy, and postulates a scale of determinism that correlates with the status of the material unit. Thus, on a galactic scale, the laws of material organization are absolutely predetermined, whereas the atom exists in a zone of indeterminacy. Ethnoi, in his view, are intermediate entities, which means that their processes are largely probabilistic.[85] Gumilev is careful to assert that a given ethnos's history leaves room for the freedom of human actions, which can change its fate; however, the principal assumptions of his theory ground personality in a genetic and biochemical predisposition, determined by mutation. When Gumilev speaks of indeterminism, he means not free will but randomness. One may be arbitrarily born with passionarity, but acting on this impulse is not a matter of free choice—it is biologically predetermined. Mutation, which is the engine of passionarity in individuals,[86] is a random event, but by producing three specific genetic types (passionarians, the harmonious, and sub-passionarians), it completely determines the future behavior of the individual in each category. In Gumilev's world, a person does not choose to be a passionarian or sub-passionarian, they merely follow their inherent nature. This is another contradiction in Gumilev's conception. He endows nature with a certain randomness (mutation, explosion), but the human subjects it produces become subordinated to these caprices as if to absolute laws. Befitting a paganist worldview, Gumilev is inclined to "ensoul" nature and "naturalize" or "desoul" the human.

Though Gumilev deals less with contemporary national consciousness than with historical ethnoi, his ideas are easily extrapolated to modern Russian sociopolitical culture, particularly its neofascist element. For that matter, one can find striking parallels between his concept of chimeric ethnoi and the platforms of racial purity advanced by Nazi ideologists in Germany. He applies to historical reality what he calls the methodology of the natural sciences, lending a quasi-scientific imprimatur to what is essentially a form of paganist (and nationalist) nature-worship—a challenge not only to Judaism but to Christianity as a kind of "Judaic conspiracy" against healthy national life in harmony with nature.

[84] Cited from Daniel W. Graham, ed., *The Texts of Early Greek Philosophy: The Complete Fragments and Selected Testimonies of the Major Presocratics* (Cambridge: Cambridge University Press, 2010), 155.

[85] Gumilev, *Etnogenez i biosfera Zemli*, 336.

[86] Gumilev, *Ethnogenesis and the Biosphere*, 261 (341).

Gumilev was the brightest representative of the second generation of Russian Eurasianists. His legacy provoked heated debates. He became a cult figure for many followers of the "Russian idea," who enthusiastically embraced his apologias for the greatness of Russia as the center of Eurasia and as a "super-ethnos." On the other hand, some nationalists accused him of "Russophobia" because of his high estimation of the Turkic peoples and their formative impact on Russian history. Most social scientists, meanwhile, took a rather skeptical view of Gumilev's works. Despite his indisputable erudition and the abundance of empirical material he cites, his general view of ethnogenesis is dictated by speculative "cosmological" hypotheses that are not subject to the criteria of verification or falsification. "Pseudoscience," "mythmaking," "folk-history"—such were some of the epithets applied to Gumilev's theory of passionarity. However, it is impossible to deny Gumilev's significant role, even as a mythmaker, in the intellectual history of the late Soviet period. Among all Russian historians, Gumilev turned out to be most successful in creating a "meta-discourse" of ethnicity that crosses the borders of disciplines and, even more essentially, the borders of science, history, myth, fiction, politics, and ideology.[87]

7. Radical Traditionalism and Neofascism. Aleksandr Dugin

Among the multiplicity of conservative movements that arose with the collapse of Soviet Marxism, one stands out as perhaps the most radical, both in political and metaphysical terms. Its radicalism is paradoxical because it calls for the resurrection of ancient esotericism as the antithesis of scientific rationalism and democratic norms; hence the movement often identifies itself as "radical traditionalism," though it goes by a number of other names, such as "continentalism," "anti-mondialism" (*antimondializm*), "revolutionary conservatism," the "third way," the "fourth political theory," etc. The closest historical analogue to this worldview would probably be the geopolitical mysticism of the Third Reich, though radical traditionalists claim equal distinction from the three dominant ideologies of the twentieth century: communism, fascism, and democracy.

The early program of this movement was delineated most clearly in the journal *Cherished Angel*, the magazine *Elements*, and the newspaper *Day. The Paper of Spiritual Opposition* (in October 1993 renamed *Tomorrow*). No other movement in Russia, except Marxism, has so thoroughly conflated political and philosophical issues, such that, for example, Aleksandr Barkashov, best known as the organizer of the radical

[87] The most comprehensive study of Gumilev's ideas and impact is Mark Bassin, *The Gumilev Mystique: Biopolitics, Eurasianism, and the Construction of Community in Modern Russia* (Ithaca: Cornell University Press, 2016).

paramilitary group Russian National Unity, used to discuss his political goals with constant reference to the terms "metaphysics," "mysticism," and "spirituality."[88]

The two preeminent spokesmen of this movement are Aleksandr Prokhanov (born 1938) and Aleksandr Dugin (born 1962). The former is a famous novelist who, in Brezhnev's time, was celebrated as the bard of the Soviet invasion of Afghanistan, and mocked by the liberal press as the "nightingale of the General Staff." As editor in chief of *Day*, he was one of the principal initiators of the anti-Gorbachev, and later anti-Yeltsin, movements, and his ideology represents a mixture of nativist, technocratic, and mystical views usually expressed in a polemical journalistic manner.

Aleksandr Dugin associated himself with the extreme nationalist factions Memory and Russian National Unity. He was the editor in chief of *Cherished Angel* and *Elements*, and authored *Paths of the Absolute* (1991), *Conspirology* (1992), *The Hyperborean Theory* (1993), *The Mysteries of Eurasia* (1996), and *Foundations of Geopolitics* (1997), to name just the earliest among his dozens of books. His writings evince a thorough acquaintance with esoteric and occult literature, but in particular he is intellectually indebted to Rene Guenon (1886–1951) and Julius Evola (1898–1974), leading figures of European right-wing esotericism before and after the Second World War, respectively, and Alain de Benoist, a theoretician of the French *Nouvelle Droit*. Further exposition of the ideology of radical traditionalism will rely principally on the early work of Dugin, who remains the most philosophically oriented of all its representatives.[89]

The fact that several neofascist periodicals in Western Europe and Russia shared the title *Elements* attests to the paganist foundations of this worldview, which sanctifies "the stormiest, the harshest, the most powerful" forces in the universe, everything that is endowed with "the potential for terrible power, capable of enacting both Great Creation and Great Destruction."[90] Radical traditionalism has affinities with romanticism and Nietzschean Dionysianism and thus opposes itself "heroically," and sometimes tragically, to any rationally structured order. From this viewpoint, contemporary civilization, obsessed with ideas of comfort and profit, has abandoned the majestic mysteries of the past; it thus falls to traditionalists to restore these archaic rituals in the most revolutionary way, by antagonizing all existing systems. The conventional, "leftist" notion of revolution presupposes a radical rupture with Tradition (usually capitalized by its adherents) and a preoccupation with the new, with a utopian vision of the future as superior to past and present. Traditionalists believe that after the American, French, and Russian revolutions, which were all leftist and "democratic," the world abandoned Tradition and sold its soul to the devil of material

[88] For instance, in an interview with Barkashov ("Slava Rossii!" *Zavtra*, no. 12 [1994]: 1–2), Prokhanov declares: "You and I are not only Orthodox mystics, not only monks and ascetics [*skhimniki*], we are politicians"—a sentiment characteristic of the metaphysical bombast and conceit of the extreme right. Here Barkashov remarks that "[s]ome historical mystery is taking place in Russia, and one must seek friends, strategic allies precisely in the mystical spirit that permeates this event" (the storming of the White House in October 1993).

[89] For a pioneering exposition of this political ideology, see Walter Laqueur, *Black Hundred: The Rise of the Extreme Right in Russia* (New York: Harper Collins Publishers, 1993), especially 139–42.

[90] "Probuzhdenie stikhii" (unsigned editorial), *Elementy*, no. 1 (1992): 3.

prosperity. This is why a new revolution is called for, this time a rightist one—which is antithetical to the conventional revolutionary formula, insofar as it purports to restore the spiritual foundations of the world, supposedly buried by decadent civilization in the name of false progress. "On the whole, we stand for the Restoration of the fullness of Tradition in its supertemporal and superhistorical essence, for the Restoration of Eternal Order, Eternal Sacred Structure, against which the 'contemporary world'—the world of materialism, skepticism, plutocracy, atheism, humanism, profanism, in short, the world of the Devil—has waged an irreconcilable struggle for many centuries."[91]

The conception of Tradition, as propagated by Dugin, has several levels of meaning. On the deepest one, traditionalism presupposes esotericism, a direct knowledge of the divine accessible only to a spiritual elite. Esotericism is not a purely theoretical discipline, but includes the practice of theosis, or deification, the mysterious transformation of the earthly into the heavenly. Dugin is anxious to distinguish the genuine traditionalist esotericism, which recognizes traditional religions and Church dogmas, from Satanic distortions of esotericism, which attack Christianity and Islam and attempt to destroy the dogmatic integrity of Tradition. Hence the existence of a second level of Tradition: exotericism, the sphere of sacred knowledge open to everyone, so long as they participate in the life of the Church. In this sense, traditionalism supports theocracy, "presupposes the restoration of the central position of the Church in the State,"[92] with all aspects of social life subordinated to Church rule, as legislated by an ecclesiastical court. A third level of Tradition requires the spiritual stratification of society and the establishment of a hierarchy of estates or castes. The recognition of different types of people, according to their spiritual origin, is a necessary condition of "truly sacred" civilization. A fourth level of Tradition mandates the restoration of the sacred sciences and arts, as opposed to secularized disciplines based upon empirical knowledge. From this viewpoint, most contemporary sciences are examples of ignorance, because they reduce reality to its material surface; whereas true knowledge must be anagogical, and lead to salvation. Hence Dugin seeks to restore "the 'hard,' sacred sciences—alchemy, astrology, sacred geography, sacred ethnography, symbolism, rituals of traditional professions, and so on."[93] Finally, Tradition is a totality, subordinating all aspects of culture and establishing strict rules and rituals of everyday conduct for all members of society.

The traditionalist concept of the "third way," opposed both to the political left and right, has nothing to do with the solidarist "third position" (discussed in the "Liberalism and Westernism" part of *The Phoenix of Philosophy*). Solidarism attempts to mediate between the extremes of communism and capitalism, a centralized economy and a free market. For Dugin, the "third way" is anti-conciliatory; it does not blend or balance left and right, but brings together the extremes of tradition and revolution. "The Third Position or the Third Way is an ideological factor that is directly opposed to the

91 "O nashem zhurnale. Kak my ponimaem traditsiiu" (unsigned editorial, but clearly by Dugin himself), *Milyi angel*, no. 1 (1991): 1.

92 Ibid., 2.

93 Ibid., 4.

position of the center in all respects .... If the center mediates and softens the positions at the edges, the Third Way sharpens and radicalizes them."[94] The very term "radical traditionalism" contains an almost oxymoronic combination of extreme leftist and rightist components. Radical traditionalists are interested in the collision of extremes, which is the potential source of maximal historical energies that will melt the world in the "eschatological fire of the final revolution."

The radical-traditionalist attitude toward socialism and communism is one of ambivalence. Between the leftist, technocratic, and materialist models of socialism (Fourier, Proudhon, Louis Blanc, and Marx) and, on the other hand, the conservative, mystical, elitist models (Plato, More, Campanella, and William Blake), radical traditionalists draw a distinction, clearly preferring the latter. If rational, evolutionary, democratic socialism (or social democracy) accommodates the progressive movement of history and consummates the capitalist tendency for general prosperity, then radical, militant, eschatological socialism, more properly called communism, attempts to reverse the direction of history, to conjoin its end with its beginning.

> Such strange utopian details in the descriptions of communist society as the communality of wives, the regulation of natural elements, the absence of labor and of private property, and so on, are nothing but a simplified, secularized notion of Paradise, of original Adamic conditions in which there exists not a multiplicity of individuals but one single Subject abiding in ontological abundance.[95]

Thus communism in Dugin's interpretation appears as a version of revolutionary conservatism appealing to the ultimate past rather than to the distant future. Dugin agrees with Shafarevich that socialism manifests mankind's obsession with death, but insists that this death is only a prologue to a resurrection in the "eschatological eon." The socialist myth, in this view, has throughout its history been adulterated by the admixture of heterogeneous ideological elements—national messianism in Jewish socialism; the idea of human rights in French socialism; the belief in evolution and progress in Russian socialism; chauvinism and xenophobia in German national socialism—but finally, socialism is regenerating its radical core and apocalyptic aspirations. "The fire of global National Revolution, Socialist Revolution, Final Revolution, approaches, which will put an end to the exhausted cycle of human history."[96]

There is much in common between Dugin's exaltation of the eschatological potentials of communism and that of Sergei Kurginian (discussed in the "Vicissitudes of Soviet Marxism" part of *The Phoenix of Philosophy*), but also a notable difference. While Kurginian proceeds from communist beliefs, increasingly introducing a mystical dimension, Dugin originates as a mystic of nationalism, and increasingly embraces socialism in its radical communist modification. These two reciprocal movements

94 Aleksandr Dugin, "Zagadka sotsializma," *Elementy*, no. 4 (1993): 11.
95 Ibid., 13.
96 Ibid., 17.

illustrate the interconnection of leftist and rightist extremes of the ideological spectrum, their gradual unification in what could be called metaphysical radicalism or eschatological extremism. With it, the difference between left and right is no longer relevant, in the same way that the absolute past and absolute future merge together in this radicalist worldview.

The connection between metaphysics and politics is dictated by the very essence of total traditionalism, which denies the liberal principle of the separation of powers and specialization of knowledge. From a liberal perspective, spiritual, political, and scientific spheres are governed by their own particular laws, and this limitation secures their relative freedom. For a traditionalist, even the most concrete and seemingly arbitrary facts in any of these spheres are conditioned by some underlying principles and therefore attest to an all-comprehensive determinism. In this way, the extreme right shares with the extreme left the hermeneutic suspicion of historical reality and the presumption of general laws governing even the most negligible events. But where Marxism, with its materialist assumptions, speaks of "laws," traditionalism, with its spiritual bias, identifies concealed "volitions" and "intentions." This is why the entirety of history is read and interpreted in terms of "conspirology" (*konspirologiia*), the science of conspiracies. The notion of conspiracy presupposes that history is designed according to some initial plan, so that all particular events—wars, revolutions, natural disasters—can be explained as part and parcel of a grand scheme. In a popular version of conspirology, the plot can be traced to an ancient Jewish and masonic attempt to take over the world, and both Soviet communism and American capitalism are seen as participants in this conspiracy, whose antagonism is merely a simulation concealing their basic collaboration. On a more esoteric level, the upheavals in the contemporary world are derived from the competition between two prehistoric civilizations—Atlantis and Hyperborea, conventional "meta-geographical" terms in theosophy and other occult sciences.

The popularity of conspirological models in post-Soviet Russia can be explained as a legacy of the long-standing habit of ideological thinking. In its spirit and method, conspirology has something in common with communist ideology: both relate to reality as to a book or system of signs in need of reading/decoding in order to determine one's proper course. The difference is that Soviet Marxism located the cherished signifieds of this all-encompassing book in the future, while conspirology relates them to the primordial past. Soviet Marxism sought to mobilize the collective will of society for the construction of a deferred paradise, while conspirology mobilizes the nation to fight back against the demonic plots that have destroyed the *original* paradise. Both are obsessed with deciphering the coded messages concealed in the most ordinary and natural things. In Stalin's time, using a newspaper containing the leader's likeness to wrap produce could serve as evidence of subversiveness, sufficient to provoke arrest and criminal prosecution. In Brezhnev's time, conspirologists argued that the use of asterisks to indicate textual breaks was a tool of Zionist propaganda, since the symbol resembles a star of David; they managed to get some periodicals to use a five-pointed star instead, but this too was subsequently opposed by still more vigilant conspirologists as the masonic star of Solomon. Conspirology represents an ideological obsession reoriented from the future to the past and preoccupied with the contemporary political implications of ancient mysteries and rituals.

From Dugin's perspective, the variety of the world's political ideologies can be reduced to three global-metaphysical systems, whose conflict determines the geopolitical configurations of the contemporary world.

The first such system is the most ancient and presupposes an absolute unity between God and man as personified in the figure of a "Divine Subject, Hero, Angelic Leader, Sacred Emperor." The entire world is the domain of his supernatural control.

> [T]he Subject of Divine nature stands in the center, on the Pole, in the middle of the sacred cosmos, which is completely subordinate to him and is therefore paradise-like .... This Divine Subject has nothing beyond himself (above himself, around himself, under himself), no higher metaphysical principle ... and therefore, he is absolutely free and inseparable from God. God is within him.[97]

This is the esoteric doctrine of immanence, which is based on gnosis, or the immediate knowledge of God as infused with earthly life. According to Dugin, this represents the noblest of all worldviews, historically realized in the sacred imperialism of the Ghibellines, in the "heresies" of the Cathars and Albigenses, in the teachings of Rosicrucianism, and (he adds) in German national socialism.

The second worldview, developed in Judaism and partly in Christianity, is based on a transcendental relationship between creator and creation. The identity of God and man is destroyed as God is elevated to a higher realm and man is expelled from paradise and doomed to dwell in the profane realm of earthly suffering. Instead of gnosis, this second worldview bases its religiosity on faith, which includes the elements of uncertainty and heavenly aspiration. Dugin therefore considers this system inferior, since it presupposes the alienation of humanity from God, though the hope of their ultimate reunion still animates the activity of the Christian Church. The paradise principle peculiar to traditionalism is irreconcilable with Judaism's principle of the transcendent nature of divinity. As for Christianity, it emerged originally in order to restore paradise on earth by merging God and man in the figure of Christ, but subsequently surrendered to Jewish transcendentalism and became a religion of sin and repentance. The Gnostic teachings condemned by the Catholic Church as Satanic and Luciferian are viewed by Dugin as the true manifestations of original Christianity, since they conceive of man in terms of his divinity and celebrate esoteric knowledge. Authentic Christianity must be purged of its Judaic distortions. The Eastern Orthodox Church, due to its proximity to the ancient pagan worldview, is more faithful to original Christianity than Western churches. As for the latter, Dugin finds affinities between their transcendental view of divinity and the Christian-democratic and social-democratic conceptions that prevail in contemporary European politics,

[97] Aleksandr Dugin, "Metafizicheskie korni politicheskikh ideologii," *Milyi angel*, no. 1 (1991): 84.

which promote a view of humanity as imperfect, sinful, and hence reliant on socially organized charity and state support.

The last system in Dugin's enumeration, "magical materialism," is presented as the most recent, and thus the most ignoble, of the three worldviews. Within it, the subject is altogether divorced from God (whether of the immanent or transcendent variety) and functions only as a particle of the material world. This view encompasses such different teachings as Soviet Marxism, American liberalism, and Fedorovian cosmism. All these have in common a belief in progress as determined by the laws of the universe's material evolution. Instead of gnosis or faith, this worldview cultivates empirical knowledge, which is a form of agnosticism, since it denies the spiritual realm and establishes efficacy as the only criterion of truth. The political applications of this worldview vary, from North Korean and Kampuchean totalitarian communism to American and Swedish models of the consumption society, where paradise is identified with purely material comfort and technological progress.

Dugin himself espouses the first worldview, which calls for a kind of paganist theocracy, a sacred empire headed by a "Divine Subject" or absolute leader. Such a society would be organized hierarchically, on the basis of esoteric privilege, with many degrees of mystical initiation. There does exist one primary division, however: the bright line between the caste of masters, designated to rule, and the rest of humanity, devoid of spiritual vision and thus treated as a herd.

> For the bearers of the Polar Subject [*nositeli Poliarnogo Sub"ekta*, i.e., those who hail the polar divinity of esoteric tradition], all people are divided into two categories: Man-gods, Divine Subjects, Supermen (the elite, the spiritual aristocracy, higher people, "Sonnenmenschen," "Sons of Light," etc.) and [on the other hand] human animals devoid of subjectivity (plebes, lower people, subhumans [*nedocheloveki*], "Tiermenschen," "Sons of Darkness"). Hence the caste, racial, or intellectual differentiation in all purely esoteric teachings.[98]

In terms of their religious orientation, Russian traditionalists proclaim their commitment to Orthodox Christianity, to Islam, and to paganism. How do they justify such an exotic mixture of historically irreconcilable traditions? The immediate impulse for the reconciliation of Christianity and Islam is the overwhelming influence of these two denominations in Eurasia, in the territory of the former Soviet Union, and the concurrent political necessity to unite them against "profane" Western civilization. In the traditionalist interpretation, Orthodoxy is closer to Islam than to other Christian denominations, since both privilege dogmatic tradition over innovation, are highly ritualistic, hostile to the spirit of the Renaissance and Enlightenment, and ardently opposed to the mixing of the secular and the sacred that is characteristic of the far more tolerant Western religiosity. Dugin finds affinities between Orthodoxy and Islam also on the theological level, since both of them are less transcendental than

98 Ibid., 85.

Judaism, which locates God beyond human perception and comprehension, and simultaneously less immanent than Western Christianity, which sanctifies worldly values, such as freedom, labor, professional achievement, education, and profit. On the transcendence/immanence scale, the three Abrahamic religions are distributed in the following way: Judaism represents the pole of transcendence and Christianity the pole of immanence, while Islam stands between them, with Eastern Orthodoxy as its closest neighbor. But in his further interpretation, Dugin collapses the Judaic and Christian poles by pointing to their shared emphasis on materialism: Judaism, in practical life, has a materialist orientation, precisely because its religious views are "too transcendental" and are alienated from earthly concerns; the "profanized" versions of Christianity prevailing in the West emphasize the human aspects of Christ and thus also fall into secularist temptations. In the final analysis, traditionalism polarizes world religions such that a Judeo-Christian civilization of the West is counterposed to, and challenged by, a united Islamic-Orthodox civilization of Eurasia. The metaphysical basis of the former is a break with Tradition, representing as it does the secularization and profanation of religious mysteries; while the Islamic-Orthodox unity seeks to preserve the dominance of the Church over the state and the immutable order of the sacred Tradition.

As for paganism, Dugin praises it even more ardently than the religions of monotheism, which counterpose the immanent and transcendent worlds. Paganism, in its original tradition, transcends the very division between sacred and profane and identifies the entire universe as

> a tissue of gnostic revelation, where each detail, each symbol is important and irreplaceable .... [B]oth of them, Being and Nonbeing [by which Dugin means the world of the transcendental], are no longer separate, but merge together .... Immanentism actually becomes the manifestation of the highest and most metaphysically convincing transcendentalism in which, however, the role of the Transcendent is filled not by a monotheistic Creator (Nonbeing) but by something transcendent in relation to the Creator Himself.[99]

Thus does Dugin, following Iurii Mamleev,[100] posit the third, the most esoteric level of mystery as something located *beyond* the God of monotheism. The truth of paganism lies deeper than the distinction between creator and creation. The root of things is not spirit distinct from matter, but something transcending this very opposition. Paganism is a manifestation of this higher unity, since it worships the universe both in its smallest parts and in its all-encompassing wholeness, and finds the truth of the whole fully present in each of its parts.

It is not clear how this paganism so cherished by Dugin differs from pantheism, which, by contrast, is furiously condemned by all traditionalists as the most cunning

[99] Aleksandr Dugin, "Velikaia metafizicheskaia problema i traditsii," *Milyi angel*, no. 1 (1991): 26, 27.

[100] See in this book the chapter "The Religion of Absolute Self and the Abyss of Negativity. Iurii Mamleev," in Part III. Mysticism, Universalism, and Cosmism.

form of materialism. "Thus the pure atheist, or 'mystical materialist,' actually endows the cosmos with a quality of divinity . . . . This gives us reason to define the given ideology as pantheism—[the idea that] 'everything is divine,' the identification of everything (Cosmos, World) with God."[101] In Dugin's classification, pantheistic materialism is the lowest of the three worldviews, but his definition of paganism, the highest of the three, coincides almost verbatim with his formula of pantheism: "The 'paganist' universe is theomorphic, or more precisely, angelomorphic."[102] This is a principal weakness of traditionalist thought: it does not provide sufficiently clear concepts to distinguish between paganism, which makes the transcendent immanent, and mystical materialism, which deifies the material world. The extremes of left (pantheism, materialism) and right (paganism) easily coincide in traditionalist metaphysics, since both are hostile to creationism, to the Judeo-Christian concept of the separation of man and God, which supports the ideology of moderately liberal and conservative movements. The first and the third worldviews in Dugin's classification are virtually identical and both are antagonistic to the second view, which prescribes tolerance and compassion, since man is weak and imperfect in his alienation from God. Paganism and materialism, on the other hand, both proclaim a heroic vision of the human being as embodying the totality of divine qualities, as sinless and self-sufficient.

In the final analysis, the traditionalist project of complete identification, "homogenization," of God and man leads to the destruction of both these entities, which in reality can be defined only in their distinction from one another. What traditionalists actually hold dear is neither the divine nor the human, but a middle sphere of mighty spirits conventionally called "angels"—hence the title of their leading theoretical journal, *Cherished Angel*. Despite their proclaimed allegiance to Christianity and Islam, traditionalists tend to privilege the angelic over the divine, since the multiplicity of angels more closely accommodates a paganist religiosity than the worship of a single God. "The gods of 'paganism' ... are not so much self-sufficient and self-regulating principles (like the God of monotheism) as Angels in an etymological sense, 'messengers,' 'spirits.'"[103] The metaphysics of angelism allows traditionalists to pursue an alternative path between poly- and monotheistic doctrines. Angels are more transcendent than corporeal polytheistic gods, and at the same time more immanent than the monotheistic God. In the monotheistic worldview, angels are entirely ancillary to God, but for traditionalism they become primary forces that reflect the multiplicity of nature in the multiplicity of spirits.

On the other hand, traditionalist angelism presupposes contempt for the "human, all too human" nature of the common man. In his programmatic introduction to the first issue of *Cherished Angel*, Dugin writes:

[101] Dugin, "Metafizicheskie korni politicheskikh ideologii," 87.
[102] Dugin, "Velikaia metafizicheskaia problema i traditsii," 27.
[103] Ibid.

> We are not interested in the slightest degree in profane and humanistic problems, even in their most honest and critical existentialist versions. It could be said that, in general, we do not address people as such. What matters to us is only the angelic dimension of being, and therefore only those souls who are aware or are at this stage have at least an intuition of their "angelomorphism," their "likeness to angels."[104]

Dugin's basic orientation is pure esotericism, or angelic elitism, as opposed to "vulgar" and democratic appeals to human dignity and human rights. However, the practical outcome of this angelic worldview, claiming to reconcile man and God, may in fact be the radical rejection of both, and ultimately the rejection of the world, which, as Dugin proclaimed in a 1994 speech, is "hopelessly bad." "The only way to get rid of it and its chimeras is its severe liquidation by any means. Total war declared against everyone who cooperates with the world, against all humanists, against anyone who is fearful or prefers American soup [i.e., from a can] to spiritual values."[105] Thus the search for "spiritual values," the angelization of the world, in its most radical extension, presupposes its utter destruction.

Traditionalist writings, though densely populated with occult terminology, should not be classified as religious philosophy, since their ultimate goal is not to provide a path to God, but to establish a hierarchy of national and geopolitical values. Orthodoxy and Islam are espoused not for their intrinsic spirituality, but as a means to consolidate Eurasian nations. In the alliance of geopolitics and metaphysics typical for traditionalists, it is geopolitics that plays the leading part. A similar symbiosis was established by Marxism in the relationship of philosophy and history. Leftist, Marxist metaphysics was interested in history as a vehicle for the transformation of the world, whereas traditionalists are obsessed with geography, since their values are radically prehistoric and antihistoric. Geopolitics, in Dugin's view, is "directly connected with symbolic geography, which regards the entire earth as a single Sacred Text, written with special signs and symbols."[106]

Using the insights of European geopoliticians, Dugin distinguishes two types of civilization: sea-oriented—"Atlantean"—and land-oriented—"continental." The antagonism between Atlanteanism and continentalism constitutes the major tension of world history. Atlanteanism, exemplified by the legendary Atlantis, by ancient Carthage, and by the contemporary UK and United States, is characterized by the spirit of trade, profit, and internationalism. Continentalism, best represented by the legendary Hyperborea, and by the historical Roman, German, and Russian Empires, emphasizes the organic unity of people in their spiritual bonds with the earth. Thus the very form of the landmass on which people stand is thought to influence the character of that people's culture and philosophy. The venturesomeness associated with the

[104] "O nashem zhurnale," *Milyi angel*, no. 1 (1991): 4.

[105] Cited from A. Kamennyi, "Dukh i pochva," *Zavtra*, no. 14 (19) (1994): 8.

[106] Aleksandr Dugin, "Ot sakral'noi geografii k geopolitike," *Elementy*, no. 1 (1992): 19.

seas that surround island nations produces an open, extroverted character, inclined to mercantilism and intercourse with other nations, while the isolating vastness of continents engenders an introverted character focused on the preservation of tradition.

Another important opposition in traditionalist geopolitics is that of North/South. "The most ancient and original layer of the Tradition unequivocally asserts the primacy of North over South."[107] North is related to the primordial paradise, to spirituality, light, purity, and eternity, whereas South embodies materiality, darkness, mixture, and temporality. The East/West opposition is derivative of this initial polarity, such that in sacred geography, East is a projection of North, while West represents the projection of South on the horizontal axis. Therefore, the contemporary geopolitical conflict between East and West can be interpreted as a modification of the original polarity between North, with its faithfulness to Tradition and "the intuition of the Sacred," and South, with its hedonism and veneration of external Nature. However, in the contemporary, post-Cold War period, the East/West opposition gives way to the initial polarity of North/South, so that Northern peoples should seek the expansion of their dominion not so much in the horizontal, but the vertical dimension. "The civilized harmony reigns when the people of the South are in harmony with the people of the North, that is, recognize their authority and their typological (not racial!) superiority."[108] As outlandish as this geopolitical speculation seems, it finds quite practical applications in the programs of prominent rightist politicians, such as Vladimir Zhirinovsky, whose political autobiography-manifesto *A Last Thrust to the South* (1993) espouses the reorientation of world geopolitics from the horizontal to the vertical lines of expansion.[109]

Peculiar to radical traditionalism is its simultaneous antagonism toward liberalism *and* critique of conservatism. Liberalism is viewed by traditionalists as a combination of rightist economic policies—the absolute freedom of markets—and a leftist political orientation—the absolute freedom of individuals ("all-permissiveness"). Traditionalism "must likewise combine elements of 'Leftist' and 'Rightist' ideologies, but we must be 'Rightist' in a political sense (that is, 'nationalists,' 'traditionalists,' etc.) and 'Leftist' in an economic sense (that is, supporters of social justice, 'socialism,' etc.)."[110] There is thus an inverse relationship between liberalism and traditionalism on all ideological levels. If liberals are oriented toward the West, then traditionalists privilege an "unequivocal orientation toward the East and solidarity with the most Eastern geopolitical sectors in the solution of territorial conflicts."[111] If liberals proclaim

[107] Ibid., no. 4, (1993): 41.

[108] Ibid., 43.

[109] "[T]he last 'thrust' to the South—Russia's access to [*vykhod na*] the shores of the Indian Ocean and Mediterranean Sea—is, indeed, the task of the salvation of the Russian nation .... It is better to divvy up spheres of influence according to the North/South principle .... [L]et it be such a world agreement, that we divvy up the entire globe, the spheres of economic influence, and act in the direction North/South" (Vladimir Zhirinovskii, *Poslednii brosok na iug* [Moscow: Pisatel', 1993], 63, 71).

[110] "Ideologiia mirovogo pravitel'stva" (unsigned editorial), *Elementy*, no. 2 (1992): 2.

[111] Ibid., 2.

internationalist and cosmopolitan doctrines, traditionalists take an "anti-mondialist" position and extol national and racial allegiance. This inversion extends to every issue in the liberal program because traditionalists take great pains to contradict liberalism "on all fronts" of the ideological struggle.

The distinction between traditionalism and other Russian conservative movements is more subtle, as they share a number of orientations. Traditionalists support the bulk of Slavophile and neo-Slavophile views, including the romantic allegiance to the past and valorization of the soil; the critique of Western rationalism and individualism; the equal rejection of Marxism and liberalism; the condemnation of the spiritual poverty of democratic societies, with their loss of national identity and erosion of tradition; and so on. However, the conservative nationalism of Solzhenitsyn's type strikes traditionalists as merely palliative, since it nostalgically appeals to Russia's prerevolutionary, tsarist past. From the traditionalist perspective, even nineteenth-century Russia was already perverted by the Enlightenment mentality that would give rise to Bolshevism; thus traditionalists "strive to return to an order that preceded not only the Revolution but also the emergence of those causes that led to the Revolution."[112] They counterpose the ideal world of tradition to both the pre- and postrevolutionary "worlds of crisis," a stance that "inevitably calls not for 'conservatism,' not maintenance of the past, but precisely Revolution, total, all-renewing, radical, but in a direction completely opposite to the Revolution of the Left."[113] In other words, traditionalism sees conservatism as insufficiently nostalgic, insufficiently radical in its nostalgia. Conservatism's desire to preserve the legacy of the past and resist any innovation made sense before the communist revolution, but now that the world is already radically changed, "liberalized," conservatism is outmoded, naive, and impotent; what is needed is not preservation of the past, but radical innovation, the restoration of a deeper layer of the past that has been buried by the destructive forces of "progress."

Another distinction of traditionalists is their universal rightist appeal, an almost paradoxical pan-nationalism or nationalist internationalism. Unlike other conservatives, with their exclusively Russian or Slavic nationalism, traditionalists attempt to unite the extreme rights of the entire world. They are more indebted to German, French, and Italian fascist or para-fascist ideologists than to the Russian Slavophiles of the nineteenth century. They cite Khomiakov and Kireevsky with sympathy, but distance themselves from the patriarchal, conservative utopianism of idyllic pre-Petrine Russia. The traditionalist spirit is not meek and conciliatory but militant and unrelenting, like the brutal-heroic aesthetics of national socialism; and as did the Nazis before them, traditionalists aspire to build an international coalition of right-wing movements to oppose the decadence of the democratic West.

As compared with conservatives, who proclaim a nativist Orthodox faith, traditionalists are far more religiously eclectic. The range of their mystical interest is

[112] Aleksandr Dugin, "Konservativnaia revoliutsiia. Kratkaia istoriia ideologii tret'ego puti," *Elementy*, no. 1 (1992): 15.

[113] Ibid.

as "cosmopolitan" as their political strategy. They praise Orthodoxy, but see in it only an external manifestation of a much deeper esoteric tradition that unites paganists, Muslims, Gnostics and other Christian heretics, and Hindu holymen. Whereas conservatives like Solzhenitsyn extol the Christian virtues of humility, self-limitation, and communality, traditionalists attribute these values to the insidious Judaization of Christianity, which took the paganist essence of Christianity as a religion of the God-man and adulterated it with the slave mentality and repentant religiosity of an outcast from paradise.

If the conservative ethics of self-limitation leads contemporary Slavophiles to a policy of isolationism, to the concentration and utilization of all native resources under the aegis of a monoethnic state, then traditionalists, with their militant mysticism, pursue imperialist and expansionist goals. "We foresee the future Eurasian empire consisting of various ethnoi, peoples, denominations, and political formations, but united around the Continental Idea."[114] This is why traditionalists, unlike Slavophiles, emphasize the historical affinities between Russia and Europe. Their goal is the unification of the entire continent of Eurasia for the struggle against the dominance of Anglo-American Atlanteanism (or, in the terminology of contemporary political science and diplomacy, against *Atlanticism*). Therefore, in contrast with conservative isolationists, traditionalists make overtures of alliance with Western Europe, especially Germany and France, in hopes of forming a powerful bloc of nations ready to surrender part of their political sovereignty to the Continental Idea.

From a radical-traditionalist standpoint, neo-Slavophilism, or conservative nationalism, is not only outdated, an insufficient reaction to democratic reforms, but is in fact fully compatible with the most aggressive impulses of Western mondialism, which tries to isolate Russia and reduce it to a purely ethnic constituency. "Whatever lies at the foundation of 'narrowly ethnic,' 'racial-nationalist,' 'chauvinistic' models of Russian statehood—ignorance, naiveté, or conscious work against one's own people and their independence—the result is fully identical with mondialist goals. Without the transformation of Russia into an 'ethnic reservation,' the US will be unable to gain *complete* control over the world."[115] Traditionalists are suspicious, not only of Russian patriots but also of Eurasianists, who identify Russia as a specific continent, neither Europe nor Asia. Traditionalists agree that, in a cultural and historical sense, Russia must preserve its unique character, but in geopolitical terms, old-style Eurasianism represents capitulation to mondialism, since Russia deliberately withdraws itself from Europe and Asia and thus leaves room for the expansion of Atlanteanism/Atlanticism. A better geopolitical formula for Russia, they believe, would be the "Heartland," the central land of the continent, the "geographical axis of history," which with the support of the "Rimland"—the peripheral, coastal states from China to France, from Japan to Italy, from India to Norway—is to oppose the Atlantic claims to world dominance.

[114] Unsigned editorial, *Elementy*, no. 1 (1992): 4.
[115] "Rossiia i prostranstvo" (unsigned editorial), *Elementy*, no. 4 (1993): 32.

Also, whereas conservatives, for instance the Russian "village prose" writers, gravitate nostalgically to the values of a preindustrial, agrarian civilization, traditionalists, like Prokhanov and Dugin himself, are ardently dedicated to technological innovation and extol the beauty of nuclear armaments and other advanced weapons of mass destruction. For them, technology, as a tool of power, is not opposed to nature, but improves and extends the majestic potential of nature's elemental forces.

To a great degree, traditionalist thinking follows the patterns of the Soviet ideological imagination, with its exaltation of heroism and courage, technological and political power, the cult of personality, and the revolutionary transformation of the world. It is as if the structures of Soviet rhetoric have been preserved, only with the content switched from left to right, like a reflection in a mirror. This is especially clear in the case of Akeksandr Prokhanov, who in the 1970s–1980s distinguished himself in glorifying Soviet military and technological expansion in specifically mystical hues, just as in the postcommunist period he has invariably glorified the militant and technological mysticism of the extreme right in hues that are unmistakably Soviet. As for Aleksandr Dugin, his militarist rhetoric, with the strongest possible concentration of aggression and hatred, far surpasses the style of late-Soviet official propaganda, and can be compared only with the most obscurantist and bellicose rhetoric of Stalin's agitprop.

The scope of this chapter is limited only to the early stage of Aleksandr Dugin's evolution as leader of the third generation of Eurasianists (after the doctrine's postrevolutionary émigré founders and Lev Gumilev). A prolific writer and a militant ideologist, Dugin later evolved in an even more extreme direction that made him a most influential theoretician of Russia's anti-Western and anti-liberal political turn in the twenty-first century. In the West, Dugin is identified as the main philosopher of Putinism and awarded such epithets as "Putin's brain" and "the most dangerous philosopher in the world."[116]

The Russian nationalist conservatism of the second half of the twentieth century has thus undergone several modifications. The first stage was the promotion of organicism and the critique of structuralism in aesthetic theories. Then came a revitalization of nineteenth-century Slavophile thought, and an attempt to prioritize this legacy over Russia's revolutionary-democratic and Marxist traditions. A third phase saw the rise of rightist political dissidentism and the reevaluation of Russian history as having been degraded by the invasion of Marxist ideas from the West and in need of the prerevolutionary national identity as a restorative. Next came the idea that capitalism

[116] https://www.foreignaffairs.com/articles/russia-fsu/2014-03-31/putins-brain; https://bigthink.com/paul-ratner/the-dangerous-philosopher-behind-putins-strategy-to-grow-russian-power-at-americas-expense; https://impakter.com/deadly-ideology-putin-eurasianism/. Only recently have Dugin's views come under consideration in academic scholarship: Mark Sedgwick, ed., *Key Thinkers of the Radical Right: Behind the New Threat to Liberal Democracy* (Oxford: Oxford University Press, 2019); Marlène Laruelle, *Russian Eurasianism. An Ideology of Empire* (Baltimore: Johns Hopkins University Press, 2019). For (highly critical) reviews of Dugin's political metaphysics, see: Charles Upton, *Dugin against Dugin: A Traditionalist Critique of the Fourth Political Theory* (Hillsdale, NY: Sophia Perennis, 2018); James D. Heiser, *"The American Empire Should Be Destroyed": Alexander Dugin and the Perils of Immanentized Eschatology* (Malone, TX: Repristination Press, 2014).

and communism are two strategies of a single conspiracy, conceived by Zionists and freemasons and designed to crush Russia as the world's last bastion of true Christian spirituality. At the same time, an alternative theory, under the influence of 1920s Eurasianism, asserted that Bolshevism was an organic extension of the Russian imperial tradition and as such promoted a future synthesis of Orthodoxy and communism. Eurasianism also found detailed biological and geographical elaboration in the theory of ethnos as a natural propensity governed by cosmic rather than social forces and destined to undergo a predictable cycle of development, from birth to extinction; the mixture of ethnoi dilutes their strength and leads to an untimely dissolution.

Finally, two modifications of nationalism resurfaced in postcommunist Russia. One is moderate conservatism, claiming the timeless values of Orthodox Christianity as a specifically Russian legacy destined to introduce the spirit of national reconciliation into a society torn apart by militant pluralism and partisanship. The other is radical traditionalism, proclaiming the restoration of a paganist, esoteric legacy and the unification of Eurasia into a single empire under Russian guidance to wage spiritual war on the secularized and materialist West. Between these two extremes, conciliatory conservatism and militant traditionalism, fall many other nuances of late- and post-Soviet nationalist thought.

Part II

Religious Thought. Orthodox Christianity

It would be difficult to extract or isolate religious thought from Russian philosophy, as the two have been integral from the outset. According to the most ancient Russian chronicle, *The Tale of Bygone Years*, Russia adopted its faith from a "philosopher" (*filosof*), a missionary sent by Byzantium in AD 986 and credited with unfolding before Prince Vladimir the mysteries of the Old and New Testaments. Most of those who founded Russian philosophy in the eighteenth and nineteenth centuries—Grigorii Skovoroda, Petr Chaadaev, Aleksei Khomiakov, and Ivan Kireevsky—were deeply religious thinkers. The central purpose of Vladimir Solovyov's philosophy, according to his own definition, was "to justify the faith of our fathers and elevate it to a higher level of rational consciousness."[1] This did not imply a return to the medieval European principle that philosophy is the servant of theology. This synthesis of religion and philosophy, as Russian thinkers at least since Solovyov understood it, was to be achieved on an individual, creative foundation, in the process of free thinking, not as an official dogmatic system of the Orthodox Church, which in Russia was traditionally quite far from philosophy and any secular forms of knowledge. For the thinkers just mentioned, the very purpose of philosophy and religion was identical: philosophy was to attain the absolute by way of thinking, religion, by way of being. The ultimate goal is one, which makes possible the synthesis of philosophy and theology.

Even in the early twentieth century, in the Silver Age, when Russian philosophy attained its broadest scope and impact, and was no longer accountable to religious censorship, it remained deeply religious, though it accentuated existentialist aspects of faith as a personal truth rather than a dogmatic tradition. This integrative character of "religious philosophy" was further intensified in the postrevolutionary period, when the majority of preeminent Russian thinkers were forced to emigrate. The writings of émigré thinkers of this period, such as Nikolai Berdiaev, Lev Shestov, Sergei Bulgakov, Semyon Frank, Dmitrii Merezhkovsky, Georgii Fedotov, and Ivan Ilyin, are imbued with a spirit of resistance to the militant materialism and atheism that prevailed in the USSR. However, the philosophical and social perspectives of Russian religious thinkers, even those with deep Orthodox affiliations, are marked by a great diversity. For example, Berdiaev's apocalyptic Christianity, with its appeal to free religious creativity and denial of Church dogmatism, finds a strong contrast and counterpart

[1] Vladimir Solov'ev, *Sochineniia* v 10 tt. (St. Petersburg: Prosveshchenie, 1914), vol. 4, 243.

in the writings of Ivan Ilyin, the foremost apologist of the political right and Russian nationalism, and is likewise quite distinct from the approach of Father Georges Florovsky, who is recognized as one of the most prominent Orthodox theologians of the twentieth century.

This part of the study is devoted to the philosophy of Christianity as grounded in Orthodox tradition. Despite its remarkable free-spiritedness, this philosophy is still inspired by Church teachings. This sets it apart from those religious ideas discussed in the previous volume, *The Phoenix of Philosophy*, in the context of existentialism and personalism. Such thinkers as Iakov Druskin or Grigorii Pomerants arrived at religious views as an outcome of their personal philosophical search, and sometimes appealed to non-Christian traditions. In contrast, the thinkers considered here are religiously grounded entirely in the Christian, and particularly the Orthodox, tradition.

1. Major Expatriate Theologians

The latter half of the twentieth century witnessed the emergence of several important expatriate spiritual writers. Although some of their works were written in English, they may definitely be inscribed in the tradition of Russian philosophy that was their cultural inheritance. Orthodox thought of this period concentrates on three major sets of problems: (1) theology and dogmatics; (2) the life of the Church, the liturgy and other sacraments; and (3) the personal experience of faith and prayer. Respectively, the three major Orthodox thinkers of the emigration—Georges Florovsky, Alexander Schmemann, and Metropolitan Anthony of Sourozh—devoted themselves to these three domains.

a. The Revival of Theology. Georges Florovsky

Georges Florovsky (1893–1979), who emigrated from Russia in 1920, had a long and illustrious scholarly career, teaching at such universities as St. Sergius Theological Institute in Paris (which he cofounded), Harvard Divinity School, and Princeton University. His first intellectual association, beginning in 1921, was with the group of Eurasianists, which he cofounded with three other thinkers; in particular, he authored three of the ten articles comprising the group's manifesto *Exodus to the East* (1921). Florovsky, however, soon broke with the Eurasian movement because of its pro-Soviet orientation, and his intellectual perspective shifted to what he called a "new patristic synthesis." Simply put, he believed that the teachings of the Eastern Church fathers should provide the foundation for a future Orthodox revival. This position informed his major works, *The Eastern Fathers of the Fourth Century* (1931), *The Ways of Russian Theology* (1937), and others, comprising sixteen volumes of his *Collected Works* published in English translation. His main treatises were composed in the 1930s–1940s and belong among the classics of Russian theology, but some of his principal articles were written later, in the 1950s–1970s, and collected in the volume *Christianity and*

Culture, where he explores the relationship between the two phenomena, an issue that was focal for Russian religious philosophy in general.

Florovsky characterizes Christianity as an "essentially historical" religion, since historical events and names, like Pontius Pilate, are included even within the Christian credo. He agrees with the English philosopher R. G. Collingwood that "what is miscalled an event is really an action, and expresses some thought (intention, purpose) of its agent."[2] Florovsky interprets this to mean that history as such began only with Christ, since before him it was merely a succession of events, and only after Christ endowed the world with purpose did history become a chronicle of "actions" in the proper (i.e., purposive) sense of this word. As Florovsky puts it, "the true history of man is not a political history ... but a history of the spirit, the story of man's growth to the full stature of perfection, under the Lordship of the historical God-man."[3] Thus the events of history ought not merely to be recorded, but also interpreted in light of their religious implications.

> Above all, the Christian historian will regard history at once as a mystery and as a tragedy—a mystery of salvation and a tragedy of sin. He pursues his professional task of interpreting human life in the light of his Christian vision of that life, sorely distorted by sin, yet redeemed by Divine mercy, and healed by Divine grace, and called to the inheritance of an everlasting kingdom.[4]

Florovsky's thought strives—typically for the conservative mode of reasoning—to mediate between extremes. In his discussion of the relationship between Christianity and the secular world, Florovsky argues the inadequacy of the two polar tendencies of "flight into the desert" and, on the other hand, the "construction of the Christian Empire."[5] He concludes that the very dilemma is a false one, since Christians are called to work within the world but not to immerse themselves in worldliness. The model of the creative interaction between Christianity and the world might be the medieval monasteries, which "were, for a long time, precisely the most powerful centers of cultural activity, both in the West and in the East,"[6] though they eschewed taking a political role. Christianity, then, does not deny worldly culture, but judges it by the measure of Christ. Thus, for Florovsky, both history and culture should be admitted into the realm of Christianity, as long as the limitations of their sovereignty are recognized and they are considered in light of their relationship to revelation.

This same equivocating tendency is evident in Florovsky's critique of the two main tendencies in contemporary theology. One of these, liberalism, attempts to demythologize Christianity by interpreting the miracles of Christ solely as edifying and psychological metaphors. At the other extreme, the neo-Orthodox tendency seeks

[2] R. G. Collingwood, *An Autobiography* (New York: Mentor Books, 1949), 127–8.
[3] Georges Florovsky, *Collected Works* (Belmont MA: Nordland Publishing Company, 1972–4), 2: 64.
[4] Ibid., 65.
[5] Ibid., 2: 28.
[6] Ibid., 30.

to limit the role of individual action in the Church, leaving its members with only the possibility to listen and to hope. Florovsky identifies these tendencies with the ancient heresies of Nestorianism and monophysitism, which respectively emphasized the human versus the divine nature of Christ.[7] The only solution Florovsky offers is to "preach the whole Christ," by which he means a theological synthesis of Christ's humanity and divinity. In effect, this entails a general return to the practice of theology as it was understood by the Church fathers. Such is Florovsky's overall message: theology is more crucial now than ever. Since the modern world is dominated by a mood of existential despair and intellectual fragmentation, theology is the one discipline that can integrate such diverse human capacities as were bestowed in the act of creation.

Theology, in Florovsky's estimation, is more important for the Church than any political or social commitment, since history must be understood through its spiritual dimension. Florovsky's main reproach to Russian Orthodoxy is that it suppressed its theological mission in favor of liturgical practice; such religious thinkers as Solovyov and Nikolai Fedorov, on the other hand, digressed too far from theology in the direction of philosophical mysticism and utopian social projects. Thus, theology, as the realm of dogmatic thinking advanced by the Church fathers, has been neglected both by the "non-thinking" Orthodox priesthood and "non-dogmatic" religious thinkers. In fact, most Orthodox priests consider theology to be a luxury, or even a betrayal of ritualistic duties, while philosophers tend to view Church dogmatics as too restrictive for the free flight of their thought. The silence of priests, and the impetuous and vague eloquence of philosophers—these were the two deviations from the theological mission of Orthodoxy. Florovsky believes that this "[n]eglect of theology in the instruction given to laity in modern times is responsible both for the decay of personal religion and for that sense of frustration which dominates the modern mood."[8] He goes even so far as to blame this anti-theological bias of Orthodoxy for the spiritual catastrophe of the Russian Revolution. When it comes to theological questions, in his view, silence is at least as dangerous as false solutions;[9] thus it is the task of Orthodoxy to revive the art of dogmatic thinking and the theological zeal of the early Eastern fathers.

b. The Liturgical Philosophy of Alexander Schmemann

Alexander Schmemann (1921–83) was one of the most influential writers on questions of the Orthodox liturgy. Having emigrated from Estonia in childhood, he lived in Paris until 1951, when he moved to the United States. In 1962, he became dean of St. Vladimir's Orthodox Seminary in New York City, where he served until his death. He was the author of approximately three thousand sermons that were broadcast to Russia twice a week and had considerable impact on the Orthodox revival there. Schmemann was a rare combination of rigorous theologian and popular preacher. Along with

7 Ibid., 1: 14–15.
8 Ibid., 15.
9 Georgii Florovskii, *Puti russkogo bogosloviia* (Paris: YMCA Press, 1988), 517.

Florovsky and Vladimir Lossky (1903–58), he is considered to be a leading Orthodox scholar in the field of Church dogmatics. At the same time, like Metropolitan Anthony of Sourozh, he is regarded as one of the most eloquent Orthodox preachers, addressing the existential and cultural challenges to faith in the postwar world.

Schmemann is an "objective" theologian in the sense that he considers the primary reality of religious life to be revelation. The objective reality of God is given through the scriptural revelation of the Bible and the corporeal revelation of Christ. "Faith is the human response to God, and this response presupposes that the initiative of the human attitude toward God that we call faith, belongs not to man but to God. God *reveals* Himself to man, man receives this revelation and responds to God."[10] This is why the atheistic demand for proof of God's existence must be answered not merely with the assertion that God is invisible, but also with the evidence of revelation, through which God becomes visible.

The majority of Schmemann's works deal with the meaning of revelation as it is presented in the Orthodox liturgy, which he considers to be the most transparent and accessible manifestation of God's reality. Three of his most important books are dedicated to the liturgy: *An Introduction to Liturgical Theology*, *The Eucharist*, and *Of Water and the Spirit*, devoted to the sacrament of baptism. He interprets the formal components of the liturgy as symbols of human communication with God grounded in the materiality of the rituals themselves.[11]

The central concept of Schmemann's theology is that of symbol. The sacraments are symbolic, but no more than the material world itself is symbolic in its relationship to the kingdom of God. Hence the function of symbol is not to represent the reality that it signifies, but actually to *become* it. The symbol is a portal from the lesser reality to the greater one. Sacraments were established in response to the fall from grace, as medicines to heal the ills of sin. Thus the purpose of the sacraments is transformative rather than representative; they act to restore the fullness of reality from which man alienated himself through sin. Etymologically, "symbol" comes from a Greek word meaning "to unite, keep together," originally referring to an object that has been divided into two pieces such that the possessor of either piece could recognize the other. In the same way, the sacrament is granted to humanity as a symbol enabling it to recognize this world, fallen and alienated, as a part of God's kingdom. In symbol,

[10] Protoierei Aleksandr Shmeman, *Voskresnye besedy* (Paris: YMCA Press, 1989), 25.

[11] Paradoxically, Schmemann sees the liturgical, ritualistic accent in Russian Orthodoxy as indicative of a certain deficiency, a lack of creative impulses. "In adopting Byzantine Christianity, Russia took no interest in either Plato, Aristotle, or the entire Hellenistic tradition, which for Christian Byzantium remained a living and vital reality …. Incredibly, Russian Christianity began without a school or scholastic tradition, and Russian culture immediately concentrated in the church and worship … and by its very nature [this church- and worship-oriented Christianity] proved alien to the idea of development and creativity. It became sacred and static, excluding doubt and seeking …. Any creativity, any seeking, any change was perceived as rebellion, almost blasphemy and anarchy, and thus the essence of culture, as a creative continuity, did not emerge." A. Shmeman, "Istoki maksimalizma v russkoi kul'ture" (a discussion on Radio Liberty). Available electronically: https://www.pravmir.ru/protopresviter-aleksandr-shmeman-istoki-maksimalizma-v-russkoy-kulture/

> the empirical (or "visible") and the spiritual (or "invisible") are united not *logically* (this "stands for" that), nor *analogically* (this "illustrates" that), nor yet by *cause and effect* (this is the "means" or "generator" of that), but *epiphanically*. One reality *manifests* and *communicates* the other, but—and this is immensely important—only to the degree to which the symbol itself is a participant in the spiritual reality and is able or called upon to embody it.[12]

For Schmemann, symbolism is connected with the very essence of religious faith, since faith is directed to the manifestation of invisible things. "Therefore, if the symbol presupposes faith, faith of necessity requires the symbol."[13]

In Schmemann's view, the reality that is manifested in the sacrament is the kingdom of God. The liturgy is the manifestation of this kingdom, not merely hoped for or believed in, but already present in human life. "For the first Christians the all-encompassing joy, the truly startling novelty of their faith lay in the fact that the kingdom was at hand. It had appeared, and although it remained hidden and unseen for 'this world,' it was already present, its light had already shone, it was already at work in the world."[14] Schmemann criticizes the tendency of later Christianity to relate this world and God's kingdom in chronological or topographical terms. According to this misrepresentation, the kingdom is "there" or "then," beyond this world or after it. The sacrament is a way of integrating here and there, now and then, in such a way that the kingdom is experienced as fully immanent and material.

The overall aim of Schmemann's theological project, despite its thematic diversity, may be summarized as an elaboration of the material substance of faith. He is critical of all kinds of religious idealism or psychologism, which identify Christianity with pure spirituality, with a transcendent realm or the internal domain of personal inspiration. "Man, as he was created by God, is both an animated body and embodied spirit, and therefore any separation of these—not just the final separation, in death, but also before death—any violation of their unity is evil, a spiritual catastrophe."[15] It is the mission of the Church to restore this unity. Against the emblematic conventionalism that developed in the Catholic and especially Protestant churches, Schmemann counterposes the realism, even materialism, of the Orthodox liturgy. For Schmemann, the core of the Orthodox tradition is its reliance on the liturgy, not in the sense that it isolates the Church from the world, but in the sense that the entire world, including the Church, is only part of God's kingdom. The liturgy is the sensible and corporeal manifestation of God's kingdom on earth, just as Christ was the corporeal manifestation of God himself. This is why one cannot divorce the liturgy from Christianity or downplay its significance by calling it a "ritualistic form." Thus, for Schmemann, the objects and actions that comprise the liturgy are spiritualized inasmuch as spirit is materialized through their sacramental manifestations.

[12] Alexander Schmemann, *The Eucharist. Sacrament of the Kingdom*, trans. Paul Kachur (Crestwood, NY: St. Vladimir's Seminary Press, 1988), 39.

[13] Ibid.

[14] Ibid., 42.

[15] Shmeman, *Voskresnye besedy*, 73.

c. The Existential Orthodoxy of Metropolitan Anthony of Sourozh

Metropolitan Anthony of Sourozh (1914–2003; secular name: Andrei Blum), commonly known as Anthony Bloom, was the son of a Russian diplomat who remained abroad after the October Revolution. An atheist in his early youth, he pursued a medical career that was not halted by his sudden conversion to Christianity. Ordained as a priest in 1948, he served for decades as the head of the Russian Orthodox Patriarchal Church in Great Britain. In 1957 he was consecrated as bishop and then as archbishop and metropolitan bishop in charge of the Russian Orthodox Church in Great Britain and Ireland. A magnificent preacher, and one of the spiritual leaders of the Russian Orthodox intelligentsia, he was for many years one of the very few bridges between the Moscow Patriarchate and Orthodoxy abroad.[16]

Figure 3 Metropolitan Anthony of Sourozh.

[16] One of the most trustworthy and authentic biographical accounts of Metropolitan Anthony was written by his longtime friend, the distinguished scholar of Russian culture Avril Pyman, *Metropolitan Anthony of Sourozh. A Life* (Cambridge: The Lutterworth Press, 2016).

Of all major Orthodox thinkers, Anthony of Sourozh puts the least emphasis on Church tradition, focusing instead on the complexities of the personal encounter between man and God. His theology is anthropologically oriented toward the existential circumstances of modernity: the psychological anxieties of contemporary humanity, its feelings of alienation, loneliness, and obsession with materialistic pursuits. Anthony does not seek to refute materialism from some "super-spiritual" or purely idealistic point of view, but argues, rather, that Christianity serves the glorification of the material world better than does atheistic materialism. "Christianity is the only perfect materialism in the sense that a materialist regards matter as a constructing material, whereas for us matter acquires an absolute significance; it is sacred because of the embodiment of Christ, in Whom the fullness of Divinity dwelled corporeally."[17] Though materialists claim to glorify man as the creator of all values, the image of man is actually denigrated, devoid as it is of those potentials for sanctification that man enjoys in Christianity. Thus communication between believers and nonbelievers might proceed, not through polemics, but on the assumption that nonbelievers' ideals and hopes are justified, but are best served by Christianity.

Metropolitan Anthony takes a similarly tolerant and conciliatory attitude toward the issue of pluralism, a phenomenon typically decried by Orthodox and conservative thinkers (Solzhenitsyn among them) as incompatible with Christian convictions. In his view, pluralism is entirely understandable: it calls into question not Christianity but Christians themselves, whose example is not compelling enough to keep others from adopting alternative value systems. Thus if one is aware of Christian beliefs but does not accept them, this is not one's own failing, but that of the Christians one knows, who do not adequately embody the truth of Christianity in such a way as to make it undeniable. Tolerance is also characteristic of Anthony's attitude toward other religions; he treats them as stages in the search for God, referring to Pascal's revelation from the *Pensées*: "Comfort yourself, you would not seek Me if you had not already found Me." This means that Christians must be attentive to how people of other religions experience God, even if their piety is expressed in the most exotic or seemingly distorted forms.

The basic concept of the metropolitan's theology is the personal and immediate encounter between an individual and God, which is attained through prayer. Anthony of Sourozh authored several books on the subject of prayer whose influence spread beyond the bounds of Orthodoxy. In these he argues that mere ritual cannot provide a true sense of God unless one knows to whom such worship is addressed. "Encounter is central to prayer. It is the basic category of revelation, because revelation itself is an encounter with God who gives us a new vision of the world."[18] One must feel God with the same certitude with which one knows a neighbor, so that prayer becomes a kind of dialogue.

[17] Mitropolit Antonii Surozhskii, "Otvety na voprosy zhurnala 'Zvezda,'" *Zvezda* (Leningrad), no. 1 (1991): 122.

[18] Anthony of Sourozh, *Metropolitan Anthony of Sourozh. A Selection of His Writing*, ed. and with an introduction by Hugh Wybrew (Springfield, IL: Templegate Publishers, 1988), 26. Other books of Metropolitan Anthony include *Courage to Pray, God and Man, Living Prayer, Meditations on a Theme*, and *Beginning to Pray*.

The difficulty, according to Anthony, is that not only may our image of God be false, but also our image of ourselves may be falsified by our social existence. Each individual presents himself as a succession of social masks, thereby becoming unrecognizable to others and even to himself. So he must also discover his true self before he can have a real relationship with God. Without self-knowledge, true dialogue with God is impossible, and many prayers go unanswered that are founded upon an incomplete understanding of the self. Anthony emphasizes the importance of silence as a mode of communication with God: "Inner silence is absence of any sort of inward stirring of thought or emotion, but it is complete alertness, openness to God."[19] True communication is both speaking and listening, and it is often easy to forget that prayer also involves listening, not just the cataloguing of requests and adorations. One should attain such a repose of soul and body that one may become aware of even the faintest whispering of God's replies. For Anthony, prayer is not just a habitual element of worship, but a continual mode of existence, of remaining open to the divine word and remaining answerable to it.

For Anthony of Sourozh, the main aspect of the relationship between man and God is mutuality. Traditionally, faith and hope are viewed as modes of the human attitude toward God, transient modes that will fall away when God reveals himself fully. However, Anthony is convinced that faith and hope are also modes of God's existence inasmuch as He is personally involved in the creation and life of each individual. "[E]very time that a man enters the world, it is an act of Divine faith in him .... God believes in us, God hopes for *everything* from us."[20] Further:

> We must bring to the world a faith not only in God, but in man ... and must trust that God did not create people in vain, that He believes in every person, that He trusts in everyone, that He loves each person until His very death on the cross; and therefore there is no man, no matter how far he is from God in his own eyes, who would not be infinitely close to God.[21]

This creed of *Christian humanism* is addressed not only to each individual but also to the entire world as it was created by God and is studied by the natural sciences. "I graduated from the science faculty; I was a doctor, and I experienced the study of physics, chemistry, biology, and medicine as part of theology, that is, as part of the knowledge of what God created, of what He reveals, of what He loves—because God created nothing by power, but created by love."[22] We have to love the world in

19 Ibid., 76.

20 Mitropolit Antonii Surozhskii, "Otvety na voprosy zhurnala 'Zvezda,'" 125.

21 Mitropolit Antonii Surozhskii, "My dolzhny prinesti v mir veru—ne tol'ko v Boga, no v cheloveka." An interview with Anthony of Sourozh by Mikhail Epstein (London, April 1989), in Mitropolit Antonii Surozhskii, *O vstreche* (St. Petersburg: Satis, 1994), 79–93. Available electronically: https://predanie.ru/book/70592-o-vstreche/#/toc6

22 Ibid.

its materiality because it was created not only with love, but "by love." Thus theology should not isolate itself from the natural sciences but incorporate them as an inquiry into God's creation.

Furthermore, non-Orthodox denominations and even non-Christian religions, according to Metropolitan Anthony, contain a certain truth about God. "As for non-Christian religions, I think that no one can invent God, and therefore any religion that speaks of God speaks from within some direct experience of the Divine. This experience may be very incomplete, but it is real."[23] Metropolitan Anthony acknowledges that he learned a great deal about Christianity and the Orthodox faith from reading and communicating with non-Christians, with secularized people, nonbelievers who were capable of love, sacrifice, compassion, and mercy. Believers have only themselves to blame for the fact that nonbelievers, meeting them, do not meet Christ in their person and therefore become alienated from faith.

Metropolitan Anthony, being a high-ranking member in the Church hierarchy, represented one of the most inclusive, existentially profound views on faith as a complete openness to the world. "Orthodoxy is as spacious as God Himself. If it is not the size of God, then it is just another religion, it is not an experience of God."[24]

Expatriate theology made an important contribution to Russian intellectual history of the 1950s–1980s in that it demonstrated that Orthodoxy is not an outdated and purely formal system of dogma. Indeed, Orthodoxy had been subject to criticisms of its strict conformity to the letter of tradition, its ostensible incapacity for spiritual renovation, its isolation from the social and cultural world. The Orthodox thinkers of the twentieth century, though immersed in dogmatic and liturgical studies, provide a framework of linkages between the formal elements of ritual and its spiritual meanings, thus giving impetus to the religious renaissance that slowly took place in Russia in the 1970s and 1980s with the waning of the ideology of atheism.

Inside the Soviet Union, meanwhile, religious thought was largely preoccupied with apologetics and with moral issues concerning the interaction of the Church with the surrounding atheistic society. To be sure, this opposition—apologetics inside the USSR, theology beyond its borders—was not absolute, since we can find examples of intermediary figures, such as Aleksandr Men, who united apologetics and proselytizing with a strong commitment to exegetical and liturgical scholarship.

2. Science and Theology. Archbishop Luka (Valentin Voino-Iasenetsky)

Within the Soviet Union, the development of religious thought was suppressed for many decades. Probably the only theological work of the mid-twentieth century in Russia was produced by Archbishop Luka (Valentin Feliksovich Voino-Iasenetsky,

23 Ibid.
24 Ibid.

1877–1961). As an Orthodox bishop, he was subjected to political persecution and spent many years in internal exile (1923–33, 1937–41). Archbishop Luka was also an outstanding practicing surgeon, a pioneer in purulent surgery, and the author of a standard textbook in this field. A laureate of the Stalin Prize in medicine in 1946, he served as archbishop of Simferopol and the Crimea from 1946 on.

The hallmark of his philosophy is the combination of his unwavering Christian faith with his immense experience in biology, physiology, and practical medicine.

> If we take religion in essence, that is, as an internal experience, as worship of God and communication with Him, then we must agree that science not only does not contradict religion, but moreover, science leads to religion. If we do not limit ourselves to the painstaking collection of facts, like Goethe's character the scientific specialist Wagner, but rather, like Faust, give space to the whole human thirst for knowledge, which seeks to comprehend the secrets of being and possess these secrets, then we will inevitably come to religion .... Science poses the same questions that religion answers. According to the law of causality, it leads us to the Primary Cause of the world, and religion answers Who this creative Cause is, not only of the world, but also of man. Science reveals the eternal Logos of Being ... [and] leads to the need for some rational meaning in life, for some higher purpose of life.[25]

Archbishop Luka produced two theological treatises: *On Spirit, Soul, and Body* (1945–7) and *Science and Religion* (completed in 1954). The first was published only in 1978, the second in 2000; they subsequently had many reprints and enjoyed significant popularity among believers due to their wealth of scientific and historical facts and mastery of logical argumentation. The first book deals in particular with corporeal images in the Bible and argues that physical matter is imbued with spirituality as soon as it becomes embodied in the human being. If the body links humanity to all nature, and soul to the animal world, then spirit is unique in a person, and links him or her with God. Archbishop Luka pays special attention to the heart, which in this view is not merely a circulatory organ, but also the source of love, devotion, and compassion. "However dubious it may seem to nonbelievers, we assert that the heart can perceive certain suggestions directly, as the words of God."[26] Archbishop Luka cites numerous examples from the Old and New Testaments on the role of the heart in higher spiritual life:

> "I will give them one heart, and I will put a new spirit in them, and I will take their heart of stone out of the flesh, and I will give them a heart of flesh." (Ezek. 11: 19)

[25] Arkhiepiskop Luka, *Nauka i religiia*. Available electronically: https://azbyka.ru/otechnik/Luka_Vojno-Jasenetskij/nauka-i-religija

[26] Cited in the most comprehensive biography of Archbishop Luka: Mark Popovskii, *Zhizn' i zhitie Voino-Iasenetskogo, arkhiepiskopa i khirurga* (Paris: YMCA Press, 1979), 439. The full text of the treatise is available electronically: Arkhiepiskop Luka, *Dukh, dusha i telo.* https://azbyka.ru/otechnik/Luka_Vojno-Jasenetskij/dukh-dusha-i-telo

"I will put my laws into their hearts." (Heb. 10: 16)

"The love of God was poured into our hearts." (Rom. 5: 5)

"God … illumined our hearts" (2 Cor. 4: 6).

The heart was an important topic in twentieth-century Russian religious thought, obviously because of its purported predisposition for intuitive and "organic" rather than rational knowledge.[27] Even more crucially, the "heart" was the key concept of hesychasm, a mystical movement in medieval Byzantine Christianity aimed at "bringing the mind down into the heart" (*nizvesti um v serdtse*). Such is exactly the vision of Archbishop Luka: the highest mind is contained in the heart, not the brain. "Scripture speaks not only of the ability of the heart to perceive the exertions [*vozdeistviia*] of the Spirit of God, but represents it as an organ that God improves and corrects as the center of our spiritual life and of knowledge of God."[28]

Archbishop Luka's original contribution is his attempt to combine the most materialistic trends in contemporary physiology, such as Ivan Pavlov's research of the nervous system, with theological doctrines. Luka makes inventive use of what could be called the "apophatic," or negative, method in natural theology. The usual approach to buttressing religion with science involves confirming the rational design of the universe—the positive, or "cataphatic" evidence of God's reason and will in natural phenomena. By contrast, the apophatic method looks for evidence of God's supernatural existence by pointing out the absence of spiritual entities in physical nature. Pavlov asserted that the human nervous system was merely a more complex version of the animal network of conditioned reflexes, and that there is nothing in the brain apparatus that could account for the existence of such "mystical" capacities as love, conscience, insight, etc. In the Soviet Union, Pavlov's physiological theory was considered the highest achievement of philosophical materialism as grounded in scientific research.

Paradoxically, Archbishop Luka draws parallels between Ivan Pavlov and Henri Bergson, who compared the activity of the brain to the mechanical workings of a telephone station, purely regulatory and devoid of intellectual content. Furthermore, Luka restores this missing link between scientific materialism and the religious worldview by arguing that the absence of spiritual elements in the physiological apparatus of the brain attests to their supernatural origin. "If in the [cerebral] cortex, no center of emotions has been found, still less should one seek it in the grey ganglions of the brain stem, which, as it is partly known, have purely physiological functions."[29] This Pavlovian discovery helps to confirm the numerous biblical references to the heart as the site of human emotions and God's inspiration as the point of their genesis. "If,

[27] Boris Vysheslavtsev, for example, devoted a study to the subject of "the heart in Christian and Indian mysticism": *Serdtse v khristianskoi i indiiskoi mistike* (Paris: YMCA Press, 1929).

[28] Arkhiepiskop Luka, *Dukh, dusha i telo.*

[29] Ibid.

therefore, one cannot consider the brain to be the organ of emotions and the sole organ of the highest knowledge, this confirms to an enormous degree the doctrine of the Holy Scripture concerning the heart as the organ of emotions in general and especially the highest emotions."[30]

Since the author was a highly esteemed and distinguished member of the scientific community who, as a practicing surgeon, had performed thousands of operations on the brain, this treatise became an important theoretical milestone. Though some readers find Archbishop Luka's reasoning somewhat naive and eclectic in its attempt to merge citations from the Bible with the highly specialized terminology of anatomy and physiology, his books' historical impact cannot be denied. Rejected by the official theological journal of the Moscow Patriarchate, Archbishop Luka's work became one of the first products of Soviet religious-philosophical samizdat. Still more importantly, it established a precedent for many subsequent attempts to reconcile religious and scientific outlooks, as demonstrated by the works of the biologist Aleksandr Liubishchev and mathematician Vasilii Nalimov.[31]

3. The Christian Intuitivism of Boris Pasternak

Another impetus for the revival of religious thought came from Boris Pasternak (1890–1960). The Nobel prize-winning author of the novel *Doctor Zhivago*, Pasternak had prior to the revolution studied philosophy under Hermann Cohen, the leader of the Marburg school of neo-Kantianism. Although he abandoned his philosophical work in favor of poetry and prose, Pasternak's critical and autobiographical essays evince a neo-Kantian predilection in his understanding of art and history. Thus for him, a book is not a material object but a "piece of hot, smoking conscience" (*kusok goriachei, dymiashcheisia sovesti*), meaning that it is the textual embodiment of the author's inner dissatisfaction with himself. Metaphor, by his definition, is "the shorthand of the spirit" (*skoropis' dukha*) since it is dictated by the brevity of human life, and joins things belonging to different planes of existence without making explicit reference to their intermediary connections.

Doctor Zhivago (1945–55), more than a novel, is a kind of investigation of the history of the Russian Revolution from a philosophical and religious standpoint. Pasternak's model was Lev Tolstoy's *War and Peace*, where narrative passages alternate with long philosophical digressions. Like Tolstoy, Pasternak focuses on the philosophy of history, but his basic assumptions are far from the Tolstoyan determinism that attempted to disclose the necessary cause behind each individual action. Pasternak's view is principally nondeterministic, since he relies on a principal difference between nature and history, the latter being the realm of human freedom. Pasternak believes that history in the true sense of the word began with Christ, since before that, humanity

[30] Ibid.
[31] On these thinkers, see Epstein, *The Phoenix of Philosophy*, 51, 99–103.

was a prisoner of the cyclical regularities of nature. Christ is the spirit of "lightness" that releases one from the "heaviness" of paganism, this "flea market of borrowed gods and conquered peoples," a "tasteless heap of gold and marble,"[32] which is characteristic of ancient Rome.

> [I]t is possible to be an atheist, it is possible not to know whether God exists, or why, and yet believe that man does not live in a state of nature but in history, and that history as we know it now began with Christ, and that Christ's Gospel is its foundation .... It was not until after the coming of Christ that time and man could breathe freely. It was not until after Him that men began to live toward the future.[33]

In this broad sense, all efforts of the human mind and will, insofar as they are imbedded in history, are derived from the primordial Christian impetus, independent of a conscious Christian identity. This was a striking message for the Soviet readers of Pasternak's novel (which circulated in samizdat until its first publication in the USSR in 1988), most of whom had been educated as atheists, and who therefore identified Christianity with otherworldly concerns, and not at all with history.

As against the didactic and moralistic interpretation of Christianity that repelled so many of his contemporaries, Pasternak emphasizes its openness to everyday life. In the Gospels, the most sublime truths are presented in the form of parables, where they are illuminated with simple things like wine, bread, fish, and olives.

> It has always been assumed that the most important things in the Gospels are the ethical maxims and commandments. But for me the most important thing is that Christ speaks in parables taken from life, that He explains the truth in terms of everyday reality. The idea that underlies this is that communion between mortals is immortal, and that the whole of life is symbolic because it is meaningful.[34]

Thus for Pasternak, Christianity is not a sublime ideal or moral greatness; it is what all history and everyday life is about, making it possible to find spirituality in the most ordinary things, in nature, and in intimate relationships.

Insofar as Pasternak emphasizes the role of Christianity in history, his outlook has not only an anti-Tolstoyan, but also a distinctly anti-Marxist slant. He is enthusiastic about the emotional spontaneity of the Russian Revolution, but refuses to give a social, materialistic explanation for this event: it is too enormous to have definitive causes. "It's petty to explore causes of titanic events .... What is truly great is without beginning, like the universe. It confronts us as suddenly as if it had always been there,

[32] Boris Pasternak, *Doctor Zhivago*, trans. Max Hayward and Manya Harari (New York: Pantheon, 1958), 43. Pasternak entrusts most of his favorite thoughts on Christianity to two of the novel's characters in particular: Nikolai Nikolaevich Vedeniapin, a former Orthodox priest and now a freethinker, and the young woman Sima Tuntsova, Iurii Zhivago's neighbor in Varykino.

[33] Ibid., 10.

[34] Ibid., 42.

or had dropped out of the blue."[35] His disagreement with the Marxist leaders of the revolution concerns not only its causes but, more importantly, its consequences. The paradox of revolution is that it is guided by the ideals of freedom, but in its execution it comes to suppress freedom. Revolution in fact reinstates those ideals and idols that had prevailed in the pre-Christian world:

> If all this rhetoric about leaders and peoples had the power to reverse history, it would set us back thousands of years to the Biblical times of shepherd tribes and patriarchs. But fortunately this is impossible .... [With the advent of Christ,] [l]eaders and nations were relegated to the past. They were replaced by the doctrine of individuality and freedom. Individual human life became the life story of God.[36]

Pasternak's own ideal, to judge from his novel, is the integration of revolution and Christianity, which would allow revolution to bring the Christian spirit of equality and compassion into social reality, while at the same time, Christianity would preserve the spirit of freedom by resisting the impulse toward dictatorship.

In general, Pasternak tends to counterpose the New Testament, with its spirit of personal freedom and brotherly love, to the Old Testament, which he associates with a Jewish inclination to prioritize God's chosen nation over the individual. Being, himself, of Jewish origin, Pasternak sought to downplay his own background in favor of his commitments to Russian culture and Christianity. Jews, in his view, are victims of the belief in their chosenness, which has isolated them from other peoples, and he summons them to join the messianic drive that emerged from the depths of their own tradition. "Don't hold on to your identity. Don't stick together, disperse. Be with all the rest. You are the first and best Christians in the world."[37]

For many Soviet people, *Doctor Zhivago* was the first introduction to the Christian worldview. If Archbishop Luka's treatises set a pattern for the reconciliation of religion and science, then Pasternak's novel argued for a conciliatory relationship between religion and history. In the Marxist view, religion is an anti-historical mode of thinking, since it enjoins humanity to relate to something outside history and establishes transcendental, heavenly goals irrelevant to the real life of society. But for Pasternak, this is a plus: history itself, he believes, is impossible without supra-historical dimensions. The historical dimension was discovered by humanity inasmuch as it made a transition from the cult of cyclic natural processes to the openness of the Christian model of redemption and salvation. The neo-Kantian component of Pasternak's thought may be identified in his vision of religion as the constructive openness of human spirit, which transcends the limits of nature and sets off in search of an unpredictable future.

35 Ibid., 182.
36 Ibid., 413.
37 Ibid., 123.

4. Christian Socialism. Anatolii Krasnov-Levitin

In the period under consideration, Anatolii Krasnov-Levitin (1915–91) was probably the most outspoken proponent of Christian socialism in the late USSR. His original surname was Levitin, and he signed some of his works with the pseudonym "Krasnov," from *krasnyi*, "red."[38] In the 1930s–1940s, he was an active member in the so-called "Living" or "Renovationist" Church (*Zhivaia tserkov'* or *Obnovlenchestvo*), which emerged in the early 1920s as an alternative to "Old" Orthodoxy. There were hardly any dogmatic or liturgical differences between the two churches, but they were opposite in their social orientation. While the Orthodox Church, under the guidance of Patriarch Tikhon, resisted the ideology and policies of the Soviet regime, the Living Church, headed by the heretical Metropolitan Aleksandr Vvedensky (1889–1946), not only tended to compromise with the authorities but proclaimed it the duty of its members to cooperate with the revolutionary regime. It criticized Orthodoxy for its traditional inertia and passivity regarding social questions, and called on the Church to actively participate in the life of the world. The Living Church represented a kind of belated protestant movement within Orthodoxy, but, unlike Tolstoyanism with its anarchic, anti-Church and anti-state orientation, it was a completely *pro*-state and politically motivated, artificial institution. At first the Soviet authorities sponsored and privileged the Living Church and attempted to eliminate "Old" Orthodoxy, but when the latter, under the leadership of Tikhon's successor, Sergei, adopted a collaborationist stance, the authorities reversed their sympathies. The traditionalist Church, with its purely ritualistic emphasis and tendency for self-isolation, was preferable to a socially active Living Church, however sincere the latter's pro-Soviet orientation. Because of this, the Living Church began to decline, disappearing almost completely by the mid-1940s.

Krasnov-Levitin, though he became a loyal member of the Orthodox Church and contributed many articles to the official journal of the Moscow Patriarchate, nevertheless preserved his enthusiasm for the ideal of a socially engaged Church. His numerous samizdat articles blaming the Church for social passivity and the government for its oppression of the Church provoked both Orthodox and Soviet authorities to repressive response, and eventually led to his imprisonment and subsequent emigration to the West in 1974. He authored a number of books on the history of the Church during the Soviet period and on his own experiences as a religious and political dissident. The title of one of his essayistic collections *Stromata*—after Clement of Alexandria's miscellany of the same name, Greek for "patchwork"—is a good indication of his variegated style of writing, which mixes autobiography, history, polemics, theology, and philosophy, though it is devoid of any claims to originality.

Krasnov-Levitin proceeds from the Gospel commandment that it is impossible for a rich man to enter the kingdom of God, and condemns all social structures based

[38] Another version of his surname, Levitin-Krasnov, is more rare in Russian, though more frequent in English sources.

on the pursuit of wealth, both capitalist and so-called socialist, which inherited from capitalism its exclusively materialist orientation. Characteristically, Krasnov-Levitin decries materialism not only in the sense of a profiteering mentality, but also in that of the official Soviet philosophy. He accepts Hegelian dialectics, but denies its compatibility with Feuerbach's materialism, the synthesis of which was claimed as the unique achievement of Marxism. The very term "dialectical materialism" seems absurd to him, as it did to many of his predecessors in Russian religious and idealistic thought. "First of all, I could never understand how one can connect dialectics, which regards everything in terms of dynamics and the interaction of opposites, with materialism—the philosophy that reduces everything to one substance—matter, derives everything from it, begins with it and finishes with it. If it's materialism, it's not dialectical; if it's dialectical, it's not materialism."[39]

Krasnov-Levitin acknowledges the enormous influence of Vladimir Solovyov on his intellectual development, especially the idea that God's kingdom must be built not only in heaven but also on earth. "The entire history of humanity is only a way for the extension of God's kingdom in the world."[40] Solovyov was famous for his sharp criticism of socialist teachings, but Krasnov-Levitin finds in him a justification of socialism as the initial stage of a just social order. "Socialism as the abolition of social inequality and injustice is … the dialectical moment in the history of humanity. After humanity reaches this threshold, it will be convinced that this is not enough, and will strive for the heavenly city; it will come to Christ, and a genuine Christian socialism will arrive."[41] Therefore, the current stage in Russian history confirms the truth of socialism, but at the same time reveals its insufficiency and the need to Christianize it.

Krasnov-Levitin's ideological position was rather rare among late-Soviet intellectuals, as it combined Christian, socialist, and revolutionary convictions. For him, the most suggestive image of Christ is found in the episode where He chases the moneylenders from the temple. Here, all three of Krasnov-Levitin's allegiances are represented: the rejection of mercantile society proceeding from spiritual grounds, but at the same time requiring forceful intervention.

Krasnov-Levitin's credo, somewhat anachronistic, recapitulates the spirit of the mid-nineteenth century, when the program of Christian socialism was first formulated by Félicité Lamennais (1782–1854), a French Catholic priest, philosopher, and political theorist. "[O]ne must find within oneself the strength to challenge capitalism and to build the free, classless, evangelical Christian society of which the great Christian Lamennais dreamed."[42] The revolutionary impetus of Krasnov-Levitin's Christian socialism goes even so far as to justify terrorism, if it is undertaken as an act of charitable self-sacrifice, for the sake of one's suffering brothers and sisters who must

[39] A. Krasnov-Levitin, *Likhie gody. 1925–1941. Vospominaniia* (Paris: YMCA Press, 1977), 242.
[40] Ibid., 233.
[41] Ibid., 239.
[42] A. Krasnov, *Stromaty* (Frankfurt/Main: Posev, 1972), 103.

be freed from oppression.[43] In any case, Russian populists and socialist-revolutionaries of the late nineteenth and early twentieth centuries are among his ideological heroes, inasmuch as their political struggle was subordinated to a religious mission.

Krasnov-Levitin praises the October Revolution, since it brought social equality to the masses. For him, Soviet communism undoubtedly has its advantages over capitalism, since it abolishes the submission of the human spirit to material profit. In a letter to Pope Paul VI in 1967, Krasnov-Levitin wrote: "The construction of industry without bosses, without private entrepreneurs, without factory owners, in short without the bourgeoisie is the great historical victory of the Russian people."[44] The fault of communism is its idealization and idolization of the state, which, according to the initial prophesies of Marx and Engels, should have withered away after the revolution, but in reality grew into a self-sufficient bureaucratic machine. The sacralization of the state and the persecution of believers are two sides of the same coin. For Krasnov-Levitin, genuine socialism would imply the restoration of the Church and gradual disintegration of the state. He sympathetically cites the belief of British Labour Party pioneer (and prime minister, 1929–35) Ramsay MacDonald that religion would help realize the building of socialism.[45]

As for Krasnov-Levitin's specific reformist ideas, he shared the program outlined by the leaders of the Living Church as early as 1918, in particular by Father Aleksandr Boiarsky, whose programmatic work *The Church and Democracy* (1918) included the following theses: collectivism is the foundation of the state, and any personal, authoritarian regime is unacceptable; capitalist property must be replaced by cooperative ownership; land must also be common property; labor is the principle of life, and everyone must work; a genuine Christian cannot be rich (if a capitalist would follow Christian norms in his economic activity, he would be bankrupt in two days), hence, no capitalists; equality of women and the elimination of all class barriers and hierarchies.

Politically, Krasnov-Levitin sympathizes with both Christian-democratic and social-democratic parties in Western Europe, but he regrets that they have lost their religious and reformative zeal. They are too preoccupied with the task of maintaining the status quo within their countries, such that the idea of an actual *Christian revolution* makes them nervous. Thus, after a critical analysis of five major modern political movements—fascism, capitalist liberalism, Christian democracy, social democracy, and communism—Krasnov-Levitin advances his own alternative, which he calls neo-humanism. He believes that this movement can integrate the agendas of both Christian and secular humanists. What distinguishes neo-humanism from traditional humanism is its focus on the individual. "[T]he old humanism brought to the fore the concept of humankind—the new humanism brings to the fore the [particular] person,

[43] There are examples of such Christianly motivated terrorism in Russian revolutionary history. Egor Sazonov (1879–1910), who in 1904 assassinated Interior Minister V. K. Pleve, confessed in a letter to family members: "I committed this deed because I felt that my conscience, my religion, my gospel, my God demanded this of me. Could I disobey? … [D]ear ones, my revolutionary and socialist beliefs and my religion have merged into one." http://www.chaosss.info/egorsazonov/

[44] Krasnov, *Stromaty*, 124.

[45] Ibid., 108.

the human personality. This is why the old humanism is abstract, divorced from life, inert, peculiar to the intelligentsia. Neo-humanism is concrete, active, dynamic."[46]

Krasnov-Levitin's ideas would probably have found more sympathy and support in South America, among proponents of liberation theology, than in contemporary Russia, where historical experience would seem to offer only evidence that Christianity and socialism are incompatible. Typologically, his views are closest to the politics advanced by the "third position" movement, which opposes itself to both communism and capitalism.[47] But most "third position" sympathizers are nonreligious, and what makes Krasnov-Levitin peculiar is that his social critique and neo-humanism claim to be founded on Orthodox Christian views.

5. Atheism as the Forerunner of Spiritual Rebirth

The traditional mode of preaching in the Church required only that the priest deliver sermons on conventional topics related to the Orthodox calendar. Both Soviet and Church authorities strove to limit the scope of the clergy's oratorical repertoire to strictly ritualistic themes. The priest Dmitrii Dudko (1922–2004) initiated the reorientation of the Russian Orthodox Church toward a dynamic interaction between the clergy and believers. He dared to break with tradition, asserting that a priest should foster deeper connections with his parish and minister to its everyday spiritual needs. In the late 1960s and 1970s, he had a great influence on the thousands of neophytes who flocked to his sermons. These events had formerly taken the form of conversations, in which Dudko answered questions from his crowded Moscow congregation, first in writing, and later in direct dialogue. Reconstructed from notes, and circulated in samizdat, these sermons appeared in the 1970s in French, English, and many other languages.

Not surprisingly, Dudko's unconventional openness led to his persecution. While still a seminary student, he was imprisoned for his religious poems for seven years. He was arrested a second time in 1979 for sermonizing to large audiences of Moscow intelligentsia and was forced, under threat of severe punishment, to apologize publicly for his "wrongful behavior, unworthy of a Christian." This capitulation alienated many of his followers and prompted him later to deep and sincere repentance, but the historical merit of his early preaching cannot be denied. Later, after the collapse of the Soviet Union, he supported the nationalist movement and expressed admiration for strong authoritarian leaders, but by this time he had become an irrelevance even to those whose lives he had transformed by bringing them to the faith.

Dudko was not a philosopher or theologian, but his thought was focused on shaping a new worldview amid the purported spiritual bankruptcy of atheism. Dudko discloses an inner contradiction of atheism, which condemns faith as an unscientific and

[46] Ibid., 149.

[47] On this trend in Soviet-era liberal thought, see Epstein, *The Phoenix of Philosophy*, 155–6.

obscurantist mode of thinking, but at the same time asserts that "no one can fully think or act without [some sort of] belief" and that "an enormous number of people believe that communism will eventually triumph all over the world."[48] Is faith in communism more substantially confirmed by experience than faith in God, which has survived for centuries? If faith in general is justifiable as a mode of thinking, the most worthy object of faith cannot be one of transitional social illusions, political or scientific fashions, but can only be found in God as the immutable, spiritual foundation of life which is grounded in the existential experience of each individual—even if many remain unaware of him. Dudko goes so far as to argue that atheism is a crime, committed first of all against the atheist himself because he kills his own soul.[49] Only a consummate criminal, whose own life is devoid of spiritual meaning, would wish that the world be destroyed. Still more criminal, in Dudko's view, is the atheistic desire that the Higher World not exist.[50]

Another recurring theme in Dudko's sermons is the moral degradation of Soviet society. The attainment of earthly goals ultimately leaves one further from the happiness that one originally set out to find, and this internal emptiness leads to immorality, the dissolution of the family, and the abuse of alcohol and drugs. Marx proclaimed that religion is the opium of the people, but when genuine religion is abolished, opium itself becomes a kind of popular religion. Dudko refutes the standard atheist argument that Christians, since the next world is their primary goal, have little interest in work and lead a dull, joyless existence. The point is that the next world is sought and attained only through life in this world. "That's why every minute of life is precious to a Christian, and the less time he has remaining, the more resolute are his actions."[51] The intensity of earthly Christian life is not diminished but augmented by its relationship to eternity.

The most original aspect of Dudko's thought is his situating of atheism in historical and eschatological perspectives. The Soviet dominion of atheism and moral degradation, in Dudko's view, is not wholly negative, because it represents a decisive test of faith. In prerevolutionary Russia, religious faith was maintained—as it is now in the contemporary West—primarily as a social and family institution, which weakens the individual's testimony of faith. The well-being of organized religion is therefore inimical to the depth and vigor of faith. The persecution of religion in the Soviet period put believers in the same—or even worse—conditions as the first Christians, and this makes them closer to Christ himself. "Russia, in its religious aspect, becomes the center of the world, the center of world history."[52] Thus the providential mission of atheism has been the preparation for the revival of faith, a "manuring of the ground." "This is the benefit of atheism. It accomplishes, so to speak, the rough work, puts itself in the role of the slave. And it labors, with all its might, thinking that it works for itself,

48 These excerpts from the Soviet *Short Dictionary of Philosophy* (*Kratkii slovar' po filosofii* [Moscow: Politizdat, 1970]) are cited in Dmitrii Dudko, *O nashem upovanii. Besedy* (Paris: YMCA Press, 1976), 53.

49 This thesis reverses Albert Camus's famous definition of religion, a transcendent world of solace and meaning beyond the Absurd, as "philosophical suicide."

50 Dmitrii Dudko, *Vovremia i ne vovremia* (Brussels: Zhizn' s Bogom, 1978), 210.

51 Dudko, *O nashem upovanii*, 128.

52 Ibid., 123.

but everybody knows that the slave works not for himself but for the master. And our master is God."[53] Thus, once again, Dudko reveals the inner irony of atheism, which inadvertently works to the benefit of its adversary, confirming the truth of Christ's parable that unburied grain cannot germinate.

In Dudko's view, the death of Christianity proclaimed by the state is like the death of Christ imminently followed by resurrection. Russia has arrived at its Golgotha: Christianity has been crucified, but one can now expect its triumph.

> Imagine what a joy it is to be with Christ on Golgotha! They say that some Catholics want especially to come here [to Russia] in order to be close to Golgotha's sufferings. Now in Russia the greatest miracle is occurring, not only the crucifixion of Christ but also His resurrection from the dead. It is unprecedented that children of inveterate atheists, who were brought up in atheism, suddenly proclaim their faith.[54]

Dudko's theme of a new resurrection imparts a joyous and festive tone to his sermons, as if Easter has burst from the framework of the annual Church calendar and is about to be celebrated on a millennial scale.

To prepare for this religious revival, Dudko insists that the role of the laity is now more important than that of the clergy, since the Church hierarchy is enslaved and subordinated by the atheistic state. He believes, furthermore, that the time has come for the unification of all Christian churches, since Christianity has reached its spiritual maturity, having learned through its own persecution the lesson of tolerance. "We must not remake each other in our own image but learn from each other."[55] In his view, the ecumenical movement, which presently involves mainly the top church officials, must be brought down into the laity and, first and foremost, adopt the spirit of humility.

The remarkable thing about Dudko's preaching is not only that he sought to address the common concerns of the laity, but that he tried to contest the provincial, peripheral role of Russian Orthodoxy, interpreting its fate as the core event of world religious history, as the central mystery of Christianity—death and resurrection. "Through our Golgotha, the entire world will be forgiven. My voice is the voice from Golgotha, a call for the salvation of the entire world."[56]

6. The Dialogue between Believers and Atheists. Sergei Zheludkov and Kronid Liubarsky

In its development, religious thought could not avoid coming into confrontation with the prevailing atheist mindset. Official ideology never ceased its attack on "religious obscurantism" and "the opium of the people," but religious thinkers were reluctant to

[53] Ibid.
[54] Ibid., 103.
[55] Dudko, *Vovremia i ne vovremia*, 319.
[56] Ibid., 212.

respond to these diatribes, since they clearly proceeded from a purely authoritative position that would not have permitted dialogue. However, with the growth of the dissident movement, the opposition between believers and atheists grew ever more philosophically relevant, since it divided many of the most prominent intellectuals. Solzhenitsyn and Sakharov provided the most famous example of such a religious divergence among dissident leaders,[57] but certain other thinkers dealt even more explicitly with the theoretical issues of this "schism." One of the most interesting cases of such polemics is the correspondence between Sergei Zheludkov, an Orthodox priest, and Kronid Liubarsky, a scientist and nonbeliever, which took place in 1974–75 while the latter was in prison. Both men were political dissidents, and it was this common ground that provided the foundation for their open and trusting theoretical dialogue.

Sergei Zheludkov (1909–84), who was forced to resign as a parish priest in Pskov in 1960, authored several samizdat books, including *Liturgical Notes* and *Why I Too Am a Christian*. He was one of the first religious writers to emphasize the significance of secular morality for the spiritual revival of the Orthodox Church. Zheludkov condemns the traditional pride of Orthodoxy, which places itself at the center of the world's religious systems. According to this scheme, Ivan the Terrible—solely on the basis of his membership in the Orthodox Church—proves to be closer to Christ than Mahatma Gandhi, since he was a Hindu. Zheludkov proposes that a person's deeds rather than their professed religious affiliation be the indicator of a Christian identity. He draws a distinction between an "elitist" *Christianity of faith*, which is granted to a chosen few through the grace of the Holy Spirit, and "universal" *Christianity of will*, which is attainable by everyone through the exercise of one's moral choice.

> Christ is the Eternal Divine Man, and the orientation of our will toward ideal humanness is the orientation toward Christ. To be sure, there can be nothing better than when Christianity of will coincides with Christianity of faith. But it happens that people who are far from the confession of the Christian faith and from religion in general, in their moods, evaluations, strivings and actions, clearly prove to be closer to Christ than we, the inveterate, baptized Christians of faith.[58]

To support his argument, Zheludkov refers to Aleksei Khomiakov, a Russian religious thinker of the nineteenth century, who wondered: "Is it not Christ whom the man who loves Truth loves? Is it not His disciple, though he does not know it, whose heart is open to compassion and love?"[59] Zheludkov uses the term "anonymous Christians," borrowed from the Catholic theologian Karl Rahner, to designate those people who are Christians despite their non-Christian or even anti-Christian convictions. Thus faith in Christ is not a necessary condition for salvation through Christ; otherwise, Christ would not be the savior of humanity, but a stumbling block (to borrow, polemically,

[57] On Andrei Sakharov and his polemics with Aleksandr Solzhenitsyn, see Epstein, *The Phoenix of Philosophy*, 162–7.

[58] S. Zheludkov and K. Liubarskii, *Khristianstvo i ateizm* (Brussels: Zhizn' s Bogom, 1982), 10.

[59] Ibid., 10.

Paul's term) for the overwhelming majority of people on their way to God. "Christianity of will is open to everyone,"[60] and the absence of faith may sometimes be the test for the purity of one's goodwill, since one is not motivated by the promise of reward.

> The irreligious sector of the Christian Church is not an abstraction, it is a joyful reality .... [The atheist] worships and serves God absolutely, so to speak, selflessly, without expectation of any reward, of any Eternity, out of, one can say, truly pure, free respect .... This is a miracle, a person's mysterious, profound, powerful connection with the Supreme Eternal Humanity of our Lord.[61]

Thus Christianity of will, which can even be irreligious, derives from the humanity of Christ himself, in whom divinity underwent kenosis—the self-emptying for the sake of his participation in human destiny. The term "anonymous Christian" applies, then, to anyone who lives according to Christ's teaching, regardless of whether this person has even heard of Christ. In fact, Zheludkov goes so far as to suggest that his opponent, Kronid Liubarsky, who sacrificed his own freedom for the cause of human freedom, is himself a model Christian.

Kronid Liubarsky (1934–96) responds from the perspective of an atheist humanist, an outlook fostered by his scientific career. He had worked as an astrophysicist and published several books in his field before his arrest in 1972 for dissident and human-rights activism. Upon his release from prison in 1977, he emigrated to Germany and founded a journal, *Country and World*, which became one of the leading periodicals of the Russian emigration. Liubarsky's arguments in favor of atheism are probably the most sophisticated of those originating in the Soviet milieu, since they combine logical, scientific, and moral criteria, abandoning the ideological presuppositions characteristic of Marxism.

Logically, Liubarsky makes use of Occam's razor, according to which "entities should not be multiplied without necessity." In other words, if facts do not require the assumption of some new principle, then such a principle should not be introduced into one's reasoning. In Liubarsky's view, the observable world does not require God to explain its functioning. "The world of the atheist is the World determined by the laws of nature and only by them, principally devoid of anything which is external to it .... This World creates itself .... It is joyous to be aware that we, as particles of this World, also incessantly participate in this act of the World's self-creation!"[62]

From Liubarsky's perspective, one of Zheludkov's assumptions—that existence on earth without faith is absurd, empty, and full of despair—amounts only to a wishful projection. That is to say that the believer imposes his own concept of God as the only source of meaning on the world of the atheist. The opposite side of the same confusion is seen in the writings of French atheist existentialists who, because of their

[60] Ibid., 16.
[61] Ibid., 17.
[62] Ibid., 25–6.

religious upbringing, described godless reality as a world of absurdity and metaphysical "nausea." The situation was different for a Soviet thinker, since his value system was, from the very beginning, free of any transcendental meanings. Thus, for Liubarsky, the world without God is quite meaningful, even more meaningful than the world with God, since the presence of a supreme being renders meaningless the initiatives of human beings. In his view, even if God does exist, He does not want humanity to be religious, lest its freedom be curtailed. Liubarsky also argues against the term "anonymous Christians"; to him this is likewise an instance of Zheludkov projecting his values on people who do not share them, and who might even be offended by the imposition. An equivalent presumption would be to call religious people actively engaged in the life of the world "anonymous atheists."

Another point of contention between the two is the origin of morality. For Liubarsky, morality has an immanent or natural explanation: it is "the aggregate of norms of behavior that maximally promote the preservation of man as a biological species, *Homo sapiens* .... A species must increase its population to expand its natural habitat, to regulate the quantity (density) of individuals in order to provide a necessary minimum of means for the existence of each individual."[63] Love for one's neighbor or the taboo against murder can be seen as natural rules of survival. Reversing Zheludkov's argument that God appears to people as love, beauty, and conscience, Liubarsky contends that these concepts are valuable in and of themselves, requiring no supplemental reference to God. Furthermore, religious concepts are not only superfluous to morality, but are even anti-moral, inasmuch as they suggest some kind of reward for virtuous behavior and are thus motivated by consideration of profit.

> I must supposedly be honest and courageous, kind and generous because I will be paid for it. It's not so important what kind of payment, it's not important that it is the salvation of my soul. The payment is great, but it is *payment* .... This is a corrupting, immoral idea. A person should be moral without any conditions, not because he or she gets something for it.[64]

In the Soviet period, it was typical for philosophical and ethical problems to be researched and experimented with in the "laboratories" of prisons and labor camps, and Liubarsky, who advances his arguments from inside a camp, often makes use of his prison experiences to illustrate his ideas. For example, he observes that his fellow prisoners, upon their conversion to Christianity, actually become less compassionate toward their comrades and lose their courage and integrity as they withdraw from "worldly affairs."

As far as religious commitments are concerned, Liubarsky prefers Judaism to Christianity because of its rationalism, its tolerance for questioning and doubting, and also its social activism. Christianity, on the other hand, suggests Liubarsky, "establishes

[63] Ibid., 28–9.
[64] Ibid., 29.

the type of thinking favorable for the emergence of totalitarianism."[65] Judaism removed God from material life, while Christianity, founded on the story of the God who became man, strikes Liubarsky as a return to a paganistic worldview, where a man can be worshipped as a god. The idea of the God-man, reversed as a Man-god, makes possible the kind of aspirations characteristic of totalitarian regimes, which would be impossible in Judaism since it draws a radical distinction between man and God.

Thus for Liubarsky, the struggle between totalitarianism and Christianity, or for example between Nazism and Catholicism, is a competition between rivals, not polar antagonists. The only genuine alternative to both religious and totalitarian thinking is scientific thinking, which is opposed to any kind of worship, be its object God or an individual perceived as God. Science does not forbid faith, but has no need of it, either. Liubarsky observes in human history a process of

> the incessant waning of the sphere of the Divine. First, springs and trees, stones and volcanoes, fell out of this sphere. Then heaven, physical heaven, fell out .... What was left was the depths of the psyche. But there will come a time when it will be clear that Conscience is Conscience, Love is Love. Not God. Will these be "worse" for it? I know that a rainbow is a solar spectrum, an atmospheric phenomenon. But do I stop admiring it for this reason?[66]

Thus the historical perspective of humanity is the transition from a reliance on myth to a completely immanent universe, which will be understood by purely scientific methods and will be improved by purely moral impulses.

In his responses to Liubarsky, Zheludkov critiques the latter's arguments on behalf of science, insofar as, in the twentieth century, science itself has overcome the materialistic and atheistic bias typical of the nineteenth. Zheludkov cites long lists of outstanding scientists who not only personally believed in God but interpreted the results of their research in a religious way, disclosing rational patterns in the organization of material substance, as evidence of an intelligent design or divine order. Following purely scientific principles, agnosticism makes more sense than atheism, since the latter's negation of faith presupposes some supernatural revelation about God's absence, which is not the case with the majority of so-called atheists. If science does not support the religious position, neither does it support the antireligious one. Moreover, Zheludkov argues that atheism is itself a religion: "[T]here are no atheists, there are idol-worshippers,"[67] since, for those who believe in God's absence, other things come to take the place of God, such as commodities or principles like Progress or Culture. Thus atheism is actually polytheism, a "religion of local eternity [*religiia zdeshnei vechnosti*]."[68]

[65] Ibid., 83.
[66] Ibid., 75.
[67] Ibid., 120.
[68] Ibid., 121.

Zheludkov involved many other people in his correspondence, both believers and nonbelievers.[69] In the course of these exchanges, a third position emerged to mediate between the extremes, and its representative was Boris Khazanov, for whom belief and nonbelief were two complementary aspects of an emerging worldview.[70] Khazanov suggests that the absence of God may be his deliberate way to promote the fullness of human responsibility on this earth, as if He had said: "Proceed as if I don't exist and learn to work things out on your own." From this standpoint, the dialogue between believers and atheists can be interpreted as a stage in the formation of a new "border theology," which takes atheism as a step toward the fuller understanding and demystification—not refutation—of God.

Zheludkov's attempt to recruit new Christians from among nonbelievers sometimes struck even his Christian associates as naive in terms of its logical argumentation. However, it proved to be one of the cornerstones of the renewed missionary consciousness within the Orthodox Church. Unlike Krasnov-Levitin, who emphasized the social responsibilities of Christians, and unlike Dmitrii Dudko, who summoned Christianity to the moral correction of the world, Sergei Zheludkov preached to both Christians and non-Christians, exhorting them to understand each other and mutually accept the moral truths of the mundane world and the transcendental beauty of Christ. In his attempt to argue the existence of God in terms accessible to believers and nonbelievers alike, and to reconcile these two groups, he stood also as one of the broadest of Soviet-era religious thinkers.

Characteristically for this new spirit of tolerance and brotherhood, Zheludkov's opponent Kronid Liubarsky was the first to acknowledge this merit of the retired priest's initiative:

> This is magnificent—this is probably the first time a Christian has made such a direct step to, I would say, "moral ecumenism" without harboring the grudge of a fatal spiritual death against us nonbelievers. This is an important step. Without it, it would be difficult to attain what Tolstoy wrote about: to unite all good people to counterbalance bad ones.[71]

Several thinkers of the younger generation, such as the priest Aleksandr Men, carried forward and refined Zheludkov's missionary project.

7. Christianity and the New Humanism. Secularization and the Intelligentsia

These polemics between Christians and atheistic humanists bring forth the next question: can Christianity and secular humanism be reconciled, and if so, how?

[69] The priest and theologian Aleksandr Men, writing under the initial Z., was one of the most persuasive participants of this correspondence.

[70] Boris Khazanov's views are discussed in the chapter on personalism in Epstein, *The Phoenix of Philosophy*, 133–6.

[71] Zheludkov and Liubarskii, *Khristianstvo i ateizm*, 75.

Overall, four possible orientations concerning Christianity's relationship to humanism can be identified. One position emphasizes the transcendental dimension of Christianity and its incompatibility with worldly commitments. Such is the traditional orientation of Russian Orthodoxy, which had promoted the withdrawal of the Church from social and political activity. At the opposite pole, there exists a similarly staunch rejection of religiosity in favor of a complete immersion in the world of human affairs. This was the founding principle of Marxist communism, realized in the Soviet period through the enforcement of mass atheism. Strangely enough, these mutually exclusive extremes were historically quite compatible. Since Orthodoxy turned away from worldly concerns, the atheist power structure permitted its existence as a ritualistic practice isolated from culture and society.

The two other positions are based on the value of tolerance, with each attempting to reconcile its own preferences with the beliefs of its counterpart. One of these positions, liberal Christianity, is open to the truth of humanism and seeks to integrate the values of non-Christians into its own worldview by finding a religious justification for nonreligious morality. Its counterpart is secular humanism, which respects the freedom of the personality and therefore accepts the Christian faith, not as ultimate truth but as one of many possible moral choices. Again, these mutually tolerant positions are more compatible with one another than with the dogmatic tendencies in their own value system, that is, conservative religiosity and atheism. In its appeal to humanistic values, open Christianity proves to be a dissident movement vis-à-vis the Church's conservatism. By the same token, secular humanism's belief in the freedom of conscience makes it unacceptable to the hard-line policy of official "class-based humanism" maintained by the Soviet authorities. Thus it is possible to group these positions not only according to the contents of their convictions, Christian and humanist, but also by the mode of their assertion: on the one hand, dogmatism justifies itself with the values of commonality, whether spiritual community or social collectivism; on the other, tolerance is founded on a belief in the sovereignty of the personality, either because it is oriented toward individual salvation, or because it promotes freedom as the highest value.

	Individuality	Collectivity
Christianity	liberal	dogmatic
Humanism	secular	atheistic

In the Soviet milieu, the position of "closed" Christianity was rarely stated in philosophical terms, since it presupposes the rejection of philosophizing as such. This is why the overwhelming majority of conceptions discussed in this part of the book belong to liberal Christian thinkers.

The generation of Christian humanists who came to spiritual maturity in the post-Stalin period was, as a rule, devoid of the socialist tenets typified by Krasnov-

Levitin. While insisting on the importance of worldly commitment, these Christians interpreted this concept as cultural and educational engagement rather than political or social activism. Evgenii Barabanov (b. 1943) was one of the early representatives of this liberal Christian trend, beginning with his contribution to *From under the Rubble* (Paris, 1974), a collection of essays compiled and edited by Aleksandr Solzhenitsyn. Barabanov was among the few contributors who, while an Orthodox thinker, did not share the Slavophilic orientation of Solzhenitsyn and Igor Shafarevich. His liberalism accounted for his inclusion in another essay collection, *Self-Awareness* (New York, 1976), which was aimed at countering the increasingly nationalistic bias among dissidents. Not surprisingly, Barabanov proved to be the only writer represented in both these mutually antagonistic publications, which signals, not some vacillation in his convictions, but rather his firm commitment to both Christianity and liberalism, and his aspiration that their organic union might reconcile the two divergent dissident tendencies.[72]

His contribution to Solzhenitsyn's volume, an article titled "The Schism between the Church and the World," suggests that the Soviet suppression of Orthodoxy has been accepted by the Church because it coincides with the age-old Orthodox tendency for social passivity and isolation. Barabanov calls the Church's exclusive self-interest "pseudo-ecclesiasticism," since, instead of serving God by serving the people, the Church opts to serve only itself and thus becomes an idol in the eyes of believers. Barabanov calls on the Church to end its isolationist stance and admit the relevance of worldly concerns. "Today, as never before, a Christian initiative is needed to counter the godless humanism that is destroying mankind, and to prevent [Christian] humanism from deteriorating into a nonreligious humanism."[73]

Barabanov's point is that conditions are unprecedentedly ripe for the reconciliation of Christianity and humanism, insofar as atheistic humanism has now come to a dead end by destroying its own humanistic foundation through an evolution to totalitarianism. The rebellion against God and Church for the sake of human self-determination led in Russia to the deification of man himself, to the "cult of personality," whereby humanism turned into the suppression of all human rights, in effect committing suicide. In his essay published in *Self-Awareness*, titled "The Truth of Humanism," Barabanov argues that the crisis of humanistic values can be overcome only through a restoration of their original Christian basis. A new Orthodoxy is needed to wash away the pseudo-ecclesiastical failings of the old Church, in the same way that a neo-humanism has arisen to oppose the perverted humanism of the totalitarian state. Neo-humanists no longer struggle against religion, but rather against the monstrous offspring of old "revolutionary" humanism. Thus it would be unforgivable for the Church to squander the unique opportunity to embrace and bless this wayward flock of secularism that has

72 Christian liberalism, a relatively rare worldview in Russian philosophy of the twentieth century, was most forcefully expressed by Georgii Fedotov (1886–1951), a prolific author who emigrated from Russia to France in 1925, and then to the United States in 1940.

73 Aleksandr Solzhenitsyn et al., eds., *Iz-pod glyb. Sbornik statei* (Paris: YMCA Press, 1974), 92.

been abused and distorted by atheism. The Church must accept what is good, even if it does not originate within the Church itself.

> It is time to see clearly: good is *indivisible* .... If we know that genuine good and the forces to accomplish it come only from God, then it would be a great impiety to restrain God in His ways of communicating these forces. Even more impious would be to deny the religious meaning of good will just because it is not confirmed by the blessing of a priest or confessor. By this we only debase our idea of God, of the Church, and of the priesthood.[74]

Barabanov distinguishes two traditions within the Orthodox Church, as exemplified by two heroes of Dostoevsky's *The Brothers Karamazov*—the elder Zosima, and the monk Ferapont. The former is a proponent of "open" Christianity, which gives religious meaning to the secular world, while the latter has contempt for anything originating outside the confines of the monastery. In Barabanov's estimation, contemporary Orthodoxy has come to a fork in the road, where it must choose between Zosima and Ferapont. Barabanov hopes that it will be able to humble itself enough to recognize the superiority of those humanists who dare to accomplish the work of God that is neglected by Christians themselves. "[T]he struggle for truth without expectation of heavenly rewards, selflessness and a spirit of sacrifice, the assertion of the will for good, the nobleness and beauty of steadfast opposition to evil and violence, an organic caring for one's neighbor, a spontaneous moral response to their suffering"[75]—such are the virtues of many nonbelievers, whose holiness should not be denied, but ought instead to be taken as an example for Christians and as a measure of their own worthiness. It is not the fault of good that it is committed by nonbelievers, but it is a deficiency of belief when it fails to accomplish the same good.

Another representative of the humanistic trend in Orthodoxy is Mikhail Meerson-Aksenov (b. 1944). A historian and theologian by education, he was involved in the Soviet dissident movement and emigrated to New York City in 1972, where he has served for decades as an Orthodox priest. His writings focus on the fate of the Russian intelligentsia, which he portrays as a secular "monastic order" that has great spiritual potential but historically devoted itself to the promotion of nonreligious values. Thus he continues the project outlined in *Landmarks* (1908), the celebrated manifesto by leading Russian thinkers critical of their country's intelligentsia for its materialist and socialist bias. Meerson explains the emergence of the intelligentsia as a specifically Russian phenomenon with reference to the consolidation of secular and religious authorities in Russia. In the West, where historically, church and state have remained distinct and even at times antagonistic, intellectuals could define themselves in relation to these two poles of authority. In Russia, where these two poles coincide in the integrity of a "holy State" and state Church, any opposition to one authority implied

[74] E. V. Barabanov and P. M. Litvinov, eds., *Samosoznanie. Sbornik statei* (New York: Khronika, 1976), 19.

[75] Ibid., 25.

opposition to both (a correlation still quite valid in twenty-first-century Russia). Thus did the intelligentsia's political opposition inevitably lead it to an antireligious bias and corresponding materialist preoccupation.

After the revolution, the configuration of these three forces—state, Church, and intelligentsia—radically changed, since the Church was not only alienated from the state but became an object of persecution. The intelligentsia, in its continuing aspiration to freethought, now came to oppose itself to the atheistic state and increasingly sought support from the spiritual tradition as embodied in Orthodox Christianity (as distinct from the hierarchy of the Russian Orthodox Church, which remained a puppet of the regime). Thus in this view, the historical evolution of the intelligentsia confirmed the projections of *Landmarks*, but it took decades of bloody lessons to prove that genuine freedom is to be found in Christianity rather than Marxism. Now, however, it is time for the Church to revise its anti-intellectual stance and both embrace the intelligentsia and assimilate its concerns.

> It seems that, divided by their previous history, the Church and intelligentsia are beginning to discover their spiritual kinship on the edge of a common grave where both of them mourn the martyrs of the faith and the martyrs of the freedom of creative spirit. They are both victims of a common enemy, of triumphant atheistic and antihuman despotism. Faced with this, what remains for them is to form an alliance for the defense of the rights of God and man on this earth.[76]

Meerson is one of the few priests to see Orthodox tradition's stubborn conformity with the rituals of early Christianity as a negative, rather than cause for praise. He argues that this conservatism has led the Church away from the historical needs of its followers. By adhering to the letter rather than the spirit of early Christianity, the Orthodox faith has lost its capacity to transform the world, as its rituals become increasingly formalistic and purely symbolic. However, as distinct from Catholicism, Orthodoxy has the advantage of dogmatic openness, despite its ritualistic rigidity. "Russian theology, at its height, asserted that Orthodoxy gives enormous spiritual freedom, since it has no systematic doctrine about the world, State, or society, and grants the Christian an initiative for creative search."[77] The Church, then, has the flexibility necessary to assimilate the intelligentsia and, more broadly, the whole process of secularization, which was a justifiable reaction to the monastic and ascetic bias of the prerevolutionary epoch of Orthodoxy. Secularization, in these terms, means intellectual and cultural freedom, which challenges any kind of dogmatism and sanctifies not only the Church but also the whole world as God's creation. Meerson believes that the American Orthodox Church, which gained its independence from the Moscow Patriarchate only in 1970, is a proving ground for the integration of Orthodoxy and the spirit of Western pluralism, with its historical dynamism.

[76] Ibid., 116.
[77] Mikhail Meerson-Aksenov, *Pravoslavie i svoboda* (Benson, VT: Chalidze Publications, 1986), 32.

8. The Philosophy of Christian Synthesis. Aleksandr Men

The most prominent Orthodox thinker of this period was the priest and theologian Aleksandr Men (1935–90). He was baptized along with his mother into the Orthodox Church by a priest who was a member of the Russian Catacomb Church.[78] In the late 1950s, when the persecutions of Christians under Khrushchev became especially violent, he made up his mind to become a priest and was ordained in 1960. What was unusual about Father Men was that, during a time when the Soviet intelligentsia was enthusiastic about the resurgence of Marxism and the prospects of political liberalization, not only did he, a member of that same intelligentsia, enter the priesthood, but also remained actively engaged in all kinds of cultural and intellectual activities. His versatility echoes that of the priest Pavel Florensky, an outstanding Orthodox thinker of the early

Figure 4 Aleksandr Men.

[78] In contrast to the official Russian Orthodox Church, controlled by the Soviet authorities, the Catacomb Church or "Russian True Orthodox Church" remained underground from the late 1920s to the end of the Soviet period.

twentieth century who died in one of Stalin's concentration camps. More remarkable still was Father Men's missionary work, an activity that was almost unheard of among Orthodox priests, since in prerevolutionary times Orthodoxy had enjoyed the official sanction of the state, and that during the Soviet period was forbidden, rendering proselytization practically impossible. For over two decades, Father Men practiced his missionary work surreptitiously and under the oppressive scrutiny of the KGB. It was only with the arrival of perestroika that he emerged as the most prominent preacher in Russia, making many public addresses and appearing frequently on television. Father Men's rise in popularity brought him the corresponding antipathy of nationalist and conservative Orthodox circles, for whom his Jewish origin and his openness to ecumenical movements made him an object of suspicion and hatred. On September 9, 1990, he was assassinated while walking to church to serve the Sunday liturgy. His martyrdom intensified the spiritual impact of his message, which was most strongly felt among the Moscow intelligentsia, thousands of whom had converted to Orthodoxy on the basis of his erudite and persuasive sermons and books.

Christianity as Historical Synthesis

Aleksandr Men was an extremely prolific writer, whose life was devoted to the completion of a project he had conceived in his youth: a seven-volume treatise on the religious evolution of humankind, titled *In Search of the Way, the Truth, and the Life*. In its scope and consistency, this work is a unique phenomenon, not only in Russia, but worldwide. Its subject matter spans the whole history of world religion prior to Christianity and encompasses various religions of the East and West, including primitive animism and magism, pagan cults of Greece and Rome, Indian and Chinese religions, and the faith of the Bible prophets. For Men, Christianity is not so much opposed to these "false" religions, but should be viewed as the crowning synthesis of their many trials and insights. "In Christianity, a long worldwide historical process of humanity's religious quest found consummation."[79] Thus Christianity may be appropriately understood not only in the narrow historical context of Judaism and

[79] Aleksandr Men', *Istoriia religii v 7 tomakh. V poiskakh puti, istiny i zhizni* (Moscow: Izdatel'stvo Sovetsko-Britanskogo sovmestnogo predpriiatiia SLOVO, 1991), 1: 9. Other volumes of this seven-volume treatise, most of them first published in Brussels by the "Zhizn' s Bogom" publishing house under Men's pseudonym of E. Svetlov, include *Magizm i edinobozhie* (1971), *U vrat molchaniia. O dukhovnoi zhizni Kitaia i Indii* (1971), *Dionis, Logos, Sud'ba. Grecheskaia religiia i filosofiia* (1972); *Vestniki Tsarstva Bozhiia. Bibleiskie proroki (VIII–IV vv. do R.X.)* (1972); *Na poroge Novogo Zaveta* (1983); *Syn Chelovecheskii* (pseudonym A. Bogoliubov) (1969). Other books by Aleksandr Men include: *Tainstvo, slovo i obraz* (Brussels, 1980); *Kak chitat' Bibliiu* (Brussels, 1981); and *Russkaia religioznaia filosofiia. Lektsii* [1989–90] (Moscow: Khram Kosmy i Damiana, 2003). Books available in English: Fr. Aleksandr Men, *Russian Religious Philosophy: 1989–1990 Lectures*, trans. Fr. S. Janos (Mohrsville, PA: Frsj Publications, 2015); Alexander Men, *The Wellsprings of Religion*, vol. 1 of *The History of Religion: In Search of the Way, the Truth, and the Life*, trans. Alasdair MacNaughton (Yonkers, NY: St. Vladimir's Seminary Press, 2018); and Father Alexander Men, *Son of Man: The Story of Christ and Christianity*, trans. Samuel Brown (Huntsville: Oakwood Publications, 1998).

Hellenism, but against the backdrop of the whole history of world religion. Men explains the purpose of his magnum opus: "[T]he entire cycle can be regarded as an attempt at religious-philosophical and historical synthesis."[80] Men's treatment of these diverse traditions is marked by a profound sympathy, as he endeavors to find within each the core of authentic religious experience, rather than disparage them, as would the conventional Orthodox approach, as perverse or mistaken. At the same time, Men manages to maintain his Orthodox values, refusing to water down his own firm commitment with syncretic or pantheistic ambivalence. Moreover, he believes that Christianity, in spite of its two thousand years of history, is still in the early stages of a ferment that will transform the world. Christianity retains too many pre-Christian prejudices, such as authoritarian intolerance, abstract otherworldliness, and ritualistic formalism and dogmatism. Christianity has a great religious history behind it and even greater historical perspectives ahead. To study the history of religion, therefore, means both to recognize Christianity's debt to its spiritual predecessors and to project into the future a refined Christianity that will increasingly begin to discover its own unique nature.

Religion and Science

Men's discursive strategy is unusual for an Orthodox scholar, as he relies heavily on contemporary science. Citing abundantly from outstanding figures in the fields of physics, biology, medicine, paleontology, and archeology, Men tailors his arguments to an audience educated in scientific atheism. For him, nature is as revelatory a text as the Bible. Thus does Men cite deficiencies in Darwin's theory of evolution to emphasize the inordinately rapid development of the human species, which, in this view, cannot be accounted for by natural selection. He also seeks to overturn the Freudian explanation of religion as suppressed desire, suggesting that this sort of explanation would be more appropriately applied to such atheistic cults as those that surrounded Stalin and Mao—expressions of a suppressed desire for communion with God.[81]

Among the sciences that Men treated as a natural source of revelation, anthropology and paleontology were most important for him, because, since Marx and Darwin, these disciplines offered some of the most persuasive arguments against religion. The Marxist conception of man (as opposed to animal) as in effect a product of labor[82] seems contradictory to Men, who cites Engels on the subject: "An animal only uses external nature … whereas man, through the changes he introduces into nature, makes her serve his goals, dominates her. This is the last essential difference between man and other animals, and by this difference man is also obliged to labor."[83] Men finds

80 Men', *Istoriia religii v 7 tomakh*, 1: 11.

81 Ibid., 15.

82 In his well-known fragment "The Part Played by Labor in the Transition from Ape to Man" (1876), Friedrich Engels asserts: "In a sense, we have to say that labor created man himself." https://www.marxists.org/archive/marx/works/1876/part-played-labour/

83 Men', *Istoriia religii v 7 tomakh*, 1: 98.

here a vicious circle: if a man has his own conscious goals which his labor serves, then without these goals there is no genuine labor. Marx himself observed that the result of labor is present ideally in the mind of the laborer before it is achieved in practice, as distinct from bees or spiders. This means that consciousness precedes labor, and is not its product. Thus, a purely economic approach to the phenomenon of human civilization is insufficient for the task of explaining the advent of consciousness, which requires a religious interpretation.

Men's theological interests were multifarious. One of his books, *Sacrament, Word, and Image*, deals with the rituals of the Orthodox liturgy. Another, *How to Read the Bible*, concerns the process of scriptural exegesis. His last completed work was a three-volume *Bibliological Dictionary*, an encyclopedia of biblical scholarship that contains 1790 entries on biblical theology and criticism, on prominent theologians and scholars, Church writers and historians, translators and publishers. Compiled from an Orthodox point of view, the dictionary, on which Men worked for over a decade, takes into account all the achievements of modern biblical scholarship.[84]

The Church and the World

Men recognized the existence of thousands of "anonymous Christians" or those who behave according to Christian morality without expressly professing a religious allegiance. However, he firmly believed in the necessity of explicit conversion, since, when it comes to faith, both extreme liberalism and extreme conservatism represent stumbling blocks on the road to God. On the one hand, conservative intolerance precludes the possibility of embracing all souls, while on the other, overly liberal standards for worship may gloss over the need for spiritual growth and commitment. A conservative standard locates God exclusively within the Church, thus denying the relevance of secular disciplines for the attainment of religious enlightenment. But a liberal standard is also detrimental, insofar as its relativism prevents it from recognizing that certain paths to God are more revealing than others. Although Men sought to find a middle ground between these poles, the predominant conservative tendency in Orthodoxy made him seem like an extreme liberal. Men did not want to efface the distinction between the Church and the world, but he did hope to broaden the scope of the Church in order that it might accommodate the best achievements of culture and science. To his followers who in the fever of newfound faith attempted to abandon their prestigious secular professions in favor of "simple" labor, like yard maintenance or domestic work, he preached the value of cultural achievement and scientific advancement as important ways of knowing God. His ideal was an "open Church," reuniting all branches of Christianity and embracing the secular treasures of humanity.

[84] Aleksandr Men', *Bibliologicheskii slovar'* (Moscow: Fond imeni Aleksandra Menia, 2002). Available electronically: https://imwerden.de/pdf/men_bibliologihesky_slovar_tom1_2002.pdf; https://imwerden.de/pdf/men_bibliologihesky_slovar_tom2_2002.pdf; https://imwerden.de/pdf/men_bibliologihesky_slovar_tom3_2002.pdf

Another point of departure from convention was his emphasis on spiritual joy over suffering. Men himself was often accused by detractors of being too joyful, but, in his view, this optimism was not merely a matter of personal disposition but was the best mode of Christian life. Christ suffered and died on the cross not so that his followers would continue to suffer after him, but to release them from the pain of sin and retribution and endow them with the joy of liberation. Sorrow is indicative of an incomplete understanding of the Christian message of love, redemption, and resurrection. Joy is Christ's gift to humanity and is indispensable to true faith.

The Problem of Evil and Theodicy

Despite the diversity of his interests, Men's central preoccupation was not liturgy or exegesis, but apologetics. Historically, this theological discipline was superseded with the ascendency of Christianity as a world religion; however, in Soviet Russia it acquired a renewed importance, since most of the population was brought up in a climate of atheism. Father Men declared very definitely that the existence of God cannot be argued rationally, but he employed every possible historical and scientific angle to argue the compatibility of religious belief with a rational worldview. He identified his position as "mysticism grounded in common sense." For him, the greatest achievement of reason is the recognition of its own limitations. Thus, Men identifies two varieties of reason: one specific and instrumental; the other comprehensive, in that it contains its own self-criticism. This latter "Great Reason," which recognizes the domain of intuition, is the foundation of theological knowledge.

> The essential difference between philosophy and dogmatic symbols must be kept in mind. Although philosophy relies on intuition, formally … it deals with ideas, not realities. The dogmatic symbol is a different matter. It cannot be deduced by the intellect, though it is expressed in the language of concepts. This is why those who ascribe the creation of the Orthodox credo to Greek rationalism are deeply mistaken …. In general, fundamental Christian dogmas are marked by intrinsic contradictions, paradoxes, and antinomies that cannot be done away with by the methods of formal logic. If the dogmas were the fruits of philosophical speculation, they would be free of these contradictions.[85]

One such contradiction can be stated as follows: if God is perfect, then why did He create an imperfect world? In answering this question, Men applies the Christian concept of kenosis, or self-emptying, which is close to the Judaic notion of God's self-contraction.

> Christianity teaches that any act of God in His relationship to the world is His self-restriction or, as the Fathers of the Church used to say, the "belittling" of the

[85] Men', *Istoriia religii v 7 tomakh*, 1: 77.

> Absolute. It is kenosis that leaves room for the freedom of creatures …. The only thing that lies beyond any explanation is the impulse for resistance to God; it is irrational by its nature.[86]

Thus God's primary qualities are generosity and self-sacrifice, first demonstrated in the act of creation and then with the deliberate martyrdom of his only son. Evil, then, is born of the abuse of the freedom granted to people by God, and an evil act is therefore a matter of taking advantage of God's generosity. What was bestowed upon humanity as a gift is mistakenly asserted as the unlimited license for egoistic self-assertion and self-aggrandizement.

According to Men, there are two principal non-Christian metaphysics of evil. The first, a monistic, Hinduist conception, ascribes evil to the Absolute itself, which creates a world of illusion because of its own deficiencies; these will be eliminated only at the end of time. The second is a dualistic, Manichaean model, which asserts the primordial coexistence of equally powerful good and evil divinities, neither of whom can be Absolute. Men argues that Christianity recognizes the partial validity of both conceptions, but situates evil not within God, nor in some anti-God, but in the sphere of creation. By endowing his creatures with free will, the generous God opens the possibility for evil action, but at the same time the possibility of its elimination through the autonomous commitment of these free beings. Thus evil can be understood only in the dynamic process of its rise and fall, which comprises the meaning of human history. The principal distinction of Christianity is that it looks at evil not as a self-sufficient substance, but as a moment of human self-determination that opens the historic perspective of evil's gradual overcoming.

Arguments against Atheism and Materialism

Men supported the concept of "ur-monotheism" (in Russian, *pramonoteizm*; in German, *Urmonotheismus*), which was outlined by Vladimir Solovyov and elaborated in detail by Wilhelm Schmidt (1880–1954) in his twelve-volume treatise *The Origin of the Idea of God*. Contrary to the conventional view that monotheism arose on the bones of polytheism, the theory of ur-monotheism concludes that even in the most primitive tribes, there is a vague idea of a unique and universal god. Schmidt provided abundant ethnographic evidence in support of this hypothesis. According to Men, this primordial monotheism was later distorted by a movement toward polytheism and magism, the belief that certain rituals can endow a person with the key to domination over nature and even over the gods themselves. This tendency evolved into the modern "religions" of materialism and technology, which also attempt to control nature and the human spirit through the implementation of certain technical or political procedures. Idol worship is the common feature of the paganist and materialist worldviews.

[86] Ibid., 81.

"Primitive paganism created the prototype of the totalitarian structure."[87] Even the most sophisticated atheist cannot do without creating other gods to replace the single God he rejects, because the need for belief is deeply ingrained in human nature. Atheism engenders its own beliefs, for example, the cult of heroes and leaders, the concepts of goodness and justice, etc., but considers them subjective predispositions ungirded by any spiritual reality. In Men's view, no one would contest that our bodily necessities derive from objective facts—thirst is not something purely subjective, but relates to the material existence of water. Thus if man has for millennia strived to find good, beauty, and something higher than himself, would it be correct to identify such aspirations with self-deception, or is there some invisible reality that corresponds to this spiritual thirst?

Men refutes the arguments usually cited by materialists against religion. One of these maintains that the immortality of spirit beyond the body is difficult to visualize and cannot be confirmed by experiment. But even for rigorous science, which constructs an abstract world of numerals and elementary particles, the non-visualization argument does not hold up. Another argument is a moral one, which insists that belief in another world weakens human will, distracting people from their earthly destination. However, very few holy books devote much space to discussions of the beyond, but instead focus on one's activities in this world, the importance of which is intensified by their definitive implications for one's posthumous fate. A third argument holds that faith in immortality is only a consolation invented because of the human fear of death. Men responds by saying that death as nonbeing holds no fear, and to the contrary, such religious versions of the afterlife as were held in the ancient East or Greece were full of horror and could in no way be confused with consolations. Religion is not designed to sweeten human life, but rather to awaken it from the temptations of temporary illusion, to foreground the far more frightening true reality. This is why, according to Men, most of the greatest thinkers and scientists, from Plato to Bergson to Teilhard de Chardin, attempted to clarify the human mind in order to substantiate the idea of immortality.

God and the World. Creationism and Evolutionism

Teilhard de Chardin (1881–1955), the Catholic philosopher, priest, and paleontologist who founded contemporary Christian evolutionism, is probably the figure closest to Men in twentieth-century religious philosophy. Men is primarily attracted to Teilhard's synthesis of theology and the natural sciences and his conception of the incessant evolution of the world from elementary physical structures, through the biological and psychological refinement of living matter, and finally to the "omega point" of highest complexity and spirituality. God's love is the spiritual center of the universe, and is both its teleological and material cause. Characteristically for an Orthodox thinker, however, Men finds some flaws in this comprehensive model of cosmogenesis. First of

[87] Ibid., 164.

all, the creative energy of matter, which in Teilhard is immanently imbued with divine energies, leaves room for pantheistic interpretations and does not sufficiently explain the radical distinction between the world and God. Evolutionism should not substitute for creationism, which presupposes the primordial transcendence of God vis-à-vis the universe, and the latter's creation from nothingness. Secondly, this immanentism has a tendency to ignore the moral problem of evil, since if God's will is present in the entirety of living matter and in all stages of human evolution, then evil must either be attributable to God (which is contrary to his definition) or excluded altogether from the divine plan of evolution. For his part, Teilhard explains evil as the marginal effect of "the game of large quantities," that is, the overall scheme of evolution cannot help victimizing various particular individuals. This naturalistic interpretation of evil as an element of chaos in the increasing harmony of the universe misses the decisive point of Christian ethics: free will. According to Men, evil should be explained in moral rather than natural terms, as the consequence of primordial sin and man's deliberate fall from grace. Again, Christian theology, however receptive it is to the natural sciences and the concept of evolution, preserves its Orthodox authenticity only by positing the radical difference of God from the world and of man from God. The world was created by God and thus remains distinct from God, with the freedom to challenge his will; creationism, as an ontological conception, is, therefore, necessarily connected with the moral conception of primordial sin.

Men's own thinking vacillates between the evolutionary mode, so attractive in terms of naturalistic theodicy, and the creationist mode, which is far more compatible with the principles of Orthodox ethics. At the same time, he finds a characteristically Orthodox concept that can be related to evolutionism, remarking that "Teilhard is very close to those Orthodox thinkers who regarded the whole world as a Theophany (a manifestation of God)."[88] Another Orthodox concept that Men relates to Chardin is *theosis* or "deification," which in the teachings of the Eastern Church fathers designates the spiritual path of the transformation of human nature and the revelation of divine nature within it. Theophany and *theosis* are the two complementary processes by which God and man encounter one another. The two natures, however, should not be confused; there exists an impassable boundary between them, which can be explicated in the traditional Orthodox distinction between God's essence and God's energies. While essence is absolutely transcendental and remains hidden from the world, energies act in the world and organize its material structure. Theophany, therefore, cannot be separated from kenosis: as God manifests himself, his energy, in the world, his divine essence is progressively drained, sacrificially emptied. In other words, we cannot perceive the relationship between God and the world except through the figure of Christ, the God-man who manifested the godhead in the world and emptied his divine nature through suffering and crucifixion. The ontological problem cannot be divorced from the ethical one: the manifestation of God in the world is simultaneously an act of creation (with respect to the first hypostasis, the Father) and an act of suffering

[88] Aleksandr Men', "O Teiare de Shardene," *Voprosy filosofii*, no. 12 (1990): 101.

and sacrifice (in the hypostasis of the Son). Creation and suffering, theophany and kenosis, are indivisible and incommensurable, like the two hypostases of God, or like the Old and New Testaments.

It would be difficult to single out in Men's legacy one particularly original idea that could be made the foundation of a coherent system. His teachings centered not on an idea but the living and holistic experience of Christ, and he sought to marshal every idea that could convey this experience. In this he was similar to his spiritual teacher, Vladimir Solovyov, to whom he dedicated his magnum opus on the history of religions. The following description of Solovyov, made by his friend the philosopher Nikolai Trubetskoi, is equally applicable to Father Men as well: "He is a Christian believer, but this doesn't keep him from finding elements of positive revelation, not only in Islam, but also in all kinds of pagan religions of the East and West. A philosopher-mystic, he nevertheless valorizes the relative truth contained in rationalist and empiricist teachings."[89]

Aleksandr Men's theological synthesis may become an inspirational impetus for the new ecumenical life of Orthodox Christianity, just as the philosophical synthesis of Vladimir Solovyov served the same ecumenical goals at the end of the nineteenth century. From the mid-1980s on, Men was by far the most popular and influential Christian leader and preacher in Russia. He was one of the founders of the Russian Bible Society in 1990, the Open Orthodox University, and the journal *The World of the Bible*. Dozens of books have been devoted to his life and legacy, many of them memoirs written by his disciples and godchildren.[90]

In one of his essays, Aleksandr Men reminds readers that Peter the Great, despite all his worldly power over the largest country in the world, suffered from a phobia of open spaces. "He built himself tiny little rooms. There is an illness like that—the fear of open spaces. In the history of religion, there is also this fear of open spaces."[91] It was precisely Men's aim to overcome this dogmatic fear, to make the space of Christianity as open as possible to Russia and the world.

9. The Generation of Neophytes and Theological Innovations

The 1970s and early 1980s in the Soviet Union was a time of rapprochement between the intelligentsia and religion. It may be seen as a period of personal conversions that preceded the society-wide turn to religious revival in the following decade. This new experience had a decisive impact on the religious thought of the 1980s. Whereas the older generation of religious thinkers had been raised as believers, the overwhelming majority of the new generation came to Christianity in adulthood, from diverse

89 E. N. Trubetskoi, *Mirosozertsanie Vl. S. Solov'eva* (Moscow: Izdanie avtora, 1913), 1: 27–8.

90 In English, the most comprehensive account of Men's life and work is Daniel Wallace, *Russia's Uncommon Prophet: Father Aleksandr Men and His Times* (DeKalb, IL: Northern Illinois University Press, 2016).

91 Alexander Men, *Christianity for the Twenty-First Century: The Prophetic Writings of Alexander Men*, ed. and trans. Elizabeth Roberts and Ann Shukman (London: Continuum, 1996), 167.

ideological and professional backgrounds. These thinkers were far more attuned to contemporary lines of discourse, such as existentialism and postmodernism, and they endeavored to justify the relevance of the Christian faith against a backdrop of cultural relativism.

In his book *Coming to Church*, the Moscow philologist Vladimir Zelinsky (b. 1942) describes the variety of these new Christians, who strikingly combine contemporary sensibilities with a religious outlook:

> A talented mathematician, an expert in patristics, the owner of an excellent library of Russian religious philosophy; or a psychiatrist, engaged in incessant prayer; or an artist, yesterday an alcoholic, now preparing to enter the theological seminary; or a computer programmer, ready at any moment to deliver lectures on the liturgy; or a theoretical physicist deeply immersed in Orthodox asceticism.[92]

This phenomenon precipitated new complications in the relationship between believers and the Church, which had been traditionally alienated from the professional interests of parishioners. Many of the new Christians were of a pro-Western orientation, but when they emigrated to the West they encountered further complications, since Western intellectuals turned out to be, on the whole, even more suspicious of religion than the Russian Orthodox Church was suspicious of intellectuals.

Another common feature of the late-Soviet Russian Orthodox neophytes was the conviction that Christianity was integral to the profile of the cultured person. "Being a Christian and being cultivated were thought to amount to virtually the same thing."[93] It was through culture, not through the Church or family traditions, that so many Soviet intellectuals found their way to religion. In the previous chapters, we have discussed how culture is "justified" from the Christian point of view. But for the "newly converted," Christianity is in turn justified from the cultural standpoint; moreover, any progression in culture inevitably brings one to the doors of the Church. For example, neither Gogol, nor Dostoevsky, nor Tolstoy would make much sense to a person unfamiliar with the Gospels or the lives of the saints. Atheism proved to be disorienting and inimical to culture, since it attempted to sever it from its spiritual roots. The Soviet system paid lip service to the "treasury of world culture," but rendered this treasure vapid by suppressing its religious content. "Culture that is authentic in its being can only be Christian culture, since only the Church is capable of embodying the ontological essence of human culture, its hidden impetus, its 'secret engine'—the transfiguration [*preobrazhenie*] of the world that has been promised to mankind."[94] Zelinsky means that culture is only the symbolic transfiguration of the world, and thus finds its existential foundation in Christianity, where such transfiguration is accomplished in the flesh, in reality, not just in a verbal or visual presentation.

92 Vladimir Zelinskii, *Prikhodiashchie v tserkov'* (Paris: La Presse Libre, 1982), 14.

93 Tatiana Goricheva, *Talking about God Is Dangerous: The Diary of a Russian Dissident* (New York: Crossroad, 1987), 48.

94 Zelinskii, *Prikhodiashchie v tserkov'*, 155.

a. Postmodernist Perspectives on Christianity. Tatiana Goricheva

Tatiana Goricheva (b. 1947) was representative of this "new wave" of Christian intellectuals. She pursued a philosophical education at Leningrad State University, where one of her most influential teachers was Boris Paramonov.[95] Initially, she specialized in (and sympathized with) German and French existentialism, and even corresponded with Martin Heidegger. Soon after her conversion to Orthodoxy in 1974, she became one of the leading members of the Russian feminist movement, as the editor of the journals *Woman and Russia* and *Maria*. In 1980, she was forced to emigrate and settled in Paris, where she founded the philosophical and religious journal *Conversation* (1983–91), probably the only periodical of the 1980s to combine religious devotion with an interest in the philosophical and cultural problems of postmodernity.

Goricheva came to Christianity from the ranks of dissident intellectuals, whose search for political freedom led them far beyond the boundaries of politics. In her own words, "[t]he dissidents have begun by freeing personality. The new Christians have to go one stage further. Now that they have overcome their anxiety and despair they no longer shape their life according to the principle of resistance. They discover other values, positive and creative."[96] While dissidents valued freedom *from* (the state, police, censorship, etc.), Christians aspire to the freedom *for* (love, brotherhood, salvation).

From this point of view, Western "freethinking" intellectuals prove to be incorrigible "lifelong" dissidents who have attained every kind of "freedom from" but have not the slightest idea of what to do with it. In her numerous articles and essays, Goricheva sharply criticizes Western civilization from the standpoint of a Christian. Her disillusionment began when she discovered that most of the Western intellectual movements that had inspired her in Russia, including feminism, were decidedly antireligious. She characterizes the spiritual climate in the West as "post-nihilistic," by which she means that it is completely indifferent to spiritual values, lacking even the commitment and inspiration of nihilism. The "death of God" led not to the triumph of natural man—to which Nietzsche and other nihilistic rebels had aspired—but rather to the death of both man and nature. Now nothing remains against which to rebel; everything is permitted—if not by law, at least by contemporary moral standards. And this drives people to a state of indifference.

Goricheva gives the example of nudism, emphasizing that the circumstance of utmost exposure strips the body of its natural seductiveness.

> Nowadays people strip themselves not because they want to tempt anybody. To the contrary, nudism attests that the body has lost its erotic aura. It is no longer connected with soul and beauty, with the world of glances and attractions. People

[95] See the chapter "The Paradoxalist Boris Paramonov. Sexual Liberation against Nationalism," in Epstein, *The Phoenix of Philosophy*, 142–8.

[96] Goricheva, *Talking about God Is Dangerous*, 45.

are not ashamed of their ugliness because they are indifferent to the opinion of others. Contemporary beaches have become a little parody of paradise.[97]

Goricheva condemns the false innocence that is attained not through repentance but through the abandonment of shame. People imagine that, with the abolition of transcendental values, they will enjoy the fullness of earthly existence, but the result is a weakening of corporeal intensity. Thus Western civilization has lost not only its spiritual depth but also its aspect of vitality, which is maintained and articulated through its tension with asceticism.

Goricheva uses concepts elaborated within postmodern philosophy to criticize its moral vacuum, which she calls cynicism, following Peter Sloterdijk's *The Critique of Cynical Reason* (1983). Born of boredom, which resembles hell, this cynicism is inspired by the devil, whose depiction in Dostoevsky's *The Brothers Karamazov* Goricheva endorses, writing, "he is devoid of the creative element, all his abominations and crimes contain nothing new."[98] Cynicism does not counterpose anti-values to values; instead it is a kind of apathy that, in Oscar Wilde's famous formulation, knows the price of everything but gives value to nothing.

However, amid this overwhelmingly negative landscape of contemporary civilization, Goricheva sees a path for a religious justification of post-nihilism. If the higher forms of civilization, religion and art, have lost their meaning—the churches reducing themselves to mere community centers, and art becoming the hyperreal reproduction of meaningless reality—then the lower echelons of reality have assumed a spiritual depth they had previously been denied. "The most brilliant things are the most ordinary things, which are by definition serial, imitative, reproductive. We find them in the prosthetic artifacts of contemporary civilization: empty cans, used bus tickets, old advertisements, and so on. It was Nietzsche who remarked that in our civilization only small things turn out well."[99] Goricheva explains this phenomenon with reference to the process of kenosis, the emptying of Christ's divine nature, which departed from higher realms of existence in order to imbue the trivial aspects of this world with grace. This is why photography today is more spiritual than painting: precisely because it is superficial by nature, it has more depth of meaning. It is not by chance that the shroud of Turin, which became the prototype of all holy iconography, may be considered the first photograph. Christ's divinity was not only manifested in his human body with his birth, but was also transmitted to the materiality of cloth upon his death—thus can the mundane objects of the world become increasingly significant, even as they become more and more worthless in human terms.

The same transformation can occur with cynicism, if it is understood as a prototype of "holy foolishness" (*iurodivost'*). Goricheva asserts that although cynicism in itself is the highest degree of ignorance, it harbors the potential for holiness insofar as it

[97] T. Goricheva, "Epokha post-nigilizma," *Beseda. Religiozno-filosofskii zhurnal* (Leningrad-Paris), no. 4 (1986): 185.

[98] T. Goricheva, "Tsinizm, iurodstvo i sviatost'," *A-Ia* (Paris), no. 1 (1985): 118.

[99] Goricheva, "Epokha post-nigilizma," 192.

challenges conventional values. She refers to ancient, Diogenic cynicism, which opposed the collective cynicism of social life via an individual, "schizophrenic" protest. In this sense, the ancient cynics are

> the predecessors of the ascetics and holy fools of Christianity. Their love of insulting people and being insulted, their sheer indifference to food, clothing, habitation, their nakedness—all this makes them close to holy fools .... Holy fools, like cynics, are completely liberated from common sense and all of life's conventions .... They are indecent to such a degree that they may be enlisted as Rabelaisian characters. They are grotesque and sometimes seem, as did the cynics, like animals.[100]

However, holy fools, as revered in the Russian religious tradition, are distinct from the ancient cynics in that they submit to the will of God and the Church. For Goricheva, "the victory over cynicism, boredom, and death is possible only through holiness. There is no more interesting and enigmatic person in this world than a saint."[101] In other words, classical cynicism makes for an interesting alternative in a society steeped in conventional values. But when cynicism itself becomes conventional, it is the saint who really stands out. The concept of the holy fool connects these two poles of spirituality and rejects conventional cynicism on the basis of a deeper cynicism, which takes as its point of reference the mystery of the other world. In Goricheva's interpretation, the saint becomes a kind of carnivalesque hero who reverses social values so radically that his or her position acquires a transcendental dimension. Her vision of the holy fool may be compared with Harvey Cox's carnivalesque interpretation of Christ as a harlequin in his famous book *The Feast of Fools: A Theological Essay on Festivity and Fantasy* (1969).

Thus, Goricheva's Christian conversion and her subsequent encounter with Western civilization resulted in a critique of secular (im)morality, but also led her to deemphasize the role of the Orthodox Church hierarchy in favor of "creative Christianity," as exemplified in the figure of the holy fool, antagonistic to both the materialism of Western civilization and the conservatism of the Russian Orthodox tradition. This innovative theological trend relied in part on German philosophy of life and existence (Nietzsche, Heidegger), but was also inclined to reinterpret Christianity through Bakhtin's theory of carnival and Berdiaev's radical eschatologism.

b. Christian Energetism. Sergei Khoruzhii

Another new trend in Orthodox philosophy focused on the theological legacy of the Eastern Church fathers. The best-known proponent of this attempt to reactivate a new philosophical-theological synthesis was Sergei Khoruzhii (in English also known as

[100] Goricheva, "Tsinizm, iurodstvo i sviatost'," 122. Characteristically, in her later work Goricheva became a leading animal rights advocate.

[101] Ibid., 123.

Horujy; 1941–2020). A scientist by education and employment (physics and mathematics), and the co-translator (with Viktor Khinkis) of the first full Russian edition of Joyce's *Ulysses*, he became famous for his critical interpretations of Russian religious philosophy. Unlike many contemporary thinkers, who rely on the legacy of the late nineteenth and early twentieth centuries, especially Vladimir Solovyov and Pavel Florensky, Khoruzhii is highly critical of this period, which he considers to be rife with distortions of the original Orthodox teachings. The latter, according to Khoruzhii, are grounded in hesychasm, the spiritual movement in Eastern Christianity that foregrounded mental asceticism and the search for divine quietness (Greek *hēsychia*) through the contemplation of God in uninterrupted prayer. These practices are focused on silence and include certain psychosomatic techniques of concentration, designed to "deify" (*obozhit'*) human nature. Hesychasm emerged in the Eastern monastic tradition in the fourth century; in the fourteenth century some of its practices were challenged as heresy, but it was defended in the works of the great Orthodox theologian Gregory Palamas, and was adopted by the Eastern Church. Following Vladimir Lossky's treatise on apophatic theology,[102] Khoruzhii finds parallels between hesychasm and the existentialist teachings of the twentieth century, such as the fundamental ontology of Martin Heidegger. Hesychasm reveals the ecstatic depth of human personality, which at any given moment is free to redefine its nature and its relationship to God, in much the same way as Heidegger's notion of *Dasein* ecstatically transcends the boundaries of the present world.

According to Khoruzhii, genuinely Christian philosophy would abandon such Platonic and neo-Platonic conceptions as "all-unity" and "the divine essence of man." It would focus instead on existential intercourse between man and God, meditating on such spiritual processes as prayer, repentance, grace, introspection, silence, the unification of mind and heart—those acts of free will that truly mediate between the human and divine as distinct entities. Thus, Platonic idealism will give way to Christian energetism. An important source for the existentialist reinterpretation of the Orthodox legacy is Gregory Palamas's differentiation of God's essence and energy, according to which essence is eternally predetermined, while energy manifests spontaneous volition and is revealed in God as grace, and in humanity as the free will to accept or reject this grace. The essentialist approach to God was emphasized by the Platonic and neo-Platonic legacy in Orthodox theology, which was later developed in Vladimir Solovyov's doctrine of "all-unity." According to this Christian Platonism, the unity of man and God is achieved objectively through the transformation of the universe and the progressive cognition of divine essences in the empirical world. Khoruzhii protests that this metaphysics of total unity gave a one-sided and distorted direction to Russian thought in the late nineteenth and early twentieth centuries, since it was based exclusively on Platonic constituents of Orthodox theology.

He defines his own task as a Palamist revival, based on the need to restore to Orthodoxy the principle of energy as the existential mode of relationship between

[102] Vladimir Lossky, *The Mystical Theology of the Eastern Church* (French original 1944) (London: J. Clarke, 1957).

man and God. He establishes direct connections between the practice of hesychasm, the theology of Palamas, and what he calls the "philosophy of Orthodox energetism."

> Freedom is the most important peculiarity of the energetic unification [of man and God], as distinct from unification through essence .... The organization and orientation of energies toward the reception of grace is spiritual work that man is free to do or not do: his freedom, along with grace, is an equally important factor in the cause of deification [*theosis*]. "Man has two wings in order to fly up to God: freedom and grace." (Maxim the Confessor)[103]

What is crucial, then, is not simply the energetic but "synergetic" approach in theology, which presupposes free collaboration and correspondence between the energy of two volitions, God's and man's. According to Khoruzhii, the notion of freedom in the theology of synergy is deeper than in secular or atheist existentialist doctrines: "[T]his is not the habitual freedom of choice between various decisions and actions limited by earthly being, but the freedom of ontological self-definition of one's own nature and essence in the broadest range—from nothing to God."[104] Khoruzhii quotes St. Macarius of Egypt (fourth c.), one of the founders of Orthodox monastic life: "You are free as God is free; and if you wish to perish, no one hinders you."[105] In Khoruzhii's view, the principle of energetism is the only reliable point where Russian philosophy can encompass the legacy of Orthodox dogmatics to produce a creative religious philosophy. It would be different from Solovyovian religious philosophy, which operates with notions of essences, norms, and ideals and is thus partly responsible for the totalitarian temptations of Russian thought. Platonism, even if integrated with Christian theology, ultimately leads to the result seen in Plato: to the construction of a social utopia that can be implemented only through the violent subordination of all society to the ideal of all-unity. The principle of synergy does not expound any fixed, collective ideals, but reveals the free cooperation of human and divine volitions on the existential plane.[106]

[103] Sergei Khoruzhii, "Problema lichnosti v pravoslavii: mistika isikhazma i metafizika vseedinstva," *Zdes' i teper'. Filosofiia, literatura, kul'tura* (Moscow), no. 1 (1992): 97.

[104] Ibid., 98–9.

[105] Ibid., 99.

[106] The position of neo-hesychasm is expressed in many of Khoruzhii's works published since the early 1990s: "Filosofskii protsess v Rossii kak vstrecha filosofii i pravoslaviia," *Voprosy filosofii*, no. 5 (1991): 26–57; *Diptikh bezmolviia. Asketicheskoe uchenie o cheloveke v bogoslovskom i filosofskom osveshchenii* (Moscow: Tsentr psikhologii i psikhoterapii, 1991) (written in 1978); "Isikhazm i istoriia," *Chelovek* (Moscow), nos. 4–5 (1991). Khoruzhii would subsequently define his field of inquiry as "synergetic anthropology." A work of his available in English: Sergey S. Horujy, *Practices of the Self and Spiritual Practices: Michel Foucault and the Eastern Christian Discourse*, trans. Boris Jakim, ed. Kristina Stoeckl (Grand Rapids: Eerdmans, 2015). An excellent introduction to his philosophy is given in the chapter "Sergey Horujy and Synergic Anthropology" in Alyssa DeBlasio, *The End of Russian Philosophy: Tradition and Transition at the Turn of the 21st Century* (New York: Palgrave Macmillan, 2014), 106–16.

Thus even within Orthodox thought, the late Soviet period demonstrates a growing diversity of inner distinctions and controversies. One of them is connected with different perspectives on the relationship of religion and culture, or Church and world. The crucial question is this: should the Church preserve its distinction and purity from the secular world, or should it recognize the elements of grace and holiness in mundane life? Another, less social and more metaphysical line of division arises between essentialist and existentialist approaches to theology. The former is represented in the works of Aleksandr Men and maintains Vladimir Solovyov's emphasis on the divinely conceived objective harmony of the universe and its evolution toward the fullness of godmanhood. The latter, represented in Khoruzhii's writings, excavates the anti-Platonic, existentialist elements in the Orthodox legacy and underscores the dynamic and personalist aspects of the human-divine synergy.

Part III

Mysticism, Universalism, and Cosmism

1. General Features of Russian Mysticism

In spite of its official status as the state church in prerevolutionary Russia, Orthodoxy had occasion to compete with numerous Christian sects of a Protestant derivation, as well as with mystical and occult systems that had a syncretic religious orientation. Russian Protestantism, with the notable exception of Lev Tolstoy and his followers, never advanced any significant systems of thought, but Russian esotericism and syncretism would achieve world renown. From Russia came such famous prophets and teachers of modern mysticism and universalist wisdom as the founder of theosophy Helena Blavatsky (1831–91), the esoteric teachers Georgii Gurdjieff (1877–1949) and Peter D. Ouspensky (1878–1947), and Nicholas (1874–1947) and Helena (1879–1955) Roerich, who introduced the powerful Oriental mysticism of Agni Yoga into the spectrum of spiritual practices.

Russian-Soviet mysticism has several distinctive features. First and foremost, it usually represents a mixture of Christian and pagan mythological beliefs (the so-called *dvoeverie* or "dual faith"). Russian pre-Christian mythology, as is well known, survived only in scattered fragments after Russia was Christianized in 988, thus leaving open a large field for mystical conjectures regarding Russian deities and their continued impact on the country's fate. These mystical restorations of Russian paganism have rarely been openly anti-Christian, attempting, rather, to combine Orthodox tradition with archaic beliefs, or more precisely, with the restorers' notions of what these beliefs must have been.

Another important feature of Russian-Soviet mysticism is its interest in expanding not only to the depths of history, but also beyond geographical boundaries—its combination of national distinctiveness with universalist claims. Russia's location spanning Europe and Asia has fueled speculation about the global destiny of the Russian nation, which was to become a keeper of universal wisdom, blending the best spiritual illuminations of both West and East.

Russian-Soviet mysticism has a strong social orientation. Rarely does it lapse into the realm of highly subjective individual contemplation; it is offered far more typically as a new social teaching, meant to inspire the whole nation and provide a just resolution to the most agonizing problems of contemporary society. This is Russian mysticism's decidedly messianic style, which seeks to appeal to the masses and organize them into an ideal society.

At the same time, Russian-Soviet mysticism has a *cosmic* dimension. Not only the individual, but even society and the earth itself are seen as too constrained to realize the great visions of national prophets. Outer space, too, must be explored and colonized, and the multiplicity of invisible spiritual worlds must be penetrated.

Russian mysticism has always been closely connected with the specific features of Russian history, but has also aspired to *overcome* history, and has thus followed apocalyptic patterns. In this view, Russia can fulfill its historical destiny only by being the first *post-historical* nation, which is fated to experience all the suffering and illuminations imposed on the world by the struggle of Christ and Antichrist on Judgment Day.

Finally, Russian mysticism has included worship of the feminine spiritual essence of the universe and even the feminine hypostasis of the divine wholeness, Sophia, in such terms as the "eternal feminine" (*vechnaia zhenstvennost'*), the "soul of the world" (*dusha mira*), and "the companion of God" (*podruga Boga*).

All of these features, which can be traced separately through such prominent mystical and occult thinkers as Vladimir Solovyov, Nikolai Fedorov, Dmitrii Merezhkovsky, Nikolai Berdiaev, Pavel Florensky, Andrei Belyi, Velimir Khlebnikov, Konstantin Tsiolkovsky, the cosmists and Orientalists, are combined in the thought of Daniil Andreev—certainly the most important Russian mystic of the late Soviet period, and the one who gives the most explicit and integrated expression of the ideas of his predecessors.[1]

2. Religious Universalism and Metahistory. Daniil Andreev and *The Rose of the World*

Daniil Andreev (1906–59) was the son of the prominent prose writer and dramatist Leonid Andreev (1871–1919), whose works boldly and insistently plumbed the depths of the human soul. Daniil confessed that his father's writings remained alien to him: Leonid had been a symbolist and expressionist, inclined toward a decadence that was in part satanically tinged, whereas Daniil received a Christian upbringing and sought religious revelations throughout his intellectual development. In the 1920s, Daniil Andreev studied at the Higher School of Literature in Moscow. He later turned to graphic art, designing maps, fonts, and calligraphy styles, to earn a living at a job that also gave him time to pursue his writing, mostly at night. In the late 1930s, he began work on his mystical novel *Wanderers of the Night* and read it to a small group of Moscow intellectuals. The book's characters aspire to transform Russia spiritually: one of them designs a Temple of the World Sun at the site where, by a strange coincidence, the new main high-rise building of Moscow State University would be built ten years

1 An excellent survey of major trends in the occult, primarily in the early twentieth century and the Stalin period, is Bernice Glatzer Rosenthal, ed., *The Occult in Russian and Soviet Culture* (Ithaca: Cornell University Press, 1997).

Figure 5 Daniil Andreev.

later. Another character delivers a lecture on the alternation of "red" and "blue" epochs in Russian history; on how, in each blue epoch, a red underground movement develops, and vice versa. For example, the early twentieth century was a blue epoch with a red (politically left) underground, while the period after the October Revolution was a politically red epoch with a blue (mystical) undercurrent. Andreev would bring such lifelong visions together in *The Rose of the World.*

In 1947, when Andreev had almost completed *Wanderers of the Night*, he was arrested, accused of a terrorist plot against Stalin, and sentenced to twenty-five years' imprisonment; under Khrushchev's rule, this term was reduced to ten years. Andreev's final decade (1948–58) proved to be the most creative period of his life. It was in the Vladimir prison that he began to hear the voices that dictated his masterpiece, *The Rose of the World*, his only religio-philosophical treatise. Andreev spent these years "communicating" with the highest spirits inhabiting Russian and other national "metacultures" as he called them; Lermontov, Dostoevsky, and Blok "guided" him in his wanderings through other worlds. During this time, he wrote on tiny scraps of paper, which were invariably confiscated, but he restored his prose and verses from memory and continued to write. It was only after Stalin's death in 1953 that Andreev was given paper and ink and allowed to write on a regular basis. Together with his prison roommates, the biologist Vasilii Parin and the historian Lev Rakov, Andreev wrote an inventive and humorous "encyclopedia" about outstanding figures of the past of the authors' own invention.

A quiet, meek, rather taciturn man, Andreev was not capable of practical leadership, although he exhibited enormous moral courage during the years of his persecution. His religious faith, strong but unconstrained by Church dogmas, enabled him to resist Soviet political pressures. (Andreev, however, was not indifferent to Church doctrines: for him, to the contrary, it would come as a tremendous tragedy when an Orthodox priest would refuse to grant him holy communion before his death because he had confessed to believing in reincarnation.) Despite chronic illness and extreme poverty, in the two years after his release from prison (1957–8), Andreev managed to complete *The Rose of the World* and died several months later. His widow Alla Andreeva was the sole custodian of the only copy, but by the late 1970s, the book was circulating in samizdat and acquired many followers, who considered it the greatest mystical revelation of the twentieth century. The first complete edition was released in 1991.

a. The Spiritual System of the World

The Rose of the World is a multifaceted book that purports to explore the structure of all existing worlds, both visible and invisible, from paradise to hell. Many of its terms and expressions cannot be found in any language; they are defined in a glossary at the end of the book. These words, Andreev claims, were introduced into his consciousness by supernatural voices, and he rationalized them as signifying the principal elements of the transphysical universe. Andreev defined *bramfatura*, for example, as the system of various material levels that constitute celestial bodies. *Shadanakar* is the name of our own planet's *bramfatura*, which consists of a great number of planes (over 240) of different kinds of matter, with various dimensions of time and space. Most of these terms do not technically belong to any natural language, but Russian and especially Sanskrit roots may occasionally be discerned in them. To Andreev's admirers, the very fact of these neologisms, their absence in any otherwise extant tongue, indicates the genuine source of his mystical inspiration, comprehensible only through spontaneous contact with the highest spirits. In this view, Daniil Andreev's entire religio-mythological system is an emanation and elaboration of the hidden meanings of these primordial words.

To designate the philosophical foundation of his system, Andreev uses such concepts as "transphysical knowledge" and "metahistory." He recognizes a multiplicity of existing worlds that are material in nature, but evolve beyond the range of human physical experience. This "metarealist" vision is not to be confused with idealism (in the Platonic sense) or materialism, since metareality comprises a multiplicity of worlds, each with its own spiritual and material dimensions. "At the foundation of the conception of the Rose of the World lies the idea of a multilayered universe. Each layer is understood as a material world whose materiality differs from that of other worlds by a range of spatial or temporal coordinates."[2] In Andreev's view, this system allows him to escape the dilemma of having to choose between materialism and idealism. Materialism is oriented toward a single version of reality, which for Andreev represents only one petal in the densely layered Rose, whereas idealism presupposes a purely abstract realm rather than many alternative realities.

Andreev's epistemology is based on the possibility of transphysical knowledge, which penetrates the layers of materiality via personal insights and metempsychosis, or memories of past-life experience. Unlike conventional epistemology, which is based on a continuous and quantitative accumulation of knowledge, Andreev's system privileges transformative moments of knowledge, which are attained by inspiration, intuition, and revelation. Just as physical knowledge of the subatomic universe is obtained through momentary glimpses of particles via experimental accelerators, transphysical knowledge also demands instantaneous intensifications of experience, which are attained only through concentrations of mental energy that cannot be sustained for more than several moments. Thus can Andreev's epistemology be described as spontaneous, indeterministic, and intensive as opposed to conventional epistemology, which is accumulative and extensive.

Another aspect of transphysical knowledge is metahistory, which addresses the temporal dimension across the Rose's many realities. Metahistory is the "totality of processes flowing in those layers of other existence, which are immersed in different streams of time and different kinds of space, but sometimes reveal themselves through the process which we perceive as history" (31). Thus the metahistory of Russia, which is the focus of Andreev's book, exposes the spiritual dynamics underlying the events of Russian history. For example, the October Revolution is partly explained as the enslavement of the feminine spirit of Russia by the demon of great-power Russian statehood. Particular historical events appear as manifestations of a larger-scale process, which Andreev formulates as the struggle between God and Anti-God (*protivobog*), the spirit of universal evil.

Thus the history of every world in Andreev's *Rose* moves according to the grand scheme of an all-encompassing telos. This narrative, however, must not be understood as deterministic, because the ultimate fate of the world and the resolution of the strife between good and evil are dependent upon the free will of each human being. Andreev elaborates the Leibnizean concept of "monads"—"indivisible and immortal spiritual units, the supreme *I*'s of people … created by God and only by God, and some of them—very few—are mysteriously born of Him" (50). In this system, monads materialize in a *shelt*, a five-dimensional body, as well as in astral and ethereal bodies. Monads acquire transitory physical existences and sometimes change their material embodiments

[2] Daniil Andreev, *Roza Mira. Metafilosofiia istorii* (Moscow: Prometei, 1991), 44. This and all further quotations are in my translation; further citations in the text refer to this edition. The first half of the treatise (six books of twelve) have been published in English translation: Daniel Andreev, *The Rose of the World*, trans. Jordan Roberts (Hudson, NY: Lindisfarne Books, 1997). More recently, another translation of selections from the treatise has been produced: Daniel Andreev, *Rose of the World*, trans. Daniel H. Shubin (Bakersfield, CA: Peace Church Challenge, 2015).

according to their individual fates, surviving physical death and reincarnating into the multiple dimensions of other worlds. Andreev believes that even elementary particles are living entities endowed with free will, but that it is presently still impossible to communicate with them. Most essential is that all monads possess absolute freedom, since they were created in the image of God. "Thus the divine creativity imposes limitations on the Creator, it circumscribes His power with a line beyond which the freedom and power of His creatures lie" (49).

Thus the existence of evil in the world proceeds from monads' ability to defy their creator. The root of evil is egoism—the intention to include all other monads, or spiritual entities, in one's own self. Only God is capable of creating monads; the devil can only try to capture them. Evil is embodied in a planetary demon named Gagtungr who represents the local manifestation of Anti-God in our universe, and who possesses three separate and interrelated identities (an anti-Trinity): the great tormentor (the pseudo-Father), the great whore (the pseudo-Virgin), and the principle of form (the pseudo-Son). The struggle between Gagtungr and the planetary Logos, who was embodied in Christ, comprises the moving force of the history of the earth. History is the progressive development of the freedom of human will, which allows an individual monad to liberate itself from evil and its consequences.

The most difficult choice for a creature who has enjoyed the freedom of the negation of God is arriving at a free acceptance of God. According to Andreev, even Gagtungr, who throughout metahistory has pursued the extremes of God's negation, may freely choose to accept God if history is to achieve its eschatological completion. "If Gagtungr, remaining the only [refuser] in the jubilant and transformed Shadanakar [the metaworld of our planet] says finally, *Yes!* to Christ and God, then Shadanakar will enter the third aeon" (272). This passage occurs at the end of Andreev's book and demonstrates the consistency of its central theme—the resolution of the metahistorical process through the free will of God-created monads.

The Rose of The World consists of twelve large parts ("books"), each divided into several chapters. In the "Short Glossary" that concludes the entire work, the central concept has the following definition: the Rose of the World is

> the coming all-Christian Church of the last centuries that will integrate in itself the churches of the past and will connect, in a free union, all religions of Light. In this sense, the Rose of the World is inter-religious or pan-religious. Its main goal is to save as many human souls as possible and to deliver them from the danger of spiritual enslavement by the coming Anti-God [*protivobog*]. (274)

Andreev sees the task of his book as promoting the rapprochement of all religions that aspire to the spiritual unity of the world. Andreev's thinking has a "bud" structure, both pluralistic and centralized, with the eidos of the rose underlying his vision on every level: multiple worlds and multiple religions are alike viewed as petals. "If old religions are petals, then the Rose of the World is the flower" (13). *The Rose of the World* is the universal teaching of pan-religion, destined to fulfill the integration of humanity, a process begun by the formation of institutions like world religions, the

League of Nations, and the United Nations. "It is a worldwide arrangement of nations [*vsemirnoe narodoustroistvo*] that aspires to the sanctification and enlightenment of the whole life of the world" (16).

Andreev introduces the concepts of the supernation (*sverkhnarod*) and its metaculture, which exist simultaneously in many material layers. Supernations include the southwestern Roman Catholic supernation, the northwestern German Protestant supernation, the Russian Orthodox supernation, and so on. Each supernation creates its own transmyth as a specific vision of alternate realities, defining the collective identity of interconnected nations. These transmyths include such artistic creations as expresses the soul of the given supernation, such as Goethe's Faust and Margarita, and Shakespeare's Hamlet and King Lear.

A supernation is flanked by two metacultural realms. The upper layer, called *zatomis*, is the metacultural abode of a supernation's enlightened souls, holy cities, and heavenly spirits. The lower layer, called *shrastr*, is home to the concentrated demonic forces of the supernation. Olympus, Sinai, and Kitezh exemplify the transmythical images of the *zatomises* in the Greek, Jewish, and Russian metacultures, respectively. Andreev explains the lack of Russian terms in his description of transphysical worlds—already named in the languages of older metacultures, primarily the Indian one—with reference to Russia's relative youth.

From the seventh book on, the author presents a kind of cohesive metahistorical explanation of Russian history from its inception to the foreseeable future. In particular, Andreev focuses on the relationship between the "Christian myth" and "ur-Russianism" (*prarossianstvo*), the indigenous Russian paganism. This duality, inherent in Russian history, is exemplified in the contrast between the elegant and cheerful exteriors of Russian cathedrals and their dark and severe interiors. Further, Andreev interprets Russia's eastward and southward expansion and the assimilation of Siberia and the Far East as a great metahistorical event that fills in the space between Catholic, Muslim, Indian, and Buddhist cultures.

Returning to deep prophecies of Russian literature (especially in Lermontov and Blok) about the "dark shepherd," the future Antichrist, Andreev demonstrates their precursory embodiment in Stalin, who proved to be a far more successful manifestation of Gagtungr's demonic will than Lenin or Hitler. Andreev exposes the mystical motives of Stalin's behavior and his life beyond the grave at the very bottom of the world.

b. The Theocratic State of the Future and the Coming of the Antichrist

Andreev's treatise has three principal thematic aspects. One is the description of the transphysical worlds. Another is the elaboration of Russian metahistory. The third aspect is the intersection of transphysical and metahistorical perspectives—Andreev's vision of future humanity, where transphysical worlds will increasingly be incorporated into earthly history, ultimately putting an end to it by thrusting it into another aeon. Compositionally, the Rose of the World is the focus of the first and last books of the treatise.

Book Subject
1 The Rose of the World (mostly sociohistorical aspects)
2–6 Transphysical worlds
7–11 The metahistory of Russia
12 The Rose of the World (mostly futuristic and eschatological aspects)

According to Andreev, the birth of the Rose of the World is predetermined, though no one can predict exactly when it will appear. Andreev is critical of the doctrines of communism, but also identifies some of its positive aspects, in particular, its envisioned harmony of the physical and spiritual components of the personality, its perspective on the balanced coexistence of civilization and nature. The transformation of the earth, the melting of polar ice and snow, the irrigation of desert land into oases, a unified cosmopolitan state, centers of new religious culture, cities of faith, triumphal gardens, theaters of mysteries, houses of meditation, philosophical institutions—such are the components of Andreev's design for the Rose of the World.

The liturgy of the Rose of the World will include not only elements of traditional religious rituals, but also the spiritual aspects of the arts and literature and the sanctified elements of nature. The sacraments of birth, childhood, friendship, love, creativity, old age, and, most importantly, femininity will be performed in the temples of the future. Andreev foresees five hierarchies of priests that correspond to his newly conceived Trinity. The first hierarchy, that of the Father, will be golden; the second, of the Virgin Mother, will be blue; and the third hierarchy, of the Son, will be white. The fourth hierarchy's service will include pantheons that revere the greatest prophets and messengers of the given nation. Temples of physical "elementals" (*stikhiali*) and the fifth, green priesthood will preach the spirituality of nature.

The Rose of the World is not only the interdenominational church of the future, but also the supreme governmental authority in a united world, where all countries will be conjoined into one federation. Andreev endows the Rose of the World with all possible perfections, but his imagination, daring and ingenious as it is in penetrating transphysical realities, proves rather plain and simplistic when it comes to specifically envisioning a social utopia, which he describes in terms similar to those of Nikolai Chernyshevsky in his novel *What Is To Be Done?*, that is, as a "crystal palace of the future" of the sort lampooned by Dostoevsky in *Notes from Underground*. Andreev depicts splendid edifices of colored marble, surrounded by luxurious gardens, which serve simultaneously as temples and public buildings. Citizens of this unified state combine physical health and spiritual sublimity, and spend their lives in absolute bliss, no longer experiencing tragedy or suffering. Technical advancement has enabled them to master all of nature's dangerous forces and at the same time to live in harmony with their environment. This lofty view of the future is reminiscent of the most common features of many humanistic utopias, but has one characteristic that is jarringly discordant with the twentieth century: it is a *theocratic* utopia. Several hierarchies of priests govern all administrative, economic, and political activities of the citizens, and even science and literature are subject to the judgment of specific world councils, which censor them according to religious and moral guidelines.

Andreev calls the leader of the Rose the "supreme mentor" (*verkhovnyi nastavnik*) and ascribes to him a combination of

> the three greatest gifts: the gift of religious prophecy, the gift of moral virtuousness, and the gift of artistic creativity .... This would be the greatest happiness for the entire earth .... He is the mystical link between living humanity and the higher world, the manifestor of providential will, the perfector of billions, and the defender of souls. To unite in the hands of such a man the fullness of spiritual and civil powers is nothing to fear. (15–16)

Strikingly, the characterization of the supreme mentor is occasionally almost identical with Vladimir Solovyov's famous description of the Antichrist in one of his last works, "A Short Tale of the Antichrist" (1899–1900). Despite knowing this work well and often making reference to it, Andreev nonetheless fails to recognize the parallels between his own supreme mentor and Solovyov's Antichrist. Moreover, in his own description of the Antichrist, who in his system will eventually become the supreme mentor and destroy the Rose, Andreev emphasizes the same all-embracing perfection. His reader is thus left with an ambivalent impression: on the one hand, Andreev glorifies the Rose of the World as the ultimate achievement of religiously united humanity; on the other, he reveals, presumably unconsciously, the demonic subtext of this theocratic dream.

The Rose of the World will not prevent Satan's arrival. Thirst for power and sexual license will put an end to the golden age, by causing the collapse of social harmony. People will worship the anti-Logos as a rebellious hero against God's tyranny. This superior and universal genius, quickly rising to the pinnacle of the arts and sciences, will be the same monad whose rough draft was Stalin. He will perform such miracles that those of Christ will pale in comparison. Under his reign, the Rose of the World will be banned, all priests and parishes destroyed. Anti-humans will rise from beneath the earth's surface, and demonic beings of higher intellect—the inhabitants of the lower worlds—will rule humanity. Suddenly a catastrophe will overtake the anti-Logos, when his monad, which had been abducted by Gagtungr thousands of years ago, is liberated by the savior; the prince of darkness will fall through all the layers of hell into the timeless depths of the galaxy.

Unprecedented terror, confusion, and bloody chaos will follow the fall of Satan. There will be sadism, sexual cannibalism, world war between demons and people, and economic collapse as power devolves to local tyrants. Nature will become an arena for horrible catastrophes. Several dozen survivors of the Rose of the World, the brothers of the Light, will gather at a single place on earth, presumably in Siberia. At this time, Shadanakar will tremble from top to bottom, and Christ will manifest himself to everyone. Andreev suggests that Jesus Christ's mission was not fully carried out the first time; that is, his death on the cross represented a failure rather than triumph of God's will. The material element of nature and of humanity has not been enlightened on a worldwide scale, but only in the flesh of Christ himself. During the centuries since his resurrection, however, Christ's spiritual powers have increased immensely. He will descend to the lowest layers of the world, and will resurrect the remainders of all souls. During this second aeon, the worlds of retribution, including the so-called hell, will be expiated and will become empty.

Gagtungr, the great demon, will remain alone in the jubilant, transformed universe. If he will finally accept God, then the third aeon, the redemption of Gagtungr, will begin, and the entire Shadanakar will disappear from the physical dimension. "It is about the coming of the third aeon that the great angel of the Apocalypse swears that time will be no more" (272).

c. The Feminine in Russian Thought. Sophiology and Materialism

Among the wide range of social, moral, environmental, historical, and theological questions that Andreev addressed, one of the most prominent is the feminine element in the universe. Many Russian visionaries and intellectuals have emphasized the feminine element in Russian popular culture. The philosopher Georgii Fedotov argued that "at every step in studying Russian popular religion one meets the constant longing for a great divine female power."[3] According to Nikolai Berdiaev: "The religion of soil is very strong in the Russian people; it lies deep down in the very foundation of the Russian soul. The land is the final intercessor. The fundamental category is motherhood. The Mother of God takes precedence of the Trinity and is almost identified with the Trinity."[4]

This preoccupation with the feminine is conventionally explained partly by geographical and historical conditions: Russia's vast open plains are often compared metaphorically to a womb that must be safeguarded from foreign invasion; for centuries, Russia sustained itself as an agricultural society, which supported a corresponding mythological vision of the earth as a divine mother. Rural rituals of fertilizing the earth survived in Russia into the twentieth century. The very names *Rus'* and *Rossiia* are of feminine gender and lead quite naturally to such folkloric and poetic expressions as *matushka Rossiia* (Mother Russia) and *Rus'-zhena* (Rus' wife).

Not all the consequences of this gender mysticism have been investigated, especially with respect to its contemporary implications. Mythological relics of femininity and maternity remained relevant to twentieth-century Russia, despite its obsession with the revolutionary utopia. It is characteristic, however, that even in the most comprehensive and informative Western investigation of feminine themes in Russian culture, Joanna Hubbs's *Mother Russia* (1988), the ideology and practice of Russian communism are not considered at all. Hubbs does not even mention the Russian concept of *materiia*

3 G. P. Fedotov, *The Russian Religious Mind* (Cambridge, MA: Harvard University Press, 1946), 362. On the connection between Russia, Mother Earth, and the Virgin, see also Andrei Siniavskii, "Mat'-syra Zemlia i Bogomater'," in his *Ocherki russkoi kul'tury, 2. Ivan-durak. Ocherk russkoi narodnoi very* (Paris: Sintaksis, 1991), 181–92. "As an expression of universal Motherhood, the image of the Mother of God sometimes merges with or stands close by the Moist Mother Earth" (189).

4 Nikolai Berdyaev, *The Russian Idea*, trans. R. M. French (Hudson, NY: Lindisfarne Books, 1992), 24.

("matter"), though materialism, as a tenet of official Soviet ideology, is probably the most important outcome of this traditional worship of Russia as mother.

One often encounters the opinion that materialism was alien to the Russian mentality and was mechanically adapted from the Western European "scientific spirit" of the nineteenth century. According to this stereotype, Russians are a mystical people, so resistant to rational knowledge of the world that they refuse to rely on objective laws. Despite the kernel of truth in such characterizations, materialism should not be confused with rationalism or empiricism. Indeed, the "average," archetypal Russian is neither a rationalist nor empiricist, but nevertheless can be regarded as a materialist; and the most unyielding materialism does not preclude a proclamation of the mystic qualities of matter.

The Russian word *materiia* is broader and more philosophically loaded than the English "matter." The Academy of Sciences' dictionary of the Russian language defines *materiia* first as "the objective reality that exists beyond and independently of human consciousness," and second as "the substance of which the physical bodies of nature are composed."[5] Only the second meaning is equivalent to the English "matter." The Russian concept of *materiia*, therefore, has not only physical but metaphysical implications, presupposing the objective nature of matter and even its priority over consciousness, a tenet that constitutes the foundation of Soviet materialism (which in its turn certainly influenced the definitions of ideologically charged terms).

The Russian philosopher Aleksei Losev (1893–1988) argued that the entirety of Russian thought, even its religious components, has a deeply materialistic bias:

> Russian philosophy is first and foremost sharply and unconditionally *ontological* .... This ontologism, however, unlike in the West, accentuates matter, something characteristic of it since mystical antiquity. The very idea of divinity as it developed in the Russian Church foregrounds elements of corporeality (e.g., the doctrine of "Sophia," the "Wisdom of God"), which P. Florensky sees as particular to Russian as opposed to Byzantine Orthodoxy.[6]

It may be supposed that philosophical materialism proceeds from this "archaic mysticism," which claims nature's maternal rights over her creatures and the reciprocal duty of the offspring to Mother Nature. The words "mother" and "matter," moreover, share a Latin origin, as Lucretius observed in *De rerum natura*. This primordial unity, which explains the mythological origin of philosophical materialism, may even be traced back to Plato, as Vladimir Toporov has explained:

> The connection between matter and mother noted by Plato responds to a profound reality of the mythopoetic consciousness .... To a certain degree, the relationship between Moist Mother Earth [*mat'-syraia zemlia*] and the Sky-Father (among

5 A. P. Evgen'eva, ed., *Slovar' russkogo iazyka*, 4 vols. (Moscow: Russkii iazyk, 1982), 2: 236.

6 A. F. Losev, "Osnovnye osobennosti russkoi filosofii," in *Filosofiia, mifologiia, kul'tura* (Moscow: Politizdat, 1991), 509.

> Slavs and in many other traditions) may be seen as a remote source of the Platonic relationship between matter ("mother") and idea/form ("father").[7]

If we accept this etymological and mythological explanation, then the entire opposition between materialism and idealism, which for Marxists constitutes the quintessential philosophical issue, can be derived from the ancient cult of the earth-mother and sky-father. Solar rays carry the energy that fertilizes the earth's womb, giving birth to the vegetable kingdom and to all living creatures. One could even argue that the essence of materialism may be traced to the worship of maternity in the form of Mother Nature.[8]

Before materialism became an official doctrine, another female-oriented philosophy had been developing in Russia, the so-called sophiology. In the late nineteenth century and the first half of the twentieth, this concept was elaborated by Vladimir Solovyov, Pavel Florensky, Sergei Bulgakov, and other thinkers who considered the Russian soul to be especially attuned to Sophia, Divine Wisdom.[9] Both *materiia* and Sophia, they argued, characterized the feminine element in the universe, but there is a major difference between them: *materiia* is nature, which gives birth to living beings; Sophia is Divine Wisdom, which generates nature. Sophia (*Hokhma* in Hebrew) speaks thus in Proverbs: "The Lord possessed me at the beginning of His way, before His works of old. I have been established from everlasting, from the beginning, before there was ever an earth .... And I was daily His delight, rejoicing always before Him" (8: 22–23, 30). Solomon says: "Wisdom I loved; I sought her out when I was young and longed to win her for my bride, and I fell in love with her beauty. She adds lustre to her noble birth, because it is given her to live with God, and the Lord of all things has accepted her" (The Wisdom of Solomon, 8: 2–3).

Sophia, or Divine Wisdom, is a mysterious entity that, under different names, is worshipped in several religious traditions: pagan, Judaic, Gnostic, and Christian. In Greek polytheism, Sophia is represented by the chaste goddess of wisdom Athena,

7 V. N. Toporov, *Tekst: Semantika i struktura* (Moscow: Nauka, 1983), 236–7.

8 According to Engels's foundational definition, materialism is connected with the ancient worship of nature: "Those who asserted the primacy of spirit to nature ... comprised the camp of idealism. The others, who regarded nature as primary, belong to the various schools of materialism .... These two expressions, idealism and materialism, originally signify nothing else but this" (Friedrich Engels, *Ludwig Feuerbach and the Outcome of German Classical Philosophy* [New York: International Publishers, 1941], 21). One can suggest that it was Russia's long tradition of dual faith, Christian and pagan, which accounts for the triumph of materialism after Christianity was undermined by the October Revolution. With the expulsion of the patriarchal religion of the heavenly Father, archaic matriarchal elements regenerated in the social unconscious and acquired the form of materialist ideology. Indeed, Paul Federn, a disciple of Freud, argued that Bolshevism is nothing but the replacement of the father's power by the principles of matriarchy. See P. Federn, *Zur Psychologie der Revolution* (Vienna: Anzengruber-Verlag, 1919).

9 Vladimir Soloviev, *La Sophia et les autres écrits français*, ed. Fr. François Rouleau (Lausanne: La Cité-L'Age d'homme, 1978); Pavel Florensky, *The Pillar and Ground of the Truth: An Essay in Orthodox Theodicy in Twelve Books*, trans. Boris Jakim (Princeton: Princeton University Press, 2004), "Letter Ten: Sophia," 231–83; Sergei Bulgakov, *The Wisdom of God: A Brief Summary of Sophiology* (London: Williams and Norgate, 1937).

born directly from the head of Zeus. In Christianity, Sophia converges with the image of the Virgin Mary. The essential quality of Sophia-Wisdom is her chastity. In Russian, as in Greek, the word "chastity" (*tselomudrie*) includes the root "wisdom"; *tselomudrie* literally means "whole wisdom." The connection between wisdom and chastity is found in many spiritual traditions. The prominent Byzantinist Sergei Averintsev emphasizes that "according to the stable mythological pattern widespread in various Eurasian cultures, wisdom belongs to a virgin or, in fact, wisdom *is* a virgin."[10]

Materialism and sophiology in Russian thought share the same mythological origin: both glorify the primary feminine elements of existence, namely nature and wisdom. Sophia represents the virginal, and *materiia* the maternal, aspects of this femininity. Both are rooted in the deepest mythological archetypes of Russian thought as the two pillars of feminine mysticism. The Soviet intensification of materialism deepened the traditional symbolic rift between the two conceptions of femininity. Materialism, as propagated by Marxism-Leninism, is not merely the glorification of the forces of *materiia*; in alliance with atheism, it strives to tear *materiia* away from its divine origins, from Sophia, and to subject it to human mastery.[11]

Originally, the image of Sophia was ambiguous. *The Thunder, Perfect Mind*, one of the Gnostic works found at Nag Hammadi in Upper Egypt in 1945 probably dating to before 350 CE, depicts Sophia as both saint and whore. Gradually, however, these aspects of the divine feminine became increasingly distinct. As mentioned, Sophia was identified with the Holy Wisdom of God and the immaculate Mother of God, the Eternal Virgin (*Prisnodeva*). Thus the sophiological preference for chastity begins to betray an ascetic bias, a one-sidedness for which materialism strives to compensate. Virginity is in conflict with the fertile, prolific forces of nature. Thus the other aspect of primordial female divinity—fertility and sensuality (called the fallen Sophia by the Gnostics)—is developed in materialist teachings, where it acts as a counterbalance to virginity, eventually beginning to overcompensate, moving into the excesses of dissipation.

Many Russian thinkers have lamented the internal division of the Russian national character, which strains in opposite directions, ascetic/angelic and sensual/animalistic, and seldom succeeds in integrating spiritual and material impulses in a human middle ground. The same tragic split occurs within the feminine elements of Russian culture; hence an important task of contemporary Russian thought is to resolve the historical antagonism between the two philosophical tendencies of sophiology and materialism.

[10] Sergei Averintsev, "K uiasneniiu smysla nadpisi nad konkhoi tsentrasl'noi apsidy Sofii Kievskoi," in *Drevnerusskoe iskusstvo: Khudozhestvennaia kul'tura domongol'skoi Rusi*, ed. V. N. Lazarev (Moscow: Nauka, 1972), 28.

[11] According to the mystic logic of materialist conception, the conjugal bond of nature and God must be severed to facilitate her incestuous marriage with her human son. Sophiology is predominantly a cult of chastity, whereas materialism, in mythological terms, is the cult of degraded maternity, since Mother Nature is raped by her own son. For this interpretation, see Mikhail Epstein, "Labor of Lust: Erotic Metaphors of Soviet Civilization," in his *After the Future: The Paradoxes of Postmodernism and Contemporary Russian Culture*, trans. Anesa Miller-Pogacar (Amherst: University of Massachusetts Press, 1995), 177–87.

d. Andreev's Mysticism of Femininity

Throughout his creative years, Daniil Andreev suffered under the pressure of official Soviet ideology's "stubborn iron materialism," but his inner resistance to this mysticism of *materiia* did not push him to the other extreme of bodiless spiritualism. Nature was at the center of his whole system, and he singled out a special category of "elementals" (*stikhiali*), spiritual entities that have an elevating effect on the human soul and are embodied in such natural elements (*stikhii*) as rivers, trees, wind, and snow. Andreev enjoyed traveling through the wildest and most remote Russian forests, because for him, nature suggested the most genuine way of knowing God and partaking in supreme wisdom. Like Rozanov and Merezhkovsky, he sought the "sanctification of the flesh," and vehemently opposed the ascetic contempt for sensuality. For him, the entire substance of nature was a manifestation of the feminine soul of the universe.

The double—materialistic and sophiological—context of Andreev's view of the feminine becomes clear from a comment he makes in *The Rose of the World* that, albeit brief, seems to encapsulate the whole spectrum of traditional Russian worship of the earth as mother and as lover. "Earth is not only our mother; in some deeper sense that still cannot be explicated, she is our lover. One should remember the precept of Dostoevsky, who urged us to kiss the earth constantly at every step" (259).[12]

Andreev attempts to elevate this "pagan" worship of the earth to the highest level of Christian theology. Chapter 3, "The Feminine," treats this question in terms of the Holy Trinity. Andreev considered himself a Christian, but he dared to dispute the doctrine of the Trinity: "I am approaching the decisive thesis .... The canonical gospels of Matthew and Luke distinctly and clearly assume the conception of the infant Jesus by the Virgin Mary from the Holy Spirit. Thus one can conclude that it was the Holy Spirit and not God the Father who was the father of the human Christ" (119). Andreev suggests that God the Father and the Holy Spirit are essentially the same hypostasis of the Trinity. "God the Father is God the Holy Spirit—these are two names for the same first face of the Trinity" (120). The third hypostasis thus represents a vacancy, which Andreev aspires to fill with the "world's feminine essence." The Trinity, in Andreev's interpretation, is nothing but Father, Mother, and Son. The second, feminine hypostasis simultaneously represents eternal virginity, maternity, spirit, and wisdom.

It is difficult to say whether Andreev was familiar with the ideas of Anna Shmidt, Dmitrii Merezhkovsky, or Sergei Bulgakov. Anna Shmidt (1851–1905) postulated that the third hypostasis of God is "God's Daughter, the Eternal Virgin."[13] Merezhkovsky did not deny that the Holy Spirit is God's third hypostasis, but claimed it to be feminine and identical to the Holy Mother, the symbolic union of divine spirit and earthly

[12] The question of the feminine, which Andreev considered the "decisive thesis" of the whole of *The Rose of the World*, is most extensively treated in book 6, chapter 3; book 7, chapter 1; book 10, chapters 2–5; and book 12, chapter 3.

[13] A. N. Shmidt, *Tretii zavet* (St. Petersburg: Petropol', 1993), 24.

flesh.[14] Bulgakov developed sophiology as a specific division within Eastern theology, but his deliberately vague doctrine of Sophia as a separate hypostasis outside the Trinity was condemned by the Orthodox hierarchy (1935), despite Bulgakov's never directly asserting Sophia as the fourth hypostasis of divinity.[15] It is likely that Church authorities censured sophiology as heresy because it seemed to pattern the Trinity after a trivial family union, and to introduce seductive sexual elements into the dogmatic core of Christianity.

Indeed, the mysterious essence of the Trinity is undermined when the Mother of God is substituted for the Holy Spirit. The concept of the Holy Spirit may have derived from the concept of *Hokhma*, or Divine Wisdom, in the Old Testament. But when the "second" hypostasis of the Son was incorporated into the concept of God in the New Testament, the "third" hypostasis had to be revised and "purged" of any feminine elements in order to avoid associations with an earthly family structure. Thus the divine wisdom of the Old Testament became the Holy Spirit of the New Testament.

Unlike the Reverend Sergei Bulgakov, the convict Daniil Andreev was not constrained in his theological imagination by Church canons. For Andreev, the incorporation of feminine elements into the Trinity had far-reaching implications for Russia; the whole material aspect of life might be spiritualized and sanctified, since maternity, which gives life to all creatures, would be a hypostasis of divinity itself.

Daniil Andreev identified this feminine essence as Zventa-Sventana, whose approximate meaning he conveys as "the lightest of the light, the holiest of the holy" (124). *Svet* means "light" in Russian, while *zventa* sounds similar to *zvezda*, "star." Generally, Andreev preferred to substitute the neologisms he claimed to have received directly from higher spirits for traditional names and terms; in this case, as in many others, he did not care to explicate the semantic difference between Sophia and Zventa-Sventana. There exist other variations on this "Universal Feminine" (*Mirovaia Zhenstvennost'*) in Andreev's vision, including Navna, or the Communal Soul (*Sobornaia Dusha*). The relation of these names and personifications to one another is sometimes obscure. Zventa-Sventana is defined as the great monad born of God, the expression of the eternal feminine, and the bride of a planetary Logos. Navna is also a monad born of God and one of the great sisters, a communal soul of Russian metaculture. When considering the cosmic, global dimensions of the feminine, Andreev preferred the name Zventa-Sventana. He reserved the name Navna for the feminine soul of Russia, alluding for instance to "the Eternally Feminine principle whose embodiment in Russia [is] Navna" (180).

> Who is she, who is Navna? She is the one who unites Russians into one nation, who calls and directs individual Russian souls higher and higher, who surrounds

[14] For a detailed account of Merezhkovsky's "new religious consciousness" and dogmatic innovations, some of which strikingly anticipated Andreev's conceptions, see Bernice Glatzer Rosenthal, *Dmitri Sergeevich Merezhkovsky and the Silver Age: The Development of a Revolutionary Mentality* (The Hague: Springer, 1975), 94–6.

[15] Bulgakov, *The Wisdom of God*, 43–62.

> Russian art with a unique fragrance, who stands above the purest and highest female images of Russian legends, literature, and music, who emits into Russians' hearts a longing for a high, special, purely Russian destination. All this is Navna. Her communal nature [*sobornost'*] consists in the fact that some part of every Russian soul ascends to Navna, preserves itself in her and merges with her inner self .... Navna is the bride of the Demiurge of Russia and is the prisoner of the Zhrugrs [the demons of great-power Russian statehood]. (89)

In his long poem "Navna" (1955), Andreev traces the sublime manifestation of this feminine spirit throughout Russian history:

> In each inspiration, in each art
> Of this nocturnal and snowy country
> Only the dawn of Thy distant presentiments
> Lightly gilds our mournful dreams.[16]

According to Andreev's mytho-historiosophy, the Russian demiurge Iarosvet was destined to marry the Communal Soul of the Russian nation and give birth to Zventa-Sventana. But this process was delayed by the interference of Velga, the great demon of a feminine nature, who removes the taboos against blasphemy and destruction. Each people has its own Velga—the goddess Kali of the Hindus, the Hebrews' Lilith, or the Gnostics' fallen Sophia—who represents another pole of the communal soul and attempts to bring society into the fold of demonic materialism. In these terms, Soviet materialistic civilization can be interpreted as an involution of Velga.

In Andreev's view, Iarosvet first appeared in heavenly Russia and encountered Navna in the tenth century, an event described as a "happy tempest": "Navna accepted him as a long-awaited groom in the blissful forest expanses of Holy Russia" (128). Yet until the nineteenth century, the feminine element was suppressed in Russian culture; such few images of women as were permitted paled in comparison with the powerful male imagery. The reason for this was that Navna was a prisoner of the Zhrugrs, who personify the demonic aspect of the state, the will to power as the dominant aspiration of patriarchal society.

Andreev pinpoints several steps in Russian literature and philosophy that mark the gradual manifestation of Zventa-Sventana. The emanation of this feminine monad into the spiritual world of our planet, Shadanakar, occurred only in the late eighteenth century. This metahistorical event was dimly reflected in the works of Goethe, Novalis, and Zhukovsky. In Russia the first embodiment of this feminine ideal was Tatiana Larina in Pushkin's *Eugene Onegin*. Then came Turgenev's women, especially Elena in the novel *On the Eve* and Lukeria from the short story "A Living Relic."

[16] Daniil Andreev, *Russkie bogi: Stikhotvoreniia i poemy* (Moscow: Sovremennik, 1989), 198.

The highest manifestations of the Eternal Feminine are found in the works of Vladimir Solovyov (1853–1900), though he failed to find a more compelling concept for this mysterious entity than the ancient Gnostic notion of Sophia. In Andreev's view, Solovyov was the first to understand that the religious revelation of the Eternal Feminine is not compatible with the Trinitarian dogma of Orthodox Christianity. This is why he expressed his vision of Sophia in a long poem, "Three Encounters," whose mystical illuminations are deliberately limited by the framework of a slightly humorous autobiographical sketch, in order to conceal their potential heretical implications. Moreover, Solovyov feared to introduce the feminine principle into the religious sphere, where it might be mixed with sexual elements, thus leading to the blasphemous equation of spiritual marriage with ritualistic depravity, seen in the practice of some Russian orgiastic sects, such as the Khlysty (flagellants).

Solovyov's fears, Andreev continues, which caused him to remain laconic and cautious about revealing his sophiological insights, were realized in the works and lamentable fate of Aleksandr Blok (1880–1921), who considered himself a spiritual disciple of Solovyov. Blok addressed his first book of poems to the Beautiful Lady, a personification of the feminine soul of the world, but in his subsequent creative work, he fell into the abyss of the demonic feminine, following the descent of the fallen Sophia, who appeared to him as an "unknown woman" (*neznakomka*), a seductive combination of virgin and whore. "Now [Blok] sings about Velga, mistaking her for Navna in his increasing blindness" (198). This error was not his alone, but the entire country's, reflecting the tragic fall of her feminine soul. From the heights of Sophia, to whom many Russian churches were dedicated, the people were slipping into the chasm of revolutionary materialism—the mystical temptation engendered by the great fornicatress, Velga.

Daniil Andreev was one of the first Russian thinkers to proclaim the primary creative role of the feminine in the spiritual growth of humankind, even though he believed that in some fields, a woman is less gifted than a man. In *The Rose of the World*, for instance, he asserts that the doors to the arts and sciences had been open wide for women for two hundred years, but that, at least in the privileged classes, there were fewer female than male geniuses in music, painting, literature, and science (123). Nevertheless, Andreev argues,

> it is indisputable that in other regards, a woman possesses gifts which a man lacks and will never have .... Motherhood, raising children, making a home, caring for the ill, the ethical rehabilitation [*vrachevanie*] of criminals, the transformation of nature, the breeding of animals, certain directions [*rusla*] in religious life, the creation of love, and finally, the creative fertilization of the soul of the man she loves—this is where a woman is indispensable and infinitely gifted ....
>
> In the spheres of the highest creativity, something occurs which is opposite to what we see in the physical world. Here the woman is the fertilizing principle, while the man is the principle of shaping and incarnation. *The Divine Comedy* is the product of two authors, and could not have appeared without both Beatrice and Dante. If we could penetrate the depths of the creative process of most great

> artists, we would be assured that it was through a woman that the spiritual seed of these immortal creations was cast into the depth of their [artists'] unconscious, into the inner recesses of their creativity. (123)

Andreev thus combines quite conventional views on the predominantly familial or domestic vocation of women with the rather original theory that women impregnate men in the spiritual sphere. According to this hypothesis, there are so few female geniuses precisely because women do not give birth to creative works, but fertilize their creators in the same way as men do not give birth to children but impregnate women. This "invisible" participation of women in the history of civilization must be acknowledged; still more crucially, the *future* of civilization must be reoriented according to the increasing role of the feminine:

> For millennia, the male, masculine element was dominant in humanity—force, audacity, pride, courage, striving afar, cruelty, militarism .... Millennium after millennium, waves of wars, rebellions, revolutions, terror, and furiously merciless massacres have rolled ceaselessly across the face on the earth. The innumerable drops in these waves are male wills and male hearts .... Meek femininity, driven into the depth of family cells, escaped destruction only because without it, man himself was as sterile as a piece of lead, and because the physical continuation of mankind is impossible without a woman ....
>
> Until now it was proclaimed that not only a man, but a woman is obliged to be manly [*muzhestvennoi*, a word for "courageous" derived from "man," *muzh*] .... But ... not only a woman, but a man too, must be feminine. (123–4)

Thus for Daniil Andreev, the feminine principle will increasingly determine the supreme goals of historical development. Nevertheless, his view does not presuppose a one-sided dominance of females in the coming epochs. The feminine is asymmetrical in relation to the masculine, in the sense that it is more "capacious" and brings the spirit of reconciliation to both sexes. The male and the female can be reunited on the basis of the feminine:

> The growth of feminine forces and their meaning for modernity are seen everywhere. This can primarily account for the general striving for peace, the reluctance to shed blood and disenchantment with violent methods of social transformation; the growth of women's social significance; the increasing gentleness of childcare; and a burning passion for beauty and love. We are entering a cycle of epochs when the feminine soul will become increasingly pure and broad, when more and more women will become deep inspirers, judicious mothers, and wise and visionary leaders. This will be the cycle of epochs when the feminine component of humanity will manifest itself with unprecedented strength, balancing the previous dominance of masculine forces in a perfect harmony. (124–5)

Andreev does not imagine the future triumph of the feminine as a mere reversal of the present patriarchal establishment; rather, he forecasts a perfect conjugal harmony of feminine and masculine elements that can be seen as an innate quality of the feminine. As Andreev conceived it, the Rose of the World will become the highest manifestation of the feminine soul of the universe. This global religious and social organization is destined to overcome

> the contradiction between two primary tendencies—ascetic spirituality, which rejects the world, and the so-called pagan tendency that extols the carnal world .... Finally, the triumph of the Rose of the World is not possible until religious humanity's striving toward the Eternally Feminine (*Vechno Zhenstvennoe*) reveals a new, deeper meaning; until the breath of Zventa-Sventana has softened and lightened the too-searing severity of the masculine principle that has hitherto completely dominated ethics, religion, and social life. (180)

One of the main goals of Daniil Andreev's work, then, is the synthesis of two Russian philosophical attitudes, materialism and sophiology—a synthesis that, for lack of a better term, I would call "materiosophy." Definitional to this term would be Andreev's wording on the "removal of the antagonism between the spiritual-ascetic and pagan tendencies, and the development of a synthetic attitude toward nature in the consciousness of the multitudes of people" (180). When reunited, these two aspects of the feminine, ascetic and pagan, spiritual and sexual, would strengthen the influence of the feminine in the future of humanity. To be sure, the feminine itself will not remain unchanged; it must embrace not only the purity of a virgin and the fertility of motherhood, but the sexual initiation of a mature woman. The integration of *materiia* and Sophia will imply "the activation of the Eternally Feminine principle, whose embodiment in Russia, Navna, had been weakened, tortured, and taken captive for many centuries" (180).

The feminine mysticism of Daniil Andreev, as of Russian philosophy in general, is clearly distinct from those varieties of contemporary Western feminism that postulate separate, self-contained spheres of female culture. Andreev stresses not so much the equality of women in historically male-dominated fields as the superiority of women in fields traditionally deprecated by patriarchal civilization. Whereas many Western feminists emphasize female perspectives in writing, reading, and criticism, Andreev emphasizes the privileged position of women in domains of intuitive or integral knowledge which cannot be reduced to scientific disciplines or critical discourse.

Russian feminine mysticism proceeds from the idea of an integral human being in whom heart and mind, body and soul, are one. According to this view, in men these capacities are usually split and highly specialized because of the division of labor. Women, however, have retained their wholeness, because it is necessary for the very act of giving birth. Whereas some Western feminists defend gender difference in the face of an overweening masculinist canon, Russian thinkers like Solovyov or Andreev are inclined to defend androgyny as part of a general desire for "all-unity" (*vseedinstvo*) as opposed to gendered specialization. Some Western feminists maintain that women must affirm their social and cultural independence from male-dominated civilization. Andreev believed, to the contrary, that not only women, but men too, must be feminine.

e. The Internal Ironies of Theocratic Thought: Utopia as Eschatology

Despite Andreev's extremely positive and optimistic view of the feminine, the underlying ambivalence of the image of Sophia as virgin and whore unconsciously penetrates his thinking. Andreev's pan-religious system contains an inner drama and inherent paradox: what he glorifies as the Rose of the World is strikingly similar to what he vilifies as the kingdom of the Antichrist. The Rose of the World is the ideal Church/State of the future, embracing all existing religions, including Christianity, Islam, and Buddhism, under the rule of one world government and one spiritual leader. This idea is reminiscent of Solovyov's utopia of global Christian theocracy led by tsar and pope, but in Andreev's vision, the future "supreme mentor" integrates the two roles. According to Andreev's prophecy, however, after several generations of peaceful rule, the Rose of the World will inevitably fall into the hands of the Antichrist, whose kingdom will finally be crushed by the Second Coming of Christ, thus ending the current aeon of world history. We have already discussed Andreev's apocalyptic vision of the end of the world (in section b). Andreev characterizes the kingdom of the Antichrist, with its horrors and blasphemies, as completely antithetical to his theocratic utopia, the Rose of the World. Nevertheless, the conceptual system underlying his description leads one to the conclusion that the Rose of the World, the kingdom of God on earth, is implicitly the kingdom of the Antichrist, or at least its antecedent. This profound irony at the very core of Andreev's theocracy was likely not fully realized by the author himself, who, from the time of his release from prison to the end of his life, had less than two years to finish his treatise. Paradoxically, the very features that culminate in the highest spirituality of the Rose of the World inexorably prepare the advent of the Antichrist.

Andreev emphasizes, for example, that the "supreme mentor" will combine artistic genius, moral righteousness, and the inspiration of a religious prophet (15). The same combination of gifts is characteristic of the Antichrist as conceived by Solovyov in his "Short Tale of the Antichrist," a work that Andreev knew well and repeatedly cited as a valid prophecy. Moreover, Andreev's Antichrist is endowed with a similar "unprecedented versatility of gifts," and he gains power through his ascension to the leadership of the Rose of the World (264–5).[17]

Among the features of the Rose of the World that are ironically mirrored in the kingdom of the Antichrist, the cult of the feminine is of central importance. As soon as the Antichrist ascends to the throne and is crowned, he "announce[s] himself to be the messenger of the Universal Feminine" (265). Solovyov never reinterpreted the Eternal Feminine ironically as a demonic cult: in his "Short Tale," he abandons and condemns his own previously affirmed ideas of total unity and universal theocracy, but leaves sophiology intact; likewise espoused to the end is the Christian justification

[17] For a more detailed analysis of the internal ironies and paradoxes of Andreev's *The Rose of the World*, see my article "Roza Mira i Tsarstvo Antikhrista. O paradoksakh russkoi eskhatologii," in Mikhail Epshtein, *Religiia posle ateizma: Novye vozmozhnosti teologii* (Moscow: AST-Press, 2013), 106–58.

of Platonic eroticism he put forth in his article "The Meaning of Love." According to Solovyov, it is through sexual love that human beings ascend to God and unite with "God's Eternal Feminine." Characteristically, Andreev considers this erotic moment in Solovyov's theology to be his greatest achievement: "[I]t is precisely the prophecy about Zventa-Sventana and the creation of historical and religious premises for the Rose of the World that constituted [Solovyov's] mission" (194).

In Andreev's eschatological vision, the kingdom of the Antichrist releases the sexual drives and raises them to the status of a religious cult. Andreev uses the name of Lilith, the demoness who was, per apocrypha, Adam's rebellious first wife, to designate the feminine counterpart of the Antichrist: "The incarnate Lilith, who pretended to be the Feminine, will alternately engage in shameless acts with the anti-Logos and in orgy-mysteries, open first to hundreds of people, and later, in principle, to everyone .... Everything will be directed toward the unbridling of the sexual element" (266–7).

Andreev seems to forget that, according to his previous arguments concerning the bisexual nature of God, the intercourse and marriage of the two divine hypostases constitute the main mystery of the religion of the Rose of the World. This idea is clearly contained, for instance, in Andreev's proposal for a future eighth ecumenical council to revise the dogma of the Holy Trinity and substitute the Feminine for the Holy Spirit as one of the three hypostases: in "the eternal union between Father and Mother ... in this love, the Third is born: the Foundation of the Universe. Father—Eternal Virgin-Mother—Son" (121). This dogmatic innovation is reminiscent of a postulate of the atheist Feuerbach, who "anthropologized" the Christian Trinity as only a reflection of sexual relationships within the earthly family. As if without realizing, Andreev humanizes (and in the process, paganizes and profanizes) the mystery of the Trinity, introducing a male-female polarity tantamount to the pagan myth of the marriage of heaven and earth.

For Andreev, the replacement of the Holy Spirit by the female aspect of divinity is the "decisive thesis" of his book, and one that he acknowledges would constitute a break with the "foundation of foundations," the Holy Trinity preached by the Christian churches: "The idea of the Universal Feminine cannot but grow into the idea of the Female aspect of Divinity, and this naturally threatens to destroy the dogmatic ideas about the hypostases of the Holy Trinity" (120–1).

The introduction of a female principle into the Trinity is not purely a theoretical proposal. The feminine, as a new dogma crucial for the religion of the Rose of the World, is also realized in the specific hierarchy of the female priesthood, which reflects the second hypostasis of the Trinity. There will be specific temples and rituals designed exclusively for priestesses, the blue hierarchy, functioning along with the golden hierarchy of God the Father and the white hierarchy of God the Son (258). Moreover, Andreev also anticipates the performance of certain cult practices, such as the blessing of young couples seeking marriage, not by Christian priests, but by the fertile forces of nature, or more precisely, by a special order of "nature-priests" under the auspices of the Rose of the World. "[O]ne should not impose wedding vows for more than several years, and it is more appropriate to ask for help not from the hierarchy of the

Christian transmyth but from Mother Earth and even from the popular Aphrodite of humankind" (255).[18]

Unconsciously Andreev reveals the side of his utopia that is, by his own value system, demonic: reverence for a sexually bipolar divinity lays the foundation for the practices of the Antichrist that Andreev himself will code as sacrilegious, and for the eventual doom of the Rose of the World. The Antichrist's main project, and the source of his power over humanity, is sexual permissiveness, for which he will offer religious justification:

> The anti-Logos will announce himself to be the incarnation of God the Father, and the woman whose appearance Lilith has taken by means of a demonic miracle to be the incarnation of the Eternal Feminine .... Around himself and the incarnate Lilith, the Antichrist will create a blasphemous cult of world fornication, and vile actions between the two of them, surrounded by fantastic effects and stupefying splendor, will be performed before the eyes of all, allegedly reflecting, in our world, the cosmic marriage of two hypostases of the Trinity. (265)

Clearly, were it not for the transformation of the Trinity into the cosmic marriage of two hypostases, sanctified and dogmatized by the Rose of the World, there would be nothing for the Antichrist to reflect or imitate. No cult of world fornication could be created from the relationship of the two traditional, Christianly understood hypostases—God the Father and the Holy Spirit. The original Trinity simply lacks any premise for such a sexual element, precludes any consideration of it, whereas Andreev's Trinity, presenting "the mystery of the union of Father and Mother" (121), clears the path for the cult of fornication. How could the sexually bipolar Trinity be reflected in ritual, except through an infinite succession of sexual unions, which is precisely what, in Andreev's system, constitutes the seductive appeal of the Antichrist and his female hypostasis?

One wonders why Andreev, who was so sensitive to the spiritual threat of feminine mysticism—which in his view Solovyov avoided, but Blok fell victim to—proved so susceptible to it himself. Perhaps *The Rose of the World*, though formally finished, should not be seen as fully complete, given the incongruity between Andreev's social prophecies and his eschatological visions. (In the end, the author, mortally ill, had less than two years after his release from prison to organize and elaborate on his inspirational fragments.) Andreev was fully cognizant that

> the intrusion of ideas about the difference of divinely male and divinely female principles into religious organizations and cults is fraught with exceptional dangers. Understood with insufficient spirituality, separated with insufficient strictness from the sexual sphere of humanity, these intrusions lead to the darkening of spirituality [via the unleashing of] the sexual element; to the blasphemous identification of cosmic spiritual marriage with sensual love and, in the final analysis, with ritual debauchery. (194)

[18] In ancient Greece, the "popular" hypostasis of this deity, Aphrodite Pandemos, was the goddess of crude, sensual love, as opposed to the ideal, heavenly love represented by Aphrodite Urania.

But this was precisely the temptation that haunted Andreev and unconsciously transformed his utopia into an apocalypse.

What Andreev proclaimed as his "decisive thesis" he also condemned as a "blasphemous cult"—for it was the selfsame feminine principle, polarized as virgin and whore. Andreev's attempt to reconcile these two aspects of the eternal mother, who is both Sophia and *materiia*, proved to be a spiritually fraught enterprise, since the opposition could not be completely erased. As soon as the desired synthesis of an all-comprehensive feminine is achieved in the project of the Rose of the World, it becomes subject to a new doubling, to the materialization of a demonic and purely sensual feminine in the kingdom of the Antichrist, and it is this theoretical irony that ultimately undermines Andreev's theocratic utopia.

Thus the mystical element of Andreev's doctrine, his veneration of the feminine aspect of divinity, comes into a very complicated and controversial relationship with the eschatological element of his doctrine, an apprehension of the "ritual debauchery" at the very essence of the demonic anti-Trinity. Andreev never managed to overcome this contradiction, but of all Russian mystics, he most expressively attested to its hidden ironies.

3. Cosmism and Active Evolutionism

a. The Sources of Cosmism

In Russian philosophical discussions of the 1970s–1980s, cosmism emerged as one of the most influential trends. It has come to designate not only a particular movement, but the overarching property and legacy of Russian philosophy as a whole. Cosmism literally means "cosmic orientation" of thought, not only because the cosmos is the object of this thought, but because the thought considers itself to be a part of the cosmos. Thought is both a cognitive reflection of cosmic reality and also a constitutive force of cosmic evolution. To offer a concise definition: cosmism is a philosophy of active evolutionism, presupposing the possibility and necessity for the human mind to regulate and transform the laws of nature. Cosmism explains historical, social, and psychological processes by the influences of cosmic energies, and asserts a reciprocal dependency of the fates of the universe on the activity of the human mind.[19]

It would be difficult to pinpoint the genesis of cosmism in the history of Russian thought, mainly because it was intimately tied to the long-standing intuitions of Eastern Christianity. Many commentators have observed that, while Catholicism evinced a predominantly historical orientation in directing the fates of the world, Orthodoxy was far more concerned with the cosmic and mystical dimension. The "theosis" or

[19] Russian cosmism must be distinguished from *cosmicism*, the philosophy developed by the American writer H. P. Lovecraft (1890–1937) in his horror narratives, which present humans as pathetically insignificant in the larger scheme of cosmic existence. Envisioning a universe ruled by evil gods, cosmicism entails, in particular, a dread before the cosmic void. Russian cosmism generally asserts an active and optimistic perspective on the transformative impact of human reason on cosmic evolution, whereas Lovecraftian cosmicism is more associated with pessimism and nihilism.

"deification of the creature" as the foremost aspiration of Christianity presupposed the transfiguration not only of human flesh, but also of the entire substance of the universe and of all living beings. This tendency may be explained by the duality of Russian Orthodoxy, which inherited a considerable pagan element with its Christian foundation; in many cases, its believers worshipped forces of nature under the names of Christian saints. Via the abovementioned "dual faith" (*dvoeverie*), Christian communities consciously or unconsciously preserved pagan beliefs and/or rituals, in effect adhering to a syncretic religion.

With Russia's vast agrarian economy, Orthodoxy of necessity accommodated the preconceptions of the peasantry, whose imagination was oriented toward cyclical processes in nature, as opposed to the linear, historical dimension of a more urbanist Western civilization. Perhaps the first monument of Russian cosmism is the so-called *Deep Book* or *Dove Book* (*Golubinaia kniga*). This collection of spiritual verses of the late fifteenth and early sixteenth centuries presents popular Christian beliefs, expressed in religious folk songs, as a huge matrix of cosmic elements. According to the *Deep* or *Dove Book*, for example, human thoughts derive from heavenly clouds, and bodies from the moist earth, with numerous other parallels drawn between the life of humankind and the workings of the universe, thus anticipating the basic presupposition of contemporary cosmism—that man and the cosmos are symbiotically joined.

In a conventional sense, the founder of Russian cosmism is considered to be Nikolai Fedorov (1829–1903), a cult figure for most later cosmists. Fedorov focused his attention on the problem of death, which, as an inevitability of nature, is also, in his view, an insult to humanity. Hence his philosophical project, which he called "the common cause" (*obshchee delo*), is directed toward overcoming death through technological and social advancement. In his understanding, Christianity is primarily a religion of resurrection, which echoes the Orthodox privileging of Easter over all other holidays, including the Nativity, the celebration of Christ's birth prioritized in Catholicism. The moral task of humanity, then, is not to wait for the Last Judgement, but to follow the example set by Christ and endeavor to make bodily resurrection possible on earth, to transform the entirety of human existence into a man-made and continuous Easter.

Several social and metaphysical reorientations proceed from this common cause. First of all, history as a succession of generations, whereby the new supplants the old, must give way to a retrospective tendency that emphasizes immortality and the resurrection of ancestors. The highest moral duty of all descendants is to revive their forebears, to reciprocate the gift of life received from them. Fedorov criticizes the civilization of his contemporaries for its procreative obsession, which has given rise to a feminized industry of conspicuous consumption oriented toward seduction. Sexuality and the cult of pleasure, comfort, and beauty distract men from the fulfilment of their highest duty. Morality, or rather "supramorality" (*supramoralizm*) as Fedorov puts it, demands that sons return their debt of love to their fathers by resurrecting them. All technological resources must be dedicated to this task of preserving and revitalizing the remains of deceased progenitors. Thus the *museum* becomes the central cultural institution of humanity and functions also as a laboratory of resurrection science, transforming the archives, as the knowledge of the past, into the practice of recreation. Furthermore, with the conquest of death, procreation becomes obsolete, and the focus of human history shifts to cosmic expansion, which will be necessary to accommodate the innumerable resurrected generations of ancestors. The religious thrust of Fedorov's project is the overturning, not just of death, but of *all* natural laws, such that humanity in its *theosis* (*obozhenie*, "deification") may attain God's omniscience and omnipotence. Fedorov often repeated that everything "granted" (*darovoe*) must be transformed into something "crafted" (*trudovoe*), that man is called to worship God by literalizing in practice all that which in scripture is usually interpreted only symbolically, as mere spiritual allegory or, at most, as miraculous intervention from another world.

The next commonly recognized figure of cosmism is Konstantin Tsiolkovsky (1857–1935), officially honored in the Soviet period as the "father of Soviet cosmonautics" and the first scientist to elaborate the technological parameters of rocketry. He was also, however, a self-styled philosopher who published numerous pamphlets on topics such as "cosmic reason." Though celebrated as a scientist, his philosophy was suppressed in the USSR for its non-materialist and mystical claims. For example, Tsiolkovsky believed that all physical matter is animate and sentient, and that every atom is a living and conscious entity—the primordial citizen of the universe. Living organisms, then, are only temporary associations of atoms, which continue to live even after the organism itself has perished. Unlike Fedorov, Tsiolkovsky espouses no project for immortality, since in his opinion, it is already the rule—on an atomic level. Atoms would prefer, he believed, to have the most perfect forms of life, for instance the human brain, as their habitat. This not only accounts for somatic death, as atoms continue to seek a superior "social" organization, but also for Tsiolkovsky's advocacy of eugenics and deliberate biological selection, that is, the disposal of inferior, and cultivation of superior, atomic associations. Two basic ideas of cosmism—the recognition of the universe as a living organism, and the active regulation of natural forces, including genetics—owe their prominence to Tsiolkovsky, who considered himself to be a disciple of Fedorov.

The third most important name in the cosmist hierarchy is Vladimir Vernadsky (1863–1945). If Nikolai Fedorov was primarily a religious thinker and Konstantin Tsiolkovsky a hybrid scientist/prophet, then Vernadsky, as a strict scientist, represents the other end of the cosmist spectrum. He was the originator of several new disciplines in the natural sciences, among them biochemistry, geochemistry, and integrative geoscience. He was the first scientist to theorize the geologic role of living matter, the "biosphere," the increasing influence of plant, animal, and human life on the evolution of planetary structures. Together with the French thinkers Édouard Le Roy and Pierre Teilhard de Chardin, Vernadsky developed the concept of the "noosphere," the collective body of human thought incorporated into the biosphere as an active factor in its transformation. In his view, the geosphere organically overlaps with the biosphere, which in turn grows into the noosphere. Thought is a form of energy, an active factor of geological evolution that allows humanity to cooperate with nature as a complementary part of a living and thinking organism.

Cosmism, like all other non-Marxist and "idealistic" teachings during the Soviet period, was rejected by official ideology, but it nevertheless enjoyed a kind of unspoken privileged status. Fedorov's project for the resurrection of the dead, for instance, was implicitly incorporated into some undercurrents of Soviet ideology, as manifested most strikingly in the construction of Lenin's mausoleum, which was designed to preserve his body until the invention of some radically new technology that could resurrect him. Despite the atheism of Marxism-Leninism and the religiosity of Nikolai Fedorov, the two systems are compatible inasmuch as both attempt to give immanent realization to transcendental aspirations. The imperative of both ideologies is technological progress, which will lead to humanity's absolute mastery of the blind forces of nature. Both systems critique capitalist civilization for its social inequality and materialistic obsessions—in Marxism, the greed of the bourgeoisie; in Fedorov, the dictatorship of fashion, which Fedorov considered corrupt and "feminine." Both strive to overcome individualism and egoism to achieve a levelling of society toward the formation of armies of workers. Labor, in each system, is the highest moral duty and value, since the task of humanity is to subordinate spontaneous and chaotic processes in nature and society to teleological and creative human reason. This is why, when such celebrated Soviet writers of a decidedly communist orientation like Maksim Gorky and Vladimir Maiakovsky glorify the immortality of omnipotent Man and the ongoing transformation of the universe through the conscientious effort of a unified humanity, they seem to pay homage to Fedorov rather than Marx. Contemporary cosmists find Fedorovian motifs in works of such prominent writers of the Soviet period as Andrei Platonov, Mikhail Prishvin, and Nikolai Zabolotsky, with the cosmos directly intervening in the lives of their characters, the energy of the human mind and will working to improve the deficiencies of the existing universe.

In the 1950s–1960s, Soviet space exploration (the first Sputnik, 1957; the first man in orbit, 1961) was motivated not only by the political ambitions of communism and the scientific genius of Konstantin Tsiolkovsky, but also by the metaphysical imagination of his teacher Nikolai Fedorov. In order to provide space for the billions of the resurrected dead and future immortals, Fedorov envisioned humankind colonizing the entire universe. The very history of Russia, as is well known, consisted in continuous colonization of new lands in all four directions of the compass, and then—as Fedorov insisted, referring to the vastness of the Russian plain—in the "fifth" direction as well, that of open space. Russia must lead humanity as the carrier of the Mind, that force that opposes the destruction and thermal death of the universe, which will inevitably come should man renounce his role as the conduit by which divine energy enters the created world.

In the 1970s–1980s, Russian cosmism was further invigorated by an increased interest in environmental matters, giving rise, in the writings of Svetlana Semenova, Nikita Moiseev, Fedor Girenok, and others, to a scientific strand that could be considered the Russian equivalent of the environmental holism of James Lovelock, Gregory Bateson, and other "New Paradigm" scientists. Here, cosmism has been influenced by ideas of negentropy, the anthropic principle, and the Gaia hypothesis.

b. The Variety of Cosmist Perspectives

Publications concerning the philosophical legacies of Fedorov, Tsiolkovsky, and Vernadsky began to proliferate in the late 1970s. At first these claimed to elaborate new areas for Marxist thought, especially with regard to the relationship between humanity and nature. At this stage, cosmism seemed like a useful add-on to Marxism, supplementing a social doctrine with a naturalistic dimension. Cosmists argued that Marx had shown the way to achieve a classless society, while Fedorov showed what to do next. That is, once communism comes fully to fruition, the energy of social struggle will be channeled into the struggle of humanity united against the brutal and random forces of nature. Ecological concerns, which were also coming to the fore at this time and thus needed to be grafted to Marxism, could comfortably be delegated to Fedorov and cosmism, according to which humankind appears to be not only a social but a cosmic being who is responsible for the well-being of nature. Such were the pretexts for incorporating cosmism into the network of Marxist ideas.

However, in the course of time, the relationship between the two systems appeared to invert itself in favor of cosmism. Increasingly, Marxism came to be inscribed within the more magnificent perspective of cosmism as one of its subordinate tools, in effect a mere technique for uniting people for the larger Common Cause. The October Revolution, Lenin and Trotsky's war communism, Stalin's collectivization and industrialization, the launch of the first satellite and the first manned spaceflight under Khrushchev—all these are reinterpreted as primitive: largely flawed, albeit productive steps in the direction of Fedorov's vision.

In the cosmism of the late Soviet period, one can distinguish a sober, scientific, or quasi-scientific type and a zealous, utopian sort grounded in religious revelationism. The moderate pole is occupied by such thinkers as Vasilii Kuprevich (1897–1969) and Nikita Moiseev (1917–2000). The latter was a prominent mathematician who in his later career embraced philosophical issues of information theory and ecology. For him, natural, social, and intellectual evolution were in fact forms and phases of coevolution building one on another. "The development of human society is as much a natural process as the formation of galaxies or the development of a virus. Today, it is important for us to see the commonality that unites all the components of this single process, and that which brings and can bring Reason to the global evolutionary process."[20]

A biologist and botanist, Kuprevich was probably the first Soviet scientist of the postwar era to officially publicize his views on the prospect of personal biological immortality. In his opinion, death represents a useful mechanism of innovation in the animal kingdom, but from a human standpoint, it is an absurdity. Since the perfection of the human can proceed through social innovation, the human species has transcended the necessity of death as a tool of biological evolution. Moreover, at our contemporary stage of technological advancement, the relatively short life span of the individual stands as an obstacle to progress, since the acquisition of a minimum knowledge within any field requires an increasingly significant proportion of a lifetime,

[20] Nikita Moiseev, *Chelovek i noosfera* (Moscow: Zhurnal Ekologiia i zhizn', 1990), 24.

making the productive period correspondingly brief. The individual has precious little time to use the knowledge he or she has acquired, let alone to contribute anything innovative or progressive. Also, in practical terms, "a human being, living several decades, is incapable of overcoming interstellar distances, just as a one-day butterfly [*babochka-odnodnevka*] is incapable of traversing the ocean."[21] Thus Kuprevich advances immortality, not as a fantastic dream, but as a necessary tool of civilization.

As a scientist, he felt obliged to speculate about the means by which immortality might be achieved, but this proved to be the most vulnerable point—not only in his, but in all the cosmists' conceptions. Kuprevich refers to the most elementary lifeforms, unicellular organisms, which are practically "immortal" by virtue of their reproductive self-division. In his view, this points to the possibility of immortality for humans, but this comparison might just as easily support the opposite argument. That is, if immortality is peculiar to simple organisms, then the probability for immortality decreases as the organism becomes more complex. A building deteriorates far more quickly than the stones from which it was made. However, Kuprevich also argues that if there is a "virus of death" operant within the body, it might be countered with a "virus of immortality," which would rejuvenate individual cells—a likelier possibility, given well-known recent advances in the science of aging.

In light of the inherent unpredictability of scientific progress, offering arguments for immortality from the standpoint of the natural sciences is risky. Fedor Girenok, a professor of philosophy at Moscow State University, exemplifies another approach to the problem, one that might be called "methodological cosmism." Faulting Fedorov's religious utopianism, he suggests a purely symbolic reading of the Fedorovian project. (Although for Fedorov himself, it was most important to treat the prospect of resurrection not symbolically but realistically, as a scientific imperative.) For Girenok, the central idea of cosmism has to do with the ontological status of human thought. Human consciousness, that is, not only reflects the laws of nature, but is a real event that occurs as part of nature. Girenok argues against the traditional opposition of human subject versus objective universe. It was Newton and Copernicus who introduced the concept of the "empty universe," but it is Russian cosmism which attempts to populate it, not only in terms of the colonization of space, but also by establishing thought as a decisive factor of cosmic life. "Russian cosmism establishes the problem which can be expressed in the following way. We cognize nature as an object, but it exists as the subject of its own changes and transformations .... Russian cosmism regards thought as real human action and cognition as a process of life, not a logical operation."[22]

Girenok finds a parallel between Russian cosmism and the postulate in quantum mechanics concerning the effects of the presence of the experimenter on the data being gathered. Another resource of his speculation is the "anthropic principle," which states that all physical constants in the existing universe, including the size of atoms and

[21] Cited from Svetlana Semenova, *Nikolai Fedorov. Tvorchestvo zhizni* (Moscow: Sovetskii pisatel', 1990), 329.

[22] F. I. Girenok, *Ekologiia. Tsivilizatsiia. Noosfera* (Moscow: Nauka, 1987), 160; further citations in the text refer to this edition.

the speed of light, are such as they are in order to make the existence of humankind and intelligence possible. Girenok also supports the theory of "negentropy," a feature common to much of contemporary cosmism. According to the second law of thermodynamics, a quantity of energy progressively decreases, which suggests that all organized forms of matter—including life and mind—will eventually dissipate. Cosmism argues that there is a force in the universe that opposes entropy, a resistance exemplified by the increasing complexity of the human organism and its creations. Thus mind is the source of cosmic energy, or *negentropy* (reverse entropy, the opposite of randomness or chaos), that brings organization, structure, and function into the universe and keeps it from exhaustion.

These three arguments—the quantum influence of the observer, the anthropic principle of the universe, and the negentropic factor of mind—are united in the philosophy of Russian cosmism, which postulates that the universe created humankind in order that humankind could recreate the universe. This reveals an interesting paradox of cosmism, which is open to critique for logical inconsistency. On the one hand, the spiritual activity of humanity is overwhelmingly determined by cosmic factors (such as solar winds); on the other hand, the entire destiny of the universe is determined by the work of the human mind. It is difficult to reconcile these two determinisms; however, almost all cosmists claim that their theory allows them to establish a harmonious interaction between the cosmos and mankind, and to posit them as mutually dependent parts of one whole.

Girenok rejects both extremes of anthropocentrism and "cosmocentrism" as obsolete concepts held over from seventeenth- and eighteenth-century science. Anthropocentrism placed man in the center of the universe, but as a result of this revolution of modernity, the universe itself proved to be inanimate, dead matter, which imposes limitations, irreversible laws defining the boundaries of human freedom. Girenok thus prefers to call his position "anthropocosmism," emphasizing the indivisibility of humanity and the universe as a self-regulating and integral system. Girenok borrowed this concept from the Ukrainian biologist Nikolai Kholodnyi (1882–1953), who in *Thoughts of a Naturalist about Nature and Man* (1944–6, published 1947) decries anthropocentrism for its "collective egoism" of mankind and proclaims a new, anthropocosmic paradigm: "Once and forever man ceases to be the center of the universe. He becomes simply one of its organic constituents, who enjoys no privileges .... [Man] becomes one of the powerful factors of the further evolution of nature in the inhabited part of the universe—the factor that acts consciously."[23] In the anthropocosmic view as expressed by Girenok, the world is determined by physical laws, but humankind adds its own definition to the world, thus consummating it (165). From this perspective, ecology appears as not only a practical need or moral obligation, but as an expression of anthropocosmic unity, where mind asserts itself as a cosmic force.

[23] S. G. Semenova and A. G. Gacheva, *Russkii kosmizm. Antologiia filosofskoi mysli* (Moscow: Pedagogika-Press, 1993), 337–8.

In his later work, Girenok reformulates the synthetic conception of anthropocosmism in favor of its cosmic component, such that humanity is ever more seen as part of a cosmic unity. Lamenting the scientific exploitation of nature, Girenok proclaims the superiority of "living knowledge," by which he means an epistemological relationship to the world founded on integrative intuition rather than analysis. He admits that this living knowledge has no instrumental value—it cannot be used to build a bridge, for example—but consists in an openness to "the intelligent silence of being" (8). Since man has dedicated himself to the interrogation and transformation of the world, it is now time for him to listen to nature without acting upon it. This presupposes not an ecological revitalization of nature by human technological means, but a renunciation of interference of any kind; instead of accommodating nature to man's needs, man will "build himself into nature" (20). "Anthropology submits to cosmology" (21). If previously Girenok (with Fedorov and Vernadsky) valorized scientific thought as the force of cosmo-urgy, now his ideal is a "simple man" who rarely reads, listens to music, or contemplates art; who instead espouses the values of "salvific non-culturedness" (18). In this view, the transition from peasantry to urbanism caused a fatal rift between humankind and nature, and what is needed now is a return from the self-destructive cultural world to the self-maintaining *natural* one.

Girenok also advances a radical critique of historicity, which presents a permanently incomplete structuring of being, even as the cosmos is always already complete and self-sufficient. History cannot be appropriated by humankind, since it has no end. Humankind has thus reduced itself to personality, which is a purely historical phenomenon; personality is self-grounding, insofar as it has no milieu other than ephemeral history. To the illusory and alienating relationship of personality/history, Girenok counterposes the ineluctable unity of man/cosmos. "The cosmos is a world in which there is no place for personality .... Personality is the principle of history (of its imagined end); man is the principle of the cosmos (which is not imagined by me). Contemporary culture remembers personality, but has forgotten about man" (14).

Accordingly, Girenok argues for a return to religious values, albeit criticizing the Christian tradition for its rationalistic and personalistic bias. What he accepts in Christian philosophy is sophiology, the mysticism of the feminine aspect of divinity which is identified as Mother Earth. The worship of the heavenly father causes humankind's alienation from the earth, insofar as it projects the Kingdom onto a transcendent plane. Girenok lauds the ancient nature cults, certain tenacious elements which still survive in Russian Christianity with its "dual faith" (*dvoeverie*). Rejecting the traditional sophiology of Solovyov, Florensky, and Bulgakov as dualistic (heaven vs. earth), Girenok instead advances cosmism as a monistic rapprochement of religion and materialism. Sophia for him is the unity of the Holy Virgin and Mother Earth. The religion of the Mother, as opposed to Judaism and Christianity—religions of Father and Son—is the creed of this mystical materialism. "The body is from moist earth, bones from stones, blood from the seas. The divine in the human comes not from God and not from man himself but from the Mother .... At the basis of the cosmic hierarchy lies motherhood, not fatherhood or creativity" (21).

Thus Girenok demonstrates one tendency in the evolution of cosmism—that of neo-paganism, the cult of Mother Nature, which draws him closer to Daniil Andreev's mysticism of the feminine. In his later works Girenok identifies his position as "archeo-avant-garde," eliminating historical and temporal dimensions.

A specific and rather weird variant of cosmism can be found in the writings of Dmitrii Panin (1911–87). An engineer by profession, he spent many years in the Gulag, where he met and worked with Aleksandr Solzhenitsyn, becoming the model for one of the main characters, Sologdin, in the novel *The First Circle*. In 1972, Panin emigrated to Western Europe, where he would publish several books on a general model of the universe. Panin professed no allegiance to the tradition of cosmism, nor did he make use of Fedorov or Tsiolkovsky in the exposition of his own system, which emphasized the active role of the Creator rather than humankind in the process of evolution. However, he can be associated with the cosmist tradition, insofar as he attempts to derive the laws of the physical universe, human psychology and morality, and the transcendental world from the same primordial principle, which he defines as *density*. Panin employs this concept at every level of explanation, whether the specific topic is time and space, good and evil, or heaven and hell. "My central hypothesis presents the Universe as a system formed by the condensation and rarefication of numerous primordial elements."[24] "All objects of the universe are densities, and spiritual and social phenomena may be defined proceeding from density."[25] Panin constructs an a priori system of postulates that has almost no inner connection except for the underlying concept of density. For example, in the beginning of his treatise *The Theory of Densities*, he offers a set of definitions:

> *Objective reality* is the totality of densities ....
> *Unity* is the interaction of densities ....
> *Cause* is the difference of densities in the unity.
> *Effect* is the result of the interaction between densities.
> *Being* is the presence of densities in a certain point in space.
> *The subject* is capable of perceiving density as a thing.[26]

According to Panin, condensation is the positive process that lays the foundation for the discrimination of good as high density and evil as low density or emptiness. God is understood as "transcendental density," which acts "immediately and independently," without the limitations of space and time, and creates everything by filling the emptiness. It is only the rarefied state of our world that gives rise to distance and intervals, as well as to various collisions between physical particles and moral wills. Time and space are likewise forms of rarefication—and of degradation of the supreme density of the Creator—since they pull apart the particles that should abide as a coherent whole.

[24] Dimitrii Panin, *Vselennaia glazami sovremennogo cheloveka* (Turne: Izdanie avtora, 1976), 5.
[25] Dimitrii Panin, *Teoriia gustot. Opyt filosofii kontsa 20-go veka* (Paris: Izdanie avtora, 1982), 7.
[26] Ibid., 8–12.

On the transphysical level, the process of condensation results in such qualities as kindness, love, mercy, generosity, while rarefication results in hatred, misery, anger, etc.[27] Accordingly, the posthumous fate of the human soul is determined by its level of density: if it has not attained a certain critical threshold, it will find itself in the hellish world of utter rarity. Characteristically, Panin acknowledges his debt to Daniil Andreev, especially in his use of such terms as "transphysical," and shares Andreev's utopian stance, calling for the establishment of an ideal society based on notions of brotherhood and chivalry. "The unification of the brotherhoods of the people of goodwill presents a greater density, which is necessary in order to overcome the resistance of the forces of evil."[28] However, Panin has no interest in metahistory, and his system is also devoid of explicit prophetic and visionary dimensions. It is constructed mostly as a dry system of theorems and general concepts, without any imagistic or narrative component. This system is an example of a purely deductive speculation around a single central concept to which the variety of specific phenomena is reduced. Theology and physics prove to be extensions of the same universal idea of "density," which illustrates the sort of extreme monism typical of syncretic thought.

One of the sources of Russian cosmism as the holistic view of noosphere, the entire universe transformed by reason and spirit, is Hegel's absolute idealism. This is the point of departure for Vitalii Kovalev (b. 1949), who pursued his philosophical studies at Moscow State University but refused to submit a dissertation because it would have obliged him to follow a Marxist methodology. Preferring the life of an independent thinker in Moscow, he collected his neo-Hegelian works on the paradigms of reason and the meaning of history in his book *The Philosophy of Posthistory* (1992).[29]

According to Hegel, Universal Spirit has progressed through the "objective" stage of Nature, further through the "subjective" stage of History, to arrive at the final stage of Absolute Spirit, in which the opposition between object and subject is overcome, thus achieving full self-awareness in philosophy. For Kovalev, this idealistic philosophy, which culminated with Hegel, now passes into the *next* stage, which he calls "diasophy," replacing philosophy's "love of wisdom" with "through wisdom" (from the Greek *dia*, "across," as in "dialectic"). Now that wisdom is no longer a mere object of love, since it has been fully realized with Hegel, it acquires a more practical dimension, gradually merging with life itself. "If philosophy is love of wisdom and the striving to possess it, then wisdom attained is already 'diasophy,' which is an absolute unity of theory and practice, cognition and life, a unity whereby absolute philosophical idealism manifests itself also as practical or active idealism."[30]

Whereas the prevailing trends in post-Hegelian philosophy of the nineteenth and twentieth centuries presented a rebellion of life and matter against reason, the truer

[27] Panin, *Vselennaia glazami sovremennogo cheloveka*, 85.

[28] Panin, *Teoriia gustot*, 115.

[29] Kovalev's later works, mostly short articles and essays on the themes of reason, history, evolution, and German and Russian philosophy, are collected on his site "Diasophy as It Is": http://www.hegel.ru/diasofia.html

[30] Vitalii Kovalev, *Filosofiia postistorii* (Moscow: ALVA-XXI, 1992), 113.

meaning of this period, according to Kovalev, was the extension of reason beyond its specific boundaries into all spheres of life, spiritualizing and idealizing the world in its entirety. This is why Marx's historical materialism and Nietzsche's philosophy of life, movements directed *against* idealism, finally demonstrated their destructive potential and hostility to *Homo sapiens*, and were overcome by the late twentieth century. Contrary to some liberal critics of Hegelian idealism as the alleged progenitor of the ideocratic systems of the twentieth century, Kovalev blames irrationalist ideology—racism, faith in revolutionary violence, etc.—for the crimes of fascism and communism. Now that communist utopianism is dying, he argues, philosophy must return to its idealist foundations and amplify them with a spiritualization of material and social life. "Diasophy … eschews the impotent intellectual conglomerations constructed by thinkers in their struggle against thought itself and generated by thought's non-recognition of itself, and addresses the speculative heights of cognition, the absolute idealism and masterful dialectics of Plato, Schelling, and Hegel."[31]

Philosophy, for Kovalev, is the highest form of human accomplishment, since reason, which organizes and penetrates all spheres of activity, comes through philosophy to understand itself and, moreover, to discover itself in everything that is not reason: nature, history, art, etc. To use reason in order to challenge and undermine Reason is a betrayal of the entire philosophical enterprise. However, these anti-idealist and anti-rationalist movements had their own significance: they highlighted those spheres of reality that still need intellectual transformation. Philosophy must not be isolated in its own speculative sphere, but should direct itself to those spheres where irrationalism has so far prevailed, so as now rather to expand reason's dominion. For example, if Nietzsche or Heidegger refutes rationality for the sake of "will to power" or "authentic being," this negation triggers reason to expand into areas previously unattainable to it. Even philosophical irrationalism is nothing but the idealization of irrationality. Thus absolute idealism did not exhaust itself with Hegel, but was carried upward by the very movements that seemed to digress from and oppose it.

Kovalev's perspectives on the historical development of reason are more eschatological than evolutionary, which sets him apart from most cosmists. In his view, historical time cannot prolong itself infinitely, since the progressive rationalization of reality occurs at increasingly dense intervals. Kovalev visualizes the timeline of history as a giant spiral whose turns bring ever more qualitative changes that are inversely proportional to their diminishing chronological spans. With the acceleration of history, each successive period will become so brief that the qualitative changes occurring within them will rapidly approach infinity. This new intensity of time change, which Kovalev calls "posthistory," will endlessly deepen the spiritual meaning of each occurrence, instead of multiplying occurrences themselves. In contrast to the American political scientist Francis Fukuyama, who in his book *The End of History and the Last Man* (1992) famously proclaimed the imminent (and likewise premised on Hegelian philosophy) end of history, Kovalev emphasizes the metaphysical rather than political meaning of this

[31] Ibid., 5.

liminality. Kovalev's posthistory—a concept he came to use as early as 1988—is not so much the end of time as the beginning of super-time. Posthistory does not represent, as in Fukuyama's envisioning, a monotonous flow of empirical time, devoid of significant historical collisions, in a uniformly democratic world suffering only from incessant boredom. Kovalev's more mystical interpretation of the "end of history" presupposes, to the contrary, that the physical dimension of time will approach zero, while history's symbolical depth will approach infinity. Instead of a positivist neutrality or apocalyptic despair about such an end of time, Kovalev proposes an "eschatology of light": "The religious task of our time consists in the preparation of souls for the encounter with Eternity, which has drawn nigh; in the promotion of a bright eschatological consciousness that understands that the end is the true beginning."[32]

Among the philosophical practices aimed at the transformation of the universe, Kovalev stipulates an important place for ecology, or more precisely, for the synthesis of diasophy and ecology, which he calls "ecosophy":

> The ecological movement can hope to achieve theoretical and practical unity in ecosophy, insofar as it represents the integration of the ecology of the natural environment, the ecology of the human body, the ecology of culture, and the ecology of spirit .... This philosophy makes a person an all-moral being, expanding the main ethical formula "Treat your neighbor as yourself" to the universal principle: "Treat the world as yourself" .... "For the world is your own self." ("What is Ecosophy?," 1989[33])

In post-Soviet Russia, religion began to supplant philosophy as the most authoritative source of wisdom and practical guidance, but Kovalev remained one of the very few thinkers to persist in assigning, as did Hegel, the mission of salvation to philosophy, even placing its internal religious potential above traditional religions. "[A] genuine religion and a genuine divine liturgy is contained in philosophy .... [P]hilosophy will save the world .... [A]ll our human world is created by thinking and is preserved by thinking .... [T]he genuine life is concentrated in philosophy."[34]

Thus does Kovalev's "diasophical" and "ecosophical" vision represent an essential link between Hegelian absolute idealism and contemporary conceptions of the noosphere, the new era of cosmic life governed by the purposeful and all-encompassing work of universal consciousness.

c. Svetlana Semenova. The Theology and Technology of Active Evolution

The best-known and most influential figure among late- and post-Soviet cosmists is Svetlana Semenova (1941–2014), the first postwar thinker to popularize Fedorov's

[32] Ibid., 31.

[33] http://www.hegel.ru/ekosofia.html

[34] Kovalev, *Filosofiia postistorii*, 4–5.

Figure 6 Svetlana Semenova.

ideas, which she did as early as the 1970s. She was the editor of the first collection of Fedorov's works to be published in the Soviet period (1982), which was also the first-ever mass edition, as prerevolutionary publications had come in the form of limited editions of several hundred copies.[35] Of all cosmists, it is Semenova who most emphatically maintained the prophetic and transformative potential of Fedorov's teaching.

Semenova considered the philosophy of cosmism in its two main branches, those of religion/philosophy and of natural science. Her early philosophical interests were connected with French existentialism, which she appreciated for the depths of metaphysical tragedy explored by Camus and Sartre, the search for human meaning in a meaningless world. However, upon discovering Fedorov in the late 1960s, she came to believe that the tragedy of the individual in an absurd world is not merely a status quo, but a condition that ought to be transcended. In her later works, she faults Camus's "solutions" to the existential dilemma as unfortunately stuck in the traditions of European culture and artistic creativity. "The artistic-playful teleology … cannot transform the natural foundation of things, abolish the tragedy of mortal human fate; [Camus's] ideal civilization so far does not dare encroach on it. [In Camus,] [t]he European idea of culture triumphs as the highest compensation and justification of the

[35] Semenova and her daughter Anastasiia Gacheva would later publish a collected works of Fedorov in five volumes: N. F. Fedorov, *Sobranie sochinenii* (Moscow: Traditsiia, 1995–2000).

natural order of existence."[36] Despite recognizing the absurdity of being, a condition rooted in the inevitable return to nonbeing, the existentialists do not propose to change being itself; instead, they seek solace in the realm of culture, where death is overcome only symbolically, for instance through the immortality of an artist's works. Of course, French existentialism, especially as represented by Jean-Paul Sartre, with his philosophy of active social engagement, did have a strong commitment to changing the world, but only politically and morally, whereas the metaphysical problem of death and absurdity was presumed to remain intact, as an eternal curse of humanity.

Thus did Semenova's encounter with Fedorov provide her with a philosophical solution to the problem of the absurd, settling accounts with her formative existentialist period. Whereas existentialism's best proposal is an individual recourse to freedom, which allows one to counterpose one's private and unique creativity to universal absurdity, Fedorov's Common Cause attacks the problem of absurdity at its source—death. With the realization of his project, the absurd is overcome, not just for the individual, and not just symbolically, but in reality, and for all humanity.

Unlike her contemporaries, most of whom take scientific perspectives, Semenova in her writings remains most faithful to the original moral and religious impetus of Fedorov's ideas. So faithful that, indeed, it is often difficult to distinguish her own thought from that of Fedorov. She seems to have understood her own task as a relatively modest one: the continuation of Fedorov's project for new centuries, incorporating both a defense of his ideas and their accommodation to the technological advancements and social transformations of the contemporary world. In her view, now that the world is even more variegated and divided than in Fedorov's time, the need for a spiritual absolute that can overcome absurdity and ever-growing relativism is that much more urgent. Humanity is divided into classes, races, nations, ethnicities, religions, genders, each of which advances its own ideology and claims to priority, but the very number of these competing ideologies attests to the difficulty of finding a common thread from which to weave a panhuman unity. Even the so-called world religions promise salvation only to the subset of the world that professes belief in their premises. Secular ideologies, both social and national, are even more limited in their scope, and of those to at least gesture at worldwide unity, the last, Marxism, divided humanity against itself in terms of class—a failure highlighting the need for an absolute that would *actually* unite the world. For Semenova, the only truly absolute project that could unite humanity, across all national and ideological divisions, is the struggle against death, the common enemy of all people. Fedorov's philosophy of the Common Cause suggests the only framework broad enough to integrate everyone and everything, including forces that are generally viewed as antagonistic, such as religion and science. The prospect of immanent immortality attained on earth combines the most far-reaching, transcendental visions of religion with the increasing technological potential of science. Thus, such specific tools of contemporary civilization as computing and digitalization can be interpreted

[36] Svetlana Semenova, *Preodolenie tragedii. "Vechnye voprosy" v literature* (Moscow: Sovetskii pisatel', 1989), 260.

as stages in the realization of Fedorov's project, since they encompass quantities of information on the immense scale needed for the resuscitation of the human body in its entirety.

However fantastic Fedorov's project may seem, Semenova insists that all the workings of civilization unintentionally pave its way. Both contemporary technology and culture are oriented toward providing a more perfect means for the reflection and reproduction of objective phenomena. Photography, television, video, audio, holography, and of course electronic media—all these technologies claim to create another reality, a hyperreality, more perfect and intransient than the one reflected. According to Semenova, these technologies may potentially constitute the precursors of the universal resurrection, which will be able to restore not only the appearance and sound, but the very existence of a person previously deceased. In her view, the legacy of the Church fathers and discoveries of contemporary science alike substantiate Fedorov's ideas.

For example, she cites from Gregory of Nyssa (335–95): "It is not improbable that this simple and non-complex nature [the soul] abides in each of [the body's] particles after its disintegration."[37] This means that, however dispersed one's bodily particles become after death, they are still related, like family members who might well achieve a reunion through the act of resurrection. In attempting which, there is no need to strive to gather every atom proper to the original body, because the magnetism of the soul in effect keeps them together. Certainly this presupposes the existence of souls that have their own free will, which would comport with the Church dogma expounded by Gregory of Nyssa, but seems incompatible with Fedorov's project, wherein the initiative of resurrection belongs not to the souls of the deceased, but to the determination of their progeny.

Equally acceptable for Semenova is to justify the possibility of resurrection with reference to "biological field" theory, a concept that was advanced in parapsychology and occult science, but that has also been elaborated by certain contemporary scientists. For example, the Belarusian physicist Aleksei Maneev (b. 1921) believes that what the ancients called "soul"—the bearer of individual consciousness—is a biological field that is emitted as a wave-like radiation by the human body and is preserved after its death. "If radiated fields (for example radio waves) continue to exist independently of their source, which however does not prevent them from bearing sufficient information, then equally possible is the existence of a bio-field that is 'radiated' at the death of an organism, but still preserves all information about it."[38] Thus might an organism be reconstructed from bio-field information, just as it was originally constructed from genetic information. Semenova goes so far as to separate the project of resurrection from material substance, proposing that memory, as the ideal reflection, might provide sufficient information to carry out the great task of the Common Cause. Memory preserves information about an object without any material connection to it, thus

[37] Semenova, *Nikolai Fedorov. Tvorchestvo zhizni*, 215.

[38] A. K. Maneev, *Filosofskii analiz antinomii nauki* (Minsk: Nauka i tekhnika, 1974): 130–1.

potentially standing as a generative model of resurrection, and one that would be more efficient than a model based on the search for actual particles of the deceased. For the most part, Semenova is open to any scientific prospect of resurrection, including the cloning of an entire organism from a single cell.

Semenova is careful to distinguish Fedorov's Common Cause from science fiction, which is based on imaginary technological projections for the future. Resurrection is not so much a technological operation as a moral effort, "a deeply intimate, sublimely and intensively loving process through which human children consciously give birth to their parents from their own selves by all their most subtle and enormously concentrated energies."[39] Just as the birth of children represents an extension of the love of their parents, the rebirth of parents is the consequence of their children's love. Semenova also responds to such critics of Fedorov as accuse him of necromancy—summoning the spirits of the dead and raising them bodily—by emphasizing, with reference to St. Paul, that the resurrected would inhabit perfected, immortal bodies rather than animate corpses. "We eagerly await a Savior from there, the Lord Jesus Christ, who, by the power that enables him to bring everything under his control, will transform our lowly bodies so that they will be like his glorious body" (Philippians 3:20–21). These "glorious" bodies will be capable of self-preservation, whereby life is sustained autotrophically, with complete nourishment generated from sunlight and air. Thus the human body will acquire the innocence of vegetable organisms, which live by photosynthesis. This capability presupposes a transfiguration of the body, which will become complete and self-creative, subject to conscious self-regulation. It is not, then, only external nature (climate, landscape) that will be subject to human conscious will, but also the organs of the body, which will be modified, even supplemented with innovative additions as dictated by the will and imagination. Fedorov called this polymorphous corporeality *polnoorgannost'*—"the complete range of organs."

With regard to sexuality, Semenova proposes a model based on an extension of genital eroticism to the entirety of the body. As opposed to Freud, who privileged the male body as the arbiter of sexual identity (since it is the site of the penis), Semenova emphasizes the eroticism of the female body, which is not focused on one organ but distributed among numerous erogenous zones. In questions of eroticism, she relies on the works of one of Fedorov's followers, Aleksandr Gorsky (1886–1943), who elaborated a theory of the erotic transformation of the universe comparable to certain later developments like Wilhelm Reich's conception of orgone, Herbert Marcuse's ideas of polymorphous sexuality, and Norman O. Brown's "love body." Gorsky ascribed fundamental importance to auto-eroticism, which in his view represents a love of one's own body in its maximally possible extension, whereby the boundaries between self and the universe become indistinguishable. From this standpoint, the object of auto-eroticism is not one's actual body, but the potential body projected by desire, one that will eventually merge with the whole of the universe. Gorsky calls this cosmic sensuality "magnetic-cloud eroticism," since the attraction of desire merges

[39] Semenova, *Nikolai Fedorov. Tvorchestvo zhizni*, 222.

with natural forces (gravity, weather, etc.), thus making eroticism a factor of cosmic evolution, and eventually transforming the entire universe into a self-governing and self-enjoying body.

Semenova writes: "The narrowly genital area of sexual reproduction breaks through and encompasses, at its highest conscious stage, the entire human organism. Magnetic-cloud eroticism, the privileging of the blossoming female body, which nourishes drowsy fantasy and creative dream, is now directed consciously and serves the human body's integration into the world."[40] Instead of limiting itself to individual reproduction, eroticism expands to encompass the continuing creation of the universe by the force of human desires, which now become absolutely conscious and instrumental, like the skills of a worker. One might note an interesting parallel between two basic conceptions of the body in Semenova's interpretation of cosmism: autotrophic nourishment and auto-eroticism. In both cases, the body becomes a self-contained microcosm that does not require other bodies for sustenance or pleasure. Thus the dialogic relationship is excluded from this universe of all-encompassing togetherness, or collectivism—which actually becomes a colossal form of solipsism, with the individual embracing the objective world as a part of itself.

Such an approach involves certain moral risks. The assumption that the external world might be made to correspond to internal desire implies the elimination of the boundary between the internal and external. This could transform the world of absolute freedom into a world of absolute violence, insofar as one person's desires would become law for all others. In postulating the ultimate unity of human consciousness and the physical world (by way of technological transformation), anthropocosmism underestimates the possible moral and psychological consequences of such a unity. Would it not be found, in particular, that the only guarantor of individual freedom, of the external world as a ground for communication and interaction between sovereign personalities, is the boundary between the internal and external?

Semenova emphasizes that Fedorov's project is not limited to a social and technological dimension, but extends to eschatology. Since resurrection will also entail the improvement of bodies and their immortality, the Last Judgement will result in *apocatastasis*—the ultimate salvation of everyone. It would be absurd to designate a perfect body for eternal suffering, but the very process of salvation will involve temporary suffering for those who, through their prior corruption, are unready for transfiguration, after which, however, no one will be condemned. Semenova also rejects traditional views that conceptualize the ideal, divine world as immutable and fixed in some blessed and shining stupor. This, she argues, is but a projection of our limited intelligence, which sees evolution as incompatible with perfection. And no wonder, as, in our earthly life, evolution is usually associated with a redressing of deficiency. "Motion, change, evolution in the limits of the natural, cosmic world (this is the only world man knows directly and physically) has always taken place through individual harm, has always brought the diminishment and death of the individual, of

[40] Semenova and Gacheva, *Russkii kosmizm*, 25.

the singular entity."[41] This is why the conventional vision of the next world, in contrast to this material, *changing* one, has always painted immortal order as beyond the flow of evolution, as absolutely static, like the ideal entities in Plato or the Heavenly Kingdom in Christianity. In Semenova's view, Fedorov stipulated, to the contrary, mobility and change as indispensable aspects of the Kingdom of God. This type of development, which is free of the degradation of individual living entities, may be called "blissful becoming"—eternal life, but not eternal stasis, which is more akin to the state of death.

Analyzing the affinities between Fedorov's doctrine and other religious teachings, Semenova reveals its correspondences with the Chinese cult of ancestors and its antinomies with Buddhist teachings about Nirvana. Fedorov was likewise critical of Judaism's conception of Shabbat, of an all-encompassing peace and rest as the ultimate state of God and humanity, which echoes the Buddhist ideal of non-activity. The only religion to sanctify the fullness of human activity, including the victory over death, is Christianity. Christ, in this context, appears less Savior than Resurrector; however, historical Christianity had misunderstood the mission of Christ. As Semenova emphasizes, Fedorov found existing churches too preoccupied with prayer and ritual, and too little interested in actually *realizing* the project contained symbolically therein.

The inner contradictions of Fedorov's philosophy are exposed in Semenova's explication of it. Fedorov claimed that the Common Cause was the true embodiment of Christ's teachings, but precisely how he understood Christ's mission, and that of God himself, remains unclear, since, in his view, the resurrection and transfiguration of the dead will be accomplished by the work of *human* mind and hands. This atheistic tendency in Fedorov's legacy becomes even more explicit in Semenova's writings. She emphasizes that Fedorov is an anti-mystical thinker; there is no place for supernatural mystery in the system of his views, no "beyond." Even those dimensions always thought to be transcendental become, in Fedorov, immanent; the next world is nothing but a model guiding human aspirations to self-preservation and immortality. Semenova is explicit in her recognition that

> the ideal of the Common Cause essentially offers a fitting solution for any ontological variant, even for the situation of extreme metaphysical despair: there is no God, and the world has no meaning. Fedorov would respond, "If this is true, then we must impart meaning to it." Therefore, if God exists, people become "active tools" of his will … if God does not exist in the form in which theistic religions present him, then the ideal of divine existence as a regulative idea of what is proper leads us to the creation of such existence, to its gradual expansion to the entire universe.[42]

This acknowledgment of the religious irrelevance of Fedorov's project is probably the most obvious of Semenova's deviations from Fedorov's original intention. In such an interpretation, Christianity is just one of the "theistic religions," an incidental

41 Semenova, *Nikolai Fedorov. Tvorchestvo zhizni*, 229.

42 Ibid., 233.

mythological pattern among resurrection stories ubiquitous in world tradition. Thus the moral and mystical dimension of Christianity, which demands spiritual transfiguration as the premise of bodily resurrection, is jettisoned from the "common cause."

Most of Semenova's works do not claim to present original ideas, but rather to synthesize the diverse sources of cosmism into a coherent system. Besides Russian thinkers, she is especially fascinated by French philosophers Henri Bergson, with his idea of creative evolution, and Teilhard de Chardin, with his concept of noosphere and his evolutionary creationism.[43] Semenova defines the common denominator of all the various cosmist tendencies as active evolutionism. In her view, the dream of human mastery of the universe was once limited to mythological and literary fantasies, but a century ago, it became a growing tendency of scientific and philosophical thought, whose joint advancement makes such "fantasies" ever more feasible. The theory of evolution challenged the traditional conception of the world as a stable whole, but humanity took another step, coming to understand evolution as a potentially conscious, even deliberate, process limited only by the human imagination.

> The idea of active evolution is the necessity of a new conscious stage in world development, when humanity directs [evolution] as dictated by reason and moral sense, takes, so to speak, the steering wheel of evolution in its own hands. It would thus be more precise to define this tendency as not so much *cosmic* as *active* evolution. Humankind, for active evolutionists, is still an interim being that is in the process of growth, far from perfection, but at the same time consciously creative, destined to transform not only the external world, but also its own nature.[44]

The assumptions behind active evolutionism echo the philosophies of Feuerbach, Marx, and Nietzsche, inasmuch as these thinkers first strive to immanentize the transcendental, by claiming that God is a creation of humanity or a symbol of its creative abilities—and then to fill the vacancy left by God by the reverse operation of transcendentalizing the immanent through the force of human creativity and will. The Common Cause of active evolution oversteps the limitations of both Marxist and Nietzschean projects, since it aspires to the unity of all humanity, not to a privileged class or a cohort of exceptional overmen.

In postcommunist Russia, anthropocosmism is especially appealing in that it offers a challenge to both communism and nationalism, aspiring to an international and intersocial unity of all humanity. However, it also challenges the project of liberal democracy. Cosmism and liberalism both reject social or national oppositions as

[43] One of Semenova's last books is an investigation—the most fundamental in the Russian language—of Teilhard de Chardin's life and thought, titled *A Pilgrim to the Future* (*Palomnik v budushchee: P'er Teiar de Sharden.* Moscow: Russkaia khristianskaia gumanitarnaia akademiia, 2009) 672.

[44] Semenova and Gacheva, *Russkii kosmizm,* 4.

criteria of privilege, but they deeply differ in their primary orientation. Liberalism inherently rejects any notion of a Common Cause or of "labor armies" obligatory for everyone, prioritizing instead the autonomous rights of each individual, protecting the uniqueness of the personality rather than subjecting it to some ideological unity or technological imperative. From the liberal standpoint, individual values are irreducible to any common task, and the project of one ideology for all humanity appears to threaten a potentially even more dangerous kind of totalitarianism than the relatively "specialized" forms already manifested historically, communism and fascism. A panhuman totality excludes all kinds of otherness, even the otherness of nature with respect to humanity. Thus the classic Soviet pejorative by which a given person could be designated as hostile—an "enemy of the people"—might now be broadened into a metaphysical accusation: an "enemy of the universe."

This is not meant to imply that the cosmist project is necessarily antagonistic to individuality. Both Semenova and Girenok emphasized that no part of the universe is expendable; even a single individual (or a single atom) contributes to its unity. But this tribute to individuality is reminiscent of many utopian projects, which require the participation of everyone for their realization. Overall, cosmism can be characterized as an extreme form of monism, one that attempts to unify various levels of existence and consciousness under the aegis of a panhuman will. Even Marxism acknowledged the principal difference between the social and the natural orders of the universe, but cosmism attempts to eliminate the boundaries between the psychological, social, natural, and technological spheres to create a universal and perfect entity that would possess simultaneously the qualities of organism, cosmos, society, and machine.

4. The Religion of Absolute Self and the Abyss of Negativity. Iurii Mamleev

Eastern and Western mysticism and spiritualism, which had a considerable impact on prerevolutionary Russian culture and later influenced Daniil Andreev's *Rose of the World*, asserted itself once again in the 1960s–1980s, penetrating many circles of Soviet society, both superficially, for example, in popular wellness and yoga classes, and on deeper esoteric levels. In the USSR, following the West with a certain lag, the entire eclectic array of various New Age practices appealed to the intelligentsia as a nonpolitical way of spiritual resistance through individual programs of self-awareness: Zen Buddhism, tantric yoga, shamanism, Helena Blavatsky's theosophy, "the fourth way" of Georgii Gurdjieff and Peter D. Ouspensky, Tibetan Buddhism, and the Agni Yoga of Nicholas and Helena Roerich.[45]

45 A broad perspective on Russian occult and esoteric movements (including cosmism) of the late and post-Soviet periods is offered in the collection: Michael Hagemeister, Birgit Menzel, and Bernice Glatzer Rosenthal, eds., *The New Age of Russia. Occult and Esoteric Dimensions* (Bern: Peter Lang, 2012).

For the most part, this kind of mysticism proved to be a passing fad, but certain underground groups, drawing inspiration from it, attempted to develop original modes of artistic and intellectual creativity. One of them included the writers Iurii Mamleev and Arkadii Rovner, who elaborated sophisticated esoteric theories. After his emigration to the United States in 1973, Rovner (1940–2019), a writer and occult thinker, founded a New York journal called *AUM*, which published esoteric materials in various genres of philosophy, prose, and poetry. Rovner attempted to build a synthesis of the mystical teachings of the West and East, generally adhering to the legacy of Gurdjieff. He authored numerous books and compiled encyclopedias on the history of mysticism, founded the Russian Esoteric Society of New York, and later, upon his return to Russia, the Institute for the Cultivation of the Inner States.

Iurii Mamleev (1931–2015) gained widespread popularity for his dark fiction, much of which was inspired by his nontraditional beliefs and mystical intuitions. Mamleev's mode of writing, which he called "metaphysical realism," is close to surrealism and expressionism in its fascination with infernal and demonic motifs, sometimes echoing Russian Symbolism and the avant-garde of the early twentieth century, especially Fedor Sologub's novels, such as *The Petty Demon* (1905).[46] One of the most intellectually extravagant and creative of Moscow's esoteric groups was the so-called Iuzhinsky circle (AKA "Mamleev's circle"), an informal literary and occult club that gathered at the two-room portion Mamleev occupied in a communal apartment in a barrack in a courtyard on Iuzhinsky Lane.[47] Several of the circle's members later achieved prominence: Evgenii Golovin (1938–2010), philologist, writer, occultist, researcher of esotericism and alchemy, the theoretician of the group; Geidar Dzhemal (1947–2016), Russian-Islamic activist, esoteric philosopher and poet, the founder and chairman of the Islamic Committee of Russia.[48] The barrack was demolished in 1968, and Mamleev emigrated to the United States in 1974 (subsequently relocating to France in 1983 and returning to Russia in 1991), but the circle continued to exist until the early 1990s.

[46] One of Mamleev's best novels (written 1966; first, expurgated publication in 1980), recently translated by Marian Schwarz as *The Sublimes*, describes a mystical circle, a grotesque gang that gathers in a village near Moscow. These philosophers, to cite a passage from a critical review, "are obsessed with the idea of seeking a divine truth—but they look for it in the bowels of the human psyche. One character cultivates 'on his scrawny, sinewy body various colonies of fungi, herpes, and pustules, which he scraped off—and ate.' A dying man thinks he's a chicken; a woman drinks the blood of live cats, another eats chocolate cake off a diseased corpse. There are sweating eunuchs, mad gravediggers, and a solipsist who caresses himself until 'his entire body seemed to be gushing sperm.' It makes Margarita at Satan's ball look like child's play, even if Mamleev shares Bulgakov's fascination with human depravity." Phoebe Taplin, "Meet Yuri Mamleev: Insanity, Murder, and Sexual Depravity on the Quest for Divine Truth." *Russia Beyond.* Available electronically: https://www.rbth.com/literature/2014/04/14/meet_yuri_mamleev_insanity_murder_and_sexual_depravity_on_the_quest_for_35879.html

[47] The history of this group is described in Marlene Laruelle, "The Iuzhinskii Circle:Far-Right Metaphysics in the Soviet Underground and Its Legacy Today," *The Russian Review* 74, no. 4 (2015): 563–80. See also Birgit Menzel, "The Occult Revival in Russia Today and Its Impact on Literature," *The Harriman Review* 16, no. 1 (2007): 1–14.

[48] Aleksandr Dugin (b. 1962), the leading theoretician of Eurasianism, joined the circle much later, in 1980.

According to Mamleev, "in Moscow in the 1960s, an entire metaphysical culture emerged, which to a certain degree reflected secret religious and mystical strivings in post-Stalinist Russia."[49] Mamleev himself was one of the most original voices of this culture, though writings of his that could be called metaphysical proper were few and brief: "The Destiny of Being" (published 1993) and "Russia Eternal" (1997).[50] Mamleev's religious-esoteric system emerged in the 1960s and drew not only on Eastern influences but also on traditional Russian spirituality.

In the West, religious systems are based on the presumption of radical difference and even opposition of man and God, with the latter postulated as existing in a special, transcendental realm beyond human reach and understanding. This is why, according to Mamleev, Church institutions and rational theology arise as means to overcome the distance between man and God. In the East, by contrast, the Absolute is thought to be immanent to humankind: "[T]here is no abyss between God and the internal highest Self of a person; moreover, in their essence they are absolutely identical."[51] This leads Mamleev to the radical conclusion that the Self is divine and that there can be no other religious object than one's own *I*. "The only object of worship and faith is the believer's own *I*."[52] Mamleev admits that this equation of God and *I* is even more radical than Hinduism's essential equation of Brahman and Atman, as stated for example in the teachings of the eighth-century Indian philosopher Adi Shankaracharya. Hinduism recognizes the principal difference between internal and external manifestations of the Absolute, between the absolute *I* of Atman and the absolute It of Brahman; their relationship is designated in the formula: "I am That" or "I am Brahman." Mamleev's formula is "I am I," which presupposes that the entire external world is only an illusion produced by the *I*, just as a dream is produced by consciousness during sleep.

Mamleev calls his system "absolute" or "ontological solipsism," since it asserts *I* as the only reality. Whereas more moderate, epistemological solipsism denies the possibility of proving the external world's objective reality, ontological solipsism denies this world's very existence. Therefore, in the new religion, love for oneself becomes the highest virtue. This does not, however, mean a proclamation of hedonism or egoism, since for Mamleev selfhood has various levels. Egoism and hedonism pertain only to the most superficial and material of these levels, those of sensual pleasure, but the religion of Self encompasses all levels of selfhood, and even presupposes the sacrifice of the lower ego to the highest *I*. Mamleev asserts the necessity for suffering, since it "reveals the closeness of the *I* to itself … its mad love for itself, and therefore sharpens the feeling of Self."[53] The suffering that the *I* inflicts on itself promotes the process of self-consciousness and deeper self-revelation. The mechanism of self-love is the incessant ascension from lower levels of ego, which is opposed to the apparent

[49] Iu. V. Mamleev, "Sud'ba bytiia." Available electronically: https://rvb.ru/mamleev/03philos/01sb/sb.htm

[50] Mamleev's works are available online: https://rvb.ru/mamleev/contents.htm

[51] Mamleev, "Sud'ba bytiia."

[52] Ibid.

[53] Ibid.

world, to the deepest levels of absolute *I*, which embraces this "surrounding" world and accepts it as an external aspect of the same selfhood.

Mamleev explains this absolutization of the Self in his philosophy with reference to the historical conditions in which it emerged: the aggressive collectivism of the Soviet regime had to be counterbalanced by a concentration on the mystical significance of selfhood. This does not mean that Mamleev is inclined to reduce his system to this historical explanation; rather, he implies that the overweening pressure of Soviet vulgar materialism and socialism made the absolute truth of this "metaphysics of the *I*" all the more obvious.

The immediate aim of Mamleev's metaphysics is "God-realization," meaning the dissolution of transient and limited human individuality in the depth of its absolute Self. The deification of this eternal and immortal *I* puts an end to all false identifications, such as "I am a student," "I am Russian," "I am young," or even "I am human." The only true identity is "I am I," which means the absoluteness of the *I* in itself.

There remains, however, a still higher revelation, which Mamleev calls the "Ultimate Doctrine" and which leads beyond this Divine Absolute. The religion of Selfhood, in his view, still lies within the esoteric tradition, while the Ultimate Doctrine indicates a path never before assayed. After the Absolute is realized, and the highest bliss, repose, and self-immersion are achieved, the horizon even beyond the Absolute may be perceived, though only through non-perception, as "the Abyss," "transcendental darkness," or "the principle of night." "Thus the negations which earlier were overcome on the way to the Absolute now play some positive role: it is as if they signify some breach or rupture in Being, a catastrophe, a way of preparation, a hole in the world."[54] This negation can be reached only after the fullness of Divinity has been achieved and transcended in human Selfhood; this aspiration for something more may be compared to "a kiss with closed eyes or a kiss of an invisible Face."[55] This eventual transcendence, which in Mamleev's view leads beyond the Absolute itself, is connected with the deepest revelation of the Russian spirit, as distinct both from the Western spirit, with its search for a transcendent God, and from the Eastern one, with its contentment in an immanent deity. The Russian idea is not only to reveal the immanence of God but to transcend God himself, to aspire to the realm of transcendental nothingness. "The anguish without 'reason' (Russian anguish!) … leads him [God] into the Transcendental abyss. He can become god-madman, god-blasphemer, god-fool, because this is God departing for the endless Night."[56]

Mamleev's description of the negative abyss evokes the conception of nothingness in such celebrated European mystics as Meister Eckhart and Jacob Boehme, who were the inspirational force behind Nikolai Berdiaev's theology of freedom. According to these concepts, God is the creator of the universe, but what precedes God himself and was never created is nothingness, or the Abyss, which accounts for indestructible

[54] Ibid.
[55] Ibid.
[56] Ibid.

human freedom. Not even God, the Creator, has the power to limit this freedom. Thus, despite Mamleev's claims of absolute originality, his Ultimate Doctrine has very respectable precedents in the Western and Russian mystical tradition. The novelty of his contribution consists not in the concept of nothingness as prior to God, but in the particular tendency of his esoteric search, which proclaims nothingness as an ultimate goal *beyond* God. Thus "religion" is superseded twice: first, when the aim of religion is attained—that is, the divine is fully realized within the Self; second, when this aim itself is negated, and the fullness of divinity is transgressed for the sake of negativity. In fact, Mamleev reproduces the logic of the movement from cataphatic to apophatic theology, from the knowledge of what God is to the knowledge of what He is not, as represented in the writings of Pseudo-Dionysius the Areopagite. But this is an ontological rather than epistemological movement: from the being of God to his nonbeing, from Pleroma to Abyss.

The person capable of such an ambivalent esoteric pursuit recalls the type of the all-encompassing panhuman (*vsechelovek*) as described by Dostoevsky in Dmitrii Karamazov or Nikolai Stavrogin: one who manages to combine the upper and lower abysses of spirit, the ideals of Madonna and Sodom. In Mamleev's description:

> This "being" simultaneously embraces both absolute fullness and absolute lack, both the will to "death" and immortality, both eternal self-preservation and the risk of "self-destruction," both absolute narcissism and an attempt to go beyond Oneself, both God and "Anti-God"—this "being" is a genuine paradox of paradoxes, and even the very fact of his existence can be called into question, because in his most important aspect he goes beyond the boundaries of reality, the boundaries of the world of the Absolute.[57]

In Mamleev's view, this transcendence beyond the Absolute lies at the foundation of the Russian national character, which accounts for its love of the shameful and hideous as displayed in the metaphysical creations of Dostoevsky, such as Svidrigailov, Stavrogin, and Dmitrii Karamazov. This space behind the Absolute is a kind of metaphysical underground in the Dostoevskian sense, except that in Mamleev, this underground does not precede the Absolute, but follows it. At this point, Dostoevsky's Christianity, as a way out of the underground, loses its salvific capacity, since it leads in the direction of the Absolute and not away from it. What is the fundamental difference between negativity "after" as opposed to "before" the positive religion of salvation? On this question Mamleev is vague, declaring merely that "all our earthly world and all other worlds, from hell to Heaven and the devil and gods and the unified Absolute, the source and principle of all of them, belong naturally to the same utterly immanent Reality."[58] One can only suppose that the supersession of the Absolute will be followed by a kind of Nietzschean reevaluation of all values, such that all that was assessed as

[57] Ibid.
[58] Ibid.

negative in the positive world will be reassessed as positive in a post-Absolute negative world, and sins will be transformed into virtues. Nietzsche did not posit this inverted world "after the Absolute," except in the historical sense of occurring in the epoch after the "death of God," but Mamleev proclaims the transcendental realm of nothingness, where this world really can exist along with the living God. This is how the Russian intuition of the panhuman differs from the German project of the superman: the panhuman does not assert their superiority over the human while remaining on earth and adhering to the principle of biological evolution; rather, in a more Eastern spirit, they entirely transcend this world and embrace both the Absolute and its negation.

Accordingly, Mamleev reassesses the conception of metaphysical art, whose task is "to replace the sacrificial, golden crown of the monarch (the crown pouring light into the external) with the dark crown of initiation, the crown of absolute deepening."[59] This means that a metaphysical writer should not eschew encounters with any spiritual (or anti-spiritual) forces, from whatever abyss they might originate, and at the same time should transcend even the most transcendent of them. Ideally, the writer's "supreme *I* must be a certain analogue of divine nothingness, some eternal coldness, transcendental in relation to any fluid reality."[60]

Writing, then, is a kind of yogic self-discipline designed for the spiritual transformation of the writer, and only the superficial and secondary outcome of this process can be "sacrificially" offered to a readership. Such is the doctrine of metaphysical egoism, which began as a reaction to the mystical collectivism of Soviet society and then developed into a system of quasi-Eastern nihilism, claiming to transcend all the Absolutes that previous religions considered to be the unsurpassable horizons of human aspiration.

[59] Ibid.

[60] Ibid.

Part IV

Postmodernist Thought. Conceptualism

1. The Origins of Conceptualism

Since the early 1990s, the notion of postmodernism has often been deployed to explain such peculiarities of late-Soviet and post-Soviet culture as the post-utopian mentality, a critical attitude toward traditional notions of truth and reality, and ironic playfulness with regard to the sign systems of various ideologies.[1] In Russia, the artistic, literary, and intellectual movement most directly related to postmodernism became known from the mid-1970s on as "conceptualism" (*kontseptualizm*), a term initially borrowed from the artistic school founded in the late 1960s by the American artists Joseph Kosuth and Sol LeWitt.

Conceptual art was connected from the very beginning with philosophy, and even claimed to be more genuinely philosophical than philosophy itself. "The twentieth century brought in a time which could be called 'the end of philosophy and the beginning of art' .... Art is itself philosophy made concrete."[2] Two lines of argument intersect in this statement by Kosuth. On the one hand, twentieth-century art is no longer limited to the creation of material forms, but seeks to question the very nature of art and redefine it with each specific work. Art thus becomes an articulation of ideas about art. "'Conceptual Art' merely means a conceptual investigation of art."[3] On the other hand, analytical philosophy, as Kosuth suggests, has long since renounced its former "philosophical" claim to enunciate the truth, to make veritable propositions about the world. Therefore, philosophy has lost its privileged "scientific" status; and

1 See, for example, "Symposium on Russian Postmodernism" (with Mikhail Epstein, Jerome McGann, Marjorie Perloff, et al.), *Postmodern Culture* 3, no. 2 (1993); available electronically: http://www.pomoculture.org/2013/09/25/symposium-on-russian-postmodernism; "Russian Critical Theory and Postmodernism: The Theoretical Writings of Mikhail Epstein. A Forum," *Slavic and East European Journal* 39, no. 3 (1995): 329–66; Epstein, *After the Future*; Mikhail Epstein, Alexander Genis, and Slobodanka Vladiv-Glover, *Russian Postmodernism: New Perspectives on Post-Soviet Culture* (New York, Oxford: Berghahn Books, 1999; new and revised edition, New York, Oxford: Berghahn Books, 2016); and Mikhail Epshtein, *Postmodernizm v Rossii* (St. Petersburg: Azbuka, 2019).

2 Joseph Kosuth, *Art after Philosophy and After. Collected Writings, 1966–1990* (Cambridge, MA and London: Massachusetts Institute of Technology, 1991), 14, 52.

3 Ibid., 84.

in a "post-philosophical" age, its function passes to art, which plays with signs and languages without any assumption as to their credibility.

These two processes, the conceptualization of art and the aestheticization of philosophy, contribute together to their rapprochement and the redefinition of conceptual art as concrete philosophy. Instead of portraying a visible object, the conceptualist artist presents its verbal description, that is, a deliberately schematized generalization that takes the place of a lifelike image. This technique paved the way for metaphysical speculation about the nature of artistic reality as nothing more (nor less) than the projection of mental forms. Russian culture proved fertile ground for the application of conceptualism due to the prevalence of ideological schemes and stereotypes throughout its history, especially during the Soviet period.

Another source of the term "conceptualism," less obvious but perhaps even more characteristic for this movement's development in Russia, is the medieval philosophical school of the same name. Among European scholastics of the thirteenth and fourteenth centuries, conceptualism functioned as a moderate version of nominalism, which asserted that all general ideas have their being not in reality but in the sphere of pure concepts. As such, this school was opposed to realism, which posited a single continuum of physical and conceptual reality, and insisted on the ontological being of such universals as love, soul, beauty, goodness, etc. Strange as it may seem, an analogous confrontation of two intellectual trends occurred in the late Soviet period, with Marxism asserting the historical reality of such general ideas as "collectivism," "equality," and "progress," and conceptualism arguing the purely nominative and mental basis of such ideological constructs. Like its medieval counterpart, conceptualism attempts to expose the realist fallacy by which objective existence is attributed to general or abstract ideas. This fallacy was the hidden assumption of the Soviet system, which conferred the status of absolute reality to its own ideological pronouncements. Virtually every facet of Soviet life was dictated by ideological presuppositions about the nature of social reality, and conceptualism attempted to expose the contingent nature of such concepts by unmasking them as constructs proceeding from the human mind or generated by linguistic practices.

In conceptualism, both as art and philosophy, concepts are self-referential units of thinking, ideas presented as ideas. The Russian *kontsept* as an aesthetic term has a more particular meaning than the English "concept" (whose less "marked" Russian equivalent, indeed, would be *poniatie*). *Kontsept* is not just a concept, but more specifically a work of art or element of such a work that presents a concept in its purity, as a self-sufficient entity. According to Ilya Kabakov, one of Russian conceptualism's founders: "Precisely because of its self-referentiality and the lack of windows or a way out to something else, [the *kontsept*] is like something that hangs in the air, a self-reliant thing, like a fantastic construction, connected to nothing, with its roots in nothing."[4]

4 Ilya Kabakov, "Conceptualism in Russia," in *Zhizn' mukh. Das Leben der Fliegen. Life of Flies*, by Ilya Kabakov (Cologne: Kölnischer Kunstverein, 1992), 249.

Conceptualism, as it emerged in the West in the 1960s, remained a narrowly artistic device and had a more limited scope, since its substitution of concept for object proceeded from visual art's need for deeper self-reflection, without some implicit criticism of Western civilization as a whole. By contrast, in Russia, *kontseptualizm* revealed much broader philosophical and critical potential, because it took aim at a logocentric and ideocratic society intoxicated with texts and concepts. The Russian version of conceptualism, which flourished in the 1970s and 1980s, established a theoretical and aesthetic distance toward the ideological discourse that dominated Soviet culture. From the start, conceptualism was not a purely artistic movement, but relied heavily on a philosophical foundation. Conceptualist poetry and visual art were theoretically self-conscious, presuming a premeditated and ironic attitude toward the language of ideas. Conceptualism might be called a meta-ideological approach to art, or a meta-aesthetic approach to ideology, since it strove to reflect upon the hidden ideological apriorisms of consciousness and to verbalize or visualize them. Insofar as people's thinking was unconsciously conditioned by ideological stereotyping in the Soviet period (as it is, to some extent or other, everywhere and at all times), conceptualists proposed to undermine this process of indoctrination by revealing it to consciousness; in a sense, that is, conceptualism worked as a psychoanalytic instrument for deconstructing the repressive Soviet superego. If psychoanalysis involves curing neuroses by bringing repressed impulses to the light of individual consciousness, the conceptualist project represented an "ideo-analysis" meant to cure the trauma of ideological obsessions by bringing them to the awareness of the collective subject.

Many of the Russian thinkers associated with conceptualism are not philosophers in the conventional sense, but rather members of the art world, or interpreters of it, or both. In this, they differ radically from all the traditional schools of thought that have relied solely on linguistic discourse for the presentation of ideas. With its visual component, conceptualism overcomes the long-standing affiliation between philosophy and literature in Russia, and also contrasts with the Western bias for philosophy couched almost exclusively in oral or written discourse. This conventional bias went unquestioned for centuries, but with the advent of conceptualism we are finally prompted to wonder: why is philosophy obliged to be verbal? Why could it not take visual or gestural form? The presupposition of conceptual art is, simply, that art may be practiced in the medium of concepts or mental projections; is this not precisely what philosophy is as well? Conceptual artists do not so much deal with visual forms per se, as with visualizations of concepts that constitute a kind of philosophical discourse translated into a system of objects and presented as works of art.

On the other hand, conceptual art problematizes not only the linguistic bias of philosophy but also the visual bias of the arts. The basis of conceptualism is a critique of *pure representation*, in the Kantian sense. For Kant, an intelligible essence does not belong to the thing-in-itself, but is imposed on it through the apriori schemes of consciousness. Similarly, the visual element in art can be understood as only a projection of the constructive imagination—an interpretation that regards the visual realm as an extension of a concept, with the concept itself capable of supplementing or even replacing a picture or image. This was done literally in the early works of Western conceptualism, where, for example, an encyclopedia article describing a chair was presented as an artistic object along with the chair itself and its reproduction in painting (Joseph Kosuth's *One and Three Chairs*, 1965; Museum of Modern Art, New York). Traditionally, the visual component is privileged over the label or verbal inscription that accompanies and designates an autonomous work of art. In conceptual art, the textual component moves into the foreground; every visual work is conceived as an illustration of its label, of the artist's textual creativity. At the same time, a conceptual work is not merely an artistic depiction of a text, like in an illustrated book, where the visual is dependent on and subordinate to the literary narrative and mimetically reflects the plot; in conceptual art, a text itself functions as a visual work or interacts independently and creatively with a visual image. Moreover, a conceptualist does not even need to create a new artifact to label and sign it, but can affix a title or signature to an existing real-world object, thereby transforming it into a concept. Thus did the Russian conceptualist artists Komar and Melamid "sign" an earthquake that occurred in Germany and send a telegram to the chancellor notifying him that they were the authors of this event. This mode allows a conceptualist to create concepts out of anything whatsoever, making this artistic practice a bona fide philosophical activity, inasmuch as it carries out the conceptualization of the world.

Conceptualist thinking reveals the futile aggressiveness of the human mind, which imposes its own ideological schemes on a reality that is inaccessible as such, and yet is continually pursued via a process of representational substitutions and innumerable references without verifiable referents. In this view, any attempt at mental coherency ultimately devolves into obsession and madness, if we define the latter as the state of consciousness divorced or isolated from reality. From the conceptualist standpoint, traditional philosophy, as the most rigorously coherent way of thinking, is closest to madness, with its solipsistic fixations on absolute ideas. The only thing distinguishing philosophy from madness is the self-irony of the philosopher; thus, in conceptualism, irony takes the place occupied by truth or verification in more ambitious philosophical systems, like German classical idealism or logical positivism. The method for relating philosophy to reality now involves not the positive correspondence or identification of concepts with objects, but the revelation of an inexorable and irreducible disjunction between them, a gap bridged only by self-referential, hence self-ironic conceptualizations. Irony becomes the only possible form of truth for conceptual philosophy, inasmuch as it lacks any criteria for verification but has innumerable criteria for philosophical self-falsification.[5]

[5] For more on conceptualism, see Epstein, *After the Future*, 30–7, 60–70, 200–3; Mikhail Epstein, "The Philosophical Implications of Russian Conceptualism," *Journal of Eurasian Studies* 1, no. 1 (2010): 64–71; Epstein, Genis, and Vladiv-Glover, *Russian Postmodernism*, 169–81, 410–27, 542–9.

2. The Archaic Postmodernism of Andrei Siniavsky

If a complete history of Russian postmodernism is ever written, then Andrei Siniavsky (1925–97), who published some of his most seminal work under the pen name Abram Tertz, would have to feature prominently as one of its founders. Siniavsky himself did not use the term, generally eschewing association with any established philosophical school; but his writing took a persistently postmodern perspective, particularly as it tended to reinterpret classical models of socialist realism in the spirit of post-utopian sots-art,[6] or "socialist art." Siniavsky emerged on the Soviet intellectual scene as a talented young critic and scholar affiliated with the Moscow Institute of World Literature. In the late 1950s and early 1960s, he managed to smuggle some of his fiction and a long essay on socialist realism to the West, where these were published under his pseudonym Abram Tertz. When this was discovered by the KGB, Siniavsky was sentenced to exile in the Mordovian labor camps. His trial in 1966 received

Figure 7 Andrei Siniavsky.

[6] This term was introduced by Vitalii Komar and Aleksandr Melamid in 1972.

international attention, since the criminal prosecution of a writer was unprecedented in the post-Stalin era, and was taken as a sign of the replacement of Khrushchev's Thaw with Brezhnev's policy of re-Stalinization. In 1973, after six years in prison and labor camp (1965–71), Siniavsky was allowed to emigrate and settle in Paris, where he worked as a professor of Russian literature and culture at the Sorbonne. There he founded, with his wife Maria Rozanova, the influential journal *Sintaksis* (thirty-seven issues, 1978–2001), which became a prominent mouthpiece for modernist and postmodernist trends in Russian culture.

Along with fictional pieces, Siniavsky authored several books of literary and cultural criticism, as well as collections of aphorisms and short essays. His nonfictional writing is difficult to classify either as scholarship or journalism; in the peculiarly Russian tradition inspired by Fedor Dostoevsky's *Diary of a Writer* and Vasilii Rozanov's *Fallen Leaves*, it is a synthesis of philosophy, artistry, and polemics, at times close to academic discourse (as in the books *Soviet Civilization* and *Ivan the Fool: Outlines of Russian Popular Belief*), at times bordering on free-flowing reflections and associations (as in *Unguarded Thoughts* and *A Voice from the Chorus*). As one commentator has observed: "Sinyavsky is philosophic but not a philosopher, he is building no system, inventing no new vocabulary. This puts him in the mainstream of the Russian tradition, in which literature and philosophy are not, as a rule, entirely differentiated."[7] Siniavsky generally preferred to publish his scholarly works under his real name, while his works of fiction and more whimsical nonfiction were offered under his pseudonym, Abram Tertz—a practice that reversed and parodied the conventional tendency of Soviet Jewish writers to take Russian pen names, since Siniavsky was a Russian who took a Jewish pen name. The relationship between his two personalities was complex enough to require a special discussion; here suffice it to say that Siniavsky preferred to express his most personal thoughts as Abram Tertz, which is typical of postmodern authors writing in a citational mode.

Religious Parody and the Aesthetics of Communism

Siniavsky's book *On Socialist Realism*, published in Paris in 1959, offers an original interpretation of the Soviet literary and artistic method, challenging both the official valorization of socialist realism and its skeptical reception in the West. Siniavsky exposes the inner contradiction of the method, which attempts to join a teleological element (socialism) with a scientific one (realism). He contends that Marxism is not only teleological but borders on religion, since it formulates an ultimate goal of history and interprets all past and present events in relation to this goal. "The specific teleology of Marxist thought consists in leading *all* concepts and objects to the Purpose, referring them all to the Purpose, and defining them all through the Purpose. The history of all epochs and nations is but the history of humanity's march toward Communism."[8] As

7 Richard Lourie, *Letters to the Future. An Approach to Sinyavsky-Tertz* (Ithaca and London: Cornell University Press, 1975), 122.

8 Abram Tertz, *On Socialist Realism*, trans. George Dennis (New York: Pantheon Books, 1960), 35.

Siniavsky sees it, even Marxist philosophy's concept of the "material base," which is supposed to determine the ideological superstructure, is inherently idealistic, since, in the words of Stalin, "[t]he base produces the superstructure so that it can serve the base."[9] Such a presupposition is at least quasi-religious in its congruence with the notion that God created man so that he might serve God.

Socialist realism is logically inclined toward classicism as an aesthetic model, with its orientation toward sublime and idealistic norms of discourse. The realistic component, which is alien to socialism, introduces an involuntary element of parody into Soviet art. "It is impossible, without falling into parody, to produce a positive hero in the style of full socialist realism and yet make him into a psychological portrait. In this way, we will get neither psychology nor hero."[10] Siniavsky would prefer both hero and parody. Grasping the inherently parodic element in socialist realism, he goes so far—in the spirit of what would later be called conceptualism—as to recommend that Soviet heroic art be enhanced via the self-conscious exploitation of parody. What a shame, in his view, that the eclectic mixture of realism and classicism officially promoted as "socialist realism" from the 1930s through the 1950s lacked the genuinely phantasmagoric proportions capable of transforming dull, didactic imitations of life into inspirationally grotesque imitations of didacticism and teleology itself.

For example, Siniavsky proposes that Stalin's death, if presented as a religious event, could have become a theme of great art, intrinsically deeply parodic.

> We could have announced on the radio that he did not die but had risen to heaven, from which he continued to watch us, in silence, no words emerging from beneath the mystic mustache. His relics would have cured men struck by paralysis or possessed by demons. And children, before going to bed, would have kneeled by the window and addressed their prayers to the cold and shining stars of the Celestial Kremlin.[11]

Such a transformation of socialist realism into a religio-parodic form was accomplished more than twenty years later in the sots-art of Komar and Melamid. The titles of many of their paintings—such as *Stalin and the Muses* and *View of the Kremlin in a Romantic Landscape* (both from the series *Nostalgic Socialist Realism*, 1981–2)—suggest an implicit reference to Siniavsky's meta-socialist project.

Instead of condemning socialist realism as false, demagogic, or simply bad art, as was done in the West, or praising its truthful reflection of life, as in the Soviet Union, Siniavsky eliminates the criterion of truth altogether, reinterpreting this canon as a system of interrelated signs that may be used for artistic purposes—not because they refer to some knowable reality, but precisely because they depart from it. He was among the first to formulate the principle of parody and conscious eclecticism as a new

9 Cited ibid., 35.

10 Ibid., 90.

11 Ibid., 92.

source for contemporary art, and he paved the way for a highly innovative postmodern assimilation of socialist realism, which in the 1960s was generally considered a dead-end movement both in the West and in dissident circles within the USSR.

In later articles and in his book *Soviet Civilization* (1988), Siniavsky continued his investigation of communism as a unique historical formation possessing its own unexplored, mystical depth. Here his concern is "not so much the history of Soviet civilization as the theory and even what I might call the metaphysics."[12] More so than other researchers in this field, Siniavsky stresses the theatrical nature of the Soviet system, which was designed as a spectacle by the great "directors" Lenin and, especially, Stalin ("in his eyes he was the only actor-director on the stage of all Russia and all the world. In this sense, Stalin was a born artist"[13]).

In his assessment of the aesthetic nature of communism, Siniavsky emphasizes the crucial role of language in the success of the Soviet regime. Official ideology coined at least three words that captured the imagination of the people by virtue of their expressiveness: "Bolshevik" (lit. "he who gives more"); "Cheka" (lit. the acronym of the early version of the KGB, the "Emergency Commission," this word resonates with *nacheku*, "on the lookout" or "on one's guard"); and "Soviet" (not technically a postrevolutionary coinage, but of course ubiquitous in the system it designated, this word literally means "a council" or "advice," and, moreover, sounds almost like *svet*, "light"). These words, in Siniavsky's semi-ironic estimation, are "the three whales on which the Soviet system … stands"[14]—an argument that prefigures the conceptualist explanation of Soviet reality as an extension of verbal models.

Absurdity, Religion, and Sexuality

Siniavsky's philosophical position is elaborated, in a deliberately unsystematic mode, in his books *Unguarded Thoughts* and *A Voice from the Chorus*. The style of these works follows that of Rozanov's philosophical journals and might support the classification of Siniavsky as an existentialist writer. Siniavsky acknowledges his debt to Rozanov in a scholarly investigation of the latter's work, and we can readily apply his characterization of Rozanov to Siniavsky himself: "He was attracted to the opportunity of being incoherent and disjointed, the possibility of contradicting himself rather than expounding some harmonious conception …. Owing to this contradictoriness, we get the sense of a very natural and living process in the growth and development of his thought."[15] The existential direction of Siniavsky's work is influenced by his position as a clandestine writer in *Unguarded Thoughts*, and then as a political prisoner in *A Voice*

[12] Andrei Sinyavsky, *Soviet Civilization. A Cultural History*, trans. Joanne Turnbull with Nikolai Formozov (New York: Little, Brown and Co., 1990), xii.

[13] Ibid., 98.

[14] Abram Terts, "Literaturnyi protsess v Rossii," *Kontinent* (Paris), no.1 (1974): 143–90. Available electronically: https://vtoraya-literatura.com/pdf/terz_literaturny_protsess_v_rossii_1974__ocr.pdf

[15] Andrei Siniavskii, *Ocherki russkoi kul'tury, 1. "Opavshie list'ia" Rozanova* (Paris: Sintaksis, 1982), 187.

from the Chorus. These "boundary situations," to use Jaspers's term, strip the personality of all usual social determinants and plunge it into the void of an absurd environment, where, as Siniavsky puts it, people "do not live—they existify [*ekzistiruiut*]."[16] Prison is a place for metaphysical discovery since here, "[m]an becomes really close and dear to one when he ceases to be known by his official tags—profession, surname, age. When he ceases even to be called 'man' and turns out to be simply the first person one meets."[17]

In these two books, Siniavsky's existentialism is of a religious variety and may be compared to that of Iakov Druskin and Grigorii Pomerants.[18] From such a perspective, God cannot be identified with the dogmatic image of any existing religious tradition, since any definition would prove to be a denial of his inconceivability and omnipresence. "Our notion of Him is so wide that it can appear as its own contradiction even within the framework of the same religious doctrine. He is unknowable yet recognizable in everything, inaccessible yet closer than the closest friend, cruel yet kind, absurd, irrational yet utterly logical."[19] Siniavsky's relationship to God is highly personal, and in some fragments he addresses *him* directly as "thou" and summons him to display his will in the most ordinary and random occurrences, which (should they be manifest) Siniavsky would take as signs of a conspiracy between himself and his God hidden also *from* himself. Siniavsky values Christianity because, in its original spirit, it is devoid of any pretension to wisdom or contemplation of eternity. It is rather "a shock regiment, a penal battalion, thrown into the hottest, deadliest sector of the front … and armed only with the readiness to die."[20] In other words, faith is neither the aloofness of meditation nor the solemnity of the temple, but an existential drive leading from despair to hope, from death to the possibility of resurrection. From Siniavsky's point of view, Christian faith is something abnormal and paradoxical, since, contrary to nature, it teaches us not to fear death, not to avoid pain, and to rejoice when we are beaten.[21]

At the other pole of life's absurdity, Siniavsky directs particular attention to sexuality, which, along with religion and art, becomes central to his philosophizing. One situation he subjects to repeated theorizing is the sexuality of prison life, where the absence of a partner makes the sexual organs absurd, since their natural meaning is derived from their union with another body. This explains why sexuality in Siniavsky's interpretation becomes an object of humor that plays on the reduction of the human to a purely organic nature: a person without clothes, for instance, seems far less natural than one who is dressed. Nakedness reveals "the proximity of sex and laughter."[22] Even without the special circumstances of loneliness and alienation, Siniavsky finds sexuality

16 Abram Tertz, *A Voice from the Chorus*, trans. Kyril Fitzlyon and Max Hayward (New York: Farrar, Straus and Giroux, 1976), 6.

17 Andrey Sinyavsky, *Unguarded Thoughts*, trans. Manya Harari (London: Collins & Harvill Press, 1965), 27.

18 See pt. 3, "Personalism and Liberalism," in Epstein, *The Phoenix of Philosophy*, 118–33.

19 Sinyavsky, *Unguarded Thoughts*, 83.

20 Ibid., 90–1.

21 Ibid., 79.

22 Andrei Siniavskii, *Sobranie sochinenii v 2 tomakh* (Moscow: SP "Start," 1992), 1: 475.

to be something absurd, owing especially to the placement of the genitals: "The very location of sex, in direct proximity to the organs of excretion, is discouraging. It's as if a squeamish, sarcastic grimace were provided by nature itself."[23] Siniavsky is sensitive to humor as an objective component of reality; his absurdity is not the tragic category of Western existentialism, but a source of comic inspiration. Sexuality is an existential joke, but the entirety of life may also be conceived in this way. "[A]t some stage you realize the frivolousness of all you have done and lived by, and this feeling is capable of driving you to despair, until it occurs to you that the whole of world history is pretty frivolous too."[24]

Existentialism and Postmodernism

We might wonder how a single thinker can combine existential and postmodern perspectives. This is one of Siniavsky's striking traits: the process of his intellectual maturation coincided with the ascendancy of existentialism on the European philosophical scene, but at the same time he grew up in an atmosphere of ideological indoctrination and Marxist scholastics, which developed his taste for linguistic and conceptual games. In my view, this convergence of existentialist and conceptualist patterns is not unique to Siniavsky; it is consistent with the inherent logic of philosophical evolution. In the history of continental philosophy, existentialism immediately preceded structuralism, whereas postmodernism grew out of post-structuralist presuppositions. Thus, existentialism and postmodernism share an opposition to structuralism's pretensions to objective scientific knowledge. Accordingly, these thought systems coincide in their gravitation toward such categories as "the absurd" and "nothingness," which challenge the structuralist infatuation with rigorous semiotic analysis. The decisive difference between them is that existentialist "nothingness" reveals itself within the depths of the self, affording the individual absolute freedom in the process of self-creation. In postmodern thought, nothingness arises from the relativity of meanings, which denies any absolute frame of reference, any real *signified* behind the *sign*. This view emphasizes not individual freedom but the contingency, and even illusoriness, of selfhood, which converges with a network of such suprapersonal mechanisms as language and the unconscious.

Siniavsky's thought, with its valorization of the absurd, establishes itself on a middle ground between existentialism and postmodernism; or, more precisely, it sets up a vibration between these two poles, alternately problematizing each of them. For example, Siniavsky is inclined to reject the existentialist project of self-realization, the heroic pessimism that recognizes the world's absurdity but aspires to imbue it with

[23] Sinyavsky, *Unguarded Thoughts*, 25. The resonance of this remark with Bernard of Clairvaux's and St. Augustine's *Inter faeces et urinam nascimur* ("We are born between feces and urine") shows the postmodernist Siniavsky's unexpected proximity to the medieval mentality, recalling Berdiaev's definition of the epoch arriving after modernity as "the New Middle Ages."

[24] Tertz, *A Voice from the Chorus*, 130.

personal meaning by the exercise of freedom. For Siniavsky, European existentialism is too "liberal," in the sense that it underestimates the strength of human dependency, of human whimsicality and obsessiveness. Siniavsky subscribes to existentialism as a theory of liberation from historical and social determinism, but faults it for undervaluing personal ties and idiosyncrasies, which no one is free to choose.

> I never know what liberal philosophers mean by the "freedom of choice" they are always talking about. Do we really choose whom to love, what to believe in, what illness to suffer? … How can we think of freedom when we are swallowed by the whole, when we see nothing, are aware of nothing except the One who chose us and, having chosen, torments or bestows favors on us? … Freedom is always negative, it implies an absence, a void hungering to be filled.[25]

Emptiness

This void hungering to be filled but never satisfied represents one of Siniavsky's metaphysical preoccupations. In his book *Strolls with Pushkin* (written in 1966–8, during his incarceration), he argues that Russia's most beloved poet, who is traditionally considered to be a model of absolute artistic perfection, lacks intellectual and psychological substance. According to Siniavsky, Pushkin's celebrated novel in verse, *Eugene Onegin*, is inherently empty, devoid of content; the narration dissolves among infinite digressions as it escapes all obligations of plot and idea. What then is the mysterious reason for Pushkin's commanding presence in Russian culture? He is invoked, after all, on every level, from the most banal idioms of common speech ("Who're you gonna blame—Pushkin?" or "Who's gonna do it—Pushkin?") to Gogol's and Dostoevsky's grandiloquent acknowledgments of his messianic role in Russian cultural history. The nineteenth-century critic Apollon Grigoriev once proclaimed: "Pushkin is our everything." Siniavsky suggests an alternative formula: "Pushkin is our nothing." And, indeed, it is nothingness that inspires the proliferation of his image in literary criticism, historical novels, memoirs, ideological schemes, and everyday life, creating an illusion that conceals the absence of Pushkin as reality.

> Emptiness was Pushkin's content. Without it he wouldn't have been full …. Loving everyone, he loved no one, and this "no one" gave him the freedom to nod to all and sundry—every nod an oath of loyalty …. Something of the vampire was hidden in so heightened a susceptibility. That's why Pushkin's [image has] such a luster of eternal youth, of fresh blood, high color: … the whole fullness of existence … [in] the empty vessel of … one who is in essence no one, remembers nothing, does not love.[26]

25 Sinyavsky, *Unguarded Thoughts*, 49.

26 Andrei Sinyavsky, *Strolls with Pushkin*, trans. Catherine Theimer Nepomnyashchy and Slava I. Yastremski (New York: Columbia University Press, 2016), 44–6.

This interpretation of Pushkin as the personification of nothingness struck critics across the ideological spectrum as an outrageous sacrilege when the book appeared in 1975 in London, and when a fragment of it was published in 1989 in Moscow. Traditionally, Pushkin had been revered either as a bard of revolutionary freedom associated with the Decembrist movement (the official Soviet interpretation), or as a poetic sage who in the course of his stormy life came to know the value of humility and experienced religious illumination (the popular interpretation in the context of the late-Soviet Orthodox revival). For Siniavsky, both Pushkin's revolutionary tendencies and his religiosity are interchangeable masks, because they adorn his absolute lack of originality. Siniavsky agrees with Belinsky's famous definition of *Eugene Onegin* as "an encyclopedia of Russian life," but the defining characteristic of an encyclopedia is to render commonplaces in a universal language, and this is where Pushkin is most skillful—as a compiler of citations smuggled in from all of world literature. Despite the public outcry, it is clear that Siniavsky never intended to disparage Pushkin, but rather to present him as a "postmodern" figure whose genius is not originality but responsiveness and universality.

In general, Siniavsky's understanding of writing privileges emptiness as both the origin and destiny of creativity. "In order to write something worthwhile one needs to be absolutely empty."[27] Language for Siniavsky is not so much a network of meanings as a network of silences artistically engrained in words. Language becomes "a means of silent communion—absolutely empty, a snare or net: a net of language cast into the sea of silence in the hope of pulling up some little golden fish caught in the pauses, in the momentary interstices of silence."[28] One can easily identify in Siniavsky's approach to language a postmodern conception of the endless play of signs that erases meaning in the exponential growth of their possible associations, preventing the attribution of any single, definitive meaning.

The Chorus and Russianness

This desemantization of the word is further illustrated by Siniavsky's central concept of the *chorus*, in which each voice is anonymous and loses all trace of intention as it is incessantly overlaid with other voices. In his book *A Voice from the Chorus*, composed during his incarceration, primarily from the disjointed speech of anonymous prisoners, there is no dialogic tension between the various voices (including the author's). Instead we sense the gaping of an indifferent void that makes interpenetration impossible. The mechanism of the chorus works to nullify the individuality of the voices, reducing them to semantic detritus. Another of Siniavsky's methods for splintering the unity of meaning is the use of brackets and parentheses, which transform the one-dimensional flow of speech into a multilayered syntactical construction that becomes a sort of grammatical chorus composed of heterogeneous pronouncements. As the author

[27] Tertz, *A Voice from the Chorus*, 234.

[28] Ibid., 291.

explains his own understanding of this style: "Prose has so far taken little account of the possibilities of brackets. By and large, brackets have always played an ancillary role and have never presumed to claim special attention. Yet a verbal construct moving on parallel and intersecting ways or levels, which can be shown graphically by means of brackets, brings writing close to certain forms of geometric art."[29]

Siniavsky argues that the Russian language, with its love of digressions and parenthetical constructions, makes a convenient vehicle for the nullification of reality, because the same "nothingness" that generated Pushkin's works exists as well in the depths of the Russian national character, as a principle of both creativity and destruction. In his assessment of Russians, Siniavsky implicitly opposes both Slavophiles, who vaunt the positive virtues of Russianness (such as diligence or hospitality), and Westernizers, who criticize their compatriots for deficiencies in the domain of civic freedom and cultural innovation. Russians, in Siniavsky's view, are absolutely incapable of accumulating valuables, but this freedom from material possessions accounts for their open-mindedness and artistic giftedness. It is likewise true, he maintains, that Russians are inclined to drunkenness and thievishness, but these same qualities are indispensable for the artist—for one, that is, who is carried away by the imagination and assimilates the property of others into his works, packing them with allusions and citations.[30] Siniavsky derives the positive qualities of the Russian people from their very negativity.

> The main point about the Russians, when all is said and done, is that they have nothing to lose. Hence the generosity of Russian intellectuals .... Readiness for anything—readiness to give up the last crumb, just because it is the last and there is nothing else, because this is the end of the road. And the frivolity of our reasoning, of our judgements. Anything will do. We have saved nothing, learned nothing. Who shall dare judge us on whom sentence has already been passed?[31]

Again, as with writing, emptiness as a national category becomes a source of endless spiritual growth, of the abundant, vague, and amorphous inspiration so typical of Russian culture. Siniavsky even argues that among the hypostases of the Christian trinity, Russians are especially open to that of the Holy Spirit, which has no anthropomorphic incarnation and thus speaks from nowhere and everywhere. "This religion of the Holy Spirit somehow accords with our national characteristics—a natural inclination to anarchy, ... fluidity, amorphousness, readiness to adopt any mould, ... our gift—or vice—of thinking and living artistically .... In this sense Russia offers a most favorable soil for the experiments and fantasies of the artist."[32]

29 Ibid., 213.

30 The contrary analogy is valid as well: thieves are seen as "artists" in their own right. "Almost as in the case of poets, what counts most in the thieves' code of behavior is style, the ability to project one's personality in terms of a show, a spectacle" (ibid., 147).

31 Sinyavsky, *Unguarded Thoughts*, 36.

32 Tertz, *A Voice from the Chorus*, 247.

Artistry. Holy Fools and Buffoons

In general, artistry (*khudozhestvo*) is the central category in Siniavsky's thought, not only in the specific domain of art itself, which he explores as a professional critic, but as an all-embracing characteristic of reality. Artistry is the world of fabricated illusions, which are more tangible than anything in the real world. Even nature is perceived as deriving from art, as a museum where all styles are exhibited simultaneously, rather than in historical succession. "Everywhere in nature we keep coming across art. Mountain architecture which foreshadows the Gothic. Clouds and puddles done in the *tachiste* manner .... A museum in which everything is preserved and renewed, in which everything—as in art—has a measure of realism and a measure of illusion."[33]

Siniavsky anticipates the conceptualist interpretation of reality as an artificial construct, but he understands "concept" as an artistic idea rather than an ideological scheme. His version of conceptualism is "soft" and sometimes borders on a more traditional aestheticism that perceives life as a theatrical play but does not reduce it to the play of signs and codes. For Siniavsky, as for Nietzsche, life is justified first and foremost as an aesthetic phenomenon. But this aestheticism is alien to Nietzsche's militantly adversarial position toward Christianity and morality. Postmodern aestheticism, as distinct from its modernist predecessor, is not hostile to traditional ideological systems and easily incorporates their fragments, including Christian "saints" and "fools," in its network of metaphoric discourse.

This does not mean that Siniavsky "aestheticizes" religion and morality. He does not privilege one discourse (artistic) over another (didactic), searching instead for a common ground that would unite artistry, morality, and religion. This he discovers in two key figures of Russian folk culture: the "holy fool" (*iurodivyi*) and "buffoon" (*skomorokh*). Religion and morality, for Siniavsky, become distorted when they acquire a stern, purely didactic character that denies the comic, ridiculous, laughing aspect of spirituality manifest implicitly in the holy fool, and explicitly in the buffoon. From this point of view, Nikolai Gogol, who in his declining years condemned his own artistic work and suppressed his comic gift in favor of religious preaching, becomes, albeit contrarily to his intentions, a holy fool precisely through this pathetic self-denial of his past buffoonery as a comic writer. Siniavsky's book *In Gogol's Shadow* is devoted mainly to the relationship between art and religion, and concludes with a paradox: the artist best fulfills his religious destiny when he faithfully serves the self-sufficient goals of his art. "In his poetic creations, Gogol seems even more religious than in his anemic and calculated Christianity."[34] This is why a simple buffoon, who is unashamed of his art, is bound to accomplish greater moral deeds than Gogol, who developed a false sense of his own importance as a prophet and preacher. "The buffoons [*skomorokhi*] Kuzma and Demyan are singing ... Only through them may Gogol save his soul [*tol'ko s nimi spasen Gogol'*]. Only through them will Russian art save its soul."[35]

[33] Sinyavsky, *Unguarded Thoughts*, 78.

[34] Siniavskii, *Sobranie sochinenii*, 2: 334.

[35] Ibid., 336.

The best illustration of the archetypal, folkloric roots of Siniavsky's thought may be found in his interpretation of Ivan the Fool, a traditional figure of Russian folktales. Foolishness, for Siniavsky, is the most profound and reliable indication of genuine wisdom. The fool does not follow the conventional path of success, but instead finds himself in the most ridiculous and humiliating situations; nonetheless, in the Russian tradition, this brings him to the ultimate triumph—finding a miraculous source of wealth and marrying a princess. It is by his vulnerability and nonconformity that he invokes the blessing of some higher spiritual force. The underlying *principle* of foolishness is the rejection of rationality and openness to the randomness of existence. Siniavsky finds that the archaic cult of foolishness has affinities with the wisdom of the most profound philosophers, whose knowledge proceeds from an acceptance of the limits of knowledge.

> The Fool's philosophy intersects here and there with the assertions of some of the greatest ancient sages: "I know only that I know nothing"—Socrates; "The wise are not learned, the learned are not wise"—Lao Tzu; and also with the mystical practices of various religions. The essence of these views is the rejection of the activity of controlling reason, which prevents the comprehension of supreme truth. This truth (or reality) *on its own* appears and reveals itself to an individual in that happy moment when it seems that the consciousness has been switched off and the soul abides in a peculiar state of receptive passivity.[36]

Foolishness illustrates the paradox of creative nothingness, since the state of receptive ignorance yields the fruits of wisdom. "If we cast everything aside and empty our minds, ceasing to expect anything at all, we can hope that the door may open a little, suddenly and of its own accord."[37] Siniavsky, in his ultimate credo, is as guided by the same expectation of miracle as are the heroes of ancient fairy tales that constitute a favorite topic of his critical research.

As the critic Alexander Genis has observed, in the contemporary humanities Siniavsky occupies the unique position of "archaic postmodernism."[38] Playing with archaic patterns of thinking, he derives from them an ambivalence and ambiguity of meaning that a less perspicacious critic might ascribe exclusively to the postmodern period.

> The world was then sufficiently metamorphic to keep turning on its side, changing one thing into another and prodding language to bring forth allegorical riddles. We are here present, as it were, at the act of the birth of art, when metaphors sprouted profusely in the still hot and steaming soil of folklore and when language, mindful of the miracle of its origin, still showed off the tricks—as well as the riddles, knavishness, deceit, invention and cunning which fill our fairy-tales and make

[36] Siniavskii, *Ocherki russkoi kul'tury, 2. Ivan-durak*, 39.

[37] Tertz, *A Voice from the Chorus*, 169–70.

[38] Alexander Genis, "Archaic Postmodernism: The Aesthetics of Andrei Sinyavsky," in Mikhail Epstein, Alexander Genis, and Slobodanka Vladiv-Glover, eds., *Russian Postmodernism: New Perspectives on Post-Soviet Culture* (New York, Oxford: Berghahn Books, 1999): 185–96.

> them so effervescent. Here it becomes clear that a poet even in the new, modern sense of the word, is a failed magician or miracle-worker who has substituted metaphor for metamorphosis, word-play for deeds.[39]

Despite Siniavsky's seeming nostalgia for the magical origin of art, he recognizes that this origin cannot be known directly, but only through the effervescence of contemporary language games. Siniavsky discloses the intellectual links between postmodern reflective relativity and the playfulness inherent in the primordial roots of the mythological imagination.

3. The Satirical Metaphysics of Aleksandr Zinoviev[40]

Although Zinoviev (1922–2006) never described himself as a conceptualist or postmodernist, his inclusion in this rubric is justified by the kinds of intellectual work that made him famous. Zinoviev emerged on the Soviet intellectual scene as a

Figure 8 Aleksandr Zinoviev.

[39] Tertz, *A Voice from the Chorus*, 200.

[40] Sections on A. Zinoviev, D. Prigov and The Canonization of Emptiness were first published in the article: "Postmodernist Thought of the Late Soviet Period: Three Profiles." *Studies in East European Thought*, 2021. DOI: https://doi.org/10.1007/s11212-021-09417-2

professional philosopher in the field of formal logic. He worked for twenty-two years (1954–76) as a professor at Moscow State University and as senior researcher of the Institute of Philosophy of the Academy of Sciences. His early publications included the monograph *Philosophical Problems of Many-Valued Logic* (1960) and numerous other investigations of a highly specialized nature. However, Zinoviev's international renown followed the publication of his philosophical novel-treatise *The Yawning Heights* (1974; published 1976), and his forced emigration to the West in 1978. He would go on to publish about thirty books of fiction and theory that brought him the reputation of a Russian Swift.

Zinoviev's literary works do not belong to the genre of fiction in a conventional sense, but are rather a mixture of philosophical discussion and idle chatter between semi-fictional characters who represent various outlooks held by Soviet intellectuals. In the view of Michael Kirkwood, a most diligent explorer of Zinoviev's work, he exemplifies "a writer who fits, more closely than anyone else I can think of, the model adumbrated in that school of literary criticism associated with Roland Barthes and Michel Foucault .... [H]e writes on matters literary, historical, political, sociological, philosophical, aesthetic, moral and religious, in a mode which defies genre classification. In that sense he is indeed a 'scriptor' producing 'écriture.'"[41] Zinoviev's method is described by the prominent Italian specialist in Russian literature Vittorio Strada as

> an absurd intermingling of voices making a parody of the dialogues of Plato. The voices didn't arrive at a definite catharsis: they remained a tangle of viewpoints revealing facets of a single *logos*: the logos of real-life communism. In moments of crisis communism goes into a series of modulations of its inner essence which constitute a kind of tragi-comic nonsense.[42]

Several features of Zinoviev's style qualify him for classification as a postmodernist thinker. Like all conceptualists, Zinoviev addressed his works predominantly to the ideological and social codes of Soviet communism, rendering their absurdity and self-contradictory nature in the form of parody. He also made broad use of pastiche, incorporating clichéd formulas of Soviet propaganda, philosophical abstractions, and psychological stereotypes, and mimicking the (il)logic of bureaucratic style. Most of his works take the form of a seemingly endless series of dialogues attributed to characters whose ideological and philosophical positions are indeterminately related to the author's own. Zinoviev exemplifies the postmodernist axiom concerning the ubiquity of citation, which goes so far as to enclose every expression in quotes in order to emphasize the transpersonal nature of thought, which depends more on linguistic structures of discourse than the subjective intentions of the thinker. Zinoviev's works

41 Michael Kirkwood, *Alexander Zinoviev: An Introduction to His Work* (London: Macmillan Press, 1993), xi.

42 Cited from Charles Janson, "Alexander Zinoviev: Experiences of a Soviet Methodologist," in *Alexander Zinoviev as Writer and Thinker. An Assessment*, ed. Philip Hanson and Michael Kirkwood (London: Macmillan Press, 1988), 11.

frequently treat the trite phenomena of Soviet reality, such as the practice of ritualistic official meetings, with incongruously lofty scientific discourse. Thus, he proposes a "newly created science of meetingology," which is to analyze the typical division between "open" and "closed" meetings. Contrary to its designation, the open meetings generally pass unnoticed by virtue of their very openness, while the closed ones attract the attention of those excluded from them, and their proceedings end up being disclosed to all interested parties. Such paradoxes, revealing the discrepancies between signs and referents etc., are typical of Zinoviev, whose entire philosophical project is to analyze the artificial and conceptual character of reality.

Extracting Zinoviev's own views from the discourse of his characters is surely as complicated as identifying Kierkegaard's views in his pseudonymous works. In Zinoviev's own words:

> The point is that my position really is embodied in the book [*The Yawning Heights*], but in such a way that the author is eliminated and characters are given the opportunity to speak and argue. That's why I don't accept everything they say. And concerning much of what I do accept, they remain silent. Nevertheless, I think that, given sufficiently attentive and repeated readings of the book, a reader can figure out the author's position .... I can in one context express and defend one judgement and in another something opposite to it. This is not a lack of principle, it is a desire to look at an issue from a different point of view, to regard another aspect of the problem .... I live in the language as in a specific reality, which is complicated, contradictory, fluid.[43]

Thus, despite the problem of determining the constantly shifting distance in the relation of narrated speech to the author's own perspectives, Zinoviev does not preclude an attempt to interpret these "fictions" as representative of his own views.

Zinoviev's logical treatises are usually ignored by critics, who focus rather on his later creative work. But one can draw curious parallels between his interest in "many-valued logic"—as opposed to two-valued logic, or the logic of mutual exclusion—and his conceptualist vision of ideology. In his treatise *Philosophical Problems of Many-Valued Logic*, Zinoviev argues that

> a whole series of reasons can be given why the number of truth values is in principle unlimited .... [F]rom an epistemological point of view there are no natural reasons which could prevent man from introducing into the number of his tools of knowledge many-valued constructions and a many-valued conception of logic .... Either human knowledge is evaluated only as true or false, or, other evaluations besides truth and falsity are possible.[44]

[43] Aleksandr Zinov'ev, *Bez illiuzii* (Lausanne: L'Age D'Homme, 1979), 16–17.

[44] Alexander Zinoviev, *Philosophical Problems of Many-Valued Logic*, trans. Guido Kung and David Dinsmore Comey (Dordrecht-Holland: D. Reidel Publishing Company, 1963), 122, 123.

This notion of many-valued logic presupposes that a statement may be both (or neither) true or false, opening it to a potentially endless array of interpretations.

Significantly, the same kind of logic is applied to the concept of ideology in *The Yawning Heights*, in which Chatterer argues: "There are no false ideologies. Nor are there any true ones. Its role in society must be described according to a quite different system of concepts. A society like ours would be unthinkable without some form of ideology. It is ideological at its very base."[45] Thus, Zinoviev's preoccupation with the many-valuedness of logic extends also to his philosophy of ideology, and in a quite postmodernist way. To designate an ideology as true or false would presuppose the existence of some external reality with which it could be compared. Such is certainly not the case with totalitarian society, where ideology *is* the reality from which reality is produced. One cannot argue about the truth or falsity of such ideological manifestations as the collective farm or communal apartment—they are forms of an imitative reality constructed by the ideological activity of the Party; they become indistinguishable from reality despite their illusory origin. Zinoviev's Chatterer expresses this ubiquitous artificiality: "These forms of imitation activity are so convenient and effective in our society … that our entire life takes on the character of an imitation of civilization …. Imitation may take on some form of reality."[46] These imitative constructs clearly correspond to what Jean Baudrillard called "hyperreality," suggesting that Western civilization has produced, in its postmodern condition, a complex of simulations that substitute for reality itself. For this French thinker, it is primarily the visual realm that produces hyperreality; but in the Soviet Union, ideology, primarily in its verbal form, was the vehicle of simulation.

A curious parallel may also be drawn between Zinoviev and another French contemporary, Louis Althusser, famous for his reinterpretation of Marxism from a structuralist and partly postmodernist perspective. Both men independently and almost simultaneously arrived at a definition of ideology as an imaginary realm that lies at the foundation of society. Althusser, in his criticism of the concept of ideology as a purely intellectual activity, writes: "Ideology in general has no history …, or, what comes to the same thing, is eternal, i.e. omnipresent in its immutable form throughout history …. Ideology represents the imaginary relationship of individuals to their real conditions of existence …. [T]his imaginary relation is itself endowed with a material existence."[47] What is postulated here is the "objectivity" and even "materiality" of ideology, which is not just composed of "beautiful lies" forged by despots or priests to enslave human minds, but presents a structural inevitability of human society. Zinoviev's Chatterer discusses ideology in much the same way:

[45] Alexander Zinoviev, *The Yawning Heights*, trans. Gordon Clough (New York: Random House, 1979), 289.

[46] Ibid., 317.

[47] Louis Althusser, *Lenin and Philosophy and Other Essays* (New York and London: Monthly Review Press, 1971), 160–2, 167.

> The birth of ideology is not within the control of human beings .... That is why ideology comes into the world complete, in possession of all its attributes. The texts have a history. But ideology of itself has no history, for its birth in this sense is an act of realization of its social function .... Ideology is accepted as a fact; it is taken into account or not as is a natural need, and not as a product of human reason or folly.[48]

Thus ideology is not the false consciousness that, according to Marx, has no substance of its own and appears only as an illusory and parasitic distortion of real production relations—it is, to the contrary, the most real thing ever. "[N]othing in history is so durable as something which has no inner foundations, such as a myth, a religion or popular prejudice."[49] Zinoviev's supposition of materiality as *subordinate* to the conceptual sphere is, again, close to Althusser's notion of "overdetermination" (*surdétermination*), which stipulated, contrary to orthodox Marxist theory, that under certain historical conditions, the ideological superstructure may be *primary*, and determine the material base. For Zinoviev, this historical condition is Soviet communism, which attempted to create the base from the superstructure, in other words, to create a socioeconomic system from ideological premises.

To the same extent that ideology becomes a system of material institutions and economic practices, material life becomes a series of ideological actions. In *The Yawning Heights*, Zinoviev illustrates this comprehensive substitution with a fictional communist city called "Ibansk," where people "do not live in the old-fashioned and commonplace sense of the word as it is applied to other people in other places. The Ibanskians do not live, but carry out epoch-making activities [*istoricheskie meropriiatiia*]. They carry out these experiments even when they know nothing about them and take no part in them."[50] Such is the suprapersonal nature of ideology, which transforms even ordinary events into signs of historical progress or regress, without the knowledge of its participants. The satiric metaphysics of Aleksandr Zinoviev originates from this discrepancy between the everydayness of subjective existence and the grandiose implications drawn therefrom by a system that attaches ideological value to every occurrence. For example, the Soviet routine of the queue is vaunted by one of Zinoviev's characters as "the highest form of social communion, expressed in deeds, not words, an absolute social equality between individuals."[51]

The predominance of concept over reality is not confined to the Soviet Union, but seems to be symptomatic of a general postmodern predisposition. At the end of Zinoviev's *Homo Sovieticus*, the hero, having fled the ideocracy of his homeland for the promised reality of the West, discovers that he has not escaped at all. Initially

[48] Zinoviev, *The Yawning Heights*, 290.

[49] Alexander Zinoviev, *Homo Sovieticus*, trans. Charles Janson (London: Victor Gollancz Ltd., 1985), 75.

[50] Zinoviev, *The Yawning Heights*, 13.

[51] Ibid., 748.

mesmerized by the magnificence of a huge glass tower in Munich, which he conceives of as the longed-for embodiment of the truly free world, he comes to a sudden disillusionment: "I remembered my Edifice and rushed to the window. It glittered in a blue heaven with such unprecedented beauty that it took my breath away. But what is that? In the most prominent place, a gigantic four-letter word shines forth in all its glory: BANK."[52] Thus even the "pure form" of this architectural wonder is subordinated to the flat concept that gives it meaning.

This is not to say that the relationship between concept and reality was the same in the Soviet Union and the West. Some investigators put a special emphasis on the use of active—as opposed to passive—negation in Zinoviev's depiction of the Soviet mentality. Taking a given assertion, for example, "I believe in God," one can oppose it with two negations: a) "I don't believe that God exists" (passive negation); or b) "I believe that God doesn't exist" (active negation). One can easily equate these respective positions with Western agnosticism in the first case and Soviet atheism in the second. Jon Elster, the political scientist who pioneered the logical analysis of Zinoviev's "fiction,"[53] cites several convincing examples of active negation as it relates to Zinoviev's preoccupation with the absurdity of Soviet ideology. In particular, from *The Yawning Heights*, Elster cites this: "The objective of the measure was to discover those elements which did not approve of putting it into practice."[54] Thus the action pursues no other end than to provoke its own negation.

In fact, this kind of active negation was typical of the Soviet mentality, which was absolutely dependent on what it sought to negate. It struggled against bourgeois conspiracies and "enemies of the people," creating these illusory targets in order to justify its own activity. Active negation is the type of negation that, depending upon its object, paradoxically maintains it rather than annihilates it. As Elster observes, ideology may be described in Hegelian terms as a kind of consciousness which is "unable by its negative relation to the object to abolish it; because of that relation it rather produces it again, as well as the desire."[55] Thus, for example, the denial of God by official Soviet atheism became an obsession that represented a constant *reminder* of God for a people that might otherwise have forgotten about religion altogether.

As a logician, Zinoviev is especially sensitive to the potential absurdity of active negation and also to the danger of failing to discriminate between it and its passive counterpart. "We merely have to distinguish between the absence of desire to do something and the presence of a positive disinclination to do it. Those aren't the same thing. One can be indifferent to something—i.e. one can lack both the inclination and

[52] Zinoviev, *Homo Sovieticus*, 206.

[53] See Jon Elster, "Active and Passive Negation: An Essay in Ibanskian Sociology," in *Alexander Zinoviev as Writer and Thinker. An Assessment*, ed. Philip Hanson and Michael Kirkwood (London: Macmillan Press, 1988), 118–44.

[54] Ibid., 119. From another translation: "The aim of the experiment was to detect those who did not approve of its being carried out and to take appropriate steps" (Zinoviev, *The Yawning Heights*, 14).

[55] Cited by Jon Elster from Hegel's *Phenomenology of Mind* ("Active and Passive Negation," 123).

the disinclination to do it."[56] This sort of indifference, argues Chatterer—who seems in many instances to represent Zinoviev's own opinion—is quite natural, and should not be confused with hypocrisy or cowardice. Passive negation is the middle way between active assertion and active negation, and for Zinoviev it represents the optimal alternative to both conformity and outright dissidence, insofar as the latter effectively upholds official ideology (albeit unintentionally). Passive negation, indeed, might even be called the essence of conceptualism, its method, in the sense that conceptualism imparts to ideology neither positive nor negative value, but demonstrates its absurdity and irrelevance, the zero-value of its meaning. Characteristically, Zinoviev, in spite of his longtime opposition to the communist regime, never spoke in support of dissidents, believing that their behavior could even contribute to the consolidation of the repressive system. "What is most curious is the organic need of the society itself for such renegades. Whereas fighting them, the society necessarily engenders them."[57]

But while Zinoviev implicitly seems to argue in favor of a "conceptualist politics" of passive negation, his explicit political stance, as evidenced in journalistic and sociological writings, is decidedly more one-dimensional. Already in his early public pronouncements after his emigration to West Germany (1978), he warns the West against the superficial opinion of communism as a system that maintains itself by force and deception. In his view, communism, as realized in the Soviet Union, responds to the deepest needs of human nature, such as the need for equality, collectivism, and social stability. Certainly one has to pay for these benefits with a modest standard of living, but without this relative poverty, communism's advantages could not be instantiated. "The merits of communism are its shortcomings and its shortcomings are its merits .... It is under the conditions of collectivism and on its basis that such tendencies develop as undermine the very collectivist way of life, destroy this great achievement of history."[58] Thus, shortly after his emigration, Zinoviev, in the spirit of his many-valued logic, looked upon communism as a mixed bag of pluses and minuses.

This "dialectical" approach is seen especially in *The Reality of Communism*, in which Zinoviev analyzes the real manifestations of communism in contrast to its ideological images publicized both by Soviet and Western propaganda. First of all, Zinoviev assumes that the Soviet system is not a deviation from the "correct" or "genuine" communism, "not one of the possible 'models,' but the naked essence of communism."[59] "According to Marxist dogma, full Communism does not yet

[56] Zinoviev, *The Yawning Heights*, 105. Another formulation of the same logical rule: "A distinction must be drawn between the absence of a standard and the existence of a negation-standard" (ibid., 618). One of the inclinations of the Soviet mentality was to believe that all social actions are either pre- or pro-scribed by the state, i.e., only assertions and active negations were legally admitted. It was hard to believe in "the absence of a standard," whether positive or negative, and to behave accordingly.

[57] Zinov'ev, *Bez illiuzii*, 112. "The population of a Communist country is on balance inclined to fight for its unfreedom against those who wish to free it." Alexander Zinoviev, *The Reality of Communism* (London: Victor Gollancz Ltd., 1984), 257.

[58] Aleksandr Zinov'ev, *Ni svobody, ni ravenstva, ni bratstva* (Lausanne: L'Age D'Homme, 1983), 74.

[59] Ibid., 104.

exist in reality, yet a science of it—'scientific Communism'—does. But in reality the situation is exactly the opposite: real-life Communism already exists in the form of numerous societies of a particular type, whereas a science of it does not."[60] Zinoviev regards communism as a specific type of civilization, potentially more powerful than capitalism: it is currently in its infancy, but promises a formidable future. The West is capable of providing a high standard of living only to some millions of people, while the majority of humanity—"the billions"—cannot achieve it, and communism offers them the best alternative: lower living standards than in the West, but sufficient for survival and, most important, available to all. "What exists in the West is only an arbitrary zigzag of history. Humanity is irritated by this deviation from the norm. Humanity feels that this [comfort and wealth] is not available to everyone and attempts to destroy it."[61] Communism is appealing to "everyone"; this is why it cannot satisfy anyone in particular. The same collective that provides social defense for an individual restrains the individual's right to self-assertion. Communist society is a well-balanced system of coercion that is beneficial to the overwhelming majority of its members, to society in general. Individual discontents with communism can never grow into a unified opposition, because people are united by their attachment to the communist system and divided by their disagreements with it.

Zinoviev argues that even the deficiencies of the communist system work for its increasing stability, which also includes "a systematic ideological conditioning of the population" that "sets the socio-biological evolution of mankind in a certain direction."[62] Therefore, *Homo Sovieticus* is "the highest form of civilization. He is superman. He is universal. If need be, he can commit anything frightful. Where it is possible, he can possess any virtue."[63] This blatant valorization might be interpreted as ironic, but in his later works, Zinoviev increasingly speaks from the perspective of a true communist believer. The books Zinoviev wrote in the perestroika period[64] evince an increasing nostalgia for the "classic communism" of the Stalinist type. This nostalgia is a conventional mood in conceptualism, which tends to reproduce totalitarian models with a subtle mixture of lyricism, irony, and the grotesque.[65]

In later works, however, Zinoviev would abandon this ambivalence and speak as a straightforward anti-liberal and anti-Westernist. If he lets any contradictions slip into his discourse now, it is not because of a love of paradox, but because his intentions are indeed mutually contradictory. Thus, he blames Gorbachev and his "acolytes," on the one hand, for careerism and phony pretensions to liberalism; on the other, for too *much* liberalism, which led to the disintegration of the great communist state. Zinoviev

[60] Zinoviev, *The Reality of Communism*, 17.

[61] Zinov'ev, *Ni svobody, ni ravenstva, ni bratstva*, 104.

[62] Zinoviev, *The Reality of Communism*, 259.

[63] Zinoviev, *Homo Sovieticus*, 199.

[64] Zinoviev, *Gorbachevism* (New York: Liberty, 1988); Zinov'ev, *Katastroika. Povest' o perestroike v Partgrade* (Lausanne: L'Age d'Homme, 1990).

[65] Suffice it to refer to a masterpiece of sots-art: Komar and Melamid's series of paintings *Nostalgic Socialist Realism* (1981–3).

famously labels perestroika "katastroika" (with the same prefix as in *catastrophe*), and in these writings is even more disdainful of Boris Yeltsin's stumbles into full-scale Western-style capitalism. Zinoviev returned to Russia occasionally in the 1990s, though he did not move there permanently until 1999, when his professorship was reinstated and he could again teach at Moscow State University.

In *The Crisis of Communism* (1990), his last book written before the fall of the USSR, Zinoviev professes an inexhaustible faith in the tenets of Marxism-Leninism, which "could as never before serve as a guiding star in the contemporary confused state of the world."[66] Typically, when Zinoviev leaves the confines of his own ironic worldview, he falls victim to the objective irony arising from the ineluctable logic of historical events, which continually seem to undermine his prophecies. One of the staunchest assumptions of his previous work was the unflappable stability of communism, but now that the disintegration of the USSR has mockingly refuted his prognoses, Zinoviev is bound to qualify his previous assertions, albeit unready to abandon them altogether. The result is unintended parody, permitting one commentator to describe Zinoviev's position just as satirically as had Zinoviev himself treated his whimsical characters: "Communist society is highly stable, except when it is not."[67] Now it is Zinoviev's turn to become a target of "Zinovievism" (to coin, or recoin, a term), the type of relentless paradoxicalism he had invented to disclose the irrationality of communist society.

Since Zinoviev's writing deals with such conceptualized reality as communism, his refusal to take a consciously ironic, "conceptualist" position toward this reality reduces his directly authorial statements to the level of his characters; the effect proves absurdist and grotesque, but now in respect to the author himself. Zinoviev is a conceptualist thinker only in that part of his writing—presumably, the most successful and compelling—that treats the myths of mass consciousness, the sophistications of enslaved intellectuals, and the paradoxical logic of ideology. As soon as Zinoviev digresses from the phantasms of communism to its reality and strikes the pose of its rigorous investigator, this pretension turns against the author, landing him in the ranks of his fictive nonsensical reasoners and philosophizers. The *logic of absurdity*, which Zinoviev brilliantly discloses in his so-called "sociological novels," like *The Yawning Heights* and *The Madhouse*, converts into the "absurdity of logic" when he tries to master it solemnly and "scientifically" in his articles and sociological treatises. As one of his commentators remarks, there are two types of clowns: those who "mourn life's deep and tragic absurdities," and those who behave like enfants terrible and unconsciously make themselves ridiculous.[68] One cannot but agree with the critic that Zinoviev belongs to both these kinds, respectively, as the author of and a character in his philosophical parodies.

66 The book was published in Russian only in 1994, already in the post-Soviet era. The passage is cited from Kirkwood, *Alexander Zinoviev*, 234.

67 Ibid., 229.

68 Janson, "Alexander Zinoviev: Experiences of a Soviet Methodologist," 23.

4. The Metaphysics of Emptiness. The Philosophical Installations of Ilya Kabakov

Ilya Kabakov (born 1933) is one of the founding members and chief proponents of conceptualism in the Soviet Union, both as an artistic movement and a philosophical worldview. He grew up in Dnepropetrovsk, the same city that produced Brezhnev and most of his political associates. Kabakov himself describes this area in southern Ukraine as "a place of marsh, quagmire, quicksand, landslides and muddy clay .... A flat, featureless never-ending plain which was the arena for incessant streams of wandering and displaced humanity."[69] This image of a cultural vacuum became one of the dominant motifs in his later artistic and philosophical work. For thirty years he lived in Moscow, earning his living as an illustrator of children's books, and at the same time laying the foundations of Soviet conceptualism together with such fellow artists as

Figure 9 Ilya Kabakov.

[69] Ilya Kabakov, "On the Subject of the Local Language," in *Zhizn' mukh. Das Leben der Fliegen. Life of Flies,* by Ilya Kabakov (Cologne: Kölnischer Kunstverein, 1992), 238.

Erik Bulatov, Ivan Chuikov, Oleg Vasiliev, Eduard Gorokhovsky, and Viktor Pivovarov. From 1987 on, Kabakov lived in Austria, France, and then New York City, and around 1996 settled permanently on Long Island. As compared with other representatives of this movement, Kabakov is most articulate and self-conscious in terms of his philosophical speculation. He is the author of numerous texts that comment on the contemporary situation in art and on general principles of conceptualist thinking.[70]

The Concept of Emptiness

Kabakov's thought is remarkable in that it concentrates on the unique features of Soviet civilization and interprets them as general philosophical categories. The central category of his worldview might be called emptiness, or void, which he views as fundamental to Soviet reality.[71] The qualities of "emptiness" and "vampirism" that (as described in Chapter 2 above) Andrei Siniavsky identified in the national genius of Pushkin, Kabakov attributes to Russia itself, which he calls a "hole in space, in the world, in the fabric of being." Emptiness in this view is not merely a lack of essential positive substance, a space waiting to be filled and organized; in Russia, according to Kabakov, unlike in Western Europe, emptiness is a principle of destruction and disorganization that actively transforms all positive being into nonbeing. "By such ineradicable activeness, force and constancy, emptiness 'lives,' transforming being into its antithesis, destroying construction, mystifying reality, turning all into dust and emptiness .... Emptiness adheres to, merges with, sucks being. Its mighty, adhesive, nauseating anti-energy is taken from the transfer into itself, which like vampirism, it gleans and extracts from the existence surrounding it."[72] If it is true that nature abhors a vacuum, then in Russia the rule is inverted: the vacuum abhors nature. One cannot interrogate emptiness for its causes and goals, because its very nature is to annihilate such categories. "Why? What was the purpose? This question can be put only to the living, the intelligent, the natural, but not to emptiness. Emptiness is the other, antithetical side of any question."[73] Because such emptiness is active, nothing can be erected in its midst without immediately falling prey to a soul-draining vampirism. In Kabakov's view, this existence-bordering-on-nonexistence is characteristic of the

[70] See especially Ilya Kabakov and Mikhail Epstein, *Katalog* (Vologda: Library of Moscow Conceptualism/German Titov, 2010). This dialogue between Kabakov and Epstein, which encompasses a broad range of metaphysical, psychological, and artistic issues, is partly translated in Ilya Kabakov, *On Art*, ed. Matthew Jesse Jackson, trans. Antonina Bouis (Chicago: University of Chicago Press, 2018), 276–355.

[71] For a detailed analysis of emptiness in Kabakov, see Mikhail Epstein, "Emptiness as a Technique: Word and Image in Ilya Kabakov," in *Russian Postmodernism: New Perspectives on Post-Soviet Culture*, ed. by Mikhail Epstein, Alexander Genis, and Slobodanka Vladiv-Glover (New York, Oxford: Berghahn Books, 2016), 363–409. This article was first published in Russian as "Pustota kak priem. Slovo i izobrazhenie u Il'i Kabakova," *Oktiabr'*, no. 10 (1993): 177–92.

[72] Ilya Kabakov, "On Emptiness," in *Between Spring and Summer. Soviet Conceptual Art in the Era of Late Communism*, ed. David A. Ross (Tacoma: Tacoma Art Museum; Boston: The Institute of Contemporary Art, 1990), 54.

[73] Ibid., 54.

entirety of Soviet civilization, whose constructive endeavors are doomed by the very fact of their being founded in the metaphysical void.[74]

Existence and Garbage

In such an environment, all constructions implicitly contain their own undoing, giving rise to another important concept in Kabakov's thought, the "dump" or "garbage." Garbage is a metaphysical category, indicating the presence of nothingness within material things; it represents something that is simultaneously nothing. Moreover, every "something" is garbage-to-be. Although this fate is inevitable for every object, its historical manifestation is especially palpable in the Soviet Union.

> I feel that man, living in our region, is simply suffocating in his own life among the garbage since there is nowhere to take it, nowhere to sweep it out—we have lost the border between garbage and non-garbage space. Everything is covered up, littered with garbage—our homes, streets, cities. We have no place to discard all this—it remains near us.[75]

Here the problem of garbage disposal is metaphysical rather than logistical: it is not that there is no dump, but rather that there is no space that is not a dump. There is no transcendental realm where the garbage might be disposed of (hell), or that promises any purification from it (heaven).

For Kabakov, however, the meaning of garbage is ambivalent. It is not just the negative aspect of physical existence, but is the core of existence itself, since reality reveals its transience in the form of garbage. As the material integrity of a thing deteriorates, its sentimental value progressively grows. An object that loses its functionality—becoming garbage—is preserved on the level of pure meaning, in memory. Thus garbage is intrinsically more ideal and spiritual than those brand-new things that serve us by their material utility. On behalf of one of his characters, "the man who never threw anything away," Kabakov writes: "[S]trange as it seems, I feel that it is precisely the garbage, that very dirt where important papers and simple scraps

[74] Kabakov's definition of "active void" obviously corresponds to Zinoviev's pinpointing of "active negation" as the constitutive factor of the Soviet system. One can even identify verbal parallels between the two authors. Thus, in a passage on Moscow as a "model communist city," Zinoviev describes the capital as a sort of "null" center of the Soviet world: "Everything here is so grey and cheerless that it even becomes interesting. It is a special kind of 'interest,' purely negative, corroding, depriving of will to action and desire to act .... Here the absence of everything that makes a person a personality attains a monstrous scope and becomes tangibly positive. This absence is cultivated here and makes progress .... Moscow is a living and very active social tissue, but a malignant one" (Zinov'ev, *Bez illiuzii*, 94–5). Zinoviev is more inclined to logical constructions, Kabakov to ontological ones; thus does Zinoviev's "active negation" become, for Kabakov, "a greedy emptiness." Characteristically, the very fact and force of negation is important for many conceptual thinkers, since it is the prerequisite of "nothingness" that transforms ideas into self-referential, fantastic, nonsensical concepts.

[75] Ilya Kabakov, *Ten Characters* (London: The Institute of Contemporary Arts, 1989), 45–6.

are mixed and unsorted, that comprises the genuine and only real fabric of my life, no matter how ridiculous and absurd it seems from the outside."[76] When things disclose their transience and "nothingness," they also increase their value. Paradoxically, the dump is not only the cemetery for deceased things, but also the realm of their immortality, where they reveal their ultimate essence and meaning.

Many of Kabakov's exhibitions showcase items of garbage accompanied by elaborately descriptive labels that would seem more appropriate for objects of great esteem, like the personal mementos of celebrated historical figures. Kabakov's metaphysical dump is an inverted museum where the objects, unlike in conventional exhibits, have no great significance, but are rather the most miserable and negligible items from someone's personal life—such as a used match, a shriveled apple core, an old receipt, or a pencil with a broken tip. A metaphysical tension arises from the relationship between the negligible materiality of these objects and their monumental verbal presentations.

Reality and Language

The relationship between reality and language is a crucial point in Kabakov's philosophy, which concentrates on Russia's peculiar logocentrism—a love of verbal expression that remains strikingly indifferent to the world of objects. "Language is a fundamental principle, an aspect of thought; the world of the dump plunges it into a new state where the word is separate from the thought, the title separate from the object; the text is separate from its meaning, the appellation is separate from that which it names; in general, every word is divorced from its signification."[77] Given that Russia is the zone of active emptiness, which imbues everything with nothingness, the activity of language is the only thing that remains real, or to use Baudrillard's term, "hyperreal," since it creates an illusory reality of significations without signifieds. Kabakov explores the language of such classic Russian authors as Gogol, Dostoevsky, and Chekhov, identifying them as precursors of typical Soviet intoxication with words, the phantasmagoric verbosity inherent in ideocratic society. In the characteristic propensity of these classics for excessive, self-referential speech, Kabakov reveals a total loss of any object of communication. "But one must talk, speak out, speak again and again …. And therein lies the reason for the neurosis in our great literature, in the minds and nerves and memories of each one of us—the neurosis of incessant talk, the preference for verbal self-realization, for the incessant, unflagging, raging sea of words … "[78]

These comments may remind us of Mikhail Bakhtin's valorization of dialogic language, but Kabakov offers a far less sympathetic interpretation of the same

[76] Ibid., 44. Compare with Zinoviev's assessment of the dump: "Love your dump … since it is your home, and you have and will have no other" (*Zhivi* [Lausanne: L'Age d'Homme, 1989], 17).

[77] Kabakov, "On the Subject of the Local Language," 239.

[78] Ilya Kabakov, *Zhizn' mukh. Das Leben der Fliegen. Life of Flies* (Cologne: Kölnischer Kunstverein, 1992), 242.

phenomenon. For Bakhtin, the dialogic relationship is the only genuine mode of human existence: addressing the other through language. For Kabakov, this obsession with dialogue attests to the lack of a relationship between words and any corresponding reality. The verbal communication people are keen to immerse themselves in is but a would-be magical incantation to keep nothingness at bay. But the very abundance of their chatter betrays the presence of nothingness all around them and intensifies their verbal neurosis. Bakhtin admires the multi-referentiality in the speech of Dostoevsky's characters, whose conversations allude to earlier conversations, themselves thickly imbedded with dialogic references. Kabakov sees this inclination for verbosity as a symptom of Russians' fear of emptiness and the implicit realization of its ubiquity. The speech of literary characters can only refer to other speech, because there is no reality beyond their words except for the void they seek to drown out with their voices—a void that is only emphasized and augmented by the emptiness of their prattle.

Kabakov's analysis shows how Bakhtin's dialogic theory can be interpreted within a broader conceptualist paradigm. For Bakhtin, to exist authentically means to communicate dialogically, which allows us to interpret Bakhtin himself as a utopian, in search of the ultimate transcendence of human loneliness, alienation, and objectification. Kabakov advances a postmodern perspective on this dialogic utopia, revealing the illusory character of the hoped-for paradise of communication, whose language is merely a self-referential miasma emanating from and papering over reality's emptiness. Bakhtin's attempt to overcome monologic solipsism is characteristic of an existentialist gesture of flight from objectivity, which inevitably falls into the even more absurd solipsism of dialogue enclosed in itself. For monologic subjectivity, there still remains the world of external objects, whereas for dialogic intersubjectivity, which assimilates everything into the process of communication, nothing real remains except for words and their meanings.

Conceptualism and Ideology

A large part of Kabakov's work is dedicated to theorizing the phenomenon of Soviet totalitarianism. Arguing that the "rupture between word and meaning creates an empty space in which lives and thrives something that can be termed 'total ideology,'"[79] he identifies a peculiar ontological/linguistic premise for the dictatorship of ideas in recent Russian history. When there is no reality to which language can refer, language itself runs the danger of substituting for reality. Like God creating the universe from nothing by the force of the Word, ideology has the power to create a reality out of language only because it proceeds from nothingness. "The word, which has been cut off from and thrown out of the nest which was its meaning, can now signify anything, depending on the direction of the ideological wind. In practice this means that a whole world of substituted meanings comes into existence."[80] Ideology itself, in Kabakov's

[79] Kabakov, "On the Subject of the Local Language," 240.

[80] Ibid.

terms, may be defined as the illusion of reality produced by language in the absence of reality as such. This accounts for the grandiose enterprises and construction projects of the Soviet era, which proceeded not from an economic basis but from abstract concepts and ideological assumptions, and often culminated in not just ineffective but phantasmagoric results. From this standpoint, ideology is linguocracy, the capacity of language to produce and impose on others a pseudo-reality that claims to be uniquely valid.

Strikingly, Kabakov defines conceptualism itself in nearly the same terms as he uses to describe ideology. First of all, he is careful to distinguish ideologically oriented Russian conceptualism from the aforementioned Western school of the same name, whose principle is "the idea instead of the thing," or "one thing instead of another"; for example, the textual representation of a chair takes the place of its visual counterpart. The principle of Russian conceptualism might be phrased as "the idea instead of no thing," since the reality to which Western conceptual representations refer does not exist in Russia. "This contiguity, closeness, touchingness, contact with nothing, emptiness, makes up, we feel, the basic peculiarity of 'Russian conceptualism.'"[81]

Conceptualism, then, shares with ideology a tendency to substitute signs or concepts for real substance. But the principal difference between them is that ideology claims its signs have real referents, while conceptualism reveals the emptiness of its own signs. Ideology conceals its own contingency, pretending to integrate signs with reality in such a way as to declare itself "true" and "all-embracing." Conceptualism exposes this "reality fallacy," disclosing the contingency of all concepts and refusing to ground itself in any reality. "Precisely because of its self-referentiality and the lack of windows or a way out to something else, it is like something that hangs in the air, a self-reliant thing, like a fantastic construction, connected to nothing, with its roots in nothing."[82] Conceptualism emerged organically in the Soviet milieu precisely because it is the underside of total ideology. The reality presented by Soviet ideology existed as an elaborate facade, a huge and expensive movie set, and conceptualism invites us to walk behind the scenes, to recognize the spectral and absurd side of this monumental construction. Whereas totalitarianism must ground itself in a monistic metaphysics of "ideas come true," conceptualism offers a series of imaginary metaphysics, which in their interplay demonstrate the relativity of each and undermine any metaphysical pretensions.

Multiple Metaphysics and Ambivalent Universals

Metaphysical systems proliferate within conceptualism by way of overcoming the metaphysical dimension of discourse, not via serious analytical criticism (as in Wittgenstein or Derrida), but through the self-ironic, self-parodic construction of systems that deliberately disclose their own contingency. Traditionally, a metaphysics

81 Kabakov, "Conceptualism in Russia," 247.
82 Ibid., 249.

bases all of reality on some general presupposition, a concept so broad as to allow all phenomena to be deduced from it. The Idea in Plato's system, Absolute Spirit in Hegel, Matter and Economic Production in Marx, the Will in Schopenhauer, Life in Nietzsche, Creative Impetus in Bergson, Being in Heidegger are examples of such grand philosophical constructions. But if we recognize, as does conceptualism, that all of these are merely concepts, that none has a privileged claim to the real, then any concept we might choose becomes equally efficient for the production of an imaginary metaphysics. Hence Kabakov intentionally chooses small and trivial objects as foundations for metaphysical discourse in order to suggest a conceptualist alternative to the grand schemes of traditional metaphysics.

One of Kabakov's most developed examples proceeds from the ordinary housefly, which acquires in his work the same status as, for instance, Hegel's Absolute Spirit.

> The work presented here, the treatise "The Fly with Wings" almost visually demonstrates the nature of all philosophical discourse—at its base may lie a simple, uncomplicated and even nonsensical object—an ordinary fly, for example. But yet the very quality of the discourse does not suffer in the least as a result of this. In this very way it is proven (and illustrated) that the idea of philosophizing and its goal consists not at all in the revelation of the original supposition (if this can turn out to be an ordinary fly), but rather in the very process of discourse, in the verbal frivolity itself, in the mutual suppositions of the beginnings and ends, in the flow of connections and representations of that very thing.[83]

Besides demonstrating the contingency of metaphysical systems, Kabakov accomplishes two other closely related philosophical tasks. By contrasting the superficiality of the topic with the gravity of his chosen genre, Kabakov not only deconstructs the methodology of serious philosophy, but elevates the trivial to the status of a topic worthy of philosophical meditation. Instead of promoting abstract concepts, Kabakov argues the merits of so humble a creature as the housefly as a principle of explanation of such important spheres as economics, politics, the arts, and civilization itself. The same device that allows him to deconstruct traditional philosophy also serves to *construct* a new range of philosophies capable of assimilating the words and concepts of ordinary language in all its infinite richness. This pan-philosophical approach can also be applied to such concepts as *chair* or *table* or *wall*, identifying them as potential universals that may provide a more vivid elucidation of the world than such traditional concepts as Life or Being.

Although Kabakov selects concrete universals that are much narrower in scope than traditional abstract founding concepts like Truth or Spirit, the specificity of his choices imparts an informational value that is lacking in the vagueness of more general terms. Thus Kabakov's metaphysics of the fly appears more informative than the traditional

[83] Ilya Kabakov, "The Fly as a Subject and Basis for Philosophical Discourse. Introduction," in *Zhizn' mukh. Das Leben der Fliegen. Life of Flies*, by Ilya Kabakov (Cologne: Kölnischer Kunstverein, 1992), 224.

all-inclusive metaphysics of Life or Spirit. In his commentary on Kabakov's installation *The Fly with Wings*, which contains the treatise "The Fly as a Subject and Basis for Philosophical Discourse," Boris Groys, another conceptualist thinker, writes:

> Our culture contains a small stock of words that lack a clear, firmly defined meaning. These words are, in a way, linguistic jokers [or "wildcards"] which, without meaning anything in particular, are thereby able to mean practically anything. Specifically, they include "being," "life," and "thought." These words mean simultaneously everything and nothing—and are equally applicable to anything at all. For this reason they have traditionally enjoyed great prestige in culture. Kabakov transforms the word "fly" into another of these joker-words which are potentially applicable to anything whatsoever .... In the ability of an ephemeral word bereft of a noble philosophical tradition to achieve the lofty status of the words which possess this tradition we may see a historic opportunity which is also open to the fly—the opportunity to construct a fly-paradise of its own, its own world of platonic, fly-essences.[84]

Thus Kabakov's multiple metaphysics presupposes the simultaneous double-movement of a concept. An ordinary concept—like that of a fly—assumes metaphysical status, while metaphysical discourse is reduced to the genre of a speech game. In this way, Kabakov's irony avoids the pitfall of intellectual cynicism, and his sincerity and lyricism regarding ordinary things avoid banal sentimentality.

Social Philosophy and the Communal Apartment

As with his metaphysics, Kabakov's social philosophy bases itself on common concepts, focusing on the opposition between public and private spaces and on the mediating role of the "communal apartment." In Kabakov's interpretation, a major historical change in the construction of social life occurred during and after the revolution, from a privileging of the personal sphere to an emphasis on the public; from home-oriented to street-oriented civilization. In the street, we are in transit and move with the crowd. Kabakov observes that nineteenth-century Russian literature abounded with imagery of the street: tramps, vagabonds, beggars, pilgrims. These "lumpen-people" constituted a psychological model by which the revolution shaped its notion of communal life and they contributed to the dissolution of privacy. In these terms, the revolution can be described as the victory of street (*ulichnye*) over domestic (*domashnie*) people. Subsequently, socialism institutionalized a new type of dwelling that introduced the social patterns of the street into the home setting: the communal apartment, which is the centerpiece of Kabakov's art and meditation. Soviet communal apartments were set up as a series of rooms ("homes"), connected by long corridors ("streets"). Different

[84] Boris Groys, "We Shall Be Like Flies," in *History Becomes Form. Moscow Conceptualism*, by Boris Groys (Cambridge, MA: The MIT Press, 2010), 102–3.

families (sometimes three generations) occupied individual rooms but shared a common kitchen and bathroom. "Everybody's lives are closely examined by the others. Everyone lives in the communal apartment as if they were under a magnifying glass. There are no secrets. Everyone knows what someone has brought with them, what is cooking, what you wore yesterday, what you are wearing today."[85]

In theory, such transparency could afford an ideal space for peoples' souls to freely mingle and create the utopian condition that many Russian thinkers had long dreamed of under the term *sobornost'*, often translated as "communality" or "togetherness." *Sobornost'* was the ultimate religious vision, for instance, of Slavophiles like Khomiakov and Kireevsky, and of symbolists like Merezhkovsky and Viacheslav Ivanov, who sometimes referred to the Greek choir as the prototype of such an ideal social body. But for Kabakov, *sobornost'*, at least as realized in the communal apartment, proves to be self-parodic. The communal apartment "reminds one of a Greek tragedy, where the choir—the collective—has to utter its opinion and its sentence."[86] The reality of this "utopia" sometimes proved even more tragic—and at the same time, comic—than the dramas of ancient theater. Many of Kabakov's works present the almost absurd intensity of "dialogical" life in the communal apartment, where people, owing to the fact that they share communal property, defend their *private* property rights with special fervor. One of Kabakov's painted boards shows a fly in the center, while the margins depict a conversation about it: "Whose fly is this?" "It's Olga's fly." Here, the metaphysical importance of the fly is emphasized once again, as it becomes the absurd subject of controversial property demarcations.

Installations as Treatises. Things among Words

Although Kabakov's philosophy is discussed here mostly on the basis of his writings, the very logic of his ideas comes from artistic experience and leads beyond words. Conceptualism, in general, exceeds the boundaries of verbal discourse, as it attempts to incorporate visual images or even material objects into a conceptual framework. This appeal to concrete objects is another side of the conceptual critique of ideology and abstract metaphysics. Conceptualism attempts to fulfill what Theodor Adorno designated as the proper, but unattainable goal of philosophical thinking:

> Philosophy, indeed theoretical thought in general, suffers from an idealistic prejudgment because it deals only with concepts, never directly with what these concepts refer to .... Philosophy cannot paste an ontic substratum into its treatises [or "its text"]. It can only talk about it in words, and in so doing it assimilates that substratum, whereas it should want to keep it distinct from its own conceptuality.[87]

[85] Ilya Kabakov, "What Is A Communal Apartment?" in *Ten Characters*, by Ilya Kabakov (London: The Institute of Contemporary Arts, 1989), 52.

[86] Ibid.

[87] Theodor Adorno, *Aesthetic Theory*, trans. C. Lenhardt; ed. Gretel Adorno and Rolf Tiedemann (London and New York: Routledge & Kegan Paul, 1986), 365.

Since it is the hallmark of conceptualist thinking to expose its own "conceptuality" as something distinct from external reality, conceptual methods make it possible to directly introduce a reality that remains separate from concepts, "an ontic substratum" you can indeed paste into a text—where it will remain its own insistent self. Concrete objects become elements of philosophical discourse, insofar as discourse itself does not attempt to assimilate them, but instead recognizes their irreducible character.

In fact, many of Kabakov's installations, such as *The Palace of Projects* or *The Fly with Wings*, present a philosophical or quasi-philosophical text in which an ontic substratum is pasted. For example, in Kabakov's installation *The Man Who Flew into Space from His Room*, the ontic substratum—a room full of enigmatic tools and detritus, with a telltale hole in the ceiling—is pasted into a textual narrative about a mad inventor who has launched himself through the roof and into the sky. (From what is left among the mysterious instruments, the "spaceship" in question appears to have been a sort of super-ambitious homemade catapult.) Kabakov's installations are often related—self-reflectively and ironically—to projects based on utopian writing. Moreover, his objective is to transform hyperbole into litotes, to connect big ideas and big words ("eternity," "immortality," or "resurrection") to tiny objects that would exemplify the internal irony of utopianism converted into material action. One of the sixty-five projects constituting the *Palace of Projects* ironically highlights the Russian philosopher Nikolai Fedorov's idea of the resurrection of all the dead:

> [T]he only worthy goal of a living person can be the resurrection of all the people who have died in the past .... In this project death is understood as something that shouldn't be, as something which delivers misery and injustice to all of humanity, which can be overcome if all of those living concentrate all their efforts on it. This theory was given the name 'The Philosophy of the Common Cause' and received widespread notice in philosophical and intellectual circles of Russian society of that time (the end of the nineteenth—beginning of the twentieth c.) .... Russian thought has always revolved around searches for ideas of a common meaning of life for all humanity, as a unified whole.[88]

In Kabakov's installation, this sublime vision is illustrated by a metal frame-table covered with plywood. On the table is a plastic box filled to about ten–thirteen centimeters of dirt. This box is "planted" with about fifty small white figures cut out of paper, vertically stuck into the dirt-ground in such a way that they touch it only with their feet without sinking into it. These tiny figures of "resurrected" people in a plastic case ironically set off the verbal grandiosity of this project. In this installation, a small object is not hyperbolically projected into the future as the predicted resurrection of all the dead, but accompanies the text as a materially insignificant, ironic illustration of the grand vision. The word and the thing together form a grotesque couple, like

[88] Ilya Kabakov, *The Palace of Projects. Artangel* (London: The Roundhouse, 1998), project 35 (no pagination).

Don Quixote and Sancho Panza. The scale relations are important here: the installation works as a semiotic machine that materially enlarges and/but semantically diminishes the text in the system of its displayed signifieds.

Kabakov's philosophy in the late 1980s and 1990s tends more and more to be expressed in the form of treatise-installations. His aesthetic provides an explanation for the historical progression of prevailing artistic modes, from icon to fresco to painting and finally to installation. The installation imitates the material surroundings of human existence in a highly literal way, while also allowing the artist to create spaces that exemplify philosophical ideas.

For example, one of Kabakov's installations, entitled *The Mental Institution, or Institute of Creative Research*, presents a series of spaces designed by his fictional characters, patients at the eponymous institution, where the treatment involves allowing them to express their disorders in creative impulses suppressed by conventional society. The patients are referred to as "authors," and the doctors as "collaborators." The works thus executed embody the patients' particular worldviews, which are treated by all concerned as innovative rather than insane. By documenting this process, Kabakov is able to present various philosophical positions in visible and spatial form, providing each with supporting textual components, including the (fictional) medical diagnoses of the patients and expositions of the original theories that inspire their creativity. One section in this installation consists of a series of paintings linked along the walls by ropes; they range in quality from outstanding to amateurish. The "author" (a patient) explains the underlying conception of the work: to demonstrate a method for levelling the unequal distribution of energies throughout the world, since "the energy of the best, 'strongest' has been transferred to the 'weak' and their quality has been levelled out, while at the same time remaining rather high."[89] Another installation, called *The Toilet*, illustrates the problem of expressing individuality within a totalitarian regime, and by extension, the general philosophical "problem of other minds." The "author" has installed two high doors whose frosted panes display the word "toilet." His accompanying text explains that within a communal apartment, the only private retreat is the lavatory, where one can escape for a time the hell consisting of other people.

It might be objected that these are presentations of the parodic philosophies espoused by fictional characters and not by the "philosopher" himself. However, it is Kabakov's prime contribution to organize these citations as a pastiche, which is a primary mode of postmodern creativity. Moreover, Kabakov's philosophy may be said to loom over all as the implicit assertion that no one of the visual philosophies in the asylum may be privileged over any other—nor may those ideas that pass as "real" in that grand lunatic asylum composed of our best universities and intellectual institutions. Kabakov's installations, by positing several possible worlds, illustrate the relativity of the concept of "reality" that exists merely as a series of philosophies, each

[89] I. Kabakov, *The Mental Institution, or Institute of Creative Research* (Malmö: Rooseum, 1991), 169.

proposing its own model of reality without providing criteria by which to verify the validity of its assertions.

Ideocracy and Madness

The theme of madness is common to conceptualist thinking, since it is addressed to life in an ideocratic society, which produces its own peculiar psychological contortions. Ideas, pushed to an extreme and exaggerated as they are in totalitarian ideology, degenerate into various kinds of obsessions. From this standpoint, ideocracy is a mental illness afflicting an entire society and replicating itself in the individual manias of its subjects. This engagement with the "disturbed consciousness" is characteristic of a number of conceptualist thinkers, since concepts themselves, insofar as they break away from reality and become self-sufficient mental units, verge on idées fixes.

Not coincidentally, *The Madhouse* is both the title and setting of Aleksandr Zinoviev's major work, which is based on autobiographical material.[90] During the earlier stage of his career, Zinoviev, as a research fellow at the Moscow Institute of Philosophy, had occasion to work with "a range of mentally disturbed people whose manuscripts had been sent by the KGB to the Institute for vetting. They were of two basic types: convinced Marxists or declared opponents of Marxism."[91] This episode illustrates three significant and interconnected points: the psychiatric cases in question arose on ideological grounds; the intelligence service (KGB) was anxious to keep these cases under surveillance; and part of this philosophy institute's mission was to "diagnose" these cases and determine whether they fell under the category of "medical" or "ideological" disturbances. This application of philosophical expertise by an intelligence agency may seem improbable, but it reveals the basic assumption of the ideocratic state: that all deviations from social and psychological norms proceed from *philosophical* errors. Having originated as a realization of a philosophical project, the Soviet system had no other criteria for judging medical and political fitness except according to philosophical principles. If a mental disorder is caused by excessive preoccupation with Marxist ideas, then it is natural to turn to Marxist specialists for help. In the ideocratic society, philosophy is fundamentally responsible for the insanity of the state and is therefore called upon to restore the mental health of its citizens.

Kabakov's general project brings philosophy out of its narrow discursive domain into the realm of ordinary speech and artistic creation. By broadening the definition of philosophy, Kabakov, more than any other contemporary thinker, responds to the uniquely Russian mode of philosophizing, which is not so much abstract thinking about the world as it is *the concrete implementation of concepts in everyday life*. Kabakov demonstrates the absurdity of an existence that submits completely to ideological designs. Conceptualism simultaneously discloses the contingent character of concepts and the conceptual character of reality. "[O]ur local [i.e., Russian] thinking, from

[90] Aleksandr Zinov'ev, *Zheltyi dom* (Lausanne: L'Age d'Homme, 1980).

[91] Kirkwood, *Alexander Zinoviev*, 15.

the very beginning in fact, could have been called 'conceptualism.'"[92] Kabakov had a powerful influence on many Russian artists, critics, and thinkers of the 1980s–1990s, who continued to develop conceptual models derived from Russia's historical tradition.

5. The Philosophy of Sots-Art and Morality of Eclecticism. Vitalii Komar and Aleksandr Melamid

The sots-art movement may be said to have been founded in 1972 by Komar and Melamid, and born of their nostalgia toward and parody of the official canon of Soviet art, socialist realism. Like Ilya Kabakov, these artists supplement their visual work with programmatic discourse, proposing that certain ideas can function as self-sufficient works of art. What is it that distinguishes the idea-as-art from the idea as an element of an ideological or philosophical system? Paradoxically, the art-idea is more quintessentially ideal than the idea embedded in theoretical discourse, because the former makes no claim to transform reality (as does the latter, in ideology) or explain it (as in philosophy). Rather than weave itself into a tapestry of justification, clarification, and argumentation, the art-idea presents itself purely as idea—idea as such. For the same reason, conceptualism establishes the concept as its basic unit, one that refers only to itself and not to some external referent.

Postmodernism encompasses many different artistic movements, including conceptualism, which has been especially influential in Russia. Within conceptualism, which works with the most diverse artistic languages and ideological systems, one can distinguish, among other subdivisions, sots-art, which concentrates on the sign system of socialist (communist) civilization. In terms of biological taxonomy, one could say that postmodernism is a "class" of aesthetic phenomena, while conceptualism is an "order" and sots-art a "family."

It is obvious, for example, that if the novels of Umberto Eco or Andrei Bitov belong to one branch of postmodernism, the conceptualist texts of Dmitrii Prigov or Vladimir Sorokin belong to another. But within conceptualism itself, even within the works of individual authors, one can distinguish between sots-art (Sorokin's *The Norm* or Prigov's poems about militiamen) and other "arts" ("Russ-art," "psych-art," etc.) that work conceptually with the sign systems of the Russian psychological novel (Sorokin's *Novel*) or the epistolary, idyllic, and elegiac genres (the poetry of Timur Kibirov).

Sots-art maintains a special relationship with Russian postmodernism as its "first love" or, more precisely, its umbilical cord, joining postmodernism with communism, from whose womb it emerged into the postcommunist world. Sots-art uncovers a certain aesthetic commonality of communist and postmodernist aesthetics: their hyperreal nature, eclecticism, derivativeness, and cold passion for ideological allegories and the clichés of the popular consciousness.

[92] Kabakov, "Conceptualism in Russia," 249.

One of Komar and Melamid's most famous politico-aesthetic concepts is the "Transstate" (*Transgosudarstvo*), which they define as follows: "Transstate is a federation of free and independent state-individuals—I-states with the right of self-government and autonomy, even including secession. Each member of the federation is a citizen-state in accordance with the Transstate fundamental law, which proclaims: 'L'etat, c'est moi.'"[93] Why the I-state? Because, they argue, the concept of the *nation*-state is outdated; the specific identity of nations became less and less distinguishable over the course of the twentieth century, and now has negligible impact on individual self-conceptions. Why, then, should not a new political reality be forged to correspond to the existential manifestations of individual selves, which are far more substantial in the contemporary world than geographical or social demarcations? Although Komar and Melamid have composed a constitution for their Transstate, appointed themselves its consuls, proclaimed its independence from all other states, and applied for membership in the United Nations, it is clear that the idea of Transstate is a purely artistic one, meaning that it has no direct political implications. This "work" takes such conventional signs of political discourse as the ratification of a constitution, the right of secession, etc., and turns them into self-sufficient aesthetic concepts that signify the signifiers themselves rather than any external signifieds. This artistic mode is typical of Komar and Melamid's work: to extract the most general concepts from conventional political, aesthetic, or journalistic discourse and present them as works of art. Contrary to the traditional notion of art as a sensuous and material activity, Komar and Melamid demonstrate that art is more essentially a domain of *mental* activity. Art is even more metaphysical than philosophy, ideology, religion, or politics, since it liberates concepts peculiar to these disciplines from their historical and material contexts. Hence, art is a concept for concept's sake.

Paradoxically, this purification of ideas through art presupposes an extreme eclecticism of genres, styles, and disciplines, whose conceptual patterns become the "material" for the production of aesthetic experience. "Eclecticism" is, indeed, one of the central terms in Komar and Melamid's theoretical glossary, serving as a synonym for the more conventional term "postmodernism"; it is how they designate their own artistic method. Eclecticism presupposes that the styles and genres differentiated by the artistic movements of the past are now ready for a secondary appropriation by some universal, though deliberately superficial and imitative, creative mind. "If modernism can be compared to an intellectual adventure, the discovery of new lands, then post-modernism reminds one of tourism."[94] Certainly, a contemporary tourist's impressions of America lack the profound (even brutal) originality of a Columbus or the first pilgrims; eclecticism, however, in spite of its touristic superficiality, has a certain metaphysical depth. Since it conjoins the signs and styles of different epochs, it acquires a supratemporal dimension. This is implicit in the very term *post*-modernism: the time

[93] Cited from Carter Ratcliff, *Komar & Melamid* (New York: Abbeville Press Publishers, 1988), 202.

[94] Vitaly Komar and Aleksandr Melamid, *Death Poems: Manifesto of Eclecticism* (New York: Galerie Barbara Farber, 1988), 25.

beyond time, the space where "now" and "always" merge into one. "Eternity cannot help but be eclectic. Eclecticism is eternity. Eternity is eclecticism."[95]

The supratemporal dimension of eclecticism gives rise to quasi-metaphysical implications. "Variation in style and eclecticism make this world, actually the transient moment of this world, like the other-world. Only in the next world do heroes of various times exist simultaneously. The Last Judgement, the purgatory, hell and heaven of various styles, fragments and fashions—that is eclecticism."[96] These religious concepts are not to be understood in a necessarily transcendental sense; the "otherworld" refers to a conceptual space where historically distant moments can be reappropriated simultaneously via aesthetic experience. Even death, which is the transcendental limit of life, becomes in Komar and Melamid's eclecticist interpretation a repeatable experience contained within life itself. "It is not true that a person dies only once. A person dies many times; all his deaths are of varying duration, but none of them are longer than his life."[97]

For Komar and Melamid this notion of eclecticism carries unexpected moral implications, challenging the conventional dismissal of postmodernism as an irresponsible, purely aesthetic, elitist play. Eclecticism presupposes that there is no such thing as a "clean conscience," since every person's conscience bears the traces of all past transgressions and possible temptations. "A clean conscience is the result of a bad memory."[98] The eclectic conscience, from this point of view, has a good memory, and thus acknowledges the continual need for repentance. Modernism aspired to perfection through the realization of an artistic utopia, but in the face of such moral smugness, Komar and Melamid ask, "When will we at last begin repenting the sins of modernism?"[99] Unlike modernism, with its transcendental pretensions, postmodernism limits itself with a measure of relativity more appropriate to human transience; for this reason, Komar and Melamid define it as "modernism with a human face."[100]

For Komar and Melamid, the concept of irony plays a crucial role in determining a postmodern morality. In order to understand this, we must realize that irony is not conceived here as something opposed to sincerity; on the contrary, the very nature of eclecticism means that the more sincere we are, the more we must recognize the inadequacy of all our pronouncements and thus take an ironic stance toward them. "If 'a thought uttered is a lie' (Tyutchev), then the more sincere a person's speech is, the more subtle an ironist he is."[101] A sincere person who understands the incommensurability of thought and speech attempts to overcome it in a positive way, by refining his or her self-expression, while the ironist maintains the same incommensurability in a negative way, by emphasizing the disjunction between levels of meaning. In order to be sincere, irony

[95] Ibid., 36.
[96] Ibid., 36.
[97] Ibid., 102.
[98] Ibid., 42.
[99] Ibid., 31.
[100] Ibid., 73.
[101] Ibid., 25.

must be addressed primarily to oneself. Modernism was aesthetically arrogant in its use of irony primarily as a tool for undermining other stylistic systems, but postmodernism embraces otherness and, therefore, becomes self-ironic. Self-irony, then, provides the condition for humility, whereby a genuine religious sensibility is restored. The historical path of a new, postmodernist morality proceeds "[f]rom irony, through self-irony, to God!"[102] Komar and Melamid's religious intuition incorporates irony as a kind of apophatic instrument that prevents the deification of any image or figure of God, the identification of God with any canon, any established idea or description.

Thus for Komar and Melamid, self-irony and morality are two sides of the same intellectual orientation. One without the other ruins the ambivalence of postmodernism and returns us to the naive and potentially dangerous modernist paradigm, where a fatally serious and exclusionary vision is sustained by a nihilistic irony addressed to all *other* conceptual systems. This is why Komar and Melamid are so sympathetic to Kierkegaard's and Schlegel's discussions of self-irony as the moving force of philosophical wisdom and religious ascension.

By taking such a position, a conceptualist may interpret even the most ostensibly serious philosophical and theological systems as implicitly ironic. It is not only the Soviet ideocracy that Komar and Melamid, following the sots-artistic mode of reasoning, reinterpret in terms of ironic nostalgia; also coming in for reconsideration are what they view as the first monuments of communist thought: Plato's *Republic* and *Laws*. Thus, to the heated debate regarding the proto-totalitarian nature of Plato's idealism, Komar and Melamid bring an unexpected twist: wasn't Plato joking? They refer to the thesis of Socrates in the *Symposium* that "the genius of tragedy is the same as that of comedy, and that the writer of comedy ought to be a writer of tragedy also," and conclude:

> Plato's remark compels one to suspect that his ideal state is the first anti-utopia, a parody whose key has been lost in the darkness of the ages. One cannot help but sense a Socratic irony in the following contention of the "comedy-writers": 'We are even the creators of the most beautiful tragedy, if not possibly the very best. For our entire state system offers a reproduction of the most beautiful and best life; we contend that this is precisely what is the most veritable tragedy.' (*Laws*, 817B).[103]

Indeed, in the *Laws*, Plato contends: "[S]erious things cannot be understood without laughable things, nor opposites at all without opposites, if a man is really to have intelligence of either."[104]

There is further evidence of the ironic component of the *Laws*, specifically, where Plato provides the project of his ideocracy with the strictest guidelines: "[The lawgiver] must divide up both the city itself and all the country into the twelve portions," etc.

[102] Ibid., 20.
[103] Ibid., 111.
[104] http://classics.mit.edu/Plato/laws.7.vii.html

Abruptly into this mercilessly rational plan of reordering the world, a nagging note enters: Plato tears himself away from the great deed of his intellect, and as if suddenly seeing it through someone else's eyes, is struck by the vanity of this legislation, its amounting to nothing but a dream:

> But we must by all means notice this—that all the arrangements now described will never be likely to meet with such favorable conditions that the whole program can be carried out according to plan. This requires that the citizens will raise no objection to such a mode of living together, and will tolerate being restricted for life to fixed and limited amounts of property and to families such as we have stated, and being deprived of gold and of the other things which the lawgiver is clearly obliged by our regulations to forbid, and will submit also to the arrangements he has defined for country and city, with the dwellings set in the center and round the circumference—almost as if he were telling nothing but dreams, or moulding, so to say, a city and citizens out of wax.[105]

Wax is the most appropriate material for the schemes of such an active and elevated madness. Kabakov does exactly the same thing in his *Palace of Projects*: he takes the thoughts of daring individuals and seers (in the example discussed above, Fedorov's universal resurrection)—ideas meant to be incarnated in cities and states, in transformations on a cosmic scale—and molds them from wax or cuts them out of paper.

Thus is the conceptualist model bigger than might be supposed, extending and addressing itself to the very roots of the ideals that inspired the development of Western civilization. It is a commonly held opinion that the Soviet implementations of Marxist ideology distorted the purity of the communist project, engendering a farcical realization of Marx's vision. But what if the farce preceded the vision? What if, that is, the very concept of utopia, as promulgated by Plato, was originally conceived as a joke, as an anti-utopian fantasy? Then we could say that what became "utopia" is the distortion of a primordial parody, a kind of anti-parody that has approached in all seriousness what was meant to be taken as humor. Thus the Soviet implementation of Marx's vision might well be understood as the perfect realization of a joke that posterity failed to get. Komar and Melamid's theory reverses the entire retrospective of Western civilization and, though it probably cannot be validated, at least bears witness to the potential scope of ironic reversals inherent in the conceptualist way of thinking.

6. Shimmering Aesthetics. Dmitrii Prigov

As we have already noted, conceptualist creativity embraces all sorts of discourse, from abstract theorizing to various forms of artistic and literary production. From the 1970s on, Dmitrii Aleksandrovich Prigov (1940–2007) was the acknowledged leader

[105] Plato, *The Laws*, trans. R. G. Bury (Cambridge, MA: Harvard University Press, 1926), 383–5.

of Moscow conceptualism, as a writer, sculptor, painter, theorist, and organizer. His theoretical statements, composed in a highly rhetorical scholarly jargon, sometimes reminiscent of structuralist discourse, are at the same time subtle parodies of this philosophical genre. Prigov is the brightest example of the "foolish philosopher," whose pronouncements seem to be quotations of some quite serious and ambitious—and often intentionally obscure—theoretical text.

Despite his parodic mode, Prigov offers a substantial contribution to conceptualist theory. Like Kabakov, he emphasizes the organic ties between conceptualism and the Russian cultural tradition, which is predominantly verbal and ideologically charged. "[T]he entire local [i.e., Russian] culture was fundamentally conceptualist and had been so for a long time. Moreover this local conceptualism had arrived at a comprehension of language as stratified layers and had fixed the level of nomination as the object of description."[106] The novelty of conceptualism, according to Prigov, is that it realizes the nominative bias of Russian culture and makes it an object of conscious aesthetic play. A conceptualist writer does not pretend to deal with human characters: the subjects of his or her work are linguistic constructions and stereotypes. "The heroes of my poems have become the different linguistic layers (quotidian, state, high cultural, low cultural, religiophilosophical), representing within the limits of the poetic text corresponding mentalities and ideologies which reveal in this space mutual ambitions and pretensions."[107] Thus does the conceptualist author establish distance between himself and the linguistic positions manifested in his works. He is no longer an actor who transforms himself into a character, but a director who is absent from the scene of his poems. The implication behind all of Prigov's poems is that they are imagined quotations of other poets who have nothing to do with Prigov himself. Like Kabakov, who produces paintings on behalf of fictional characters, Prigov produces verses as if they were written by, for example, a Chinese poet, or a woman poet, or a Soviet conformist requisitely extolling the beauty of Moscow and condemning Reagan's imperialist policies.

However, the distance between Prigov and his masks is indeterminate and flexible—hence his term for his method: "shimmering aesthetics." The reader never knows in advance whether the poet is sincere or parodic in his pronouncements, because the degree of his identification with his character changes from line to line, from word to word.

> Taking the place of the conceptual, a shimmering relationship between the author and the text has developed, in which it is very hard to define (not only for the reader but for the author, too) the degree of sincerity in the immersion into the text and the purity and distance of the withdrawal from it. I.e., the fundamental

[106] Dmitrii Prigov, "Conceptualism and the West," in *Poetics Journal Digital Archive*, ed. Lyn Hejinian and Barrett Watten (Middletown, CT: Wesleyan University Press, 2015), 1161–2.

[107] Dmitri Prigov, "What More Is There To Say?," in *Third Wave. The New Russian Poetry*, ed. Kent Johnson and Stephen M. Ashby (Ann Arbor: University of Michigan Press, 1992), 102.

content becomes the drama between the author and the text, his flickering between the text and a position outside of it.[108]

Prigov identifies "shimmering aesthetics" as an advanced stage of conceptualism, even referring to it as "post-conceptualism," since the parody and pastiche traditionally associated with conceptualism are now enriched with "new sincerity." This kind of sincerity is post-conceptual insofar as it never clearly distinguishes itself from an ironic simulation of sincerity. In other words, "shimmering aesthetics" presupposes a tension between conceptual and non-conceptual modes of expression. Whereas early conceptualism was "hard," its later permutations have "softened": there has been a movement away from a strict preoccupation with ideological codes and their alienating ironic reproduction, and toward a more lyrical engagement with the way ideology is manifested in the idioms of poetic characters, whom Prigov calls "heraldic heroes" ("the Fed'ral Agent, Reagan, the Fireman, the Jew," etc.[109]).

This post-conceptualist tendency could be seen as a rapprochement between post-structuralist and existential modes, since they are both opposed to the hard codes of structuralism. "[O]ur relation to the word is rife with personal-existential tension, [and] local [i.e., Russian] conceptualism—even during its most heroic period—was tinged with personality and emotionalism."[110] Prigov's theory postmodernizes existentialism by intensifying personal sincerity to the point of mania or absurdity, where it becomes a linguistic cliché. Thus many of his poems are variations on topics from Russian classic poetry, with Prigov inserting his own personality into the position of Pushkin's or Lermontov's lyrical heroes and pushing their lyricism to the self-parodic extreme of heart-rending confession. This device "permits not only the authenticity of each of them to be revealed within the limits of the axiomatics postulated by them, but also the absurdity of the total ambitions inherent in the desire of each of them to capture and describe the entire world in their terminologies."[111] At the same time, this melodramatic absurdity not only ridicules the heroes' lyrical excesses, but becomes an element of the author's lyrical self-revelation—even as it is well-nigh impossible to pinpoint the moment where the conceptual and existential merge.[112]

In light of Prigov's theorizing, two important stages in the formation of Russian conceptualism can be distinguished, and applied to the evolution of postmodernism as a whole. In its first stage, postmodernism sharply opposes itself to modernism in its attempt to demystify its ideological codes and totalizing claims. But this very project of demystification still bears the imprint of modernist radicalism and utopianism; by fighting fire with fire, postmodernism remains captivated by its vanquished enemy. In

[108] Ibid., 102.

[109] Ibid., 102.

[110] Prigov, "Conceptualism and the West," 1162.

[111] Prigov, "What More Is There To Say?," 102.

[112] The most comprehensive collection of Prigov's theoretical writings is a volume of his collected works in five volumes: Dmitrii Prigov, *Mysli. Izbrannye manifesty, stat'i, interv'iu* (Moscow: Novoe literaturnoe obozrenie, 2019), 792pp.

its second stage, postmodernism establishes an independent identity precisely through its lyrical and nostalgic empathy with all stylistic systems, past and present, including modernism. Instead of a "hermeneutics of suspicion," which is still modernist in its presupposition of a privileged perspective, postmodernism develops a hermeneutics of trust, of semi-ironic empathy, which approaches all texts and codes with a presumption of their existential authenticity and therefore rejects the demystification project as a matter of hubris. Mature postmodernism is suspicious of suspicion itself, because it sees the entire network of cultural symbols as a multilayered play of mystifications.

7. The Canonization of Emptiness. The Medical Hermeneutics Inspectorate

The conceptualist movement generated such an abundance of philosophical and quasi-philosophical theories that we have space to discuss only a few of them. Among other artist-thinkers, mention must be made of Andrei Monastyrsky (b. 1949), the leader of the "Collective Actions" group, and Sven Gundlakh (b. 1959) of the "Death-Caps" (*Mukhomory*) group, whose work in the late 1970s and 1980s significantly influenced the development of later conceptualism.

Among the conceptualist groups of the succeeding generation, the Medical Hermeneutics Inspectorate (*Inspektsiia 'Meditsinskaia germenevtika'*; 1987–2001) was—as its name suggests—the most philosophically motivated. For its three founding members, Pavel Peppershtein (b. 1966; the group's most active theorist), Sergei Anufriev (b. 1964), and Iurii Leiderman (b. 1963; separated from the group in 1991), hermeneutics is not so much a theory of exegesis as a mode of behavior, encompassing self-reflection and self-interpretation. The group seeks to restore hermeneutics to its original status as one of the medical disciplines, a practical diagnostics focused on bodily symptoms rather than artificial, conventional signs. Instead of taking texts as their objects of interpretation, they concentrate on real things and situations, performing what they call "inspections." Any experience or behavior can function as an inspection of itself, insofar as it includes self-reflective and self-descriptive components. It is both diagnostic and pathological as it attempts to reveal an abnormality as well as conceptualize it. However, inspection is not merely psychological introspection; it presupposes collective participation in the hermeneutic process, according to which members of the group reinterpret the entirety of a given situation as a text with specific rules of grammar. For example, the "inspectors" might spend time drinking wine with their friends in a restaurant, but this pastime simultaneously constitutes a hermeneutic procedure, an "inspection" of the restaurant and of the wine. The inspection culminates in a real text—a report describing the semiotics of the situation or object under examination, including evaluations of each element, such as waiters, napkins, and glasses, in terms of their relative merits, using the traditional Russian system of grading from one to five. The absurdity of assessing such minutiae offers a parody of ideological and pedagogical gestures, which proceed from a typically totalitarian mania for evaluation. Inspection is meta-ideological discourse—"ideological" because it adds a connotative plane to any denotation, and "meta" because these connotations (evaluations) themselves become the objects of description.

For non-inspecting participants of such outings, the practice of inspection can result—since it is never disclosed in advance and therefore cannot be distinguished from "normal" behavior—in a kind of permanent doubling of experience, a total hermeneutization of the world. Once subjected to inspection, every ensuing action reveals a potential for self-reflection and description; every gesture can be interpreted as an exegesis of the gesture itself; by drinking wine, one also assesses what it means to drink wine. Hence inspection might be said to have a quasi-messianic potential: like angels, who introduce the invisible transcendental dimension into earthly life, inspectors introduce the invisible semiotic, metalinguistic dimension to routine reality. Unlike angelic mediation, however, inspection has no privileged or fixed criterion for evaluation, since every judgment is contingent on the properties of the given situation or object: the "wineness" of the wine, and so on. Curiously, this activity restores the primordial etymological meaning of the term "hermeneutics," derived from the name of Hermes—but inspectors play messengers to no gods.

Medical hermeneuts do not self-identify as philosophers or theoreticians of aesthetics, but call themselves specialists in the area of "evolving aesthetic categories." They are not interested in concepts whose theoretical status is already established, but in such elements of everyday life and colloquial language that have the potential to become aesthetic categories. For example, they theorize the category of "the small," such that the phenomenon of medical hermeneutics itself can be identified as "a big, thick discourse-narrative about the small."[113] According to these hermeneuts, in classical antiquity, the small was categorized as something unworthy of attention, but with Christianity it came to be counterposed to the world of the large as a domain of specific value. Consider, for example, the place of the child in the Christian tradition, or the image of the "little man" (*malen'kii chelovek*, the socially humiliated and intellectually limited) in nineteenth-century Russian literature. In the twentieth century, however, large things, such as superpowers, messianic ideas, and colonial expansions, have so compromised themselves, proved so dangerous and oppressive, that the small has replaced the large in terms of its significance and value. For example, the rights of minorities have become a central issue of social justice, and local traditions have had increasing influence on the formation of cultural identities. Now it is the small that is really large, and therefore the very distinction between small and large loses its relevance.

Now that this difference is erased, the category of nothingness takes precedence in culture. Medical hermeneutics proclaims the "empty canon" as the center of contemporary civilization, since postmodernism has drained it of all substance by demonstrating its relativity. If postmodernism, in its revolutionary forms (deconstruction, multiculturalism), did its best to undermine and empty the grand

[113] Sergej Anufriew, Jurij Leiderman, and Pavel Pepperstein, *Auf sechs Büchern Inspektion "Medhermeneutik"* (Dusseldorf: Kunsthalle Düsseldorf, 1990) [parallel texts in Russian and German], 66.

Western canon, now the time has come to emphasize the canonical nature of emptiness itself.[114] We must recognize "the role of the classicizing principle in schizophrenic space."[115] The accent is to be put not on heterodox alternatives to the dominant canon, such as multicultural challenges to Eurocentrism, but on the orthodox observation of the canon of emptiness, or the rules of desemantization. "Empty canon" implies a grammatically correct and pragmatically effective, albeit semantically blank, discourse that maintains the spirit of "orthodoxy."

Orthodoxy is one of medical hermeneutics' key concepts, designating the correctness of discourse as such, without any verifying or falsifying relationship to reality or other discourses. "Orthodox practice is the behavior of language on the border; the canon of emptiness is the border unfolding not in the direction of 'unknown' or 'known' but within itself."[116] In other words, the border, as the semantic difference between objects, concepts, and words, now functions not as a mode of organization of cultural information, but as absolutely empty space in need of its own cultivation. Difference is different from what it differentiates and has no cultural or informational meaning; it is the "zero modality" of discourse that enables all signs but is devoid of any specific significance. If deconstruction works with existing texts and demonstrates their ambivalence or obscurity, what medical hermeneutics proposes is the construction of texts within this emptiness, a place its proponents call the "orthodox hut" (*ortodoksal'naia izbushka*), presupposing that it has an inner space which itself must be filled and canonized. This practice of construction within emptiness is designated by the Russian word *obustroistvo* ("arrangement"), which is different from other politically loaded words with the same root—for instance *stroitel'stvo* ("construction," used Sovietly especially in the context of "building communism") or the famous *perestroika* ("restructuring")—in that it emphasizes not constructing, deconstructing, or reconstructing anything outside, but structuring inner space, literally "constructing around from within." Only after the positive meanings of culture are deconstructed can the genuine construction within emptiness recommence.

This process can lead to a new ideologization of the cultural canon, as well as its historization, lyricization, and utopianization, which are principally different from ideology, history, lyricism, utopianism in themselves, as these have already been deconstructed. "Emptiness is a characteristic of the 'unknown' after the desacralization of the Empty Center that was produced by postmodernism. Ideologization can occur only after the critique of ideology made by postmodernism. Therefore, we locate ourselves in a zone of cultural self-knowledge that is only possible after postmodernism."[117] The relationship of ideologization to ideology can be compared with the relationship of inspection to participation: it is a double action that includes its own hermeneutic assessment.

[114] In Russian, the term "canon" refers not so much to a certain body of texts as to the rules or code of their organization, the underlying principles or stereotypes of a specific cultural epoch; for example, the "medieval canon" or the "realism canon."

[115] Anufriew, Leiderman, and Pepperstein, *Auf sechs Büchern Inspektion "Medhermeneutik,"* 54.

[116] Ibid., 55.

[117] Ibid., 56.

Furthermore, ideologization and other possible "-izations," like historization or lyricization, indicate a new, post-inspectional stage of hermeneutics, where the very form of participation, such as ideology, exists only as the projection of a hermeneutic mind that is grounded in emptiness. Ideology is produced as one of many elements in "orthodox" practice; that is, according to the rules governing the relationship of ideological signs. Medical hermeneutics is concerned not with ideology as such, but with an ideological canon, as well as historical and lyrical canons—purely grammatical structures devoid of any political or psychological meaning. In this case, hermeneutics abolishes, "emptifies" the textual object that had still been present in deconstruction, and produces its own textual armature as a system of rules for correct writing. Any genre, any type of discourse, can be reproduced hermeneutically as an empty canon, thus realizing the Kantian idea of the aesthetic as a pure form of purposiveness without purpose. What hermeneutics produces, therefore, is not a new ideology designed to influence politics and transform reality, but artistic forms of ideologization devoid of any specific content. In the same way, the lyrical verses produced by hermeneuts have nothing lyrical about them; rather, they inspect and expose the textual strategies of lyricism. They are devoid even of the parodic or ironic intention characteristic of earlier conceptualism and certainly avoid the nostalgic overtones and "new sincerity" of later conceptualism. For hermeneuts, these canons of irony or sincerity are already empty, and what is intended is the mere restoration of the canon of lyricism as a purely formal matrix.

Postmodernism was justified as a self-critical stage in the development of Western culture, but now that practically everything has been deconstructed, a new constructivism can come into play: the construction of ideological, historical, and lyrical worlds that cannot be deconstructed, since their "default meaning" is no meaning at all. To canonize emptiness means to reinstate the entire richness of world culture in a new modality impervious to deconstruction; the variety of canons having been stripped of their validity, now, devoid of meaning and purpose, all forms of culture can be recanonized in their emptiness, resurrected into the afterlife. Pavel Peppershtein and Sergei Anufriev's subsequent evolution toward "psychedelic realism" manifests this trajectory of their art and theory: reality itself turns out to be one of many hallucinations, and far from the most reliable and convincing one.[118]

8. Postmodernism versus Soviet Utopianism and Western Demythologization. Boris Groys

Among proponents and interpreters of Russian conceptualism, Boris Groys (b. 1947) stands as the most philosophically oriented, and the postmodern condition of philosophy itself comprises one of the main subjects of his thought. He was initially trained in mathematical logic in Leningrad. After his emigration to Germany in 1981, he established himself as a philosopher, art critic, and curator. He is currently

[118] The most comprehensive collection of Pavel Peppershtein's early writings, both theoretical and fictional, is *Dieta starika. Teksty 1982–1997 gg.* (Moscow: Ad Marginem, 1998).

a professor of Russian and Slavic studies at New York University and senior research fellow at the Karlsruhe University of Arts and Design in Germany.

Groys was the first to suggest the term "conceptualism" to describe the new aesthetic movements appearing in Moscow in the late 1970s. His article "Moscow Romantic Conceptualism," published in the first issue (1980) of the journal *A to Z*, offered a general overview of Moscow conceptualist art as a combination of a Western conceptualist mode with a Russian utopian vision. Later, the qualifier "romantic" turned out to be irrelevant, and Groys found a more appropriate term, "post-utopian," to designate a specifically Russian version of what is known as postmodernism in the West.

In order to understand the post-utopian sensibility, one has to address the nature of Russian utopianism, which is the theme of Groys's book *The Total Art of Stalinism*. The central idea is that socialist realism, which emerged as a result of the severe suppression of all nonrealistic avant-gardist modes of creativity, is actually a continuation and realization of the avant-garde project. Avant-garde art presupposes a radical break with and complete transformation of reality, as humanity moves beyond nature and history into a utopian space where the laws of matter will be abolished in favor of the sovereign imagination. During the 1910s–1920s, such avant-gardists as Velimir Khlebnikov, Vladimir Maiakovsky, Kazimir Malevich, and Vladimir Tatlin challenged the tradition of realism and proclaimed themselves the spiritual masters of the world (thus, Khlebnikov appointed himself "Chairman of Planet Earth" [*Predsedatel' zemnogo shara*]). However, their rebellion was mostly negative, their imagination being abstract and transrational; according to Groys, it was only Stalin who managed to realize the avant-garde project and become an actual master of the world. Stalin himself represents the ultimate achievement of avant-garde art. "The usurpation of God's role and the reconstruction and reinterpretation of the myth of God the Artist who shapes 'life' and 'overcomes the resistance of the material' are all hidden avant-garde mythologemes."[119] Stalin's suppression of avant-garde art was, in Groys's terms, motivated by his desire to be the sole artist in a country that provided an inexhaustible supply of material for his imagination. This also explains the injunction that the austere schematicism of avant-garde projects be replaced by realism: now that reality conformed to a utopian vision, art no longer needed to oppose itself to life, but rather to simulate life itself, to authentically reproduce a reality that had been perfected through revolution.

The official formula of socialist realism demands "the reproduction of reality in its revolutionary development," which presupposes that reality itself becomes politically transformed before it becomes an object of realistic representation. Politics under Stalin was the implementation of his artistic design, which is why art necessarily became an instrument of party and state policy. Critics of totalitarian art typically attend to only one of its aspects, namely, its subordination to political ideology. Groys discloses another aspect of the same symbiosis: politics itself was subordinated to an art project—which would explain the failure of this politics to account for socioeconomic factors,

[119] Boris Groys, *The Total Art of Stalinism. Avant-Garde, Aesthetic Dictatorship, and Beyond*, trans. Charles Rougle (Princeton: Princeton University Press, 1992), 70. This book was originally published in German in 1988 under the title *Gesamtkunstwerk Stalin* (*Stalin as an Integral Work of Art*).

its sole pursuit of a vision of the harmonious aesthetic transformation of reality. Groys further posits this artistic factor as the decisive impetus for communist revolution.

> Because it took place in a technologically and culturally backward country, the Russian Revolution was often viewed from rationalist Marxist positions as a paradox. Russia, however, was aesthetically far better prepared for revolution than the West; that is, it was far more willing to organize all life in new, as yet unseen forms, and to that end it allowed itself to be subjected to an artistic experiment of unprecedented scale.[120]

Groys's view of the communist state as a work of art might seem rather whimsical, unless we recall Plato's republic, which from the outset was conceived as an artistic projection. Tellingly, Plato too banishes poets from his republic, since their subjective insights can only distort the objective perfection and absolute harmony of the ideal state. Plato's invectives against myth in favor of objectivity clearly anticipate Stalinist persecutions of avant-gardist mythmaking in favor of socialist realism, which superseded the transformative stage where myth had served as the blueprint for a new, postrevolutionary reality. Instead of nostalgically valorizing the avant-garde of the 1920s as an epoch of free artistic innovation, Groys suggests that this movement contained the seeds of totalitarianism; thus, ironically, it perished by its own triumph, inspiring Stalin's surrealist policy and becoming obsolete when it became reality.

Groys's approach makes it difficult to distinguish the point at which utopian becomes post-utopian. On the one hand, socialist realism is "both reflected and consummated avant-garde demiurgism,"[121] with Stalinism being "merely the apogee of triumphant utopianism";[122] on the other hand, as utopia claimed to be realized, it evidently entered some post-utopian stage in which socialist realism converged with Western postmodernism. "Hence, beginning with the Stalin years, at least, official Soviet culture, Soviet art, and Soviet ideology become eclectic, citational, 'postmodern.'"[123] Some of Groys's statements give rise to confusion, since he identifies both utopianism and post-utopianism with postmodernism: "The utopianism of Soviet ideology consists, as it were, in its postmodernity."[124] Obviously socialist realism as the "realization" of utopianism is only the initial stage of postmodernism, which organically passes into postmodernism's second stage, when eclectic and citational gestures become a matter of deliberate irony and defamiliarization.

According to Groys, late-Soviet postmodernism arose as a proliferation of self-parodic, small-scale totalitarianisms, by means of individual reconstructions and deconstructions of large-scale totalitarianism. "[T]he death of totalitarianism has made us all totalitarians in miniature."[125]

[120] Ibid., 5.
[121] Ibid., 72.
[122] Ibid., 76.
[123] Ibid., 108.
[124] Ibid., 108.
[125] Ibid., 115.

> It proved impossible to break free of Stalin without reiterating him at least aesthetically. Consequently, modern Russian art has approached Stalin as an aesthetic phenomenon in order to repeat him and thus liberate itself from him. By constructing both text and context, practicing both construction and deconstruction, simultaneously projecting utopia and transforming it into antiutopia, it is attempting to enter the mythological family so that it may relate to Stalin not with *ressentiment* but with a feeling of superiority.[126]

In other words, late-Soviet postmodernism manifests a posttraumatic attempt to overcome the trauma of totalitarianism by its endless parodic repetitions. Groys gives the example of Ilya Kabakov, who creates some of his works on behalf of fictional characters whose artistic pretensions imitate the megalomania of avant-garde art, but whose fate in reality echoes the smallness of Dostoevsky's or Gogol's "humiliated and oppressed" heroes. Kabakov's metaphysics of the fly is another example of micro-totalization, which at the same time relies upon the reconstruction of philosophical discourse in order for its ironies to be realized.

According to Groys, the peculiarity of Russian postmodernism lies in the use of ironic reconstructions of totalitarian modes in order to simultaneously deconstruct them. This stems from a realization that no privileged perspective exists that might excuse the thinker from complicity with political mythology. Thus the task is to make self-conscious the mythological presuppositions of one's own discourse. This symbiosis of mythmaking and myth-negation provides the basis for Groys's critique of Western postmodernist theory, which in his view focuses exclusively on negative, "deconstructive" aspects, hoping thus to earn itself an "alibi" vis-à-vis crimes of political mystification.

This tendency can be traced to Roland Barthes's *Mythologies*, where only "rightist" and "bourgeois" mythology is recognized as such, since "wherever man speaks in order to transform reality and no longer to preserve it as an image … myth is impossible …. Revolution announces itself openly as revolution and thereby abolishes myth."[127] To such a contrast between revolution and myth, Groys offers the reasonable objection that "what all significant known myths tell about is the creation and transformations of the world";[128] the leftist myth of revolution should thus be far more powerful than its conservative, "bourgeois" counterpart.

Groys finds postmodernism obsessed with the theoretical claims of deconstruction, as if this practice represented some ultimate guarantee against mystification and further ideological manipulation. All pretensions to complete demystification are false and may create new mythological illusions by their very claims of neutrality and objectivity. In particular, Groys demonstrates that Deleuze and Guattari's emphasis

[126] Ibid., 119.

[127] Roland Barthes, *Mythologies*, trans. Annette Lavers (New York: Hill and Wang, 1987), 146, 147.

[128] Groys, *The Total Art of Stalinism*, 117.

on language "as a machine, producing certain effects, amenable to a certain use"[129] only superficially leads to the deconstruction of myth; in reality, it repaves the way for the totalitarian myth of literature as "'a cog and a screw' of one single great Social-Democratic mechanism" (Lenin[130]), and of writers as "engineers of human souls" (to use Stalin's famous phrase). In other words, the rejection of the mythological semantics of language and of the unconscious, which "poses no problem of meaning, solely problems of use,"[131] and their reduction to pure instrumentality and machinery, leads to the formation (or re-formation) of the myth of the state-machine, literature-as-engineering, and so on. When the activity of an individual is denied as a mere illusion and replaced by the elusive "otherness" of the "unconscious" and "unsaid," this role of "the other" is easily usurped by a "super-individual," like Stalin, who "succeeds in creating an artificial unconscious, an artificial context, and new and as yet unseen machines of desire called, say, 'Soviet people.'"[132] Therefore, the philosophy of "otherness" and "difference," or theoretical post-humanism, does not eradicate myth as such, but rather tends to replace a "conservative" myth of autonomous personality with a potentially far more dangerous "revolutionary" myth of self-creating collectivity, inevitably exemplified and headed by an artist-demiurge.

Groys finds equally suspicious the postmodernist refutation of external determinisms of historical reality in favor of internal determinisms of linguistic and psychological mechanisms. A human being as a slave of discursive models is no freer than a slave of objective circumstances. The major efforts of twentieth-century Western philosophy went to debunk the metaphysics of objective knowledge, but in its place was established a metaphysics of the objectively unknowable, the supreme impersonal authority that governs human subjectivity from within (like Freud's unconscious, Jung's archetypes, Heidegger's Being, Foucault's episteme, or Deleuze's desiring-machine). With postmodernism, the "external" as a force of objectification and alienation becomes even more intimately incorporated into human identity than when it was presumed to comprise a world of objects; thus the possibility of resistance to this internalized hegemony of structures becomes even more problematic.

Groys's critique of post-structuralism does not proceed from some naive pre-structuralist or traditionally rationalist point of view. More or less accepting the philosophical premises of post-structuralism, he nevertheless attempts to reveal its inner contradictions and the deficiencies rooted in the metaphysicality of its own discursive assumptions.

> The problem is not to understand that the search for authenticity was an illusion, the spontaneous and natural don't exist, and we live in a world of copies which have no originals and words which were never pronounced for the first time. Such

[129] Gilles Deleuze and Felix Guattari, *Anti-Oedipus: Capitalism and Schizophrenia*, trans. Robert Hurley, Mark Seem, and Helen R. Lane (New York: Viking Penguin, 1977), 109.

[130] Robert C. Tucker, ed., *The Lenin Anthology* (New York: W. W. Norton & Company, 1975), 149.

[131] Deleuze and Guattari, *Anti-Oedipus*, 109.

[132] Groys, *The Total Art of Stalinism*, 120.

> understanding has a shortcoming of no small importance: it considers itself to be original and authentic, i.e. true. The problem is to realize the mechanism of production of the authentic and spontaneous.[133]

Thus, even the post-structuralist project of suspicion grounds itself in a presumption of privileged insight, a place beyond reproach from which to judge, and Groys's corrective project entails the analysis of such presumptions of authenticity.

Groys proposes a concept of reduction or "epoche," a Husserlian term signifying an abstention from judgment. Consciousness itself is the product of ascesis or abstention, insofar as consciousness refuses to be a separate and self-contained entity and attempts to be open to the being of the other. What makes consciousness different from all other kinds of being is that it withdraws its own being, abstaining from self-assertion, and becomes a form of receptivity to the being of other entities. Knowledge is also a form of ascesis, since it subordinates the being of its bearer to the being of what is known.

Postmodernism pushes these ascetic procedures to the extreme by establishing a citational mode for all kinds of discourse. Whatever I pronounce is a quotation originating in someone that is not-I; even more crucially, whatever I *am* is engendered by something that is not-I. This ascetic orientation can be traced to the Kabbalistic notion of self-contraction, by which God limited his own being to make room for the world; the same ascetic procedure is easily recognized in the Christian notion of kenosis, by which God's son descends into the material world by renouncing his divine attributes and becoming subject to human suffering. According to Groys, this "kenotic analysis" should be applied to all products of culture: "The creative act is therefore kenosis, i.e., the descent of the sacred prototype into the profane and through this descent the sanctification of the profane itself."[134] Thus, in Groys's terms, Kabakov profanes the sacredness of philosophical discourse by addressing it to a fly and sanctifies the fly by making it worthy of philosophy. This postmodernist gesture essentially repeats the gesture of Christ, who profaned his divinity by his embodiment as a human being, and simultaneously sanctified human flesh by the act of resurrection. Whether we categorize this parallel as a Christian substantiation of postmodernism or a postmodernist interpretation of Christianity, what is most essential is that ascesis as a mode of self-profanation works on all levels. For Groys, this model also explains the Nietzschean and Freudian problem of how and why life and the unconscious give rise to consciousness. If rationality, according to both thinkers, is something oppressive to the vital impetus of will and libido, why do they produce a force that inhibits them? "If consciousness, culture, art, and so on arise as a result of the sublimation of natural forces, then, when these forces confront resistance, where does this resistance come from? … This force cannot be simply a 'censorship of consciousness,' as in Freud, since this very consciousness is recognized as a product of sublimation."[135] Thus Groys

[133] Ibid., 212.
[134] B. E. Grois, "Filosofiia i vremia," in *LOGOS. Leningradskie mezhdunarodnye chteniia po filosofii kul'tury*, kn. 1. *Razum. Dukhovnost'. Traditsii* (Leningrad: Leningrad University Press, 1991), 31.
[135] B. E. Grois, *Dnevnik filosofa* (Paris: Beseda—Sintaksis, 1989), 217.

posits a mechanism of ascesis by which the libido has come to control itself by the construction of cultural limitations. Nietzsche denounces asceticism as a denial of life force, but for Groys, one increases one's life-force by one's deliberate self-limitation. "[A]scesis produces life-power, increases it. Nietzsche is entitled to condemn such force growing through ascesis as 'low and slavish,' but he cannot deny its superiority .... Nietzsche himself partially indicates this when he repeats habitual maxims like 'he who cannot obey cannot command' and so on."[136]

Proceeding from this idea of ascesis to the postmodern condition, we might say that the sin of metaphysics can only be overcome by acknowledging the inevitability of this sin. One cannot deconstruct mythology without constructing other mythologies by the selfsame act. This is the post-structuralist mode. The Russian formula involves constructing mythology in order to deconstruct it; the tension between these two aspects of mythological discourse gives rise to self-effacing parody, which proves to be the exemplary mode of asceticism, for two complementary reasons: first, because through construction of this quasi-mythology, the postmodern author denies his own originality and discloses the patterns of preexisting mythologies (both rightist and leftist); second, because he recognizes the impossibility of implementing mythological designs, and ridicules his own attempt. Parody is a gesture of self-denial that makes no pretense to generosity, but acknowledges its own falsehood, and thereby becomes a double self-denial. The fault Groys finds in Western postmodernism is its insufficient asceticism; that is, it has achieved the first stage of self-denial (citation) but failed to realize that citation only constitutes a mode of self-assertive activity by which unoriginality is celebrated as a form of originality. However, Groys underestimates the sophistication of some Western postmodern reflexivity, since his concept of ascesis works in the same direction as, for example, the concept of *humour* as a self-effacing irony in Deleuze or *différance* as a mode of postponement in Derrida.

The central concern of Groys's later philosophizing is the problem of the "new." He attempts to broaden the postmodernist paradigm, which, in his view, "concludes that one cannot use new signs, since if they are not taken from tradition, they are meaningless. This is why in philosophy, science, art, and so on, [postmodernists] propose to use exclusively old signs."[137] Groys would prefer to transform the postmodernist paradigm by making newness conceivable, even inevitable, but not as a progressive category that refers to the growth of objective knowledge. The new may only be understood as what is fashionable, so that the source of a trend's popularity must be contained in something other than truth. "Fashion is a historical mode in which the new succeeds the old without any appeal to the true, the natural, and so on."[138] This is the major point of Groys's book *On the New*, which was published in Germany in 1992.

Groys's concern with the new reflects the postmodernist preoccupation with otherness; indeed, his concept of the new may be regarded as leading beyond the

[136] Ibid., 217.
[137] Ibid., 22.
[138] Ibid., 19.

postmodernist paradigm itself, as its other. Another embodiment of this otherness, posited in space rather than time, is his understanding of Russia as the other of the West, as a living organism that cannot be analyzed by Western modes of abstract reason, in the same sense in which, for Kierkegaard, otherness appears as "individual existence"; for Schopenhauer, as dark, primordial "will"; for Nietzsche, as "life"; for Marx, as "matter"; for Freud, as "libido," and so on. Russian philosophy advanced its own concept of otherness as embodied in Russia itself. It is no accident that Russian philosophy was born with Chaadaev and Khomiakov in the 1830s, at exactly the same time when the philosophy of German idealism underwent its first major crisis:

> This was the time when the unconscious was first discovered as a non-objectified Other that lies beyond reflection, dialectics, thinking, or cognition; moreover, thinking itself was understood, in light of this discovery, as only a function of the Other—the world, will, existence, economic practice, and so on. Thus, thinking was unable to reflect and substantiate itself, as had recently been the case with German idealism. Therefore, one can consider Chaadaev's and the Slavophiles' Russia just another name for the European post-idealist unconscious.[139]

Similarly, Groys explains the poor reception of psychoanalysis in Russia by the fact that "Russia cannot have a subconscious, because it is itself a subconscious."[140] Thus is revealed Russia's crucial importance for postmodernist thought, not because Russia advances postmodernist theories, but because it is an implicit object of such theories. Historically, Russia preceded other non-European nations as the mysterious "other" that would subsequently be identified with numerous African, Asian, and South American cultures. The duality of the Russian intelligentsia illustrates the postmodern situation in which a thinker finds otherness in the depth of his or her own self. If Westerners dreamed of Indians, Africans, and so on as external, exotic, and impenetrable others, then the Russian intelligentsia, while possessing the European mentality, finds this exoticism not in the external world, but in the Russian identity.

Among all Russian philosophers of the postmodern, Groys is probably the most postmodern in his view of philosophy itself. He distinguishes between theory and philosophy. "Philosophical thinking, as distinct from the theoretical sort, is not the thinking of an individual subject about the universal, but is the thinking of a universal subject, of fate itself, about the particular."[141] The active subject of thinking is now not an individual, but a nexus of mechanisms hidden in language and the unconscious. Thus philosophy becomes the process of the self-disclosure of these mechanisms through their application to particulars of existence. The individuality of the philosopher is effaced in the process of philosophizing, which is defined by Groys as "the great

[139] B. E. Grois, "Poisk russkoi natsional'noi identichnosti," *Voprosy filosofii*, no. 1 (1992): 56.
[140] B. E. Grois, "Rossiia kak podsoznanie Zapada," *Paralleli (Rossiia—Vostok—Zapad). Almanakh filosofskoi komparativistiki*, no. 1 (1991): 15.
[141] B. E. Grois, "Znanie, bezumie, individual'nost'," *Beseda. Religiozno-filosofskii zhurnal*, no. 6 (1987): 122.

defeat." This is a postmodern criterion of truth—not mere indifference to its absence, but the recognition of one's defeat in its search. Though truth is absent, its image is present. "It is not correct to think that there is no image of the truth on earth. The great defeat is this image of truth."[142] To accept this defeat—the extinguishment of one's own individuality—is what makes one a philosopher, one of the most exquisite heroes of ascesis.

9. Academic Postmodernism. Valerii Podoroga

A more academic version of philosophical postmodernism evolved in the Laboratory for Postclassical Research at the Institute of Philosophy of the Russian Academy of Sciences (Moscow). The adjective "postclassical," essentially paraphrasing "postmodernist" or "post-structuralist," was meant as a more neutral and officially acceptable designation of the newest trend. Founded and headed from 1987 on by Valerii Podoroga, this group included Mikhail Ryklin, Elena Petrovskaia, Mikhail Iampolsky, and certain other younger authors. They published a collection of books on philosophy titled *Ad Marginem* that were methodologically inspired by contemporary French thinkers (Jacques Derrida, Gilles Deleuze and Felix Guattari, Jean Baudrillard, and others). In 1997, the Laboratory was renamed the Sector for Analytic Anthropology.

This philosophical school developed mostly in the post-Soviet period, beyond the temporal scope of this book, so here we will outline only its basic and initial features. Valerii Podoroga (1946–2020), who from 1974 to the end of his life worked at the Institute of Philosophy in Moscow, adopted much in his methodology from Maurice Merleau-Ponty's phenomenology of perception and Merab Mamardashvili's theory of consciousness.[143] Podoroga's early publications (1980s) focused on the problem of language, culture, and power in Benjamin, Adorno, and Foucault, with language understood in phenomenological rather than analytic perspective. Podoroga's mature method, which he would later call "visual anthropology," includes phenomenological, hermeneutical, and deconstructionist readings of German philosophers and Russian writers, with a special emphasis on the corporeal and spatial quality of texts as "landscapes."

In his first book, *The Metaphysics of Landscape: Communicative Strategies in the Philosophical Culture of the Nineteenth and Twentieth Centuries* (1993),[144] Podoroga investigates the thinking of Kierkegaard, Nietzsche, and Heidegger as a variety of landscapes, which possess their own plasticity, an array of visible and tangible forms. In fact, Podoroga's book should rather be titled *The Landscapes of Metaphysics*, rather than *The Metaphysics of Landscape*: the point is not that these philosophers think

[142] Ibid., 123.

[143] On Merab Mamardashvili (1930–90), see Epstein, *The Phoenix of Philosophy*, 103–11.

[144] Valerii Podoroga, *Metafizika landshafta. Kommunikativnye strategii v filosofskoi kul'ture XIX-XX vv.* (Moscow: Nauka, 1993; 2nd, expanded edition, Moscow: Kanon+, 2013).

about spaces, but rather that their thinking itself is spatial. According to Podoroga, the process of reading includes the perception of the text as a spatial pattern manifesting the internal landscape-qualities of textuality as such.

Podoroga proceeds from Humboldt's assumption that language is woven from space and from Novalis's suggestion that any landscape is an ideal body for the expression of a certain structure of thought. He further introduces the concept of the "world line," which presupposes that each philosopher outlines his own vision of the world, which is as picturesque as a landscape, but encompasses not some local terrain, but rather the world-scape as a whole: "For Heidegger, for example, such a line would be that of a fold or bend, a tectonic, earthly line; for Nietzsche, a line of dance (Dionysus), a cosmic line of 'eternal return'; for Kierkegaard, a line of cascade, the discrete line of faith."[145] Thus does Podoroga attempt to interpret metaphysical insights as a kind of eidetic experience to identify the corporeal design and gestures behind an abstract thought—a project resonant with the post-structuralist paradigm of "corporeal thinking."

Podoroga's first book represented an exemplary specimen of Russian academic postmodernist writing. His style—like that of other post-structuralist authors—Foucault, Derrida, or Lyotard—is highly idiosyncratic, dense with the very metaphorical patterns and eidetic "apriorisms" that the book itself attempts to examine. Podoroga's subsequent (2007) designation of his method as "analytic anthropology" is somewhat misleading, because it has nothing to do with logical analysis in the tradition of analytic philosophy but is rather a blend of phenomenology and deconstruction, as evidenced by Podoroga's later books.[146] The term "anthropology" also appears redundant, insofar as this method relates to specifically human intellectual and sensuous capacities no less and no more than any kind of phenomenology, or, more broadly, than cultural studies or cognitive science. Podoroga works in a field that could be defined as philosophical "perceptology." He performs close readings of literary and visual texts (such as paintings and films, in particular, those of Sergei Eisenstein) so as to reconstruct the sensuous, haptic, psychomotor experiences that are peculiar to human perception. In his own version of post-structuralism, Podoroga focuses on reading and thinking as inseparable from perception, from panhuman (not just individual) psychosomatic subjectivity as mediated by literary and artistic sign systems.[147]

* * *

Postmodernism is often criticized for its alleged aesthetic snobbery and moral indifference. Consider Solzhenitsyn's invectives against "spiritually impotent"

[145] Ibid., 1.

[146] V. Podoroga, *Mimesis. Materialy po analiticheskoi antropologii literatury v dvukh tomakh*. Vol. 1. *N. Gogol', F. Dostoevskii* (Moscow: Kul'turnaia revolutsiia; Logos-altera, 2006); V. Podoroga, *Antropogrammy* (Moscow: Logos, 2014).

[147] On Podoroga, see *Russian Studies in Philosophy* 54, no. 4 (2016), special issue: "Contemporary Russian Philosophers: Valery A. Podoroga." Available electronically: https://www.tandfonline.com/toc/mrsp20/54/4. See also Alyssa DeBlasio, "Valery Podoroga (1946–2020)," *Filosofia: An Encyclopedia of Russian Thought*. Available electronically: http://filosofia.dickinson.edu/encyclopedia/podoroga-valery/

postmodernism in the early 1990s: "For the postmodernist the world does not contain real values. There is even an expression, 'the world as text' …. Culture is supposed to be closed in on itself …. The artist has no responsibility to anyone in these games. The rejection of any ideals is seen as a virtue."[148] But in fact, Russian postmodernists, not unlike their Western counterparts, do emphasize the moral implications of philosophical contingency, which undermines totalitarian and hegemonic discourse and promotes self-irony as a mode of epistemological humility. Russian culture proved to be a fertile ground for the application of postmodernist philosophy, owing to the prevalence of ideological schemes and stereotypes throughout its history, especially during the Soviet period. To be sure, the West's "track record" in correlating sign systems to observable reality (e.g., through scientific research, economic practice, etc.) is hardly perfect, and it has certainly had its episodes of ideological "reality-creation." But in Russia this latter practice is so much more pronounced as to represent a difference in kind: reality has routinely been constructed from ideological signs and dogmatic systems.

For this reason, conceptualism may be viewed as the predominant Russian-Soviet mode of thinking, as the self-awareness of practices underlying Russian history and its ideocratic institutions. Russian conceptualism offers a radical challenge to totalitarian claims of absolute truth, to the kind of ideological madness that prescribes ideas for the transformation of reality. Russian conceptualism may be considered an ironic imitation and inversion of the solipsistic activity of the collective supermind, which is not only imprisoned by its allegiance to absolute ideas, but in turn makes society itself a prison or lunatic asylum.[149]

[148] A. Solzhenitsyn, "Igra na strunakh pustoty" ("Playing on the Strings of Emptiness"), 1993. https://www.rulit.me/books/igra-na-strunah-pustoty-calibre-0-8-64-read-262937-3.html. The citation in the text represents my own translation from the original, but an English translation of this piece did appear as "The Relentless Cult of Novelty and How It Wrecked the Century" in the *New York Times Book Review*, February 7, 1993, 3, 17.

[149] The author of this study can also be characterized as a postmodernist thinker. His book publications on postmodernism include: Mikhail Epstein, *After the Future: The Paradoxes of Postmodernism and Contemporary Russian Culture*; Ellen Berry and Mikhail Epstein, *Transcultural Experiments: Russian and American Models of Creative Communication* (New York: Palgrave McMillan, 1999); Epstein, Genis, and Vladiv-Glover, *Russian Postmodernism*; and Mikhail Epshtein, *Postmodernizm v Rossii* (St. Petersburg: Azbuka [the series "New Cultural Code"], 2019); a full bibliography of Epstein's works on postmodernism is given on pp. 582–6 of this last edition.

Mikhail Epstein's contribution to postmodern theory is explored in the following publications: "Russian Critical Theory and Postmodernism: The Theoretical Writings of Mikhail Epstein. A Forum," *Slavic and East European Journal* 39, no. 3 (1995): 329–66. (Dale Peterson. "Introduction: Mikhail Epstein's Russian Postmodernism," 329–32; Edith W. Clowes, "Simulacrum as S(t)imulation? Postmodernist Theory and Russian Cultural Criticism," 333–43; Anesa Miller-Pogacar, "Varieties of Post-Atheist Spirituality in Mikhail Epstein's Approach to Culturology," 344–56; and M. Epstein, "Response: 'Post-' and Beyond," 357–66); Victor Terras, "Sweet Moments of Recognition: Epshtein on Postmodernism," *Slavic and East European Journal* 41 (1997): 477–81; Thomas Epstein, "Mikhail Naumovich Epshtein (Mikhail Epstein)," in *Dictionary of Literary Biography*, vol. 285. *Russian Writers since 1980*, ed. M. Balina and M. Lipovetsky (Detroit: Bruccoli Clark Layman/Thomson Gale, 2004), 61–8; Caryl Emerson, "Foreword," in Mikhail Epstein, *The Transformative Humanities: A Manifesto* (New York, London: Bloomsbury Academic, 2012), xi–xxiii; and M. N. Lipovetskii, ed., *HOMO SCRIPTOR: Sbornik statei v chest' 70-letiia M. N. Epshteina* (Moscow: Novoe literaturnoe obozrenie, 2020).

Epilogue: The End of Soviet Philosophy and Strategies for the Future

1. The Critique of the Russian Ideocratic Tradition

By the turn of the 1990s, as the Marxist ideocratic regime was coming to an end, and various nationalistic and Eurasianist, religious, cosmist, and postmodernist intellectual movements were asserting themselves, the question emerged: what would come to succeed Marxism as the dominant philosophical trend? Would it be, unlike Soviet materialism, a kind of new idealism that would proceed from the grounds of Russian prerevolutionary religious philosophy, from the legacy of Vladimir Solovyov and the Silver Age?

Indeed, with the perestroika and glasnost of the late 1980s, Russia rediscovered its philosophical heritage, and for the first time, or after a long historical pause, opened formerly banned or barely available books by Petr Chaadaev, Vladimir Solovyov, Nikolai Fedorov, Dmitrii Merezhkovsky, Vasilii Rozanov, Nikolai Berdiaev, Lev Shestov, Pavel Florensky, Sergei Bulgakov, and Semyon Frank; and religious and mystical works by Lev Tolstoy, Helena Blavatsky, Georgii Gurdjieff, Nikolai Uspensky, Nicholas and Helena Roerich, Daniil Andreev, and others.[1] After decades of total domination by Marxist dogma, there was enormous enthusiasm for this kind of spiritually transformative reading. It appeared quite likely that, from atheistic materialism, Russian thought would, in a kind of dramatic reversal, quickly move to some form of religious idealism, which would exemplify the quintessential "Russian idea" for the twenty-first century.

However, some of the younger and most perceptive critics of Soviet Marxism, such as Evgenii Barabanov (b. 1943), Sergei Khoruzhii (1941–2020), and Boris Paramonov (b. 1937), vehemently disagreed with such a perspective.[2] They pointed, not to the break between ideocratic Soviet Marxism and the eschatological "Russian idea" as professed by idealist and anti-Marxist thought, but to the affinity of these trends. According to these critics, moreover, the very phenomenon of *religious philosophy* is suspect,

[1] James P. Scanlan, ed., *Russian Thought After Communism: The Rediscovery of a Philosophical Heritage* (London: Routledge, 1994).

[2] See the sections on Barabanov and Khoruzhii in the part "Religious Thought. Orthodox Christianity" of this book, and the chapter on Boris Paramonov in Epstein, *The Phoenix of Philosophy*, 142–8.

both on religious and philosophical grounds. Vladimir Solovyov had considered the mission of his philosophy to be "to justify the faith of the Fathers"—but, does faith need rational justification? And should reason pursue the same truth that is already given in revelation?

As discussed in the introduction to this book, the legacy of Platonism is paradoxically shared by such ideological antagonists as prerevolutionary idealists and Soviet Marxists. It is as if there were some kind of division of intellectual labor between them: Russian communism emphasized the material and social aspects of the Platonic utopia, while religious thinkers emphasized its ideal and spiritual aspects. But the ultimate project of Platonism is not separation but unification of both worlds: the full materialization of ideal norms. Therefore, it assumes the complementarity and even fusion of the ideal and the material.

The Russian intelligentsia of the latter half of the nineteenth century made its way from old-style idealism to fashionable materialism, and in the early twentieth century strove to return from shallow materialism to religious idealism. These two counter-movements were later repeated, in the same order, in the early-Soviet obsession with "dialectical materialism" (1920s–1950s) and the disenchantment with materialism (1960s–1980s). But these seemingly opposite directions actually evolved within a single Platonic paradigm of *socially active idealism*. Materialists and sophiologists unconsciously converge in their adherence to the Platonic ideocratic project, and unintentionally work together to idealize and ideologize human existence, on the one hand, and to materialize these most abstract ideas in social practice, on the other.

Aleksei Losev (1893–1988), justly considered the last representative of classical Russian idealism, was also the first to identify the Platonic subtexts of Soviet ideocracy. As a commentator remarks, Losev saw "the newly evolving 'materialism' [as] elaborating its own 'kingdom of ideas,' its own mythology and dogma .... Therefore, Platonism was for Losev the secret hero of the political storms of the late nineteenth and early twentieth centuries .... Socialist mythology, ... according to Losev, naturally implemented Platonism in its sociopolitical practice."[3] Losev himself was ambivalent about the meaning of Platonism; he criticized its paganism and affiliation with the political system of slavery, but at the same time interpreted Orthodoxy as a genuinely Christian Platonism.

One can surmise that this ambivalence was inherent not only in Losev's work, but in the entire tradition of Russian philosophy, which aspired to a Christian modification of Platonism, but actually slipped into its pagan version, the ideology of state socialism and, accordingly, the totalitarian system of enslavement to the state. Marxist philosophers used to criticize Russian religious thought ("idealism") as the manifestation of a reactionary, bourgeois, or feudalist worldview, incompatible with scientific and social progress. Late-Soviet critics, including Barabanov, Khoruzhii, and Paramonov, to the contrary, blame Russian idealism for its secret or unconscious

[3] L. A. Gogotishvili, "Mifologiia khaosa (o sotsial'no-istoricheskoi kontseptsii A. F. Loseva)," *Voprosy filosofii*, no. 9 (1993): 48, 49.

complicity with the communist revolution, its alleged laying of the groundwork for this social cataclysm via the dissemination of apocalyptic forebodings. In this view, Russian society proved so receptive to the messianic revelations of Marxism and the mystique of the last bloody battle and coming golden age, precisely because Solovyov, Fedorov, Merezhkovsky, and Berdiaev had already tuned the nation's soul to the key of eschatological expectations that would be fulfilled, or at least precipitated, by their contemporaries and compatriots—by Russia as the vanguard of post-history. Among the great Russian philosophers, there was hardly a one (with the partial exception of Vladimir Solovyov) who evinced an evolutionary approach; none of them developed a system justifying the gradual improvement of existing conditions. They were all, rather, either metaphysical radicals, valorizing cataclysmic solutions for historical problems (e.g., Fedorov and Berdiaev); or existential skeptics who doubted the bourgeois values of rationality and productivity (e.g., Rozanov and Shestov).[4]

From the standpoint of this critique, Russian idealist philosophy was anti-Marxist and anti-communist only because it was inherently anti-bourgeois, and regarded Marxism and socialism as mere extensions of capitalist, philistine ideals. Thinkers like Fedorov and Berdiaev condemned Marxism not for its revolutionary ambitions, but because it seemed *insufficiently* revolutionary, promising only better modes of production instead of the spiritual transformation of the earth. The anti-communist stance of these thinkers, that is, expressed an even more ardent hatred for the existing world than that harbored by communists; the total eschatological renovation they envisioned threatened to claim even more victims than the metaphysically more moderate and materialistically motivated Marxism of Lenin and his followers.

Now that Platonism, in its Marxist guise, has been overcome by Russian thought, is it still possible to find inspiration in Platonism as such, in its most sublime idealistic and religious interpretations? Or does the experience of Russian history convincingly show that Platonic idealism has exhausted itself as a spiritual resource, and that all attempts to Christianize it are just wishful illusions?

The critics mentioned above, and many other thinkers, agree that both the "Russian idea" and Soviet ideocracy have alike come to an end as philosophical principles. The question then arises: if philosophy in Russia has reached the point of no return, not only to ideocratic Marxism, but also to religious idealism, what is the task of the new philosophy?[5]

The projections of the aforementioned critics diverged. At the time it was argued, on the one hand, that Russian philosophy should *secularize* itself, abandoning both the theological claims of prerevolutionary idealism and the political mysticism and ideological claims of Marxism. Hence Russian philosophy needs to undergo the same process of epistemological self-criticism and analytical self-limitation that Western

4 See, for example, Evgenii Barabanov, "Russkaia filosofiia i krizis identichnosti," *Voprosy filosofii*, no. 8 (1991): 102–17.

5 A large-scale discussion of this question, and much evidence for an answer to it, are offered in Alyssa DeBlasio's book *The End of Russian Philosophy: Tradition and Transition at the Turn of the 21st Century* (New York: Palgrave Macmillan, 2014), 106–16.

philosophy has undertaken in a variety of movements over the last centuries, with Kant, Husserl, Wittgenstein, and Derrida. In other words, intellectuals have to desacralize their labor, to produce analysis rather than metaphysical fantasies, to abandon any claims to spiritual and political power, and even relinquish the overambitious and ultimately ridiculous title of "intelligentsia," fraught as this concept is with so many delusions of self-aggrandizement.

An additional measure may also be required, according to such authors as Evgenii Barabanov and Boris Groys. They believe that, insofar as Russian philosophy has long been immersed in a neurosis of distinctiveness, it must submit to a kind of psychoanalytic treatment in order to demystify its metaphysical pretensions, to expose the inferiority complex behind them, and heal Russian philosophy's birth trauma—caused, in this view, by medieval Russia's abrupt exposure to the Enlightenment in the eighteenth century. In this context, the most compelling part of the Russian intellectual legacy is not its influential and celebrated accomplishments, whether those of religious idealists like Vladimir Solovyov or revolutionary materialists like Nikolai Chernyshevsky and Aleksandr Herzen, but rather the work of academic philosophers—neo-Kantians, positivists, intuitivists, phenomenologists—who may have lacked original theoretical constructions, but were at least modest, sober, and accurate in their epistemological analyses.

Another point of view, most persistently elaborated by Sergei Khoruzhii, is that Russian religious idealism was not purely Orthodox at all, nor even properly Christian, but essentially idealistic in a Platonic sense. According to Khoruzhii, the "false" notion that Platonism prepared the ground for Christianity and remains its most authentic philosophical foundation has haunted European thought for centuries, pervading neo-Platonism, rationalism, German idealism, and other major systems. Khoruzhii sees Russian thought as not the sole victim of the Platonic distortion of Christianity, but quite possibly the most sorely afflicted. Thus Vladimir Solovyov's philosophy of "all-unity" (*vseedinstvo*), which was the source of inspiration for practically all other trends in Russian religious thought, is based on the Platonic and neo-Platonic vision of ideal unity, progressively incorporated into the diversity of earthly entities, which reveals the affinity of Solovyov's theocratic utopia with Plato's ideocratic republic.

It should be noted that Solovyov, and especially such of his followers as Sergei Bulgakov, Pavel Florensky, and Aleksei Losev, who occasionally even critiqued their teacher, sought to overcome or improve on the one-sided idealism of Plato with notions of "religious materialism," "concrete idealism," or "sophiology." These improvements presupposed that the world of ideas must manifest and embody itself materially, just as Christ-God became Christ-Man. As Khoruzhii observes, however, the relationship between God and man in Christianity is not the same as the relationship between ideas and objects in Plato. According to the teachings of the Eastern Church fathers, God and man are absolutely different in essence, but communicate through energies (existence, volition). Therefore, argues Khoruzhii, a genuinely Christian philosophy should abandon such Platonic and neo-Platonic conceptions as the "total unity of an ideal world" or "divine essence of man." It should focus instead on existential intercourse between man and God, meditating on such spiritual processes as prayer, repentance, grace, introspection, silence, the unification of mind and heart—those acts of free will that truly mediate between the human and divine as distinct entities.[6] For this reason, Khoruzhii believes that the "energetical" or existential core of the Orthodox tradition, concerned with the unique dynamic of personal volition and the acquisition of grace, must still be reexamined and restored, as the premise on which the future of Russian religious philosophy can be built.

Thus, two distinct and apparently incompatible projects are advanced for the reform of Russian philosophy: one, Barabanov's, calls for its total secularization, its separation from theology and ideology; the other, Khoruzhii's, suggests an even closer, deeper alliance with the ascetic and existential core of Orthodox Christianity. What both solutions have in common is their rejection of the Platonic dominance in the Russian philosophical tradition, both in its explicit form (religious idealism) and in its undercurrents (Marxist ideology and state ideocracy).

2. New Metaphysical Radicals

The development of Russian thought from the 1950s to the 1980s clearly testified against materialist ideology and communist ideocracy. However, the years following the collapse of the Soviet system witnessed a resurgence of the Platonic type of ideocratic discourse, which reveals even more radical tendencies than did Russian philosophy of the early twentieth century. We use here the term "radicalism" in the same sense that allowed Karl Popper to apply it equally to Plato and Marx: "[U]ncompromising *radicalism* .... Both Plato and Marx are dreaming of the apocalyptic revolution which will radically transfigure the whole social world."[7] The material substance of Russian historical existence came to be so exhausted by the Soviet ideocratic experiment, so rarefied, that in the 1990s the kingdom of absolute ideas again bubbles up beneath its translucent surface, tempting thinkers to construct new systems of all-unity, to accommodate heaven on earth. As Evgenii Barabanov observes: "[I]n a situation of an acute identity crisis, in the anguished attempts to restore the torn threads of forgotten traditions, the *ideological* and *utopian* paradigms of Russian philosophical thought are acquiring a second life. Again the 'Russian idea'! Again the 'special way,' again 'originality,' again doctrinal preaching instead of the pupil's desk."[8]

Indeed, if we attempt to summarize post-Soviet developments in Russian thought, we discover a general tendency for the radicalization of its metaphysical ambitions. This tendency may be identified in such diverse movements as nationalism and Eurasianism, with the radical traditionalism of Aleksandr Dugin; Marxism, with the eschatological communism of Sergei Kurginian; and religious philosophy, with the

6 Thus, for Khoruzhii, the most authoritative source of Christian existentialism as opposed to Platonic idealism is Gregory Palamas (1296–1359), the Orthodox monk, theologian, and intellectual leader of hesychasm, an ascetical method of mystical prayer.

7 Popper, *The Open Society and Its Enemies*, vol. 1, *The Spell of Plato*, 164.

8 Barabanov, "Russkaia filosofiia i krizis identichnosti," 48.

increasing popularity of Nikolai Fedorov's cosmism and "resurrectionism" and Daniil Andreev's "interreligious" doctrine of *The Rose of the World*.

Even movements that would seem to be pre-inoculated against metaphysical assumptions, such as structuralism, culturology, and conceptualism, reveal in the 1990s a growing propensity for universalist claims. For example, the later works of Iurii Lotman and Vasilii Nalimov are rife with a metaphysics of chance, contiguity, and indeterminism. Georgii Gachev builds far more ambitious cosmosophical constructions than did his predecessors in culturology, Mikhail Bakhtin and Dmitrii Likhachev.[9] The conceptualist group "Medical Hermeneutics" is much more concerned with metaphysical generalizations, albeit parodic ones, than were the conceptualists of the 1970s–1980s. Is it a coincidence that these new, radical metaphysical discourses have proliferated with the collapse of the Soviet ideocratic system?

It should be kept in mind that this system was not merely a political and legislative entity, but was founded on a metaphysical, even eschatological, vision, officially called Marxism but stemming also from the prophetic philosophizing of the late nineteenth and early twentieth centuries. The collapse of the Soviet regime thus left something more than just a need for governmental reform: it left a metaphysical vacuum, eager to be filled. If the prevailing mood among intellectuals in the late Soviet period was to challenge and demystify ideocracy, then the collapse of that ideocracy generated numerous emulations and simulations among various intellectual groups, which have attempted, at least in theory, to build a new ideocratic regime on a more firm, nationalistic and/or religious foundation. Traditionally in Russia, political platforms have been constructed on a framework of the most general, "filosofical" ideas (the Russian *filosofiia* being a fuzzier term than its English equivalent). In the early 1990s, competing metaphysical theories rushed in to fill the demolished and excavated site with a foundation for a new political architecture. *The death of one "big" totalitarianism gave birth to a number of smaller ones.* Many politicians, of both leftist and rightist orientation, including the leaders of the most influential Duma parties, such as Vladimir Zhirinovsky of the Liberal-Democratic Party, Dmitrii Ragozin of Rodina, and even the communist leader Gennadii Ziuganov, more or less consistently wielded metaphysical ideas to justify their ambitions for intellectual leadership.

This overall tendency, characteristic of the Russian mentality in general but exacerbated in the 1990s by increasing political instability, can be called "metaphysical radicalism." Political radicalism flows from the very core of this type of metaphysics, which, following the Marxist paradigm, does not limit itself to explaining the world, but attempts to change it. At the same time, no politics aspiring to radically transform the world can limit itself to the social, economic, and legislative dimensions, but must also entail metaphysical assumptions. In Western, liberal-democratic countries, politics usually pursues the less expansive goals of partially improving existing systems, and is thus separate—at least, on the conscious or open level—from metaphysical

[9] See the individual chapters devoted to Lotman, Nalimov, and Gachev in *The Phoenix of Philosophy*.

considerations. Since Russia's historical dynamics are not evolutionary but disruptive and catastrophic, each break in political continuity necessitates renewed and quite overt metaphysical speculation and indoctrination designed to justify the entirely new social order. It is the privilege of metaphysics to address the world as a whole, as it is the objective of political radicalism to transform this whole completely. Thus metaphysical and political radicalism are mutually dependent, as the totalitarian experiments of the twentieth century have shown: both communist and fascist radicalism advanced strong metaphysical claims. Russian philosophy, which during the 1950s–1980s had resisted the stranglehold of Soviet ideocracy, in the 1990s sought the foundation for a new type of ideocracy, potentially based on the ideas of nationalism, radical traditionalism, cosmism, religious fundamentalism, or eschatological communism. The options are varied.

Metaphysical radicalism is a specific type of philosophical discourse that ignores the Kantian critique of metaphysics and claims to "transcend" the epistemological limits imposed on human cognitive capacities. However, this philosophical mode cannot be identified with the naive metaphysics that Kant criticized; it aspires not to truth but to power. This is not a precritical, descriptive metaphysics, but a post-critical, prescriptive one, a metaphysics that draws on suppressed desires and taps the collective unconscious. Western intellectuals are familiar with this type of fiery speculation through the works of New Left thinkers such as Herbert Marcuse, but the principal distinction of most Russian "New Right" thinkers is their appeal not to the future, but to the absolute past, to the resurrection of ancestors or the restoration of Tradition.

Metaphysical radicalism may be approached from the standpoint of the imperative mood, which, as Roman Jakobson observed, is not subject to criteria of verification: "[I]mperative sentences cardinally differ from declarative sentences: the latter are and the former are not liable to a truth test."[10] Unlike the phrase *This is done*, the phrase *Do this!* cannot be challenged by the question "Is it true or not?" The same may be said of "metaphysics in the imperative mood," which evades critical challenges to its truthfulness. Kant's critique of philosophical dogmatism was crucially conclusive with respect to metaphysical "declarations," but to what extent can it help to demystify the metaphysical "imperatives" that began to proliferate in the nineteenth and twentieth centuries precisely as a result of Kantian limitations on theoretical reason?

The alliance between metaphysics and politics has potential benefits for both: as *practice*, it concentrates on a single goal, a single direction of change; as *theory*, it posits itself beyond truth and falsehood. As alluded to above, one of Marx's most famous statements on the mission of philosophy is his eleventh thesis on Feuerbach: "The philosophers have only *interpreted* the world, in various ways; the point, however, is to *change* it."[11] This proposition features a curious asymmetry: the transition from

[10] Roman Jakobson, *Language in Literature*, ed. Krystyna Pomorska and Stephen Rudy (Cambridge, MA: The Belknap Press of Harvard University Press, 1987), 68.

[11] Karl Marx, "Theses on Feuerbach," trans. W. Lough. Available electronically: https://www.marxists.org/archive/marx/works/1845/theses/theses.htm

"interpreting" to "changing" is achieved at the price of "variousness," which is omitted in the second part of the thesis. That is, while the world can be interpreted in *various* ways, presumably there is only *one* way for its practical transformation. Totalitarian implications are thus inherent in the very project of philosophy as practical/political action.

There are, to be sure, strong tensions among the representative trends of metaphysical radicalism originating from diverse ideological sources. For example, radical traditionalists, inspired by such far-right thinkers as René Guénon (1886–1951) and Julius Evola (1898–1974), condemn Fedorovian cosmism as a leftist, technocratic heresy obsessed with the idea of progress and active, self-governed human evolution. Neofascist ideologists of Vladimir Zhirinovsky's camp, meanwhile, condemn radical traditionalists like Aleksandr Dugin for their romantic alienation from the contemporary scene and their obsession with the past.[12] Nonetheless, these antagonisms serve to underscore the substantial unity of metaphysical radicalism, not in the specific content of the individual projects that fall within its scope, but in the very mode of imperative thinking that establishes a set of ideas about what the world *should* be, while utterly rejecting the world as it is. Nikolai Fedorov, the founder of Russian cosmism, asserted that "philosophy must become the knowledge, not only of what is, but of what ought to be, that is, from the passive, speculative explanation of existence, it must become an active project of what must be, a project of universal action."[13] Not only Fedorovians, but radical traditionalists and neo-Marxist utopians, too, could subscribe to this statement of what philosophy should do in the face of the world's problems and what the world should become in the name of philosophical ideas. The formula for the political implications of this metaphysical radicalism can be found in Nietzsche's prophecy: "The time of the struggle for domination of the globe is upon us; it will be undertaken in the name of basic philosophical teachings."[14] Russian metaphysical radicals invoke, as a model, the fate of Nietzsche's own teachings: German recruits going into the trenches of the First World War with volumes of *Zarathustra* in their rucksacks.

The ideological incompatibility among Marxist, nationalist, and religious discourses, which sharply divided them in the late Soviet period, in the 1990s became less relevant as these positions merged in the overarching type of radicalist discourse. Consider the words of Sergei Kurginian, one of the chief ideologists of the post-Marxist revival of communism, and the principal political advisor of the conservative, procommunist

[12] See, for example, the criticism of radical traditionalism in the neofascist journal *Attack* (*Ataka* [c.1995, no. 12]: 32–4), whose editor Sergei Zharikov was the main ideologist and minister of culture in the "shadow" government of Vladimir Zhirinovsky.

[13] Fedorov, cited from V. V. Zen'kovskii, *Istoriia russkoi filosofii* (Paris: YMCA-PRESS, 1950), 2: 135.

[14] Friedrich Nietzsche, *Schriften und Entwürfe 1881–1885*, ed. F. Koegel (Leipzig: Naumann, 1897), 110. The fact that two world wars with catastrophic outcomes were inspired in part by the ideas of the Übermensch and the will to power stands as a reminder of the risk, the deadly danger, of mixing philosophy and politics.

forces in the Soviet leadership that organized the failed putsch of August 1991, hoping to preserve the Soviet Union as a communist superpower:

> We regard communism not only as a theory but as a new metaphysics which leads to the creation of a new, global religious teaching .... It contains many fundamental features vitally important for civilization, features of a new world religion with its own saints and martyrs, apostles and creed .... Among the indisputable predecessors of communism we identify Isaiah and Jesus, Buddha and Lao-Tze, Confucius and Socrates .... Today there is no alternative to the communist meta-religion.[15]

Kurginian further insists that Russia has experienced, from time immemorial, "the need for an idea with global-messianic potential capable of unifying Eurasia. She found this in communism .... The red field, communist eschatology, and communist mysticism have existed, exist, and will exist in Russia and, most probably, these ideas ... will find their place within the Eurasian expanses, merging with Orthodox, Sufi, Buddhist, and perhaps Catholic mysticism."[16]

This example of the discourse of metaphysical radicalism reduces or even erases any difference among communist, nationalist, and religious rhetorical strategies. Another striking example comes from the leader of the Communist Party, Gennadii Ziuganov, the strongest rival of Boris Yeltsin in the struggle for Russian political and ideological leadership in the 1990s: "From the standpoint of ideology and worldview, Russia is the keeper of the ancient spiritual tradition: its fundamental values are *sobornost'*[17] (collectivism), the supreme power of the State [*derzhavnost'*], sovereignty [literally: self-sufficiency of statehood], and the goal of implementing the highest 'heavenly' ideals of justice and brotherhood in earthly reality."[18] Remarkably, within a single sentence, phrases imbued with religious meaning—"spiritual tradition," *sobornost'*, and "heavenly ideals"—merge together with such nationalist bywords as *derzhavnost'* and "statehood," and with "collectivism" and "brotherhood," key terms in communist jargon.

Thus we can single out metaphysical radicalism as one of the most powerful tendencies in post-Soviet thought, as a kind of meta-discursive strategy transcending the ideological differences among previously oppositional movements.

15 S. E. Kurginian, B. R. Autenshlius, P. S. Goncharov, Iu. V. Gromyko, I. Iu. Sundiev, and V. S. Ovchinskii, *Postperestroika* (Moscow: Politizdat, 1990), 59–60, 66.

16 Sergei Kurginian. *Sed'moi stsenarii* (Moscow: Eksperimental'nyi tvorcheskii tsentr, 1992), 3: 201, 228.

17 In Russian, the term *sobornost'*, coined by Aleksei Khomiakov, one of the founders of Slavophilism, means "togetherness" or "the spirit of communality," and has a theological origin and connotation (the spiritual experience of the Russian Orthodox Church). By glossing it with "collectivism," as if this were its synonym, Ziuganov in effect equates religious and communist views—which was indeed one of the central points of his ideological program ("Christ as the first communist").

18 *Sovetskaia Rossiia*, September 24, 1994.

3. Conceptualism versus Metaphysical Radicalism

Another major strategy sharing the contemporary intellectual scene with metaphysical radicalism is conceptualism. Like its counterpart, it suggests a universal mode of speculation: a critical attitude toward traditional notions of reality and an ironic playfulness with regard to the sign systems of various ideologies—a ludic method that empties all metaphysical assumptions of their contents to reveal a bare skeleton of abstract discourse contingent on a system of arbitrary beliefs. Conceptualism exposes the "reality fallacy" of all "master discourses," discloses the contingency of all concepts and refuses to ground itself in any one "Reality." Conceptualists view totalitarian thinking, with its claims to all-encompassing truthfulness, as a kind of madness: a network of internally connected though arbitrary propositions *presumed* to coincide with external reality. When turning its attention to more properly philosophical ideas, conceptualism playfully relativizes or paraphrases metaphysical discourse, using its rhetorical models to describe such trivial objects as flies or garbage. This is not merely an attempt at the ironic deconstruction of traditional philosophy; it is also a project for the proliferation of new, multiple metaphysics, each of which consciously demonstrates the contingency of its central concept, be it Absolute Spirit in Hegel's writings, or a housefly in Kabakov's treatise "The Fly as a Subject and Basis for Philosophical Discourse."

Unlike radical metaphysics, which exists "in the imperative mood," conceptualist simulative systems of thought could be called "metaphysics in the *subjunctive* mood," which also serves to distinguish them from pre-Kantian dogmatism, or "metaphysics in the *indicative* mood," that is, metaphysics claiming to adequately describe reality as it is. Russian conceptualists, not unlike their Western allies, emphasize the moral implications of philosophical contingency, which undermines dogmatic and hegemonic discourse, and promotes self-irony as a mode of epistemological humility.

The Russian version of conceptualism established a theoretical distance between itself and a great number of metaphysical schemes that dominated late-Soviet and early post-Soviet culture, including Marxist, nationalist, mystical-esoteric, and other "grand" and "foundational" discourses. With the collapse of the Soviet Union, as the official ideology lay in ruins, the critical sharpness and topicality of conceptualism diminished for a while, but conceptualists did not remain jobless for long: other ideologies (religious fundamentalism, national messianism, etc.) came to contend for the "yawning heights" of state ideocracy, and their aggressive rhetoric escalated to such a degree of automatization and self-repetition that conceptualism could resume "working" with them.

If in the 1970s–1980s conceptualism was neatly opposed to more academic and serious types of humanistic discourses, such as neo-rationalism or culturology, the 1990s witnessed a tendency for their consolidation. Just as Marxism, nationalism, and religious fundamentalism have begun to gravitate toward a unified discursive strategy of metaphysical radicalism, so do structuralism, culturology, and conceptualism, which were clearly divided in the 1970s–1980s, tend to unify in opposition to metaphysical radicalism. This unity is based, first and foremost, on the post-structuralist notion of the cultural relativity and contingency of all discourses—a theoretical tenet that was not alien to structuralism and culturology, but was most consistently and convincingly articulated in conceptualism.

Thus, by the mid-1990s, one could see a sharp polarization between metaphysical-radicalist and post-structuralist (or conceptualist, in the broadest sense) types of discourses, with a corresponding neutralization of the internal differences within both. The divide between Russian metaphysical radicals and deconstructionist-conceptualists can be compared with that, among Western intellectuals, between "metaphysicians" and "ironists" as described by Richard Rorty:

> The metaphysician is someone who takes the question "what is the intrinsic nature of (e.g., justice, science, knowledge, Being, faith, morality, philosophy)?" at face value. He assumes that the presence of a term in his own final vocabulary ensures that it refers to something which has a real essence .... The ironist, by contrast, is a nominalist and a historicist. She thinks nothing has an intrinsic value, a real essence .... [Ironists are] never quite able to take themselves seriously because they are always aware that the terms in which they describe themselves are subject to change, always aware of the contingency and fragility of their final vocabularies, and thus of their selves.[19]

If the metaphysician's "final vocabulary" includes such concepts as "true," "good," "right," "the Church," "the Revolution," "professional standards," "progressive," "creative," etc., then the terms preferred by the ironist are those that deny the very possibility of a "final vocabulary," including "perspective," "conceptual framework," "historical epoch," "language game," "redescription," "vocabulary," and "irony." The ironists share the conceptualist position with regard to the "eternal values," "self-evident truths," and "global imperatives" advanced by metaphysical radicals.

But, however meaningful, this parallel with Western intellectual types needs certain adjustments. Russian metaphysical radicals are not just "metaphysicians" in Rorty's sense, that is, "realists" as opposed to "nominalist" "ironists." Metaphysical radicals not only believe in "real essences," they summon us to transform the world in accordance with their vision of these essences. As for conceptualists, they are not only "aware of the contingency and fragility of their final vocabularies, and thus of their selves"—they also purposefully and sometimes aggressively question and undermine all existing vocabularies, directing their "redescriptions" against both rightist and leftist metanarratives whenever these lay claim to "intrinsic value."

This "extremism" on both sides appears to deepen the split between metaphysical radicalism and conceptualism and diminish the chances of their mediation and neutralization in the framework of a purely scientific or scholarly discourse. At first

[19] Richard Rorty, "Ironists and Metaphysicians," in *The Truth about Truth. De-Confusing and Re-Constructing the Postmodern World*, ed. W. T. Anderson (New York: Putnam, 1995), 101–2.

glance, metaphysical radicalism and conceptualism seem wholly incompatible, even antagonistic, since the former pushes the claims of metaphysics to the extreme of prophecy and propaganda, while the latter reduces it to an act of linguistic buffoonery. Indeed, metaphysical radicals have nothing but contempt for "futile" and "foolish" conceptualist games, whereas conceptualists pointedly ridicule the "dangerous" pretensions of philosophically intoxicated radicals.

But, essentially, the current *radicalization* and *conceptualization* of metaphysical discourse may be regarded as two aspects of the same process.

4. The Symbiosis of Radical Metaphysics and Conceptualism

The more radical metaphysical assumptions become, the more they reveal their potentially conceptualist nature. It is not by chance that Russian conceptualism emerged as the ironic duplication of the discourse of Soviet Marxism: as new, post-Marxist modes of radical discourse become politically influential, conceptualism easily assimilates them for its ironic repertoire of empty cultural codes.

The conceptualist dimension in post-Soviet thought cannot be reduced to a merely parodic gesture. The point is that radical discourse itself increasingly reveals internal conceptual qualities; the more an idea is pushed to extremes, the more it exposes its lack of referent and the pure schematism of its abstract speculation. For example, on the political scene, the phenomenon of the ultra-rightist Vladimir Zhirinovsky (b. 1946) may be explained as an intersection of radical and conceptualist modes, making him something like a postmodern or "performance-art" Führer. Calling his party "Liberal-Democratic," for example, represents a kind of semi-intentional buffoonery, as the party's program is fiercely nationalist and *anti*-liberal. The title of Zhirinovsky's autobiography-manifesto, *A Last Thrust to the South* (1993), moreover, could easily have been taken from the conceptualist verse of Dmitrii Prigov. The very idea of Russian soldiers washing their boots in the Indian Ocean presents a combination of political radicalism—the nationalist aspiration to maximally extend the Russian Empire, all the way to the continent's southern margin—and the aesthetics of conceptualism: an idea that is ruthlessly consistent in logical or ideological terms demonstrates its irrelevance and ridiculousness.

The regeneration of totalitarianism after the death of totalitarianism cannot but incorporate a conceptualist self-subversive mediation. This is why the new radicalism is doomed from the very outset to be conceptually loaded, though rarely—unlike conceptualism proper—to the point of self-realization. Some subtle observers find in Zhirinovsky's extremist escapades a kind of conscious clownery that does not so much act aggressively as play with the signs of aggressiveness. In most cases, however, radicalism acquires a conceptualist dimension inadvertently, whereas conceptualism quite purposefully engages with radical discourse to demonstrate both the opulence and poverty of pseudo-metaphysical ideologies thus constructed.

Such a deliberate symbiosis of radicalism and conceptualism may outline the perspective for a new Russian metaphysics, one that would give a postmodern, self-reflective dimension to a traditionally Russian holistic way of thinking.[20] Dmitrii Galkovsky's novel-treatise *The Endless Dead End* is a paradigmatic example of the radicalist-conceptualist mode of thinking. Galkovsky's thought turns out to be a mediation between metaphysical radicalism and the conceptual shaking and draining thereof. Born in 1960, Galkovsky graduated from the philosophy department of Moscow State University in 1986. By his own account, he completed *The Endless Dead End* (whose title could also be translated as *The Infinite Deadlock*) in the late 1980s, but it was published only in 1997. This multilayered text consists mainly of an indeed interminable self-commentary on Galkovsky's own essay about the Russian philosopher Vasilii Rozanov (1856–1918). It represents, in fact, a series of comments on the entirety of Russian culture of the nineteenth and twentieth centuries, focusing primarily on, besides Rozanov, Aleksandr Pushkin, Nikolai Gogol, Fedor Dostoevsky, Lev Tolstoy, Anton Chekhov, Vladimir Solovyov, Vladimir Lenin, and Vladimir Nabokov. The almost one thousand comments have a tree structure, with large and smaller branches forming a kind of hypertext.

Galkovsky gives his method an intricate description: "the sedimentation of a mentally ungraspable idea in the philological sphere at the expense of reconciling it with one's own realism and even cynicism."[21] Galkovsky seeks to combine aspects of two characters from Dostoevsky's *The Devils*, the revolutionary Petr Verkhovensky and the buffoon Captain Lebiadkin, in his fictional and autobiographical counterpart Vladimir Odinokov, and in his real-life behavior as a tabloid metaphysician and refined boor and clown. Galkovsky's two essential themes are "I will destroy you all" and "I am of no use to anyone," an oxymoron reflected even in his protagonist's name Vladimir Odinokov (whose etymology amounts to "world-ruler" plus "lonesome"). Galkovsky combines philosophical wistfulness and pathos with "mad raving will," cynically inverting his own metaphysics with vulgar, streamlined, practical, "Lenin-like" decisions that are immediately parodied and undergo a fine-tuned aesthetic sorting, which is followed by the opposite: escape behind the looking glass, disappearance. "I am a thinking parody .... [A] parody that becomes aware of itself as parody disappears .... The chain of parodies continues into infinity, becomes more and more complex and grandiose. It reaches the Absolute, that is, it parodies infinity."[22] The treatise-novel is constructed as a never-ending split between pathways of thought, crossroads multiplying, becoming self-referential dead ends. Essentially it claims to be a microcosm of Russian culture, modeled as an infinite series of inversions and ruptures. Every decision is taken to a metaphysical extreme and therefore contains the mechanism of its own derangement.

One can imagine a kind of monolithic, though ambivalent, philosophical discourse where the seam between radicalist and conceptualist ingredients becomes

[20] On the origins and the progression of these totalitarian trends in Russian thought, see Mikhail Epstein, *Russian Spirituality and the Secularization of Culture* (New York: FrancTireur-USA, 2011); and Mikhail Epstein, "Russkaia sverkhideia: tselostnost'. Vse ili nichego," *Zvezda*, no. 1 (2017): 239–50.

[21] Dmitrii Galkovsii, *Beskonechnyi tupik* (Moscow: Samizdat, 1997), 21.

[22] Ibid., 659.

indistinguishable. The tendency for such symbiotic philosophizing is evident in the 1990s, both on the side of metaphysical radicalism, which cannot but locate itself in a postmodern, post-totalitarian space; and conceptualism, which demonstrates an increasing proclivity for almost sincere, invariably grandiose and self-derisive, self-*erasive* metaphysical speculation.[23]

While Western postmodern discourse remains predominantly critical and self-critical, as seen in the pervasive influence of deconstruction with its demystifying and anti-metaphysical claims, Russian postmodern thought tends to emphasize and even overstress its metaphysical disposition, finding *the antidote to metaphysical indoctrination in its very excesses.* Where Western thought prefers to mediate opposites and ground itself in "neutral," scientifically sound terms, Russian thought deliberately moves in the polar directions of excessive prophecy and relentless irony, pendulating between two opposites instead of attempting their rapprochement and stable synthesis.

The originality of Russian intellectual culture lies in the colorful interplay of extremes radiating out in both directions. In the eighteenth century, the great Russian scientist and poet Mikhail Lomonosov expressed his patriotic belief that "the Russian land can give birth to its very own Platos." And it did, begetting metaphysicians of the most radical sort, such as Vladimir Solovyov, Nikolai Fedorov, Nikolai Berdiaev, Aleksandr Bogdanov, Konstantin Tsiolkovsky, Andrei Platonov, Nicholas Roerich, and Daniil Andreev—all those who felt the need to raise the dead, to make humankind

[23] It is on the crossroads of radicalist and conceptualist discourses that the author of this study situates some of his own writings, such as *Cries in the New Wilderness: From the Files of the Moscow Institute of Atheism*, trans. and intr. Eve Adler (Philadelphia: Paul Dry Books, 2002). The original Russian title is *Novoe sektantstvo: tipy religiozno-filosofskikh umonastroenii v Rossii, 1970–80-e gody* (New Sectarianism: The Varieties of Religio-Philosophical Consciousness in Russia, 1970s–80s) (Holyoke, MA: New England Publishing Co., 1993; third, revised and expanded edition: Samara: Bakhrakh-M, 2006). *New Sectarianism* is filled with the voices of metaphysical radicals and sectarians, from the mystical Thingwrights and the absurdist Folls to the messianic Khazarists and the doomsday Steppies. As a counterpoint to this medley of comic, grotesque, poetic, banal, poignant, and harrowing voices is the voice of the commentator, Prof. Gibaidulina, who struggles to maintain the purity and objectivity of her scientific atheism in the face of a bewildering variety of religious experiences. Another example of radicalist-conceptualist discourse is Mikhail Epshtein, *Velikaia Sov'. Filosofsko-mifologicheskii ocherk* (Great Owland. A Philosophical and Mythological Treatise) (New York: Word/Slovo, 1994; second, revised and expanded edition: Samara: Bakhrakh-M, 2006). In Russian, *Sov'* refers both to "Soviet" and "owl" (*sova*). *Great Owland* is an experimental myth that explores the deep patterns of the Soviet mentality and metaphysics, following Roland Barthes's suggestion that the best weapon against myth is to mystify it in turn, producing an artificial, second-order myth. The book describes a Northern people who believe the Great Owl to be their totemic ancestor, and explores the customs and rituals of these nocturnal owl-people, and the very nature of "owlism," an archaic and occult source of twentieth-century ideocratic systems. The foundations for this radicalist-conceptualist type of philosophical discourse are laid out by my conceptual persona or philosophical stand-in Iakov Abramov (1893–1966), in his teaching on "unidiversity," or "pan-difference" (*vserazlichie*): "Uchenie Iakova Abramova v izlozhenii ego uchenikov. Publikatsiia M. N. Epshteina," *LOGOS. Leningradskie mezhdunarodnye chteniia po filosofii kul'tury. Kniga 1. Razum. Dukhovnost'. Traditsii* (Leningrad: Izdatel'stvo LGU, 1991), 211–54. Partly translated into English: "The Teachings of Iakov Abramov As Interpreted by His Disciples. Compiled, edited, and commented on by Mikhail Epstein," trans. A. Miller-Pogacar, *Symposion. A Journal of Russian Thought* 3 (1999): 29–66. Available electronically: https://www.emory.edu/INTELNET/abramov.html

immortal, to attribute soul to matter, to unite the worm with God, to build the ideal state, to create heaven and earth anew, to make the sun fall from the sky and burn in the human breast. As a necessary counterweight to this metaphysical radicalism, the Russian intellectual climate also gave birth to conceptual game-playing, by which all these lofty ideas expose their grotesqueness. Whenever the ecstasy of the "great tradition," the "final battle," "white Communism," the "Eurasian mystery," right- and left-wing "internationales," "Aryan Platonism," or "Orthodox-Islamic fundamentalism" crops up, there is also no lack of apophatic mimicry and nominalistic deflation of these grandiose "realities." Whenever Fedorovism or Roerichism rears its head—manifesting itself in the various Mamleevs, Dugins, and Kurginians—there one also finds an array of Prigovs, Sorokins, and Komar and Melamids to counteract them. When a metaphysical nationalist like the artist Ilya Glazunov produces his iconic, "monumental" panoramas, one also encounters the conceptualist Ilya Kabakov, with his trashy "communal apartment" installations and creative therapy for patients in an insane asylum.

This is also true of traditions in philosophy proper, where the two extremes are represented by the idealistic metaphysics of Vladimir Solovyov (1853–1900) and the intellectual buffoonery of Vasilii Rozanov (1856–1919): these two most important philosophers of their time openly despised one another. Both have certain polar prototypes in the writings of Dostoevsky, to whom each was quite indebted: the pious monk Aleksei Karamazov and the scandalous "Underground Man." Solovyov contemptuously compared Rozanov with Mikhail Saltykov-Shchedrin's satirical character Porfirii "Little Judas" Golovlev, while Rozanov, for his part, likened Solovyov to a rope dancer, sardonically ascribing to him the urge to climb to heaven before an audience. These philosophical extremes cannot be eliminated. They can in part be mediated through moderate realism, pragmatism, or phenomenology, but the volatile and explosive mix of the most radical metaphysics and the most defiant mockery and travesty can scarcely be eradicated from the Russian intellectual scene.

Conclusion

1. The Circular Paths of Ideocracy

The eight intellectual movements discussed in the two volumes *The Phoenix of Philosophy* and *Ideas Against Ideocracy* do not exhaust the diversity of Soviet philosophy of the post-Stalin era. Certain distinguished thinkers have worked in numerous special fields—for example, the history of philosophy; the philosophy of science, logic, and psychology; the study of Eastern philosophy and religion—that we have not addressed, preferring to focus on philosophical schools and methods of, and approaches to, the most universal problems of philosophy, rather than specific thematic divisions and disciplines.

In general, there are two main vectors in the intellectual evolution of this epoch: anti-totalitarian and neo-totalitarian. The disintegration of the dominant Marxist metanarrative, of the entire system of Soviet ideocracy, led to the emergence of new philosophical currents, such as neo-rationalism and structuralism, personalism and liberalism, and cultural studies (culturology), all explored in *The Phoenix of Philosophy*. These directions are in principle deeply anti-totalitarian, oppositional not just to Marxism, but to any form of *totalist* thinking, as they are based on critical reflection, the scientific approach, comparative analysis of cultures, and the fundamental values of personal and public freedom.

The first three of four movements presented in *Ideas Against Ideocracy* indicate a different vector—toward the possible formation of new ideocratic discourses. This danger is most strongly expressed in nationalism and Eurasianism, discussed in the first part. It is not an abstract possibility, but the political reality of Russia of the twenty-first century, when the authoritarian regime is forming a new ideology based on patriotism and traditionalism, on the ideas of anti-Westernism and anti-liberalism. It was within Eurasianist theory that the very concept of "ideocracy" as a state governance was advanced:

> An ideocratic state has its own system of beliefs, its own ruling idea [*ideia-pravitel'nitsa*] (the bearer of which is the governing stratum united in a single state and ideological organization), and therefore must, by all means, actively organize and govern all aspects of life. It cannot allow any disobedient,

> uncontrollable and irresponsible factors—primarily private capital—to interfere in its political, economic, and cultural life.[1]

The tradition of Eurasianism in Russia is one hundred years old, counting forward from the collection *Exodus to the East. Presentiments and Accomplishments. The Affirmation of the Eurasians* (book one, Sofia, 1921). Subsequent landmarks include the works of Lev Gumilev in the 1960s–1980s and of his radical successor Aleksandr Dugin, who brought Eurasianism all the nearer to neofascist archaism and mysticism. But it was not until the twenty-first century that Eurasianism, increasingly demonstrating its ideocratic potential, became an ideological justification for Russian anti-Western politics.

Another foundation of post-Soviet ideology is the revival of Orthodoxy. The Church is actively involved in social life, typically on the side of the state, and seeks to expand its sphere of clerical influence on education and secular culture. The religious philosophy of the 1960s–1980s as described in this book's second part was free of this ideocratic component; acting as a form of spiritual liberation from the oppression of state atheism, it was for the most part close to the liberal ideals of the era. But it cannot be denied that it had the potential to develop into a religious ideology, given the "symphonic" Church-state traditions of both Russia and the Orthodox world in general. In Eastern Christianity, in the absence of a universal center of faith like the Vatican in Catholicism, national churches find their organizational support in the state.

Finally, universalism and cosmism, as presented in the third part of the book, are likewise not alien to ideocratic demands. The Universal Church of the Rose of the World—a mystical project of Daniil Andreev—is the basis of a new, all-planetary ideocracy of the future. Ironically, this projected "inter-religion" will result in the martyrdom of its believers and the coming to power of the Antichrist as ruler of humankind. Nikolai Fedorov's philosophy of the Common Cause also includes elements of ideocracy in its union with technocracy; hence the cosmist assertion of the common civic duty of all people to form labor armies and do their part in the war on death. If the Eurasianist utopia or Orthodox fundamentalism fails to achieve predominance in Russia in the twenty-first century, then the techno-cosmic utopia of Fedorov and Tsiolkovsky may well fill this vacancy, with super-technologies promising universal resurrection, with immortal artificial intelligence capable, in theory, of transforming all the cosmos into a noosphere.

These three directions described in separate parts of the book—nationalism and Eurasianism, Orthodox philosophy (in some of its varieties), and religious universalism and cosmism—are united by their reliance on certain social and religious communities or mass movements. In the first case, this is a unity of a nation or group of nations (Eurasia); in the second, a religious and ecclesiastical community, "togetherness," "spiritual collegiality" (*sobornost'*); in the third, a community of all mankind as a planetary unity, bound by the common idea of active evolution and transformative technology.

[1] Trubetskoi, "Ob idee-pravitel'nitse ideokraticheskogo gosudarstva."

Only the fourth trend described in this book (in the last part), conceptualism, represents a consistent alternative to any temptations and delusions of ideocracy, as it develops the technique of ideocracy's relativization, the deconstruction of any metanarrative. Of course, history shows that some versions of postmodernism may have their own ideocratic and even socialist component, as in the radical versions of political correctness and multiculturalism.[2] But it is in Russian postmodernism that these political tendencies have been least expressed. Conceptualism has been a reliable technique for the nominalistic deconstruction of any ideologies and systems of ideocracy.

Thus, the construction of these two volumes reveals an inverse symmetry. The first volume, *The Phoenix of Philosophy*, begins with an analysis of Marxist ideocracy and moves on to three oppositional movements based on rationalist, personalist-liberal, and culturological approaches. The second book, *Ideas Against Ideocracy*, begins with an analysis of three movements that emerged in opposition to Marxism, but have their own ideocratic potential, and ends with the philosophy of postmodernism and conceptualism, which is consistently anti-totalitarian and critical of any ideology. Thus do the two volumes create a two-vector, self-contradictory, inherently ironic movement: a) away from communist ideocracy; b) toward the formation of anti-totalitarian, anti-Marxist movements; c) some of which are fraught with the potential for new ideocracy; d) toward the critique of ideocracy as such.

2. The Comedy of Ideas and the Tragedy of Ideocracy

The French poet and thinker Paul Valéry (1871–1945) once said that after Dante's *Divine Comedy* and Balzac's *Human Comedy*, the time had come to inaugurate a third, "intellectual" comedy treating the adventures and transformations of human thought. Comedy, in the Dantean and Balzacian sense, is the most monumental of all genres, the genre least dependent on the will of its authors, and most on the condition of their society, which, as it were, dictates to them, turning them into its literary secretary (this image comes from Balzac's preface to his Comedy). Every society gets the comedy it deserves.

Valéry himself did not write the "third" comedy, although he had all the necessary qualifications for it: the broadest erudition, the subtlest intellect, and a great artistic talent. But he still lived in the Balzacian world of the "human comedy," where human beings, their characters, passions, and interests were the moving force of all events. Dante, for his part, had lived in a society welded together by Christian faith and organized on the model of the Church; its moving force was the authority of divine revelation, which had laid out the path leading from the sinful depths of earthly life

[2] The profound difference between Western multiculturalism and the theory of transculture, which grew up on the basis of late-Soviet culturology, is highlighted in Berry and Epstein, *Transcultural Experiments*.

to the bright crystal heavens of paradise. The *Divine Comedy* was as much a necessary expression of medieval, "feudal" society as was the *Human Comedy* of property-owning, "bourgeois" society. And these works were written in the very countries that classically modeled the corresponding social-spiritual organization: pre-Renaissance Italy and postrevolutionary France.

The model of the third type of society, called "socialist" or "communist," emerged in postrevolutionary Russia. It was precisely here that a new moving force appeared at the foundation of society: the force of *ideas*. It was ideas that brought the Russian Revolution, waged the Civil and "Great Patriotic" Wars, established plants and factories—not only in order to produce something material, but also to assert the productivity of the socialist ideas themselves. The rule of ideas, ideocracy, is fraught with paradoxes: it means to unleash and intensify the class struggle for the sake of the classless society; to wipe out the wealthy for the sake of the common wealth; to devalue labor in support of the value of labor; to fight militantly in the struggle for peace; to die of hunger in the struggle for the harvest; to annihilate matter in the struggle for materialism. Every idea bears within itself a staggering comedy that has caused a lifetime's worth of tragedy to millions. Socialist society was the only modern society constructed according to a previously laid plan, based on ideas born in the minds of its thinker-founders; it was the most speculative and "premeditated" society on earth. It was a society without God and without a market—spiritually and materially poor, but rich in ideology—the kingdom of ideas personified in its rulers.

In socialist and atheist Russia, the things that feudal and bourgeois society lived by lost their prestige and reality. A tense and conscious battle was waged against God—or rather, against the *idea* of God, since his actual existence was denied. Likewise, a struggle was conducted for the *idea* of plenty, although articles of material luxury and even necessities themselves disappeared. But in any case, it was ideas alone that had an acknowledged and palpable reality, ruling over human beings. Everything that existed outside of ideas, whether acknowledged or denied, lost its living reality and receded into the background. Ideas were all there was: they would neither feed us in this life, nor save us in the next one, but they did give us the feeling that our life was rightly lived, our death not in vain.

Thus, the third comedy, the comedy of ideas, arises precisely from the self-consciousness of socialist society, whose inner spring is neither the will of God nor the private interests of human beings, but ideas in which the faith and passion of immense human masses are concentrated. Russian intellectual history of the twentieth century is a history of thought struggling desperately to escape the prison of an ideocratic system created by the strenuous and sacrificial efforts of thought itself. What makes Russian thought unique, both comic and tragic, is its internal tension, its struggle against itself, against its own ideocratic constructions. The truth-seeking intelligentsia and the power-asserting ideocracy—both belong to the same breed of the credo "thought is power." This is how Francis Bacon's "knowledge is power" can be transcribed into the language of Russian and Soviet ideology. Thinking, unlike knowledge, constructs ideas meant not to adequately reflect the world but radically transform it. Thus does thought as a force of spiritual liberation rise to resist the triumph of thought as a force of political domination. One speculative capacity, the "intelligentsia," opposes itself to another speculative capacity, the "ideocracy"—but the former also creates the latter. This self-contradictory movement of thought, shattering its own foundations, gives an unprecedented, deeply paradoxical, and sometimes sarcastic character to Russian philosophy.

3. Philosophy and the Philosophical

There is another paradox in Russian intellectual history: the preeminence of *the philosophical* over *philosophy* as such. State, ideology, economics, politics and geopolitics, literature, art, warfare, space exploration—all these spheres in Russia and the USSR were abundantly philosophical, though philosophy as such was not as developed and sophisticated as it was in the West. In a certain sense, Western philosophy, as a discipline, "outsourced" itself to its "disciples," Russian writers and revolutionaries, leaving it to Fedor Dostoevsky and Lev Tolstoy, to Vladimir Lenin and Lev Trotsky, to test in literary and political practices a host of Western philosophical ideas, from those of Plato, Rousseau, and Hegel to Feuerbach, Marx, and Nietzsche. While *philosophy* remained in the West to prosper as an academic subject, its impact generated an excess of *the philosophical* in Russia, where the adjective absorbed the noun.

The same can be said of the predominance of the verb "to philosophize." As Nikolai Berdiaev observed: "It is characteristic of the Russian people to philosophize [*filosofstvovat'*]. An illiterate Russian peasant likes to pose questions of a philosophical nature—about the meaning of life, about God, about eternal life, about evil and untruth, about how to realize the Kingdom of God .... The fate of the philosopher in Russia is painful and tragic."[3] This is a typical Russian paradox: while philosophy as an action, as "philosophizing," was widespread even among "commoners," the fate of the professional philosopher was tragic.

Why? Precisely because *the philosophical* and *philosophizing*, as attributes and actions of the state and society, overpowered *philosophy* as a noun, as an academic discipline. Russian philosophy had a very modest impact on the West, but the impact or "blowback" of *the philosophical* was immense. Nineteenth-century Russian literature influenced Western culture with its philosophical ideas and problems, just as in the twentieth century, the USSR influenced the West with the philosophical ideas (Marxism, materialism, dialectics, collectivism, socialism, communism) that determined Soviet ideology, politics, and economics. To take just one historical period: in the USSR of the 1920s–1930s, philosophy as such, as an independent academic subject, was in a subdued position, as a servant of party ideology. But the sphere of *the philosophical* was rampant, spreading even to such distant domains as theater (Stanislavsky), physiology (Pavlov), and agriculture (Michurin), with all such activities glorified and sponsored by the state as "philosophically correct," as faithful to "materialism" and "realism."

3 N. Berdiaev, *Russkaia ideia* (St. Petersburg: Azbuka-klassika, 2008), 59.

Paradoxically, in the quintessentially *philosophical state* that was the USSR, the *state of philosophy*, with the repression of all independent thought and thinkers, was miserable. The fateful and often disastrous originality of Russian philosophy consisted precisely in its dissemination to other areas, in an act of "kenosis" or self-transcendence that can be viewed both as an aggressive philosophical appropriation of politics, economics, ideology, and literature—and as philosophy's sacrificial devotion to the world beyond its professional boundaries.

Thus until the end of the Soviet epoch, Russia never played an important role in world philosophy, but philosophy did play an enormous role in Russia, especially in the twentieth century. Now that the system of Soviet ideocracy has not only been theoretically dismantled, but also historically transcended, one could hope for a reversal of these trends. As philosophy plays a lesser political role in a Russian society increasingly motivated by economic and technological interests, Russian philosophy, rethinking its unique experience of self-denial and self-liberation, may assume a more prominent role on the international scene. It remains to be seen how these dramatic lessons of the twentieth century—the monumental tragicomedy of a superpower both created and ruined by the force of ideas—will guide Russian thought in the twenty-first century.[4]

[4] On the most recent developments in Russian thought, see Mikhail Sergeev, Alexander Chumakov, and Mary Theis, eds., *Russian Philosophy in the Twenty-First Century. An Anthology* (Leiden, Boston: Brill, Rodopi, 2020). My own philosophical positions are laid out in Mikhail Epstein, "From Analysis to Synthesis: Conceiving a Transformative Metaphysics for the Twenty-First Century," ibid., 74–100.

Bibliography

Abramov, A. I. "Otsenka filosofii Platona v russkoi idealisticheskoi filosofii." In *Platon i ego epokha*, edited by F. Kh. Kessidi, 212–37. Moscow: Nauka, 1979.

Adorno, Theodor. *Aesthetic Theory*. Translated by C. Lenhardt. Edited by Gretel Adorno and Rolf Tiedemann. London and New York: Routledge & Kegan Paul, 1986.

Agurskii, Mikhail. *Ideologiia natsional-bol'shevizma*. Paris: YMCA Press, 1980.

Althusser, Louis. *Lenin and Philosophy and Other Essays*. New York and London: Monthly Review Press, 1971.

Andreev, Daniel. *The Rose of the World*. Translated by Jordan Roberts. Hudson, NY: Lindisfarne Books, 1997.

Andreev, Daniel. *Rose of the World*. Translated by Daniel H. Shubin. Bakersfield, CA: Peace Church Challenge, 2015.

Andreev, Daniil. *Roza Mira. Metafilosofiia istorii*. Moscow: Prometei, 1991.

Andreev, Daniil. *Russkie bogi: Stikhotvoreniia i poemy*. Moscow: Sovremennik, 1989.

Anthony of Sourozh. *Metropolitan Anthony of Sourozh. A Selection of His Writing*. Edited and with an introduction by Hugh Wybrew. Springfield, IL: Templegate Publishers, 1988.

Anufriew, Sergej, Jurij Leiderman, and Pavel Pepperstein. *Auf sechs Büchern Inspektion "Medhermeneutik."* Düsseldorf: Kunsthalle Düsseldorf, 1990.

Arkady Dragomoshchenko, Mikhail Epstein, Jerome McGann, Marjorie Perloff, et al. "Symposium on Russian Postmodernism." *Postmodern Culture* 3 (1993), no. 2. Available electronically: http://www.pomoculture.org/2013/09/25/symposium-onrussian-postmodernism

Averintsev, Sergei. "K uiasneniiu smysla nadpisi nad konkhoi tsentrasl'noi apsidy Sofii Kievskoi." In *Drevnerusskoe iskusstvo: Khudozhestvennaia kul'tura domongol'skoi Rusi*, edited by V. N. Lazarev, 25–50. Moscow: Nauka, 1972.

Averintsev, Sergei. *Ritorika i istoki evropeiskoi literaturnoi traditsii*. Moscow: Shkola "Iazyki russkoi kul'tury," 1996.

Barabanov, Evgenii. "Russkaia filosofiia i krizis identichnosti." *Voprosy filosofii*, no. 8 (1991): 102–17.

Barabanov, E. V., and P. M. Litvinov, eds. *Samosoznanie: Sbornik statei*. New York: Khronika, 1976.

Barthes, Roland. *Mythologies*. Translated by Annette Lavers. New York: Hill and Wang, 1987.

Bassin, Mark. *The Gumilev Mystique: Biopolitics, Eurasianism, and the Construction of Community in Modern Russia*. Ithaca: Cornell University Press, 2016.

Bassin, Mark, Sergey Glebov, and Marlene Laruelle, eds. *Between Europe and Asia: The Origins, Theories, and Legacies of Russian Eurasianism*. Pittsburgh: University of Pittsburgh Press, 2015.

Berdiaev, N. *Russkaia ideia*. St. Petersburg: Azbuka-klassika, 2008.

Berdyaev, Nikolai. *The Russian Idea*. Translated by R. M. French. Hudson, NY: Lindisfarne Books, 1992.

Berry, Ellen, and Mikhail Epstein. *Transcultural Experiments: Russian and American Models of Creative Communication*. New York: Palgrave MacMillan, 1999.

Borodai, Iurii. "Krest'ianskii trud i sel'skaia obshchnost'. Filosofsko-ekonomicheskie predposylki perestroiki agrarnogo proizvodstvsa." In *Chto s nami proiskhodit? Zapiski sovremennikov*, edited by V. Lazarev, 110–37. Moscow: Sovremennik, 1989.

Bulgakov, Sergei. *The Wisdom of God: A Brief Summary of Sophiology*. London: Williams and Norgate, 1937.

Chalmaev, V. A. *Ogon' veshchei*. Moscow: Sovetskaia Rossiia, 1989.

Clover, Charles. *Black Wind, White Snow: The Rise of Russia's New Nationalism*. New Haven; London: Yale University Press, 2017.

Collingwood, R. G. *An Autobiography*. New York: Mentor Books, 1949.

Cox, Harvey. *The Feast of Fools: A Theological Essay on Festivity and Fantasy*. Cambridge, MA: Harvard University Press, 1969.

DeBlasio, Alyssa. *The End of Russian Philosophy: Tradition and Transition at the Turn of the 21st Century*. New York: Palgrave Macmillan, 2014.

DeBlasio, Alyssa. "Valery Podoroga (1946-2020)." *Filosofia: An Encyclopedia of Russian Thought*, March 2019. Available electronically: http://filosofia.dickinson.edu/encyclopedia/podoroga-valery/

Deleuze, Gilles, and Felix Guattari. *Anti-Oedipus: Capitalism and Schizophrenia*. Translated by Robert Hurley, Mark Seem, and Helen R. Lane. New York: Viking Penguin, 1977.

Deutsch, Babette, and Avrahm Yarmolinsky, eds. *Modern Russian Poetry*. New York: Harcourt, Brace, and Company, 1961.

Dudko, Dmitrii. *O nashem upovanii. Besedy*. Paris: YMCA Press, 1976.

Dudko, Dmitrii. *Vovremia i ne vovremia*. Brussels: Zhizn' s Bogom, 1978.

Dugin, A. "Konservativnaia revoliutsiia. Kratkaia istoriia ideologii tret'ego puti." *Elementy*, no. 1 (1992).

Dugin, A. "Metafizicheskie korni politicheskikh ideologii." *Milyi angel*, no. 1 (1991).

Dugin, A. "Ot sakral'noi geografii k geopolitike." *Elementy*, no. 1 (1992), nos. 3–5 (1993–4).

Dugin, A. "Velikaia metafizicheskaia problema i traditsii." *Milyi angel*, no. 1 (1991).

Dugin, A. "Zagadka sotsializma." *Elementy*, no. 4 (1993).

Elster, Jon. "Active and Passive Negation: An Essay in Ibanskian Sociology." In *Alexander Zinoviev as Writer and Thinker. An Assessment*, edited by Philip Hanson and Michael Kirkwood, 118–44. London: Macmillan Press, 1988.

Emerson, Caryl. "Foreword." In *The Transformative Humanities: A Manifesto*, edited by Mikhail Epstein, xi–xxiii. New York, London: Bloomsbury Academic, 2012.

Engels, Friedrich. *Ludwig Feuerbach and the Outcome of German Classical Philosophy*. New York: International Publishers, 1941.

Engels, Friedrich. "The Part Played by Labor in the Transition from Ape to Man." Translated by Clemens Dutt. Available electronically: https://www.marxists.org/archive/marx/works/1876/part-played-labour/

Epshtein, Mikhail. *Novoe sektantstvo: tipy religiozno-filosofskikh umonastroenii v Rossii, 1970–80-e gody*. Holyoke, MA: New England Publishing Co., 1993; third, revised and expanded edition: Samara: Bakhrakh-M, 2006.

Epshtein, Mikhail. *Postmodernizm v Rossii*. St. Petersburg: Azbuka, 2019.

Epshtein, Mikhail. "Roza Mira i Tsarstvo Antikhrista. O paradoksakh russkoi eskhatologii." In *Religiia posle ateizma: Novye vozmozhnosti teologii*, by Mikhail Epshtein, 106–58. Moscow: AST-Press, 2013.

Epshtein, Mikhail. *Velikaia Sov'. Filosofsko-mifologicheskii ocherk*. New York: Word/ Slovo, 1994; second, revised and expanded edition: Samara: Bakhrakh-M, 2006.

Epstein, Mikhail. *After the Future: The Paradoxes of Postmodernism and Contemporary Russian Culture*. Translated, and with an introduction, Anesa Miller-Pogacar. Amherst: University of Massachusetts Press, 1995.

Epstein, Mikhail. *Cries in the New Wilderness: From the Files of the Moscow Institute of Atheism*. Translated, and with an introduction, by Eve Adler. Philadelphia: Paul Dry Books, 2002.
Epstein, Mikhail. "Emptiness as a Technique: Word and Image in Ilya Kabakov." In *Russian Postmodernism: New Perspectives on Post-Soviet Culture*, edited by Mikhail Epstein, Alexander Genis, and Slobodanka Vladiv-Glover, 363–409. New York, Oxford: Berghahn Books, 2016.
Epstein, Mikhail. "From Analysis to Synthesis: Conceiving a Transformative Metaphysics for the Twenty-First Century." In *Russian Philosophy in the Twenty-First Century. An Anthology*, edited by Mikhail Sergeev, Alexander Chumakov, and Mary Theis, 74–100. Leiden, Boston: Brill, Rodopi, 2020.
Epstein, Mikhail. "Labor of Lust: Erotic Metaphors of Soviet Civilization." In *After the Future: The Paradoxes of Postmodernism and Contemporary Russian Culture*, by Mikhail Epstein, translated by Anesa Miller-Pogacar, 177–87. Amherst: University of Massachusetts Press, 1995.
Epstein, Mikhail. "The Philosophical Implications of Russian Conceptualism." *Journal of Eurasian Studies* 1, no. 1 (2010): 64–71.
Epstein, Mikhail. *The Phoenix of Philosophy: Russian Thought of the Late Soviet Period (1953–1991)*. New York, London: Bloomsbury Academic, 2019.
Epstein, Mikhail. "Postmodernist Thought of the Late Soviet Period: Three Profiles." *Studies in East European Thought*, 2021. DOI: https://doi.org/10.1007/s11212-021-09417-2
Epstein, Mikhail. "Russkaia sverkhideia: tselostnost'. Vse ili nichego," *Zvezda*, no. 1 (2017): 239–50.
Epstein, Mikhail. *Russian Spirituality and the Secularization of Culture*. New York: FrancTireur-USA, 2011.
Epstein, Mikhail. "The Teachings of Iakov Abramov as Interpreted by His Disciples. Compiled, edited, and commented on by Mikhail Epstein." Translated by A. Miller-Pogacar. *Symposion. A Journal of Russian Thought* 3 (1999): 29–66. Available electronically: https://www.emory.edu/INTELNET/abramov.html
Epstein, Mikhail, Alexander Genis, and Slobodanka Vladiv-Glover. *Russian Postmodernism: New Perspectives on Post-Soviet Culture*. New York, Oxford: Berghahn Books, 1999; new and revised edition, New York, Oxford: Berghahn Books, 2016.
Epstein, Thomas. "Mikhail Naumovich Epshtein (Mikhail Epstein)." In *Dictionary of Literary Biography, vol. 285. Russian Writers since 1980*, edited by M. Balina and M. Lipovetsky, 61–8. Detroit: Bruccoli Clark Layman/Thomson Gale, 2004.
Evgen'eva, A. P. *Slovar' russkogo iazyka*, 4 vols. Moscow: Russkii iazyk, 1982.
Federn, P. *Zur Psychologie der Revolution*. Vienna: Anzengruber-Verlag, 1919.
Fedorov, N. F. *Sobranie sochinenii*. Moscow: Traditsiia, 1995–2000. Available electronically: http://nffedorov.ru/wiki/
Fedotov, G. P. *The Russian Religious Mind*. Cambridge, MA: Harvard University Press, 1946.
Florensky, Pavel. *The Pillar and Ground of the Truth: An Essay in Orthodox Theodicy in Twelve Books*. Translated by Boris Jakim. Princeton: Princeton University Press, 2004.
Florovskii, Georgii. *Puti russkogo bogosloviia*. Paris: YMCA Press, 1988.
Florovsky, Georges. *Collected Works*. Belmont, MA: Nordland Publishing Company, 1972–74.
Galkovsii, Dmitrii. *Beskonechnyi tupik*. Moscow: Samizdat, 1997.
Genis, Alexander. "Archaic Postmodernism: The Aesthetics of Andrei Sinyavsky." In *Russian Postmodernism: New Perspectives on Post-Soviet Culture*, by M. Epstein, A. Genis, and S. Vladiv-Glover, 185–96. New York, Oxford: Berghahn Books, 1999.
Girenok, F. I. *Ekologiia. Tsivilizatsiia. Noosfera*. Moscow: Nauka, 1987.

Gogotishvili, L. A. "Mifologiia khaosa (o sotsial'no-istoricheskoi kontseptsii A. F. Loseva)." *Voprosy filosofii*, no. 9 (1993): 39–51.

Goricheva, T. "Epokha post-nigilizma." *Beseda. Religiozno-filosofskii zhurnal* (Leningrad-Paris), no. 4 (1986): 84–97.

Goricheva, Tatiana. *Talking about God Is Dangerous: The Diary of a Russian Dissident.* New York: Crossroad, 1987.

Goricheva, T. "Tsinizm, iurodstvo i sviatost'." *A-Ia* (Paris), no. 1 (1985): 118–23.

Graham, Daniel W., ed. *The Texts of Early Greek Philosophy: The Complete Fragments and Selected Testimonies of the Major Presocratics.* Cambridge: Cambridge University Press, 2010.

Grois, B. E. *Dnevnik filosofa.* Paris: Beseda—Sintaksis, 1989.

Grois, B. E. "Filosofiia i vremia." In *LOGOS. Leningradskie mezhdunarodnye chteniia po filosofii kul'tury*, kn. 1. *Razum. Dukhovnost'. Traditsii*, 5–32. Leningrad: Leningrad University Press,1991.

Grois, B. E. "Poisk russkoi natsional'noi identichnosti." *Voprosy filosofii*, no. 1 (1992): 52–60.

Grois, B. E. "Rossiia kak podsoznanie Zapada." *Paralleli (Rossiia—Vostok—Zapad). Almanakh filosofskoi komparativistiki*, no. 1 (1991): 15–31.

Grois, B. E. "Znanie, bezumie, individual'nost'." *Beseda. Religiozno-filosofskii zhurnal*, no. 6 (1987): 84–123.

Groys, Boris. *The Total Art of Stalinism. Avant-Garde, Aesthetic Dictatorship, and Beyond.* Translated by Charles Rougle. Princeton: Princeton University Press, 1992.

Groys, Boris. "We Shall Be Like Flies." In *History Becomes Form. Moscow Conceptualism*, by Boris Groys, 97–104. Cambridge, MA: The MIT Press, 2010.

Gumilev, L. N. *Drevniaia Rus' i velikaia step'.* Moscow: Mysl', 1989.

Gumilev, L. N. *Ethnogenesis and the Biosphere.* Moscow: Progress Publishers, 1990.

Gumilev, L. N. *Etnogenez i biosfera Zemli.* 3rd pr., Leningrad: Gidrometeoizdat, 1990.

Gumilev, L. N. *Etnosfera: Istoriia liudei i istoriia prirody.* Moscow: AST, 2004.

Gumilev, L. N. *Noosfera i khudozhestvennoe tvorchestvo.* Moscow: Nauka, 1991.

Hagemeister, Michael, Birgit Menzel, and Bernice Glatzer Rosenthal, eds. *The New Age of Russia. Occult and Esoteric Dimensions.* Bern: Peter Lang, 2012.

Hegel, G. W. F. *The Philosophy of History.* Translated by J. Sibree. New York: Dover Publications, 1956.

Heiser, James D. *"The American Empire Should Be Destroyed": Alexander Dugin and the Perils of Immanentized Eschatology.* Malone, TX: Repristination Press, 2014.

Horujy, Sergey S. *Practices of the Self and Spiritual Practices: Michel Foucault and the Eastern Christian Discourse.* Translated by Boris Jakim. Edited and with an introduction by Kristina Stoeckl. Grand Rapids: Eerdmans, 2015.

Hubbs, Joanna. *Mother Russia: The Feminine Myth in Russian Culture.* Bloomington: Indiana University Press, 1988.

Ianov, Aleksandr. *Russkaia ideia. Ot Nikolaia I do Putina. Kniga vtoraia: 1917–1990.* Moscow: Khronograf, 2014.

Isaev, I. A., ed. *Puti Evrazii. Russkaia intelligentsiia i sud'by Rossii.* Moscow: Russkaia kniga, 1992.

Jakobson, Roman. *Language in Literature.* Edited by Krystyna Pomorska and Stephen Rudy. Cambridge, MA: The Belknap Press of Harvard University Press, 1987.

Janson, Charles. "Alexander Zinoviev: Experiences of a Soviet Methodologist." In *Alexander Zinoviev as Writer and Thinker. An Assessment*, edited by Philip Hanson and Michael Kirkwood, 10–25. London: Macmillan Press, 1988.

Kabakov, Ilya. "Conceptualism in Russia." In *Zhizn' mukh. Das Leben der Fliegen. Life of Flies* by Ilya Kabakov, 240–9. Cologne: Kolnischer Kunstverein, 1992.

Kabakov, Ilya. "The Fly as a Subject and Basis for Philosophical Discourse. Introduction." In *Zhizn' mukh. Das Leben der Fliegen. Life of Flies* by Ilya Kabakov. Cologne: Kolnischer Kunstverein, 1992.

Kabakov, Ilya. *The Mental Institution, or Institute of Creative Research*. Malmö: Rooseum, 1991.

Kabakov, Ilya. *On Art*. Edited by Matthew Jesse Jackson. Translated by Antonina Bouis. Chicago: University of Chicago Press, 2018.

Kabakov, Ilya. "On Emptiness." In *Between Spring and Summer. Soviet Conceptual Art in the Era of Late Communism*, edited by David A. Ross, 53–60. Tacoma: Tacoma Art Museum; Boston: The Institute of Contemporary Art, 1990.

Kabakov, Ilya. "On the Subject of the Local Language." In *Zhizn' mukh. Das Leben der Fliegen. Life of Flies* by Ilya Kabakov. Cologne: Kolnischer Kunstverein, 1992.

Kabakov, Ilya. *The Palace of Projects. Artangel*. London: The Roundhouse, 1998.

Kabakov, Ilya. *Ten Characters*. London: The Institute of Contemporary Arts, 1989.

Kabakov, Ilya. "What Is A Communal Apartment?" In *Ten Characters* by Ilya Kabakov. London: The Institute of Contemporary Arts, 1989.

Kabakov, Ilya. *Zhizn' mukh. Das Leben der Fliegen. Life of Flies*. Cologne: Kolnischer Kunstverein, 1992.

Kabakov, Ilya, and Mikhail Epstein. *Katalog*. Vologda: Library of Moscow Conceptualism/ German Titov, 2010.

Kamennyi, A. "Dukh i pochva." *Zavtra*, no. 14 (19) (1994).

Khoruzhii, Sergei. *Diptikh bezmolviia. Asketicheskoe uchenie o cheloveke v bogoslovskom i filosofskom osveshchenii*. Moscow: Tsentr psikhologii i psikhoterapii, 1991.

Khoruzhii, Sergei. "Filosofskii protsess v Rossii kak vstrecha filosofii i pravoslaviia." *Voprosy filosofii*, no. 5 (1991): 26–57.

Khoruzhii, Sergei. "Isikhazm i istoriia." *Chelovek* (Moscow), nos. 4–5 (1991).

Khoruzhii, Sergei. "Problema lichnosti v pravoslavii: mistika isikhazma i metafizika vseedinstva." *Zdes' i teper'. Filosofiia, literatura, kul'tura* (Moscow), no. 1 (1992): 94–105.

Kireevskii, I. V. *Kritika i estetika*. Moscow: Iskusstvo, 1979.

Kireevsky, Ivan. "On the Necessity and Possibility of New Principles in Philosophy." In *Russian Philosophy*, edited by James M. Edie, James P. Scanlan, and Mary-Barbara Zeldin, 1: 171–213. Knoxville: The University of Tennessee Press, 1987.

Kirkwood, Michael. *Alexander Zinoviev: An Introduction to His Work*. London: Macmillan Press, 1993.

Komar, Vitaly, and Aleksandr Melamid. *Death Poems: Manifesto of Eclecticism*. New York: Galerie Barbara Farber, 1988.

Kosuth, Joseph. *Art after Philosophy and After. Collected Writings, 1966–1990*. Cambridge, MA and London: Massachusetts Institute of Technology, 1991.

Kovalev, Vitalii. *Filosofiia postistorii*. Moscow: ALVA-XXI, 1992.

Kozhevnikov, A. Iu. *Russkii patriotizm i sovetskii sotsializm*. Moscow: Prometei, 2017.

Kozhinov, Vadim. *Razmyshleniia o russkoi literature*. Moscow: Sovremennik, 1991.

Krasnov, A. *Stromaty*. Frankfurt/Main: Posev, 1972.

Krasnov-Levitin, A. *Likhie gody. 1925–1941. Vospominaniia*. Paris: YMCA Press, 1977.

Kurginian, Sergei. *Sed'moi stsenarii*. Moscow: Eksperimental'nyi tvorcheskii tsentr, 1992.

Kurginian, S. E., B. R. Autenshlius, P. S. Goncharov, Iu. V. Gromyko, I.Iu. Sundiev, and V. S. Ovchinskii. *Postperestroika*. Moscow: Politizdat, 1990.

Laqueur, Walter. *Black Hundred: The Rise of the Extreme Right in Russia*. New York: Harper Collins Publishers, 1993.

Laruelle, Marlene. "The Iuzhinskii Circle: Far-Right Metaphysics in the Soviet Underground and Its Legacy Today." *The Russian Review*, 74, no. 4 (2015): 563–80.

Laruelle, Marlène. *Russian Eurasianism. An Ideology of Empire*. Baltimore: Johns Hopkins University Press, 2019.

Lipovetskii, M. N., ed. *HOMO SCRIPTOR: Sbornik statei v chest' 70-letiia M. N. Epshteina*. Moscow: Novoe literaturnoe obozrenie, 2020.

Lobanov, Mikhail. *Stranitsy pamiatnogo: literaturno-kriticheskie stat'i*. Moscow: Sovremennik, 1988.

Losev, A. F. "Osnovnye osobennosti russkoi filosofii." In *Filosofiia. Mifologiia. Kul'tura* by A. F. Losev, 509–13. Moscow: Politizdat, 1991.

Lossky, Vladimir. *The Mystical Theology of the Eastern Church*. London: J. Clarke, 1957.

Lourie, Richard. *Letters to the Future: An Approach to Sinyavsky-Tertz*. Ithaca and London: Cornell University Press, 1975.

Luka, Arkhiepiskop. *Dukh, dusha i telo*. Available electronically: https://azbyka.ru/otechnik/Luka_Vojno-Jasenetskij/dukh-dusha-i-telo

Luka, Arkhiepiskop. *Nauka i religiia*. Available electronically: https://azbyka.ru/otechnik/Luka_Vojno-Jasenetskij/nauka-i-religija

Mamleev, Iu. V. "Sud'ba bytiia." Available electronically: https://rvb.ru/mamleev/03philos/01sb/sb.htm

Maneev, A. K. *Filosofskii analiz antinomii nauki*. Minsk: Nauka i tekhnika, 1974.

Marx, Karl. "A Contribution to the Critique of Hegel's Philosophy of Right. Introduction." Translated by Annette Jolin and Joseph O'Malley. Available electronically: https://www.marxists.org/archive/marx/works/1843/critique-hpr/intro.htm

Marx, Karl. "Theses on Feuerbach." Translated by W. Lough. Available electronically: https://www.marxists.org/archive/marx/works/1845/theses/theses.htm

Meerson-Aksenov, Mikhail. *Pravoslavie i svoboda*. Benson, VT: Chalidze Publications, 1986.

Men', Aleksandr. *Bibliologicheskii slovar'*. Moscow: Fond imeni Aleksandra Menia, 2002. Available electronically: https://imwerden.de/pdf/men_bibliologihesky_slovar_tom1_2002.pdf; https://imwerden.de/pdf/men_bibliologihesky_slovar_tom2_2002.pdf; https://imwerden.de/pdf/men_bibliologihesky_slovar_tom3_2002.pdf.

Men', Aleksandr. *Istoriia religii v 7 tomakh. V poiskakh puti, istiny i zhizni*. Moscow: Izdatel'stvo Sovetsko-Britanskogo sovmestnogo predpriiatiia SLOVO, 1991.

Men', Aleksandr. "O Teiare de Shardene." *Voprosy filosofii*, no. 12 (1990): 89–102.

Men, Alexander. *Christianity for the Twenty-First Century: The Prophetic Writings of Alexander Men*. Edited and translated by Elizabeth Roberts and Ann Shukman. London: Continuum, 1996.

Men, Alexander. *The Wellsprings of Religion*, vol. 1 of *The History of Religion: In Search of the Way, the Truth, and the Life*. Translated by Alasdair MacNaughton. Yonkers, NY: St. Vladimir's Seminary Press, 2018.

Men, Father Alexander. *Son of Man: The Story of Christ and Christianity*. Translated by Samuel Brown. Huntsville: Oakwood Publications, 1998.

Men', Fr. Aleksandr. *Russian Religious Philosophy: 1989–1990 Lectures*. Translated by Fr. S. Janos. Mohrsville, PA: Frsj Publications, 2015.

Menzel, Birgit. "The Occult Revival in Russia Today and Its Impact on Literature." *The Harriman Review* 16, no. 1 (2007): 1–14.

Michurin, V. A. "Slovar' poniatii i terminov teorii etnogeneza L. N. Gumileva." In *Etnosfera: Istoriia liudei i istoriia prirody*, edited by L. N. Gumilev. Moscow: AST, 2004. Available electronically: https://www.e-reading.club/chapter.php/86668/107/Gumilev_-_Etnosfera__istoriya_lyudeii_i_istoriya_prirody.html.

Mitrokhin, Nikolai. *Russkaia partiia: Dvizhenie russkikh natsionalistov v SSSR. 1953–1985 gody*. Moscow: Novoe literaturnoe obozrenie, 2003.

Moiseev, Nikita. *Chelovek i noosfera*. Moscow: Zhurnal Ekologiia i zhizn', 1990.

Nietzsche, Friedrich. *Schriften und Entwürfe 1881–1885*. Edited by F. Koegel. Leipzig: Naumann, 1897.

Osipov, Vladimir. *Tri otnosheniia k rodine: Stat'i, ocherki, vystupleniia*. Frankfurt: Posev, 1978.

Palievskii, P. V. *Literatura i teoriia*. 2nd ed. Moscow: Sovremennik, 1978.

Panin, Dimitrii. *Teoriia gustot. Opyt filosofii kontsa 20-go veka*. Paris: Izdanie avtora, 1982.

Panin, Dimitrii. *Vselennaia glazami sovremennogo cheloveka*. Turne: Izdanie avtora, 1976.

Pasternak, Boris. *Doctor Zhivago*. Translated by Max Hayward and Manya Harari. New York: Pantheon, 1958.

Peppershtein, Pavel. *Dieta starika. Teksty 1982–1997 gg*. Moscow: Ad Marginem, 1998.

Plato. *The Laws*. Translated by R. G. Bury. Cambridge, MA: Harvard University Press, 1926.

Podoroga, Valerii. *Antropogrammy*. Moscow: Logos, 2014.

Podoroga, Valerii. *Metafizika landshafta. Kommunikativnye strategii v filosofskoi kul'ture XIX-XX vv*. Moscow: Nauka, 1993; 2nd, expanded edition, Moscow: Kanon, 2013.

Podoroga, Valerii. *Mimesis. Materialy po analiticheskoi antropologii literatury v dvukh tomakh*. Vol. 1. *N. Gogol', F. Dostoevskii*. Moscow: Kul'turnaia revolutsiia; Logos-altera, 2006.

Popovskii, Mark. *Zhizn' i zhitie Voino-Iasenetskogo, arkhiepiskopa i khirurga*. Paris: YMCA Press, 1979.

Popper, Karl R. *The Open Society and Its Enemies*. London: Routledge and Kegan Paul, 1966.

Prigov, Dmitrii. "Conceptualism and the West." In *Poetics Journal Digital Archive*, edited by Lyn Hejinian and Barrett Watten, 1161–5. Middletown, CT: Wesleyan University Press, 2015.

Prigov, Dmitrii. *Mysli. Izbrannye manifesty, stat'i, interv'iu*. Moscow: Novoe literaturnoe obozrenie, 2019.

Prigov, Dmitri. "What More Is There To Say?" In *Third Wave. The New Russian Poetry*, edited by Kent Johnson and Stephen M. Ashby, 101–4. Ann Arbor: University of Michigan Press, 1992.

Pyman, Avril. *Metropolitan Anthony of Sourozh. A Life*. Cambridge. The Lutterworth Press, 2016.

Ratcliff, Carter. *Komar & Melamid*. New York: Abbeville Press Publishers, 1988.

Rorty, Richard. "Ironists and Metaphysicians." In *The Truth about Truth. De-Confusing and Re-Constructing the Postmodern World*, edited by W. T. Anderson, 100–6. New York: Putnam, 1995.

Rosenthal, Bernice Glatzer. *Dmitri Sergeevich Merezhkovsky and the Silver Age: The Development of a Revolutionary Mentality*. The Hague: Springer, 1975.

Rosenthal, Bernice Glatzer, ed. *The Occult in Russian and Soviet Culture*. Ithaca: Cornell University Press, 1997.

"Russian Critical Theory and Postmodernism: The Theoretical Writings of Mikhail Epstein" (a forum). *Slavic and East European Journal* 39, no. 3 (1995): 329–66.
Scanlan, James P., ed. *Russian Thought after Communism: The Rediscovery of a Philosophical Heritage*. London: Routledge, 1994.
Schmemann, Alexander. *The Eucharist. Sacrament of the Kingdom*. Translated by Paul Kachur. Crestwood, NY: St. Vladimir's Seminary Press, 1988.
Sedgwick, Mark, ed. *Key Thinkers of the Radical Right: Behind the New Threat to Liberal Democracy*. Oxford: Oxford University Press, 2019.
Semenova, Svetlana. *Nikolai Fedorov. Tvorchestvo zhizni*. Moscow: Sovetskii pisatel', 1990.
Semenova, Svetlana. *Preodolenie tragedii. "Vechnye voprosy" v literature*. Moscow: Sovetskii pisatel', 1989.
Semenova, Svetlana. *Sozidanie budushchego. Filosofiia russkogo kozmizma*. Edited by A. G. Gacheva. Moscow: Nookratiia, 2020.
Semenova, S. G., and A. G. Gacheva, eds. *Russkii kosmizm. Antologiia filosofskoi mysli*. Moscow: Pedagogika-Press, 1993.
Sergeev, Mikhail, Alexander Chumakov, and Mary Theis, eds. *Russian Philosophy in the Twenty-First Century. An Anthology*. Leiden, Boston: Brill, Rodopi, 2020.
Shafarevich, I. R. *Russofobiia. Dve dorogi—k odnomu obryvu*. Moscow: Tovarishchestvo russkikh khudozhnikov, 1991.
Shafarevich, I. R. *Sotsializm kak iavlenie mirovoi istorii*. Paris: YMCA Press, 1977.
Shimanov, G. M. "Kak ponimat' nashu istoriiu i k chemu v nei stremit'sia" (1974). Available electronically: http://chri-soc.narod.ru/sh_kak_ponimat_nashu_istoriu.htm
Shmeman, A. "Istoki maksimalizma v russkoi kul'ture" (a discussion on Radio Liberty). Available electronically: https://www.pravmir.ru/protopresviter-aleksandr-shmeman-istoki-maksimalizma-v-russkoy-kulture/
Shmeman, Protoierei Aleksandr. *Voskresnye besedy*. Paris: YMCA Press, 1989.
Shmidt, A. N. *Tretii zavet*. St. Petersburg: Petropol', 1993.
Siniavskii, Andrei. *Ocherki russkoi kul'tury*, 1. *"Opavshie list'ia" Rozanova*. Paris: Sintaksis, 1982.
Siniavskii, Andrei. *Ocherki russkoi kul'tury*, 2. *Ivan-durak. Ocherk russkoi narodnoi very*. Paris: Sintaksis, 1991.
Siniavskii, Andrei. *Sobranie sochinenii v 2 tomakh*. Moscow: SP "Start," 1992.
Sinyavsky, Andrei. *Soviet Civilization. A Cultural History*. Translated by Joanne Turnbull with the assistance of Nikolai Formozov. New York: Arcade Publishing. Little, Brown and Co., 1990.
Sinyavsky, Andrei. *Strolls with Pushkin*. Translated by Catherine Theimer Nepomnyashchy and Slava I. Yastremski. New York: Columbia University Press, 2016.
Sinyavsky, Andrey. *Unguarded Thoughts*. Translated by Manya Harari. London: Collins & Harvill Press, 1965.
Skovoroda, Gregory. "Socrates in Russia." In *Russian Philosophy*, edited by James M. Edie, James P. Scanlan, and Mary-Barbara Zeldin, 1: 17–8. Knoxville: The University of Tennessee Press, 1987.
Slovar' russkogo iazyka, 4 vols, edited by A. P. Evgenieva. Moscow: Russkii iazyk, 1982.
Solov'ev, Vladimir. *Sochineniia v 10 tt*. St. Petersburg: Prosveshchenie, 1914.
Soloviev, Vladimir. *La Sophia et les autres écrits français*. Edited by Fr. François Rouleau. Lausanne: La Cité-L'Age d'homme, 1978.
Solzhenitsyn, Aleksandr. "Igra na strunakh pustoty" (1993). Available electronically: https://www.rulit.me/books/igra-na-strunah-pustoty-calibre-0-8-64-read-262937-3.html

Solzhenitsyn, Aleksandr. "Nashi pliuralisty." *Vestnik russkogo khristianskogo dvizheniia*, no. 139 (1983). Available electronically: http://www.rodon.org/sai/np.htm

Solzhenitsyn, Aleksandr. *Rebuilding Russia. Reflections and Tentative Proposals*. Translated and annotated by Alexis Klimoff. New York: Farrar, Straus and Giroux, 1991.

Solzhenitsyn, Aleksandr. "'Russkii vopros' k kontsu XX veka." *Novyi mir*, no. 7 (1994). Available electronically: https://magazines.gorky.media/novyi_mi/1994/7/russkij-vopros-k-konczu-xx-veka.html

Solzhenitsyn, Aleksandr. *Sobranie sochinenii v 20 tomakh*. Vermont-Paris: YMCA Press, 1981.

Solzhenitsyn, Aleksandr et al., eds. *Iz-pod glyb. Sbornik statei*. Paris: YMCA Press, 1974.

Solzhenitsyn, Alexander. "Repentance and Self-Limitation in the Life of Nations." In *From under the Rubble* by Alexander Solzhenitsyn, Mikhail Agursky, Evgeny Barabanov, Vadim Borisov, F. Korsakov, and Igor Shafarevich, 105–43. Translated by Michael Scammell and A. M. Brock. Boston, Toronto: Little, Brown and Company,1975.

Solzhenitsyn, Alexander. "A World Split Apart." Harvard University commencement address, delivered June 8, 1978. Available electronically: https://www.americanrhetoric.com/speeches/alexandersolzhenitsynharvard.htm

Strauss, Leo. *On Tyranny. Including the Strauss-Kojève Correspondence*. Edited by Victor Gourevich and Michael S. Roth. New York: The Free Press, 1991.

Surozhskii, Mitropolit Antonii. "My dolzhny prinesti v mir veru—ne tol'ko v Boga, no v cheloveka." An interview with Anthony of Sourozh by Mikhail Epstein (London, April 1989), in Mitropolit Antonii Surozhskii, *O vstreche* (St. Petersburg: Satis, 1994), 79–93. Available electronically: https://predanie.ru/book/70592-o-vstreche/#/toc6

Surozhskii, Mitropolit Antonii. "Otvety na voprosy zhurnala 'Zvezda.'" *Zvezda*, no. 1 (1991): 122–8.

Taplin, Phoebe. "Meet Yuri Mamleev: Insanity, Murder, and Sexual Depravity on the Quest for Divine Truth." *Russia Beyond*, 14 April 2014. Available electronically: https://www.rbth.com/literature/2014/04/14/meet_yuri_mamleev_insanity_murder_and_sexual_depravity_on_the_quest_for_35879.html

Terras, Victor. "Sweet Moments of Recognition: Epshtein on Postmodernism." *Slavic and East European Journal* 41 (1997): 477–81.

Terts, Abram. "Literaturnyi protsess v Rossii." *Kontinent* (Paris), no. 1 (1974): 143–90. Available electronically: https://vtoraya-literatura.com/pdf/terz_literaturny_protsess_v_rossii_1974__ocr.pdf

Tertz, Abram. *On Socialist Realism*. Translated by George Dennis. New York: Pantheon Books, 1960.

Tertz, Abram. *A Voice from the Chorus*. Translated by Kyril Fitzlyon and Max Hayward. New York: Farrar, Straus and Giroux, 1976.

Toporov, V. N. *Tekst: Semantika i struktura*. Moscow: Nauka, 1983.

Trubetskoi, E. N. *Mirosozertsanie Vl. S. Solov'eva*. Moscow: Izdanie avtora, 1913.

Trubetskoi, N. S. "Ob idee-pravitel'nitse ideokraticheskogo gosudarstva." *Evraziiskaia khronika* (Berlin), no. 11 (1935). Available electronically: https://www.gumilev-center.ru/ob-idee-pravitelnice-ideokraticheskogo-gosudarstva/

Tucker, Robert C., ed. *The Lenin Anthology*. New York: W. W. Norton & Company, 1975.
Upton, Charles. *Dugin against Dugin: A Traditionalist Critique of the Fourth Political Theory*. Hillsdale, NY: Sophia Perennis, 2018.
Vysheslavtsev, Boris. *Serdtse v khristianskoi i indiiskoi mistike*. Paris: YMCA Press, 1929.
Wallace, Daniel. *Russia's Uncommon Prophet: Father Aleksandr Men and His Times*. DeKalb, IL: Northern Illinois University Press, 2016.
Whitehead, Alfred North. *Process and Reality*. Glencoe, IL: Free Press, 1979.
Zelinskii, Vladimir. *Prikhodiashchie v tserkov'*. Paris: La Presse Libre, 1982.
Zen'kovskii, V. V. *Istoriia russkoi filosofii*. Paris: YMCA-PRESS, 1950.
Zheludkov, S., and K. Liubarskii. *Khristianstvo i ateizm*. Brussels: Zhizn' s Bogom, 1982.
Zhirinovskii, Vladimir. *Poslednii brosok na iug*. Moscow: Pisatel', 1993.
Zinov'ev, Aleksandr. *Bez illiuzii*. Lausanne: L'Age d'Homme, 1979.
Zinov'ev, Aleksandr. *Katastroika. Povest' o perestroike v Partgrade*. Lausanne: L'Age d'Homme, 1990.
Zinov'ev, Aleksandr. *Ni svobody, ni ravenstva, ni bratstva*. Lausanne: L'Age d'Homme, 1983.
Zinov'ev, Aleksandr. *Zheltyi dom*. Lausanne: L'Age d'Homme, 1980.
Zinov'ev, Aleksandr. *Zhivi*. Lausanne: L'Age d'Homme, 1989.
Zinoviev, Alexander. *Gorbachevism*. New York: Liberty, 1988.
Zinoviev, Alexander. *Homo Sovieticus*. Translated by Charles Janson. London: Victor Gollancz Ltd., 1985.
Zinoviev, Alexander. *Philosophical Problems of Many-Valued Logic*. Edited and Translated by Guido Kung and David Dinsmore Comey. Dordrecht-Holland: D. Reidel Publishing Company, 1963.
Zinoviev, Alexander. *The Reality of Communism*. London: Victor Gollancz Ltd., 1984.
Zinoviev, Alexander. *The Yawning Heights*. Translated by Gordon Clough. New York: Random House, 1979.

Appendix: Original Russian and Other Foreign-Language Titles

A to Z (journal) – *A-Ia*
Akhmatova, Anna
Requiem – Rekviem
Andreev, Daniil
The Rose of the World – Roza mira
Wanderers of the Night – Stranniki nochi
Barabanov, Evgenii
"The Schism Between the Church and the World" – "Raskol tserkvi i mira"
"The Truth of Humanism" – "Pravda gumanizma"
Belov, Vasily
Business as Usual – Privychnoe delo
Blok, Aleksandr
"The Scythians" – "Skify"
Boiarsky, Father Aleksandr
Boomerang – Bumerang
Cherished Angel – Milyi angel

The Church and Democracy — Tserkov' i demokratiia
Chernyshevsky, Nikolai
Conversation - Beseda
Country and World - Strana i mir
Day. The Paper of Spiritual Opposition - Den'. Gazeta dukhovnoi oppozitsii
What is to Be Done? - Chto delat'?
Dostoevsky, Fedor
The Brothers Karamazov - Brat'ia Karamazovy
The Devils - Besy
Diary of a Writer - Dnevnik pisatelia
Notes from Underground - Zapiski iz podpol'ia
Dugin, Aleksandr
Conspirology - Konspirologiia
Foundations of Geopolitics - Osnovy geopolitiki
The Hyperborean Theory - Giperboreiskaia teoriia
The Mysteries of Eurasia - Misterii Evrazii
Paths of the Absolute - Puti Absoliuta
Elements - Elementy
Exodus to the East. Presentiments and Accomplishments. The Affirmation of the Eurasians - Iskhod k Vostoku. Predchuvstviia i svershenia. Utverzhdenie evraziitsev
Florovsky, Georges
Christianity and Culture - Khristianstvo i kul'tura
The Eastern Fathers of the Fourth Century - Vostochnye ottsy IV veka
The Ways of Russian Theology - Puti russkogo bogosloviia
From under the Rubble - Iz-pod glyb
Galkovsky, Dmitrii
The Endless Dead End - Beskonechnyi tupik
Groys, Boris
"Moscow Romantic Conceptualism" - "Moskovskii romanticheskii kontseptualizm"
On the New - O novom
Gumilev, Lev
"The Biography of a Scientific Theory, or an Auto-Obituary" - "Biografiia nauchnoi teorii, ili Avtonekrolog"
Ethnogenesis and the Earth's Biosphere - Etnogenez i biosfera Zemli
Ilarion
"The Sermon on Law and Grace" - "Slovo o zakone i blagodati"
Kabakov, Ilya
"The Fly as a Subject and Basis for Philosophical Discourse" - "Mukha kak predmet i osnovanie filosofskogo diskursa"
The Fly with Wings - Mukha s kryl'iami
The Man Who Flew into Space from His Room - Chelovek, kotoryi uletel v kosmos iz svoei komnaty
The Mental Institution, or Institute of Creative Research - Sumasshedshii dom, ili Institut kreativnykh issledovanii
The Palace of Projects - Dvorets proektov
The Toilet - Tualet
Kholodnyi, Nikolai

Thoughts of a Naturalist about Nature and Man – *Mysli naturalista o prirode i cheloveke*
Komar, Vitaly and Alexander Melamid
Nostalgic Socialist Realism – *Nostal'gicheskii sotsrealizm*
Stalin and the Muses – *Stalin i музу*
View of the Kremlin in a Romantic Landscape – *Vid na Kreml' v romanticheskom peizazhe*
Kovalev, Vitalii
The Philosophy of Posthistory – *Filosofiia postistorii*
"What is Ecosophy?" – "Chto takoe ekosofiia?"
Krasnov-Levitin, Anatolii
Stromata – *Stromaty*
Landmarks* – *Vekhi
Lobanov, Mikhail
"Enlightened Philistinism" – "Prosveshchennoe meshchanstvo"
Luka, Archbishop
Science and Religion – *Nauka i religiia*
On Spirit, Soul, and Body – *Dukh, dusha i telo*
Mamleev, Iurii
"The Destiny of Being" – "Sud'ba bytiia"
"Russia Eternal" – "Rossiia vechnaia"
The Sublimes – *Shatuny*
Maria* – *Mariia
Memory – Pamiat'
Men, Aleksandr
Bibliological Dictionary – *Bibliologicheskii slovar'*
How to Read the Bible – *Kak chitat' Bibliiu*
Sacrament, Word, and Image – *Tainstvo, slovo i obraz*
In Search of the Way, the Truth, and the Life – *V poiskakh Puti, Istiny i Zhizni*
Palievsky, Petr
"The Artistic Work" – "Khudozhestvennoe proizvedenie"
"The Internal Structure of the Image" – "Vnutrenniaia struktura obraza"
Panin, Dmitrii
The Theory of Densities – *Teoriia gustot*
Pasternak, Boris
Doctor Zhivago – *Doktor Zhivago*
Podoroga, Valerii
The Metaphysics of Landscape: Communicative Strategies in the Philosophical Culture of the Nineteenth and Twentieth Centuries – *Metafizika landshafta. Kommunikativnye strategii v filosofskoi kul'ture XIX-XX vv.*
Pushkin, Aleksandr
Eugene Onegin – *Evgenii Onegin*
Rozanov, Vasilii
Fallen Leaves – *Opavshie list'ia*
Russian National Unity – Russkoe natsional'noe edinstvo
Self-Awareness* – *Samosoznanie
Shafarevich, Igor
Russophobia – *Rusofobiia*
Socialism as a Phenomenon of World History – *Sotsializm kak iavlenie mirovoi istorii*

Schmemann, Alexander
The Eucharist – Evkharistiia
An Introduction to Liturgical Theology – Vvedenie v liturgicheskoe bogoslovie
Of Water and the Spirit – Vodoiu i dukhom
Schmidt, Wilhelm
The Origin of the Idea of God – Der Ursprung der Gottesidee
Siniavsky, Andrei
In Gogol's Shadow – V teni Gogolia
Ivan the Fool: Outlines of Russian Popular Belief – Ivan-durak: ocherk russkoi narodnoi very
On Socialist Realism – Chto takoe sotsialisticheskii realizm
Soviet Civilization – Sovetskaia tsivilizatsiia
Strolls with Pushkin – Progulki s Pushkinym
Unguarded Thoughts – Mysli vrasplokh
A Voice from the Chorus – Golos iz khora
Sloterdijk, Peter
The Critique of Cynical Reason – Kritik der zynischen Vernunft
Sologub, Fedor
The Petty Demon – Melkii bes
Solovyov, Vladimir
"The Meaning of Love" – "Smysl liubvi"
"A Short Tale of the Antichrist" – "Kratkaia povest' ob antikhriste"
"Three Encounters" – "Tri vstrechi"
Solzhenitsyn, Aleksandr
Matrena's House – Matrenin dvor
"Repentance and Self-Limitation in the Life of Nations" – "Raskaianie i samoogranichenie kak kategorii natsional'noi zhizni"
Sorokin, Vladimir
The Norm – Norma
Novel – Roman
The Tale of Bygone Years – Povest' vremennykh let
The Tale of Igor's Campaign – Slovo o polku Igoreve
Tolstoy, Lev
War and Peace – Voina i mir
Tomorrow – Zavtra
Turgenev, I. S.
"A Living Relic" – "Zhivye moshchi"
On the Eve – Nakanune
Woman and Russia – Zhenshchina i Rossia
The World of the Bible – Mir Biblii
Young Guard – Molodaia gvardiia
Zelinsky, Vladimir
Coming to Church – Prikhodiashchie v tserkov'
Zheludkov, Sergei
Liturgical Notes – Liturgicheskie zametki
Why I Too Am a Christian – Pochemu i ia khristianin
Zhirinovsky, Vladimir
A Last Thrust to the South – Poslednii brosok na Iug

Zinoviev, Aleksandr
The Crisis of Communism – Krizis kommunizma
Homo Sovieticus – Gomo sovetikus
The Madhouse – Zheltyi dom
Philosophical Problems of Many-Valued Logic – Filosofskie problemy mnogoznachnoi logiki
The Reality of Communism – Kommunizm kak real'nost'
The Yawning Heights – Ziiaiushchie vysoty

Name Index

Notes: References to notes comprise the page number plus the note number e.g. 13 n.8 refers to note 8 on page 13
References to figures are in italicized text
Page numbers in bold refer to the pages specifically devoted to the given author.

Adi Shankaracharya 152
Adorno, Theodor 189, 211
Akhmatova, Anna 37
Althusser, Louis 175–6
Amalrik, Andrei 35–6
Andreev, Daniil **110–18**, 111, **122–31**, 139–40, 150, 215, 220, 228, 232
Anthony of Sourozh/Anthony Bloom 67, *69*, **69–71**
Anufriev, Sergei **200**, **203**
Aristotle 1–3, 3 n.7, 15, 67 n.11
Averintsev, Sergei 3, 121

Bakhtin, Mikhail 14, 16–17, 105, 184–5, 220
Balzac, Honoré de 233
Barabanov, Evgenii **90–1**, 215–16, 218–19
Barkashov, Aleksandr 47, 48 n.88
Barthes, Roland 173, 206, 228 n.23
Baudrillard, Jean 175, 184, 211
Belinsky, Vissarion 2, 168
Berdiaev, Nikolai 63, 105, 110, 118, 153, 215, 217, 228, 235
Bergson, Henri 74, 99, 149, 187
Blavatsky, Helena 109, 150, 215
Blok, Aleksandr 10, 111, 125, 130
Borodai, Iurii 28
Brezhnev, Leonid 48, 51, 162, 181
Bulgakov, Sergei 63, 120, 122–3, 138, 215, 218

Camus, Albert 82 n.49, 143
Chaadaev, Petr 2, **9**, 63, 210, 215
Chalmaev, Viktor 18–19
Chekhov, Anton 184, 227
Chernyshevsky, Nikolai 116, 218
Cochin, Augustin 34

Danilevsky, Nikolai 19
Dante Alighieri 233
Darwin, Charles 95
Deleuze, Gilles 206–7, 211
Derrida, Jacques 186, 209, 211–12, 218
Dostoevsky, Fedor 14, 16, 18, 102, 111, 116, 122, 154, 162, 167, 184, 206, 227, 229, 235
Druskin, Iakov 64, 165
Dudko, Dmitrii **81–3**, 88
Dugin, Aleksandr **47–50**, **52–6**, **60**, 151 n.48, 219, 222, 229, 232

Elster, Jon 177
Engels 33, 80, 95, 120 n.8
Epstein, Mikhail 71 n.21, 84 n.57, 88 n.70, 121 n.11, **157 n.1**, 160 n.5, 182 nn.70–1, **213 n.149**, 227 n.20, **228 n.23**, 233 n.2, 236 n.4
Evola, Julius 48, 222

Faulkner, William 14
Federn, Paul 120 n.8
Fedorov, Nikolai 66, 110, 132–6, 138–9, 142–6, 148, 190, 197, 215, 217, 220, 222, 228–9, 232
Fedotov, Georgii 63, 90 n.72, 118
Feuerbach, Ludwig 79, 129, 149, 221, 235
Florensky, Pavel 3, 93, 106, 110, 120, 215, 218
Florovsky, Georges 10, **64–6**
Foucault, Michel 173, 207, 211–12
Frank, Semyon 63, 215
Freud, Sigmund 33, 95, 146, 208, 210
Fukuyama, Francis 141–2

Gacheva, Anastasiia 143 n.35
Galkovsky, Dmitrii **227**
Genis, Alexander 171
Girenok, Fedor 134, 136–9, 150
Gogol, Nikolai 102, 167, 170, 184, 206, 227
Goricheva, Tatiana **103–5**, 105 n.100
Gorsky, Aleksandr 146
Gregory of Nyssa 145
Groys, Boris 188, **203–10**, 218
Guattari, Felix 206, 211
Guenon, Rene 48, 222
Gumilev, Lev **37–47**, *37*, 60, 232
Gumilev, Nikolai 37
Gundlakh, Sven 200
Gurdjieff, Georgii 109, 150–1, 215

Hegel, G. W. F. 1, **4**, 5–6, 17, 39, 79, 140–2, 187, 224, 235
Heidegger, Martin 6, 33, 103, 105–6, 141, 187, 207, 211–12
Herzen, Aleksandr 2, 16, 218
Hubbs, Joanna 118

Ianov, Aleksandr 21 n.25, 36
Ilarion 17
Ilyin, Ivan 63–4
Ivanov-Razumnik, Razumnik 9–10
Ivanov, Viacheslav 3, 189
Ivan the Terrible 15, 19, 84

Jakobson, Roman 13, 221
Jaspers, Karl 42, 165

Kabakov, Ilya 158, *181*, **181–93**, 197–8, 206, 208, 224, 229
Kant, Immanuel 1, 159, 218, 221
Karamazov, Dmitrii 154, 229
Khazanov, Boris 88
Khlebnikov, Velimir 14, 110, 204
Kholodnyi, Nikolai 137
Khomiakov, Aleksei 18, 58, 63, 84, 189, 210
Khoruzhii, Sergei **105–8**, **107 n.106**, 215–16, 218–19, 219 n.6
Khrushchev, Nikita 3, 93, 111, 135, 162
Kierkegaard, Søren 174, 196, 210–12
Kireevsky, Ivan 2, 17 n.12, 18, 58, 63, 189
Kirkwood, Michael 173

Kojève, Alexandre **5–6**
Komar, Vitalii 160, 163, **193–7**, 229
Kosuth, Joseph 157, 160
Kovalev, Vitalii **140–2**, 140 n.29
Kozhevnikov. *See* Kojève, Alexandre
Kozhinov, Vadim 14–18, 17 n.12, 44
Krasnov-Levitin, Anatolii **78–81**, 88–90
Kuprevich, Vasilii 135–6
Kurginian, Sergei 50, 219, 222–3, 229

Lamennais, Félicité 79
Leiderman, Jurij 200
Lenin, Vladimir 5, 12, 16, 19, 115, 134–5, 164, 207, 217, 227, 235
Lermontov, Mikhail 111, 115, 199
Le Roy, Édouard 133
Lifshits, Mikhail 14
Liubarsky, Kronid **83–8**
Lobanov, Mikhail 18–19
Losev, Aleksei 119, 216, 218
Lossky, Vladimir x n.2, 67, 106
Lovecraft, H. P. 131 n.19
Luka (Valentin Voino-Iasenetsky) **72–5**, 77

Maiakovsky, Vladimir 134, 204
Mamai (the Tatar khan) 17
Mamleev, Iurii 54, **150–5**, 229
Marcuse, Herbert 146, 221
Marx, Karl 4–5, 26, 39, 50, 80, 82, 95–6, 134–5, 141, 149, 176, 187, 197, 210, 219, 221, 235
Meerson-Aksenov, Mikhail 91–2
Melamid, Aleksandr 160, 163, **193–7**, 229
Men, Aleksandr (Father Men) 72, 88, 88 n.69, *93*, **93–101**, 108
Merezhkovsky, Dmitrii 63, 110, 122, 123 n.14, 189, 215, 217
Mihajlov, Mihajlo 26
Mitrokhin, Nikolai 21 n.25
Moiseev, Nikita 134–5
Monastyrsky, Andrei 200

Nalimov, Vasilii 75, 220
Nevsky, Aleksandr 18
Nietzsche, Friedrich 48, 103–5, 141, 149, 154–5, 170, 187, 208–12, 222, 222 n.14, 235

Odinokov, Vladimir 227
Orwell, George 17
Osipov, Vladimir 19–20
Ouspensky, Peter D. 109, 150

Palamas, Gregory 106–7, 219 n.6
Palievsky, Petr **13–14**, **18**, 44
Panin, Dmitrii 139–40
Paramonov, Boris 103, 215–16
Pasternak, Boris **75–7**
Pavlov, Ivan 74, 235
Peppershtein, Pavel **200**, **203**, 203 n.118
Peter the Great 12, 19, 101
Plato 1–5, 50, 106–7, 119, 141, 148, 187, 196–7, 205, 218–19, 235
Platonov, Andrei 134, 228
Pleve, V. K. 80 n.43
Podoroga, Valerii **211–12**
Pomerants, Grigorii 26, 35–6, 64, 165
Pope Paul VI 80
Popper, Karl R. 4 n.8, 219
Prigov, Dmitrii Aleksandrovich 193, **197–9**, 226
Prokhanov, Aleksandr 48, 48 n.88, 60
Pushkin, Aleksandr 14, 16, 124, 167–9, 182, 199, 227

Roerich, Helena 109, 150, 215
Roerich, Nicholas 109, 150, 215, 228–9
Rorty, Richard 225
Rovner, Arkadii 151
Rozanov, Vasilii 2, 122, 162, 164, 215, 227, 229

Sakharov, Andrei 20, 32
Sartre, Jean-Paul 33, 36, 143–4
Sazonov, Egor 80 n.43
Schmemann, Alexander **66–8**
Schmidt, Wilhelm 98
Semenova, Svetlana 134, **142–50**, *143*, 143 n.35
Sergius of Radonezh 19
Shafarevich, Igor **32–6**, 43–4, 50, 90
Shestov, Lev x n.2, 63, 215
Shimanov, Gennadii 20
Shmidt, Anna 122
Shragin, Boris 26, 36
Siniavsky, Andrei 26, 36, *161*, **161–72**, 182
Skovoroda, Grigorii 2, 63
Solovyov, Vladimir 2–3, 63, 66, 79, 98, 101, 106–8, 110, 117, 120, 125, 127–30, 138, 215–18, 227–9
Solzhenitsyn, Aleksandr 12–13, **20–32**, *21*, 36, 58–9, 70, 90, 139, 212
Sorokin, Vladimir 193, 229
Stalin, Joseph 3, 12, 17, 19, 36–7, 51, 94–5, 111, 115, 117, 135, 163–4, 204–7
Stavrogin, Nikolai 154
Strada, Vittorio 173
Strauss, Leo 5–6

Teillard de Chardin, Pierre 38, **99–100**, 133, 149
Tertz, Abram 161–2
Patriarch Tikhon 78
Tolstoy, Lev 75, 102, 109, 215, 227, 235
Toporov, Vladimir 119
Toynbee, Arnold 39
Trotsky, Lev 135, 235
Trubetskoi, Nikolai 10, 101
Tsiolkovsky, Konstantin 110, 133–5, 139, 228, 232

Ustrialov, Nikolai 10

Valéry, Paul 233
Vernadsky, Vladimir 38, 133, 135, 138
Vvedensky, Aleksandr 78
Vysheslavtsev, Boris x n.2, 74 n.27

Whitehead, A. N. 1, 5

Yeltsin, Boris 32, 180, 223

Zelinsky, Vladimir 102
Zheludkov, Sergei **83–8**
Zhirinovsky, Vladimir 57, 220, 222, 226
Zinoviev, Aleksandr *172*, **172–80**, 183 n.74, 184 n.76, 192
Ziuganov, Gennadii 220, 223, 223 n.17

Subject Index

Notes: References to notes comprise the page number plus the note number e.g. 13 n.8 refers to note 8 on page 13
Page numbers in bold refer to the pages specifically devoted to the given subject.

Absolute Idea/absolute idealism 4, 6, 140–2, 160, 213, 219
Absolute Self/selfhood 152–5
Absolute Spirit 5, 140, 187, 224
absolutism 32
abstractionism 45
absurdity 18, 31, 86, 135, 143–4, 164–6, 199–200
Abyss 45 n.80, 125
  of negativity 150–5
active evolutionism **131–50**
active negation 177–8, 178 n.56, 183 n.74. *See also* passive negation
active void 183 n.74
aesthetics/aestheticism 13, 158–9, 170, 193–4, **197–201**, 203–4, 226–7
  of communism **162–4**
agnosticism 53, 87, 177
all-unity (*vseedinstvo*) 2, 106–7, 127, 219
analytic anthropology 212
angels/angelism **55–6**, 201
antagonism 51, 56–7, 121, 127, 222
anthropic principle 134, 136
anthropocentrism 15, 30, **137**
anthropocosmism 137–8, 147, 149
anti-systems 42–4
anti-Westernism 16, 231. *See also* Westernism
apocalypse 50, 63, 110, 118, 128, 131, 142, 217, 219
apologetics 72, 97
apophatic/negative method 74, 106. *See also* cataphatic/positive method
art-idea/idea-as-art. *See* sots-art/socialist art
artistry 13–14, **170–2**
ascesis/asceticism 104, 106, 208–9
Asia 11–12, 16, 59, 109
atheism/atheists 11, 18, 20, 23–4, 32, 44, 49, 55, 63, 67, 69, 72, **81–3**, 89, 91, **98–9**, 102, 134, 177, 234
  and believers **83–8**
  scientific 34, 95, 228 n.23
atom/atomic 22, 46, 133, 136, 145, 150
avant-garde/avant-gardism 14, 44–5, 151, 204–6
axis time 42

Battle of Kulikovo (1380) 17
The Bible 67, 73, 75, 95
biological evolution 135, 155, 179
biological field theory 145
biosphere 38–9, 43, 45, 133. *See also* geosphere
black hole (personal consciousness) 45, 45 n.80
blasphemy 124–5, 128, 131
Bolshevism/Bolsheviks 10–11, 19, 23, 25–6, 33, 58, 61, 120 n.8, 164
border theology 88
bourgeois 16, 32, 80, 134, 177, 206, 217, 234
  cosmopolitanism 12
  Lobanov’s critique of 18
brain 74–5, 133. *See also* heart; nervous system
bramfatura 112
Buddhism 128
  Nirvana 148
buffoon (*skomorokh*) **170–2**. *See also* holy foolishness/holy fools
Byzantium 17, 19, 63, 67 n.11

canon 163, 201–3, 202 n.114
capitalism **36**, 49, 51, 60, 79–81, 179–80

cataphatic/positive method 74, 154. *See also* apophatic/negative method
Catholicism 87, 92, 131–2, 232
chastity and wisdom (*tselomudrie*) 121
chauvinism 37, 50
China 9, 11, 25 n.34, 42, 59, 148
Chorus 168–9
Christ 52, 54, 65–8, 70, 75–6, 79, 82–5, 97, 101, 104–5, 117, 132, 146, 148, 208, 218. *See also* God
  Antichrist 110, **115–18**, 128–31
Christianity 44, 46, 49, 52, **54–5**, 59, 63, 70, 72, 83, 87, 101, 123, 128, 132, 138, 148–9, 154, 165, 218. *See also* Hindu/Hinduism; Islam; neophytes; non-Christian; New Testament; Old Testament; Protestant/Protestantism
  American Orthodox Church 92
  anonymous Christian 84–6, 96
  believers/nonbelievers 24, 70, 72, 81, **83–8**, 90–1, 102
  Byzantine Christianity 15, 67 n.11, 74
  Catacomb Church 93 n.78
  Christmas/Easter celebration 16, 132
  communion 95, 112, 168, 176
  death and resurrection **83** (*see also* resurrection)
  dual faith (*dvoeverie*) 120 n.8, 132, 138
  Eastern Christianity 2–3, 106, 131, 232 (*see also* Orthodoxy)
  Florovsky on 64–6
  heresies 43, 52, 66
  intuitivism **75–7**
  liberal 89–90
  and new humanism **88–92**
  Orthodox Christianity 10–11, 18, 20, 44, 53, 61, 64, 81, 92, 101, 125, 219
  Orthodox Church 11, 30, 63, 78, 84, 88, 91, 93, 105
  Russian Christianity 16, 67 n.11, 138
  Russian Orthodox Church 34, 69, 81, 92, 102, 223 n.17
  Russian True Orthodox Church 93 n.78
  sacraments **67–8**, 116
  Synthesis (*see* synthesis, Christian)
  teachings of Eastern Church fathers 64, 100, 105, 218
  Western Christianity 15–16, 54
Christian socialism **78–81**
civilization(s) 3, 10, 16, 29, 39, 43, 49, 96, 116, 134, 136, 143, 145, 183
  agricultural 36
  Atlantis/Atlanteanism/Atlanticism 51, 56, 59
  contemporary 31, 42, 48, 104, 132, 144, 201
  continental/continentalism 56
  decadent 10, 49
  Islamic-Orthodox 54
  Judeo-Christian 54
  role of feminine 126
  socialist (communist) 193
  Western (technological) 3, 9, 36, 53, 103–4, 132, 159, 175, 197
classicism 163
collective identity 29, 115
collectivism 80, 89, 147, 153, 155, 158, 178, 223, 235
The Common Cause (*obshchee delo*) project 132, 135, 144–6, 148–50
communality (*sobornost'*)/togetherness 30, 124, 147, 189, 223, 223 n.17, 232
communication 70, 147. *See also* language
  with God 67, 71
  verbal 184–5
communism 2–3, 9, 11–12, 12 n.6, 20, 30, 32, 36, 47, **50–1**, 61, 80–2, 89, 116, 118, 134–5, 141, 149–50, 173, 178, 180, 193, 202, 216, 221–3, 235
  aesthetics of 162–4
  communist revolution 43, 58, 205, 217
  real-life 179
  scientific 179
  vs. national self-arrangement **24–6**
conceptual art 157–60
conceptualism (*kontseptualizm*) 157–9, 163, 178–9, 181, 187, 189, 192–3, 203–4, 213, 220, 233
  conceptualist thinking 160, 182, 190, 192
  and ideology 185–6
  meta-ideological/meta-aesthetic approach 159

and Russian culture 198–9
vs. metaphysical radicalism **224–9**
Western 160, 186, 204
condensation process 139–40. *See also* density
consciousness 2, 17, 27, 35, 43, 63, 88, 96, 112, 119, 127, 142, 160, 177, 208
disturbed 192
human 119, 136, 146–7
individual 145, 159
juridical 28
moral 23, 28
national 18, 25, 46
personal 45, 45 n.80
self-consciousness 29, 152, 159
conservatism 57–8, 60–1, 89, 92, 96, 105
enlightened 28–9, 32
moral 21–35
revolutionary 47, 50
conspiracy/conspirology (*konspirologiia*) 46, **51**, 61, 165, 177
Continental Idea 59
continentalism 47, 56. *See also* radical traditionalism
conventional epistemology 113
cosmism 4, 38, 45, 53, 55, 82, 85, 110, 220, 222, 232. *See also* The World
and active evolutionism **131–50**
perspectives of cosmists 135–42
sources of cosmism 131–4
theology and technology of 142–50
The Church and 96–7, 108
cosmic energy 38, 137
cosmogenesis 38, 99, 131
methodological 136
Russian cosmism 131 n.19, 132, 134, 136–7, 140, 222
cosmopolitan/cosmopolitanism 12, 17–18, 20, 58–9, 116
Stalin's campaign against 17
creationism 55
Creator and creation 52, 54, 66, 114, 139, 153 (*see also* God)
and evolutionism **99–101** (*see also* evolutionism)
self-creation 46, 146, 166
culture, Russian 2–3, 67 n.11, 118, 158, 162, 198, 213, 227–8
calendar 36
Christianity 102
feminine elements of 121, 124, 127
folk 14, 170
myth 10
culturology 4, 220, 224–5, 231, 233 n.2
cynicism 104–5, 188, 227

death 24, 34, 43, 50, 68, 99, 105, 132–5, 144, 148
of Christ/Christianity 83, 104, 117, 132
death instinct (Shafarevich) 33, 50
death of God 103, 155
virus of death 136
Decembrist revolt (1825) 15–16, 168
Deep Book/Dove Book (*Golubinaia kniga*) 132
degradation 15, 28, 32, 41–2, 82, 139, 148
deification. *See* theosis/deification
democracy 20, 27, 29–30, 32, 36, 47, 50, 80, 149
democratic socialism. *See* social democracy
demythologization 65, **203–11**
density **139–40**. *See also specific processess*
determinism/indeterminism 46, 51, 75, 137, 167, 207, 220
diasophy **140–2**
dissident(s)/dissident movement 20, 31–2, 60, 78, 84–5, 89, 103, 164, 178
Divine/divinity 52–3, 66, 70, 72, 104, 118, 123, 129, 131, 138
Divine Wisdom (*see* feminism/feminine, Sophia (Divine Wisdom))
female 121, 129
Self 152–3
sexually bipolar 130
dogmatism/dogmatic thinking 63, 66–7, 89, 92, 107, 221, 224
dual faith (*dvoeverie*) 109, 139

eclecticism 163–4
morality of 193–7
ecology/ecological crisis 15, 137–8, 142

ecosophy 142
egoism 114, 134, 152
collective egoism 137
metaphysical 155
emigration 22, 27, 64, 78, 85
empiricism 2, 119
emptiness/void 82, 139, 167–8. *See also* Nothingness
canonization of 200–3
empty universe 136
metaphysics of **181–93**
energetism **105–8**
Enlightenment 14, 34, 53, 58, 96, 115
entropy 31, 41–2, 45–6, 137. *See also* negentropy
epistemology 113
erotic/eroticism 129
auto-eroticism 146
genital 146
magnetic-cloud eroticism **146–7**
eschatology/eschatologism 50, 130, 147, 217, 219, 223
eschatological extremism 51
eschatology of light 142
esoteric/esotericism 47–9, 51–2, 54, 56, 59, 109, 150 n.45, 151. *See also* exotericism
eternity 82, 87, 142, 165, 190, 195
ethical monism. *See* monism
ethnicity **37–47**
chimeras/chimeric 39 n.57, 42–3, 42 n.70
ethnic evolution 41
ethnogenesis 37, 42
ethnoi/ethnos 38–44, 46
ethnology 38
Eurasia/Eurasian 11, 38, 47, 53–4, 56, 59, 121, 223. *See also* neo-Eurasianism
Eurasianism/Eurasianists 6, **10–13**, 10 n.3, 20, 38, 47, 59–61, 64, 215, 219, 231–2
Europe/European 11–12, 16, 36, 41, 59, 109, 182
egocentrism 17
jurisprudence 28
philosophy 1, 5, 166
evil(s)/Devil 24–5, 31, 43, 48–9, 68, 91, 100, 104, 113–14, 131 n.19, 154
demoness 124–5
Satan 49, 52, 117
and theodicy **97–8**, 100
evolutionism **99–101**
active evolutionism **131–50**
biological evolution 135, 155, 179
evolutionary creationism 149
existence 36, 38, 41–2, 82, 85–6, 89, 104–5, 113, 133, 137, 144–5, 150, 152, 158, 171, 175–6, 182, 185, 222
of anonymous Christians 96
of evil 114
feminine elements of 121
and garbage/dump 183–4
God's 67, 71, 74, 88, 97
human 132, 185, 191, 216
existentialism 64, **69–72**, 102, 143–4, **165–7**, 199
exotericism 49. *See also* esoteric/esotericism
expansionism of Russia 25
extremism 51, 225

fascism 11, 35, 47, 80, 141, 150
feminism/feminine 103, 134, 138–9. *See also* Mother Nature; Mother Russia
Aphrodite Pandemos (goddess) 130 n.18
Communal Soul (*Sobornaia Dusha*) 123–4
demonic feminine 130
Lilith 124, 129
Velga 124–5
Eternal Feminine (*vechnaia zhenstvennost'*) 110, 123, 125, 127–8
feminine elements 118, 120–1, 123–4
feminine spirit of Russia 110, 113, **118–21**
fertility and sensuality 121–2, 126, 129
Iarosvet 124
mysticism of femininity **122–7**
Navna 123–5, 127
Sophia (Divine Wisdom) **6–7**, **120–1**, 123, 125, 127, 131, 138
Tatiana Larina 124
Universal Feminine (*Mirovaia Zhenstvennost'*) 123, 128–9
Western feminism/feminists 127
Zventa-Sventana 123–4, 129
France 11, 15, 17, 59, 151, 234

freedom 20, 27, 29, 32, **34**, 46, 54, 77, 89, 92, 103, 107, 144, 231
absolute 57, 114, 147, 166
human 75, 85, 114, 137, 154
revolutionary 168
French Revolution of 1789 34
fundamentalism 12, 28–9, 32, 221, 224, 229, 232

geopolitics 47, 52, **56–7**, 57 n.109, 235
geosphere 133. *See also* biosphere
Germany 34, 36, 46, 59, 160
gnosis/Gnostic/Gnosticism 43–4, 46, 52–3, 59, 121, 124–5
God **29**, 54, 70, 74, 77, 82–3, 85–7, 95–7, 105, 114, 122, 133, 138, 148, 153, 165, 177, 196, 204, 234. *See also* Christ
Anti-God (*protivobog*) 98, 113–14, 154
communication with 67, 71
death of God 103, 155
faith in 4, 20, 67, 71, 82, 84
God-realization 153
God the Father 122, 129–30
and *I* 152
kingdom of God 67–8, 78–9, 148, 235
and man 52, 55–6, 59, 65, 71, 87, 100, 106–7, 152, 163, 218
Mother of God 118, 121, 123
and nature 121 n.11 (*see also* Nature)
objective reality of 67
qualities of 98
revelation of 65, 67, 70–1 (*see also* revelation/revelationism)
and self-knowledge 71
Siniavsky's relationship to 165
transcendental density 139
and the World 99–101
Golgotha **83**
Gospels 76, 78, 102, 122

heart 73–5. *See also* brain; nervous system
hedonism 27, 57, 152
hermeneutics 51, **200–3**
hesychasm 74, **106–7**
Hindu/Hinduism 59, 84, 98, 124. *See also* Christianity; Islam
Absolute 152
Brahman/Atman 152
Hokhma (Divine Wisdom) 120, 123
holism 2, 134
holy foolishness/holy fools (*iurodivyi*) 104–5, **170–2**. *See also* buffoon (*skomorokh*)
Holy Spirit 84, 122–3, 129–30, 169
Holy Trinity 122, 129
homogenization 34, 55
Huguenots 15, 36
human/human being 11, 17–18, 55–6, 73, 86, 88, 113, 127, 131, 178, 234
anti-human 117
consciousness 119, 136, 146–7
cosmicism (*see* cosmism/cosmopolitanism)
death of mankind 33, 50
free will 34, 46, 98, 100, 106, 113–14, 145, 219
human body 38, 104, 142, 145–7
humanism 22, 30, 49, 80–1, **88–92**
humanity 4, 11–12, 16–18, 22, 24–5, 27, 30, 33–4, 38, 53, 66–7, 70, 73, 75, 77, 79, 84–5, 87, 96–7, 106, 114–15, 117, 127, 130, 132–5, 137–8, 144, 148–50, 179, 204
humankind 4, 19, 22, 80, 94, 134–5, 137–9, 152
human rights 27, 32, 50, 56, 85, 90
life span 135
neo-humanism 80–1, 90
panhuman (*vsechelovek*) 17–18, 144, 150, 154–5, 212
personality 15, 22, 33, 46, 81, 106 (*see also* personality)
polnoorgannost' 146
self-determination 29, 34, 90, 98
soul 43, 110, 122, 140, 145, 207
vs. Christ 66
Hyperborea 51, 56
hyperreality 145, 175
hypostasis 100–1, 110, 122–3, 129–30, 130 n.18

iconic sign 13
idealism/ideas 5, 33, 113, 120, 120 n.8, 140–1, 160, 196, 215–16, 218. *See also specific idealisms*
Being 5, 33, 153, 187, 207

developmental stages of 4
German 210, 218
Marx on 5
image (*obraz*) 13–14
holistic intuition 14
immanence/immanent 52–5, 86–7, 100, 134, 144, 149, 152–3
imperialism 16, 52
indigenous ethnic groups 42. *See also* tribe(s)
individualism 11, 14–15, 27, 58, 134
individual behavior 22–3, 27
individuality 13, 30, 33, 39 n.58, 150, 153, 168, 191, 210–11
inspection **200–2**
integrity (*tsel'nost'/tselostnost'*) 2, 4, 19, 49, 86, 91, 183
intelligentsia, Russian 10, 18, 81, 92–3, 101, 210, 216, 218, 234–5
obrazovanshchina 26
and people **26–7**
secularization and **88–92**
internationalism 10, 12, 22, 25, 56, 58
intuitivism, Christian **75–7**
irrationalism 142. *See also* rationalism
Islam 44, 49, 53–6, 101, 128. *See also* Christianity; Hindu/Hinduism
Ismailism 44
isolationism/isolationists 25, 59

Jews/Jewish 15, 17–18, 20, 26, 34–6, 43–4, 77, 94
monotheism 45
national messianism 50
Judaism 17, 44, 46, 52, 54, 86–7, 94, 138
Shabbat 148
judicial system/judicialism **27–9**

kenosis (self-emptying) 85, 97–8, 100–1, 104, 208, 236
Khazar/Khazarian Kaganate 17, 44
kontsept, Russian 158. *See also* conceptualism (*kontseptualizm*)

labor 19, 36, 80, 95–6, 127, 134, 216, 232, 234
language 112, 164, 168, 207, 211–12
and literature 13
and reality **184–6**
Siniavsky on 168–9
large people (*le grand peuple*) **34**, **36**, 44. *See also* small people
The Last Judgement 132, 147, 195
legalism 27
legal state (*pravovoe gosudarstvo*) 27
liberalism/liberals 4, 20, 25–7, 34, 36, 53, 57–8, 65, 80, 90, 90 n.72, 96, 149–50, 179, 231
liberation 17, 19, 81, 97, 167, 232, 234
literature 13–14, 17, 23, 115
Caucasus in Russian literature 16
monologic 17
polyphony 17
samizdat 19–20, 75–6, 78, 81, 84, 112
liturgical philosophy **66–8**
The Living Church 78, 80
living knowledge 138
logocentrism 184
love **71–2**, 86, 99
children/parent's love 146
love of wisdom 6, 140
of verbal expression 184

madness 160, 192–3, 197, 213, 224
Manicheanism 43–4, 46, 98
manifestation 4, 6, 17, 31, 33, 45, 52, 54, 59, 68, 100, 114, 124, 127, 152, 178, 183, 194, 216. *See also* Theophany
Marxism/Marxist 4–5, 12, 19–20, 22, 25–7, 33–4, 39, 47, 51, 53, 56, 58, 60, 77, 79, 85, 92–3, 95, 120, 134–5, 140, 144, 149, 158, 161–2, 175, 178, 192, 197, 215, 217, 219–20, 222, 224, 226, 231, 233, 235
anti-Marxist 33, 76, 215, 217
and cosmism 135
material base 163
materialism (materialist ideology) 2–3, 5, 49, 54–5, 68, 74, **98–9**, 112–13, 125, 127, 138, 141, 153, 215–16, 218, 235
atheistic 70, 215
demonic 124
dialectical 79, 216
Levitin's disfavor of 79
magical 53
militant 5, 63

mystical 55, 138
and nature 119–20, 120 n.8
pantheistic 55
philosophical 74, 119
and sophiology **118–21**
vulgar 39, 153
materiia (matter) 118–19, 122, 127, 131
materiosophy 127
Medical Hermeneutics Inspectorate (*Inspektsiia 'Meditsinskaia germenevtika'*) **200–3**, 220
metaculture 111, 115, 123
metahistory of Russia **110–31**
metaphysics 43, 48, 55–6, 153, 164
ambivalent universals and multiple 186–8
of angelism 55
of emptiness **181–93**
metaphysical art 155
metaphysical radicalism/radicals 51, **219–24**
and conceptualism **224–9**
metaphysical realism 151
and politics 51
satirical **172–80**
minorities 26, 201
modernism/modernity 14, 70, 137, 195–6. *See also* postmodernism
monads **113–14**, 117, 123–4
mondialism 59
anti-mondialism 47, 58
monism 30–2, 140, 150
against pluralism 30–2
monotheism 45, 54–5, 98
morality **86**
of eclecticism **193–7**
immortality 99, 105, 132–6, 144, 148, 190, 229
and law 27–9
moral conservatism **21–35**
nonreligious 89
and religion 29–30, 96, 170
supramorality (*supramoralizm*) 132
Mother Earth 36, 130, 138
Mother Nature 119–20, 121 n.11, 139
Mother Russia (*matushka Rossiia*) 118–19
multiculturalism 42, 201–2, 233, 233 n.2
mutation 40, 44, 46
mystery 16, 20, 48 n.88, 54, 83, 105, 129–30, 148
mysticism 20, 48, 59–60, 66, 109–10, 150, 223, 232
of femininity **122–7**, 130, 138–9
gender 118
myth/mythology 87, 118, 120–1, 176, 204–7, 209, 228 n.23
chimera (mythical animal) 42 n.70
cultural 10
Russian pre-Christian 109
socialist 50, 216
transmyth 115, 130

National Bolshevism 23
nation/nationalism 4, 12, 12 n.6, 19–20, 21 n.25, **22–3**, 25, 35, 37, 50, 58, 61, 64, 149, 219, 221, 224, 231–2. *See also* Russian nationalism
and class 11
conservative 58–9
militant 29
national guilt and repentance 23–4
nationalists 12–13, 18–21, 27, 37, 47, 57, 60, 81, 222–3, 226, 229
nationality 16, 22
national socialism 11, 19
national spirit 14, 17–18, 25, 45
self-arrangement *vs.* communism 24–6
natural sciences 31, 38, 46, 71–2, 99–100, 133, 136, 143
Nature 57, 122, 127, 129, 131–2, 137–8
and God 121 n.11
and humanity 135, 137–8
and materialism 119–20, 120 n.8
natural elements 122
Universal Spirit 140
Nazi(s)/Nazism 19, 35–6, 45–6, 58, 87
negentropy 41, 134, 137. *See also* entropy
neo-Eurasianism **37–47**. *See also* Eurasia/Eurasian
neofascism 47–61, 222
neo-Kantian 75, 77, 218
neologism 39 n.59, 112, 123
neo-paganism 139
neophytes 81, **101–8**. *See also* Christianity
neo-Platonism 15, 106, 218

neo-Slavophiles/-Slavophilism 32, 58–9. *See also* Slavophilism
and nationalists of 1960s–1970s 18–21
revival in aesthetics 13–18
nervous system 74. *See also* brain; heart
new patristic synthesis 64
New Testament 63, 73, 77, 101, 123. *See also* Old Testament
nihilism/nihilists 34, 45, 131 n.19, 155, 196
non-Christian 15, 64, 72, 84, 88–9, 98. *See also* Christianity
non-Jews 35. *See also* Jews/Jewish
noosphere 38, 133, 140, 142, 149, 232
Nothingness 33, 41, 45, 100, 153–5, 166, 168–9, 171, 183–5, 183 n.74, 201. *See also* emptiness/void

occult 51, 56, 109–10, 110 n.1, 145, 151, 228 n.23
October Revolution of 1917 **9–10**, 25, 35, 80, 111, 113, 120 n.8, 135
Old Testament 15, 29, 35, 63, 73, 101, 123. *See also* Christianity; New Testament
organism(s) 19, 40, 145–6
of human/humanity 25, 137
living 20, 133, 210
symbiosis 4, 43
unicellular 136
organs. *See specific organs*
Orthodoxy 10, 15, 21, 23, 52–54, 56, 58–9, 66, 70, 72, 78, 83–4, 89–92, 94–6, 100, 106, 109, 123, 131–2, 216, 232
otherness 150, 196, 207, 209–10

pagan/paganism/paganist **53–5**, 76, 98–9, 101, 109, 115, 122, 129, 132
pan-philosophical approach 187
pantheism 54–5
passionate drive/passionarity **39–40**, **39** nn.59–60, **44–7**
harmonious 40, 46
passionarians 39 n.59, 40–1, 46
sub-passionarians 40–1, 46
passive negation 177–8. *See also* active negation
patriotism 19, 21, 23, 41, 231
personality 4, 89, 116, 138, 150
human 15, 22, 33, 46, 81, 106
nation as **21–32**
symphonic 11
phenomenology 4, 211–12, 218, 229
philosophy 1, **5–6**. *See also specific philosophies*
ancient 3
defined by Whitehead 1
European 1, 5, 166
and history 6, 75
liturgical **66–8**
and philosophical 235–6
and politics 6–7
and religion 63 (*see also* religion)
Russian **x n.2**, **1–4**, 9, 63–4, 107, 127, 131, 210, 216–19, 221, 235–6
Western 1, 207, 235
The Phoenix of Philosophy: Russian Thought of the Late Soviet Period (Epstein) ix n.1, 14, 50, 64, 231, 233
physiology/physiological theory 73–5, 235
Plato-Marxism 5
Platonism 4–5, 4 n.8, 7, 106–7, 112, 216–18
pluralism/pluralists 4, 26, 61, 70
monism against 30–2
socialist 30
polemics 12, 27, 30, 33, 36, 70, 78, 84, 88, 162
polytheism 87, 98, 120
post-conceptualism 199
post-Hegelian philosophy 6, 140
posthistory 141
post-Marxist philosophy 6, 222, 226
postmodernism 102–5, 157, 185, 191, 193–5, 199–203, 213 n.149, 228, 233. *See also* modernism/modernity
academic **211–13**
archaic **161–72**
vs. utopianism and demythologization **203–11**
postrevolutionary movements 9–10
post-Soviet Russia 4, 7, 15, 51, 142, 211
priests, hierarchies of 116
profane/profanism 49, 52–3

Protestant/Protestantism 43–4, 68, 78, 109. *See also* Christianity
pseudo-ecclesiasticism 90
psychoanalysis 159, 210
Puritans 34, 36

racism 37, 141
radicalism 47, 199
  metaphysical 51, **219–29**
  political 220–1, 226
  traditionalism/traditionalists **47–61** (*See also* traditionalism/ traditionalists)
rarefication 139–40. *See also* density
rationalism 2, 12, 14–15, 47, 58, 86, 119, 218. *See also* irrationalism
realism 14, 44, 68, 162, 204
  metaphysical 151
  psychedelic 203
  socialist 162–4, 193, 204–5
reality 13–14, 68, 104, 158, 160, 167, 174–7, 179–80, 189–94, 203–7, 213, 223–4, 231
  godless 86
  God's 67
  historical 9, 46, 51, 158, 207
  and language 184–6
  objective 119, 152
  Soviet reality 164, 174, 182
  truth and 171
Reason 97, 135, 141, 153
reduction/epoche 208
relativism 31–2, 96, 102, 144
religion 20, 26, 31, 52, 72, 99, 101, 142–3, 152, **154**, 164–6. *See also specific religion*
  of absolute self 150–5
  and morality 29–30, 96, 170 (*see also* morality)
  pan-religion 114, 128
  and philosophy 63–5, 219
  religious belief 2, 20, 26, 97
  religious faith 30–1, 68, 82, 112
  religious idealism 68, 215–19
  religious parody 162–4
  religious thought 63, 72, 74–5, 83, 101, 216, 218
  and science 95–6, 144
religiosity 30, 52–3, 55, 59, 89, 134, 168
Renaissance 24, 30, 53, 72
resurrection 16, 47, 50, 83, 117, 132–4, **145–8**, 165, 190, 197, 208, 220–1, 232
revelation/revelationism 65, 67, 70, 87, 95, 100–1, 112–13, 135, 152–3, 160, 199, 217, 233
revolutionary conservatism 47, 50. *See also* radical traditionalism
revolutionary violence 26, 141
Roman Empire 10
romanticism 11, 48
The Rose of the World (Andreev) 110–17, 122, 124–5, 127–31, 150, 220
Rosicrucianism 52
ruling idea (*obshchaia ideia-pravitel'nitsa*) 5, 11, 231
Russian Empire 10–11, 34, 56, 226
Russian nationalism 9–10, 21, 21 n.25, 25, 64. *See also* nation/nationalism
Russianness 23, 35, **168–9**

sacred sciences 49
salvation 25, 29, 49, 77, 83–4, 89, 103, 142, 144, 147, 154
scientific spirit 119
Scythians 9–10
second law of thermodynamics 137
secularization 32, 54
  and intelligentsia **88–92**
self-awareness 4, 140, 150, 213
self-denial 209, 236
self-destruction 24, **33–4**, 42, 46
self-limitation **24**, 27, 30, 59, 209, 217
self-preservation 36, 40, 146, 148
self-realization 6, 30, 166, 184
self-sacrifice 19, 28–9, 79, 98
semiotic approach 13
sermons/preachings 32, 66, 81–3, 94, 170, 219
sexuality 132, **164–6**
  sexual identity 146
  sexual reproduction 147
shrastr (layer of supernation) 115
sign (*znak*) 13, 51, 166
sin 10, 52, 67, 97, 100, 209
skepticism 4, 49

Slavophilism 2, **11–14**, 18, 20. *See also* neo-Slavophiles/-Slavophilism
Kozhinov's view on 14–15
Slavophiles **9**, 16, 24–5, 58–60, 169, 189
Slavs 17, 35, 38
small people (*le petit peuple*) **34–6**, 44. *See also* large people
Smenovekhovstvo (Change of Landmarks) **10**–12
social democracy 50, 52, 80
socialism 11, 19, **33–4**, 37, **50**, 52, 58, 162–3, 188, 217, 235
Christian **78–81**
social philosophy **188–9**
social science 22, 29–31
socioeconomic system 11, 22, 176
solipsism 147
epistemological 152
monologic 185
ontological 152
sophiology **118–21**, 123, 127, 138, 218
sots-art/socialist art 161, 163, **193–7**
Soviet Union 11, 20, 32, 53, 72, 74, 81, 101, 175, 177–8, 183, 223–4
space exploration, Soviet 134
specificity of Russia 11, 13, 17
spirit/spirituality/spiritual life/spiritualism 14, 18, 25–7, 29–30, 36, 38, 48–9, 53, 56, 61, 68, 72–3, 76–7, **81–3**, 89, 99–100, 103, 106, 116, 122, 125, 128, 150, 152, 155
spiritual system of the World **112–15**
St. Bartholomew's Day massacre 15
structuralism 4, 12–14, 60, 166, 199, 220, 224–5, 231
post-structuralism 207–8, 212
structuralists 13, 166, 175, 198
supernation (*sverkhnarod*) 115. *See also specific layers*
supernatural 4, 52, 74, 87, 112, 148
Supreme Mind 4
symbol/symbolism 49, 67–8, 151
syncretism 95, 109, 132
synergetic approach 107, 107 n.106
synthesis, Christian 6–7, 12, 61, 63–4, 66, 79, **93–101**
The Tale of Igor's Campaign (song) 16
Tatar-Mongol hordes 15, 17, 38
technology 60, 98, 132–4, 232
of active evolution 142–50
teleology 143, 162–3
terrorism 79, 80 n.43
theocracy 49, 53, 128, 131
theocratic state of future 115–18
theodicy, evil and **97–8**, 100
theology 38, 63
revival of **64–6**
science and **72–5**, 140
and technology of active evolution **142–50**
theological innovations **101–8**
Theophany (manifestation of God) 100–1. *See also* manifestation
theosis/deification 30, 49, 100, 131–3
theosophy 51
Third Position movement 49, 81, 88
Third Way 47, **49–50**
total ideology 185–6
totalism/totality 1–2, 4, 14, 25, 49, 55, 113, 150
totalitarian/totalitarianism 4 n.8, 6–7, 11, 20, 26–7, 29, 32, 36, 87, 90, 107, 179, 185, 191–2, 200, 204–7, 213, 216, 222, 224
Tradition **48–9**, 54, 57, 215, 221
traditionalism/traditionalists 12, 49, 51, 54–9, 61, 219
transcendence/transcendental/transcendentalism 4, 24, 52–4, 77, 86, 88–9, 104–5, 134, 138–9, 153, 183, 195
self-transcendence 236
transcendental density 139
transcendental nothingness 153
transculture 233 n.2
transphysical 140
transphysical knowledge 112–13
transphysical worlds 115–16
Transstate (*Transgosudarstvo*) 194
tribe(s) 9, 15, 19, 38. *See also* indigenous ethnic groups
Trinity 116, 118, 122–3, 129–30
anti-Trinity 131

truth 27, 31, 35, 53–4, 63, 70, 76, 83–4, 89–90, 119, 151 n.46, 160, 175, 187, 209, 211, 213, 216, 221, 224–5, 234
Turks 38
"tyranny and wisdom" 6–7

Ultimate Doctrine 153–4
universalism 110–31, 232
ur-monotheism (*pramonoteizm/Urmonotheismus*) 98
utopia/utopianism 1, 26, 33, 36, 43, 141, 190, 197, 199, 202–11
  communist 141
  religious 136
  socialist 43
  utopian 3 n.7, 19, 48, 66, 140, 185, 189–90, 222
  vs. postmodernism 203–11

vampirism 182
Virgin Mary 121–2
virgin/virginity 121, 125, 127
visual anthropology 211

Westernism 9, 20, 32, 49. *See also* anti-Westernism
Westernizers 9, 16, 27, 169
White Guard movement 9
The World. *See also* cosmism/cosmopolitanism
  the Church and 96–7, 108
  spiritual system of 112–15

Young Germany movement 34

zatomis (layer of supernation) 115

www.ingramcontent.com/pod-product-compliance
Lightning Source LLC
Chambersburg PA
CBHW060251100726
47907CB00003B/847
9781501380914